At the Pivot of East and West

EXPERIMENTAL FUTURES
Technological Lives, Scientific Arts, Anthropological Voices *A series edited by Michael M. J. Fischer & Joseph Dumit*

At the Pivot of East and West

Ethnographic, Literary, and Filmic Arts

MICHAEL M. J. FISCHER

Duke University Press Durham & London 2023

Printed in the United States of America on acid-free paper ∞
Designed by Aimee C. Harrison
Typeset in Untitled Serif and Changa by Copperline Book Services

Library of Congress Cataloging-in-Publication Data
Names: Fischer, Michael M. J., [date] author.
Title: At the pivot of East and West : ethnographic, literary, and filmic arts / Michael M. J. Fischer.
Other titles: Experimental futures.
Description: Durham : Duke University Press, 2023. | Series: Experimental futures | Includes bibliographical references and index.
Identifiers: LCCN 2022043417 (print)
LCCN 2022043418 (ebook)
ISBN 9781478019893 (paperback)
ISBN 9781478017189 (hardcover)
ISBN 9781478024460 (ebook)
ISBN 9781478093756 (ebook other)
Subjects: LCSH: Anthropology and the arts—Southeast Asia. | Documentary mass media and the arts—Southeast Asia. | Arts and society—Southeast Asia. | Documentary films—Southeast Asia—History and criticism. | Southeast Asian literature—History and criticism. | Social change in motion pictures. | Social change in literature. | BISAC: SOCIAL SCIENCE / Anthropology / Cultural & Social | LITERARY CRITICISM / Comparative Literature
Classification: LCC NX180.A58 F56 2023 (print) | LCC NX180.A58 (ebook) | DDC 306.4/70959—dc23/eng/20221229
LC record available at https://lccn.loc.gov/2022043417
LC ebook record available at https://lccn.loc.gov/2022043418

Cover art: Entang Wiharso, *Rope from the Sky* (detail), 2021. Acrylic paint and glitter on canvas, 420 × 800 cm. Courtesy of the artist and Black Goat Studios.

The open access edition of this work was made possible by generous funding from the MIT Libraries.

TO MY HOSTS AND GUIDES IN THE
LITERARY, THEATRICAL, AND FILMIC ARTS
for affordances and accompaniments
during the pandemic of 2019–2022
providing key notes, entertainments,
and further beckoning into the
third spaces of situated *hantu* (ghosts)
and global *gentayanagan* (wanderings)
worlds of *bayangan* (both shadow and imagination)
neither here nor there, always both

Contents

Acknowledgments

This book, along with *Probing Arts and Emergent Forms of Life*, was written in the spring of 2020 as the COVID-19 pandemic was breaking across the world and the dire predictions of the Buddhist sermon that concluded *Probing Arts were coming to pass*. The immersion in these two volumes was supported by my wife, Susann Wilkinson, not only with good food and general comfort, but with a daily mantra and reminder of how lucky we were to have a roof over our head, heat and electricity, access to food, and the ability to quarantine in a safe environment. The COVID-19 pandemic was a more virulent reprise of experiences with the earlier SARS pandemic, avian influenza pandemics, and threat of a MERS pandemic experienced in Singapore (Fischer 2013), and, of course, of the Ebola and Zika pandemics elsewhere (in West Africa and Brazil, respectively). We had run just ahead of COVID-19 after a wonderful exploration of Batak country in Sumatra, after which I had spent five weeks in Singapore until the Chinese New Year, at which the Buddhist sermon was a part. I left just as the pandemic was arriving (having been identified in late November or in December 2019 in Wuhan, China). We managed a second wonderful trip to Ecuador, leaving there in early March just as the terrible outbreak of COVID-19 overwhelmed medical services in Guayaquil.

All the more thanks to these textual and visual artworks as spaces to inhabit and explore. I would like to thank in particular those whom I was able to meet, hang out with, or interview, or exchange notes with. Tan Pin Pin and Sandi Tan did public presentations I was able to attend at Singapore's National Archives and at the Brattle Theater in Cambridge, Massachusetts. Jasmin Ng spent a delightful long afternoon with me filling in some background on both, as well as on her own remarkable career, at the Forty Hands Cafe in Tiong Bahru, across from Books Actually (the home also of Kenny

Leck's Math Paper Press) in Singapore, places well known to any booklover who has lived there. I corresponded briefly also with Sophia Siddique Harvey as well as Sandi, giving all three filmmakers drafts of my writing for comment, and was also delighted to meet with Dr. Sharon Siddique, who was then at the Singapore University of Technology and Design's LKY Centre for Innovative Cities, and who provided welcome wisdom, context (and contacts) about the joy of Sophie, Sandi, and Jasmine's filmmaking in the early 1990s. Kevin Martens Wong similarly spent a lovely evening talking about his project to keep the Kristang language alive (I visited one of his classes), as well as talking about his novel *Altered Straits*. Daniel Hui accompanied filmmaker Thorsten Trimpop and myself on a scouting trip to Papua New Guinea (PNG) for Thorsten's next film. I thank Thorsten for many conversations about film, both in and following a class on ethnographic and experimental film that we taught together at MIT. The trip to PNG filled in some contexts in relation to trips Susann and I had made to Sulawesi to visit Toraja and Bugis communities (trips made possible by Prof. Muhammad Nasrun at Tadulkao University in Palu, and by Prof. Sulfikar Amir of Singapore's Nanyang Technological University, who arranged an international Science, Technology and Society conference at Hasnuddin University in Makassar). The PNG trip also provided some broad contexts for the trip we made to Australia to attend a spectacular 4S (Society for the Social Study of Science) meeting in Sydney (with a side trip to Uluru, immersion in the precolonial history of Sydney, and two extraordinary museum shows of Aboriginal art, including a retrospective of the bark carvings of John Mawurndjul at Sydney's Museum of Contemporary Art and the Art Gallery of South Australia). Prof. Nazry Bahrawi, then still at the Singapore University of Technology and Design, introduced me to a circle of Malay writers, playwrights, and literary figures in Singapore, expanding my interest in Malay plays and generally the wider Malay world. I thank Li Lin Wee for introducing me to Boo Junfeng, and Junfeng for spending time with me at the Goodman Arts Center talking about his Art in Transit project, described in the afterword, his film *Apprentice* about the death penalty in Singapore, and his then upcoming plans to direct the National Day Parade in a new way.

Since finishing this book, more works have been published within the scope of these explorations, and I have tried to accommodate some of them, including especially Sandi Tan's second novel, Laksmi Pamuntjak's third novel, and Intan Paramaditha's first novel. Special thanks to Laksmi Pamuntjak and the flurry of emails we exchanged as this book was going into final proofs.

I thank Ken Wissoker at Duke University Press, editors Lisl Hampton, Ryan Kendall, Joshua Gutterman Tranen, Kim Miller, Philip Thomas, and Ihsan Taylor for shepherding the book; designer Aimee Harrison; and the several reviewers for the press. Two of these reviewers, who provided extensive comments, have made themselves known to me, and I gratefully thank them both: Greg Clancey, Professor of History, head of Tembusu College, and leader of the STS cluster at the National University of Singapore, has been my host and intellectual companion throughout my decade-plus engagements with Singapore—a consummate historian of science and technology in Asia and longtime engaged resident in Singapore; and Byron Good, Professor of Anthropology and Social Medicine at Harvard and Gadjah Mada University in Yogyakarta, who has been an intellectual companion since graduate school and with whom I co-teach and have learned to think especially about things psychological and affecting mental health, and who with Professor Mary-Jo DelVecchio Good has provided constant touch points for thinking about Indonesia, medical sociology, Turkey, Iran, and the Middle East. Quite apart from reading the manuscript, all three of them are constant internal audiences for what I write about this part of the world. They are, of course, not responsible for any remaining defects, and their rights to disagree are both inviolable and cannot shake deep friendship.

Introduction

Reader's Guide and Manifesto

When history and historiography fail to articulate the atrocities and absurdities . . . whe[n] history fails to address man-made and natural atrocities, fiction arises to bear witness to the immemorial and unthinkable. . . . It is fiction that is capable of facilitating history's power of imagination and judgment . . . —DAVID DER-WEI WANG, *WHY FICTION MATTERS IN CONTEMPORARY CHINA*

The first violent film I saw was not a kinky B movie, nor did I see it at an appropriate age. The image of the slashing woman, stuck in my head for many years, comes from *Pengkhianatan G30S/PKI* . . . Every elementary school student of the period was required to see [it]. —INTAN PARAMADITHA, "THE WILD CHILD'S DESIRE"

This spring, memory laws arrived in America. Republican state legislators proposed dozens of bills designed to guide and control American understanding of the past. —TIMOTHY SNYDER, "THE WAR ON HISTORY IS A WAR ON DEMOCRACY"

I turn from textbook theories
toward listening to strangers in my office
their mute underworlds
articulating
through speech and body.
—LYDIA KWA, "UNSPOKEN" IN *SINUOUS*

Pivots come from geopolitical strategies
(followed as well in competitions via art
markets, science, and education).

Knots come from the psychology of
unexpected outcomes of action.

Hinges come from changes of consciousness
that are accumulative and slow, often recognized
as dramatic shifts only post facto.

This volume complements and expands an earlier volume, *Probing Arts and Emergent Forms of Life* (Fischer 2023), on the arts as complements *alongside* or *in conversation with* ethnographies, and as partial keys to: forms of emergent consciousness, common sense, *sensus communis,* epistemes, habitus, and structures of feeling in the globally interconnected, politically, semiotically, and media-fraught, Anthropocenic twenty-first century. Anthropology is positioned often as a target because it can deploy potent ethnographic tools to analyze, clarify, and make legible the social dramas surrounding films, controversial novels, pandemics, global protests, popular culture inter-references, and historical accounts that have not been settled, and periodically return to haunt the living.

The first three epigraphs above signal some of the political and cultural stakes of witnessing through other means, when erasures of history are enforced by either propaganda of governments or psychological repression of personal trauma, or both. Intan Paramaditha's reference to "Wild Child," the 1959 song by The Doors, is particularly sharp:

> Natural child, terrible child
> Not your mother's or your father's child
> You're our child, screaming wild

It is her metaphor for the rebellious and "lost" generation after the fall of Suharto in Indonesia.[1] It is a generation with analogues across the globe, from the 1968 generation in France and the United States, to the 1360/1980s generation in Iran (Behrouzan 2016). The title of her novel, alluded to in this book's dedication, *Gentayanagan* (translated into English as *Wanderings*), can refer to wanderings between worlds of all sorts, mystical as well as epistemological, cultural as well as historical. But the accent in the novel is less historical hauntology (verticality) and more cosmopolitan youth or young adult (horizontality)—their references beyond the national, their changing of generational experience, their constraints and potentials, enthusiasms and frustrations. As Lydia Kwa puts it, this requires listening for the often mute knots of being caught in circumstances, social forces, family pressures different from those of parents, and gender relations that are intersectional, unpredictable, and pressured, buffeted by geopolitical, global, and planetary shifts, mediated by new algorithmic communication technologies.

By linguistically fraught, I am thinking of such diagnoses as digitally enabled "post-truth" conditions of "equiprobability, where virtually any statement can be challenged at very low, or no cost" (Cesarino 2020), and where cryptographic models of proxy social media dissemination disappear sources as part of hybrid warfare and politics that are inserted into national political systems (Leirner 2020; Fischer 2023). By anthropology as a target, one thinks of resistance to the compensatory politics of attention to those who have had low social and economic capital, seen as inimical to radical neoliberalism and so subject to attack as relativist, sentimental, impractical, opposed to progress (as measured in GDP without serious concern for accompanying growth of inequalities or environmental damage). This issue of anthropology as a target has been trenchantly addressed in a series of sharp essays on Brazil by Brazilian anthropologists pointing out their struggles, along with those of filmmakers, other social scientists, and cultural producers against the presidential regime of Jair Bolsonaro (Almeida 2020; Cabral de Oliveira and Marini 2020; Cavignac 2020; Neiburg and Ribeiro Thomaz 2020).

Films and novels, like ethnographies, provide workspaces for tracing how taken-for-granted common sense changes over time, creating fissures and frictions in the process. Watching new fragments of common sense form and coalesce, while other bits of familiarity fall away, can simultaneously track signals of the future, which is why some novels and films seem prescient. It is as if they are corralling the signs before they surface in public awareness. It is as if they have a kind of foresight. Thus sometimes, it is said, rather than art representing reality, reality seems to follow art. Art can reveal events foretold. Some generations experience rapid social change, and either its accompanying disorientation and alienation, or, alternatively, they can experience heightened hopes for further speedy change toward anticipated outcomes. Friction and differences in experience-grounded common sense can be exacerbated in such speed of change, not just between generations but also between different strata of society: between on the one hand political leaders, elites, and academics, and on the other hand citizenry. Such differences constantly raise questions of proper governance, transparency, accountability, and legitimacy.

Indeed, a thread that runs through many cultural, and postcolonial, discussions in Asia is the competition between forms of authoritarian, centralized governance and unified nationalism versus forms of democratic, decentralized governance and celebrating the strength of diversities of experience. Each political stance has its theoretical advantages and disadvantages, but also each has its hold on different segments of the populace. Indonesia provides a recent clear example of attempts to decentralize, with legacies still in place of entrenched authoritarian local governance and Cold War anti-communist defensiveness. Such is the defensiveness of those "who still cannot utter the acronym for the Indonesian Communist Party—PKI," as Laksmi Pamuntjak writes early in her extraordinary 2013 novel, *Amba: The Question of Red*, "without flinching, without feeling obliged to show disgust" (Pamuntjak 2014, 26). There are two levels of such competition, that of realpolitik (driven by the forces of the political economy) and that of philosophy (rhetorical framings of politics and its legitimations). These competitions are often evoked in the names of Han Fei, the Chinese legalist scholar of the Warring States period (476–221 BCE), who is said to be a touchstone for Xi Jinping, the current leader of China, versus John Locke and Jeremy Bentham, the founders of theories of liberal and social democracy. The Singapore of "Harry" Lee Kuan Yew (popularly known as LKY), the country's Cambridge-educated prime minister from 1959 to 1990 (then senior minister and minister mentor from 1990 to 2011), was somewhere in between. Singapore served as a partial model for China's previous leader, Deng Xiaoping (paramount leader from 1978 to 1989), who visited it in 1978, opened China to capitalist reforms, and whose statue along the Singapore River in front of the Museum of Asian Civilizations commemorates his visit and his call for China to emulate Singapore. In 1985 Deng invited Singapore's former deputy prime minister, the London School of Economics–educated Robert Goh Keng Swee, to advise on special economic zones (SEZs), which became the initial growth engine for Shenzhen and Guangdong province's "capitalism with Chinese characteristics" (Vogel 1989, 2011). Lee Kuan Yew began as a social democrat (his People's Action Party was for a time part of the Socialist International, an organization of European social democratic parties), but increasingly adopted a more meritocratic disciplinary vision akin to Han Fei's, as for instance in his address to the Socialist International Congress in Uppsala in 1966 (Lee Kuan Yew 1966). Both Singapore and Indonesia (since the fall of Suharto, who ruled from 1967 to 1998) are cautiously liberalizing and democratizing within the pressures and constraints of a global neoliberal economy, in the pivot geopolitically between East and West, between China and the United States.

In *Probing Arts*, I explored how artworks (installations, exhibitions, novels, painting, dance, video, and film) provide para-ethnographic access to changing worlds, anticipating changes as much as registering them, and often doing so as much through their tactics and strategies of composition as their ostensive content (see Fischer 2023). Art worlds and comparative literature discussions often revolve around strategies of composition or questions of form, and how they relate to the historical conjunctures out of which they arise. Anthropologists, likewise, have long debated their own arts of writing—to what extent is the pen a form of power over the people being described; to what extent can ethnographic writing be dialogic or polyphonic; to what extent can ethnographic writing adequately stage (as in theater) competitions for hegemonic power, legitimacy, and common sense; what poetic, genre, and stylistic competencies do linguistic, cultural, postcolonial, and de-colonial translations require? Insofar as ethnographic writing attempts to do something other than simply transmit information, the arts of ethnographic writing are a matter of constant discussion, and the forms have changed as the subject matter and goals have.[2]

In this volume I explore how documentary filmmakers and novelists deal with many of these same issues. What makes some experimental films ethnographic? Given that cultural and postcolonial or de-colonial forms increasingly depend on digital platforms, are the lecture-videos of Hito Steyerl and the digital films of Harun Farocki or Xu Bing as important to present-day ethnographic film debates as Third Cinema was to ethnographic film debates in the 1960s and 1970s? Are there novelistic tools of character development (life histories), social analysis (gender, power, genres of speech, visual and spatial markers, class formations), and compositional tactics (omniscient narrator, linguistic code switching, use of visuals, parallel columns, sidebars, or alternating chapters with different narrators to present counterarguments and different perspectives) that can energize ethnographic writing? And can the arts become textual twins (similar but different) to ethnographies, illuminating, interrogating, and reenergizing one another? Indeed, filmmakers, novelists, and playwrights often talk about the importance of their "research"—interviewing, hanging out, observing, sometimes participating—in identical or similar ways as do ethnographers. Verbatim theater puts on stage actual, if edited and shaped, interview transcripts, just like the long-form interviews that ethnographers collect and sometimes also experiment with as publishable forms of encounter, dialogue, or document.[3]

In *Probing Arts*, feminage (feminist cutting and sewing) of modernist Dada puppets and female pirates, and young girls' self-cutting (in Sally Smart's art) conversed with the language of intestines, multiple eyes, and post-wayang superheroes in an Indonesia struggling (in Entang Wiharso's art) to fend off terror past and present (see Fischer 2023). Park Chan-kyong's *Belated Bosal* sent the Buddha off on a funeral pyre in a post-Fukushima irradiated forest; and his *Anyang Paradise City* mixed Asian Gothic, shamanic, and post-*minjung* (people's) art to deal with the national psychological traumas of the 1988 Greenhill Textile Mill fire (in which twenty-two female workers died locked in a dormitory, ironically when the labor movement was at its height) and the 2014 Sewol Ferry sinking (killing 245 high school students and fifty-four others on their way to Jeju Island). Ayoung Kim used her animist and animation art to analogize the Yemeni refugees on Jeju Island twisting in limbo with spinning cubes of precious metals mined and torn from the mother rock in Mongolia. Charles Lim's decade-long video and installation project provided a sea-based view of Singapore's technocratic sublime, including its underground and undersea expansions and its "safe seas" missiles. Malay Archipelago life reemerged in Zai Kuning's ghost ships, *ghazal* music, and *orang laut* (sea peoples) operas. Kumar Kiran and Chandralekha reinvented Indonesian and Indian dance as inquiries into masculinity and femininity, historical codes, tantric roots, repression, and expressive potentials.

I made a claim in *Probing Arts* for a new language of art emergent in Asia that I called synthetic realism, akin perhaps to synthetic biology and its bio-artists (Fischer 2023). Synthetic biology is the redesigning of organisms for new abilities, or the creation of novel organisms that have never previously existed.[4] Synthetic realism, in what I suggest is perhaps a new language of art, is open on the one hand to the technological future, and simultaneously to a critique of the transnational present. It is partly made up of gritty survivorship of war, both World War II and the Cold War, with its guerrilla insurgencies and brutal security-state responses. And it is partly made up of an ability to metabolize transnational cultural and de-colonial circulations both to comment on local-regional dilemmas, and to participate in synthesizing new forms of gaming. Gaming, artificial intelligence, bodily practices, and growing molecular and ecological knowledge all contribute to emergent Asian sensibilities that do not eschew, but rather recruit, shamanic wisdom, shape-shifting animal companions and symbolic hybrids along with attunement to the "movementality" of the Earth (earthquakes, volcanoes) as well as extraction and mining, and engage with transgressive visceralities, desires, winds, religious shadows, and ghosts of the unsettled dead.

All these continue in the present volume but with different media. Documentary filmmaker Tan Pin Pin maps Singapore's urban life through ambulatory sound with and without people, and with literal and figurative time capsules. Women novelists re-narrate Southeast Asian political worlds with surround-sound cinematic motifs, the colors of fauvist and cubist painting, and emotional and psychodynamic intelligence. Daniel Hui's experimental films dissociate, become multiple, and stage gendered psychodramas of political leadership and film directing. Daren Goh reinvents the detective story for the age of artificial intelligence and psychopharmacology, pushing Weberian hyperrationalities beyond the dialectics of Enlightenment, not toward old-style strong-man dictatorships, but locating structures of feeling as social democracy policy goals slide into post-human meritocracy. Analytic monsters reinvent merlions and antabogas (the Ananta Shesha of Hindu texts) as bioengineered, hive minds, and Gestalt social psychologies, and re-narrate archipelagic battles of the geopolitical past and future. Nuraliah Norasid fuses the Greek Medusa with the Chinese White Snake to deliver a critique of racism, ethnic stratification, and erasure of ethnic cultural histories in the meritocracy.

Ethnographic nuggets come as lightning strikes or illuminations of recognition and often sound an alert or fire alarm (*aprés* Walter Benjamin [1928] 1979, 84; see also Löwy 2005), a warning, a call for help, or for doing something new. I had such a flash of illumination when I googled Matisse's *Woman with a Hat* and instantly recognized through its colors what novelist Laksmi Pamuntjak was describing about the portrait of her protagonist's mother in the novel *Fall Baby* (2019). The protagonist, Siri, provides an account of the colors, but only with a better understanding of the goals of fauvism did I fully grasp *and feel* the synesthesia of grief in the nonnaturalist colors of green with some red. I felt it as not just conceptually clear but emotionally powerful. It was for me a moment of illumination, but it also clarified some things in the plot about the dynamics of Siri and her mother with their quite different psychologies, secrets, defense mechanisms, and melancholias in relation to a missing husband and father. I had a similar flash of illumination when Sandi Tan described in published interviews that she wrote the female-perspective novel, *The Black Isle* (S. Tan 2012a) while listening to a loop of favorite film scores. Again, when I tracked down the films she mentioned, their scores and soundtracks suddenly unlocked for me the emotion-rhythms of her novel that was not just another fictive family saga re-narrating Singapore's history. They deepened my ability to track the obsessive and charismatic features of "the Singapore story," and its gendered power and legitimacy struggles, for Singapore but also beyond Singapore.[5] *Flashpoints* are as important as lightning strikes. Flashpoints illuminate deep-play social dramas unfolding in state reactions and public counterreactions to certain artworks that seem to violate often hidden, variable, and moveable, but also tacitly accepted, if contested, "out of bounds" (colloquially called "OB") rules, such as *To Singapore, with Love* (Tan Pin Pin 2013) or Salman Rushdie's *Satanic Verses* (see Fischer 1990, 2014; Fischer and Abedi 1990).[6]

Ethnographic nuggets or revelatory illuminations can come also in the form of dance, through which generation-defining changes in cultural, gender, and de-colonial sensibilities are both registered and shaped. In *Probing Arts*, I opened a discussion about this with Kirin Kumar and Chandralekha's choreographies (recognizing different forms of masculinity, femininity) and with Edith Podesta's *Indices of Vanishment* (Fischer 2023, ch. 6). The latter is a choreography that is almost calligraphic, with ink line-drawing minimalism and conceptual vigor, that is narratively about the emotions of a couple having to move out of their long-occupied flat. The topic of displacement and moving from long-occupied homes comes up again in the present volume in Jing-Jing Lee's novels. Podesta's choreography might be read along with them. Podesta's calligraphic dance reappears in this volume's first chapter on film, in a scene in Tan Pin Pin's film *Singapore GaGa* (2005) about silences, ambient noises, and visuals—all being different kinds of ethnographic brushstrokes. There are two more dance explorations that resonate across *Probing Arts* and *In the Pivot of East and West*: Oliver Tarpaga's *Declassified Memory Fragment* on contemporary violence (that both Singapore and Indonesia have deeply embedded in their body politic as danger points like touching a hot stove); and Steven Page's account of Bangarra Dance Theatre in the documentary film *Firestarter* (Blair and Minchin 2020), using dance as an anti-racist pedagogy and monitoring index of cultural and social change.

Artists have the initial advantage. They are allowed to present unfinished, enigmatic, and unexplained works. Anthropologists return the serve, but are required by peer review and editors to frame and explicate, often reductively, things evasively called theory or narrative (modernization, globalization, neoliberalism). Not that theory is bad, but it must be built up from the ethnography and empirical ground-truthing, not deduced from itself. Theory and ethnography are dialectically related. Less can often be more: an editor-friend advises to focus on "the film not the footage." But for the anthropologist the footage *is* the film. It is what one goes to films to see, or at least what I go for. The footage is or contains the object of desire, however much, in Lacanian fashion, the object may be elusive. It is the traces, the semantic slippages and allusions that are the substance of the conjuring. "The film" is but a frame device, sometimes suggesting a point of view, or a "take," on the richer complexity ("real world"), to which one again returns. Or perhaps better is the analogy with the move in documentary filmmaking to dispense with voice-overs (the theory, narration, or interpretation that overwrites the ethnography.) As Carlos Fausto, the Brazilian anthropologist who has written one of the most exciting books of the past several decades on Amazonian art, puts it: "The complexity that interests me here is . . . that of the form itself and its power to evoke its non-visible parts and convoke an act of looking, setting off an imaginative projection" (Fausto 2020, 22). What is "most exciting" for me about Fausto's book is its dedication to and respect for the ethnographic material (the footage, not the film)—not in some romantic or nostalgic way, but in a way that also pursues historical change, migrations, borrowings, and exchanges.[7] A second important book in a similar vein is Edgar Garcia's interpretive survey of the poetics of North American petroglyphs, Anishinaabe pictographic birchbark scrolls, Nahuatl dialectical parallelism, Maya glyphs as productive, hermeneutically powerful art forms that are not mere "mnemonic cues but also creative prompts" (Garcia 2020, 100). At issue in both books is an artistic creativity that engages and creates social and ecological worlds, that resists cataloguing but demands imaginative participation.[8]

A really good film, theater piece, novel, art installation, or ethnography can be a serious play-space, a place for mind storming and immersion in other worlds. Ethnographic and anthropological commitments to probing what is "actually the case" place simple constraints on such forms, raising the bar above journalistic "human interest" vignettes (that at best ignite more in-depth interest); travel literature's usually thin engagement with locals (better for the ethnography of the travelers' own culture than of local, native points of view); or speculative fantasy fiction's relaxation of reality constraints (as opposed to "hard" science fiction which probes the limits of the feasible). These commitments to the real, the actual, the empirical, and ground truth can enliven other forms of future-thinking such as scenario-building, ecological-, systems-, and design-thinking, and artificial intelligence. Ethnographic (and comparative) thinking and open-ended participant observation (reality-checking, asking questions *in situ*) can aid in policy work. It can help, for instance, in redesigning the internet (against government and corporate intrusiveness, bias in algorithms and in very large-scale data governance) so as to keep decision-making driven by "big data" from turning human beings into surplus and ghost labor—as already Germaine de Staël worried in 1813 about the mechanisms of Napoleonic bureaucracy (Staël 1818), and Mary Gray and Siddhart Suri in more recent times about Silicon Valley (Gray and Suri 2019)—and to protect against political tyranny sold as management efficiency. These last worries are raised by various theorists of efficient tyranny from Plato's philosopher-king and Khomeini's variant thereof, as well as Han Fei's "realist legalism" and Xi Jinping's or Lee Kuan Yew's variants; or Taylorist and neoliberal management-speak variously analyzed for the present by Luc Boltanski and Eve Chiapello in *The New Spirit of Capitalism* (1999), by Naomi Klein in *The Shock Doctrine* (2008), and several other recent books (Zuboff 2019; Gray and Suri 2019; and McGhee 2021).

Singapore plays an important role in contemporary debates on all these issues, as if in a battle royale, or superpower-ideological competition, with Han Fei in one corner and John Locke or Jeremy Bentham in the other. The Singapore model is discussed intensively by those who would reform and strengthen China (Deng Xiaoping's call for China to emulate Singapore in opening up to capitalism with Chinese characteristics; Xi Jinping's return to Han Fei–inspired strong central control plus imperial expansion via Belt and Road projects across Central and Southeast Asia, similar initiatives along the Pacific Rim to New Guinea, Indonesia, and Australia, and across Africa and Latin America). The Singapore model is likewise discussed by Western theorists who fear the end of the promises of social democracy, that those promises are being overwhelmed by increasingly specialized, mutually implicated systems, and fragility of critical infrastructures of twenty-first-century society. But it is in novels, films, and ethnographies that these theories are broken down into actual lives, scenarios, and alternative outcomes.

In the following three sections, I expand a bit about pivots (in geopolitical space), knots (of the psyche and social psychology), hinges (of history), and portals (to the future). They are metaphors or concepts that may be helpful in thinking about historical changes in consciousness, common sense, the *sensus communis*, habitus, culture, structures of feeling, and communities of practice.[9] Concepts are, in fact, metaphors, transposable frameworks that allow movement across particular examples.[10] They usually fail after a time through obsolescence, overuse, erosion by changes in the worlds to which they are applied, or sheer academic industry needs for novelty, like any other capital, needing renewal and faster or wider circulation. They can be analytics for a time, temporary logical operators. They perform better in the plural: always try in a sentence to pluralize the nouns to see if that makes a logical difference. Singularizing tends to be a philosopher's sleight of hand to imply substance and to overcome having to deal with contingency, limitations, and situatedness.

For "pivots" in geopolitical space, art markets and commissions serve as initial loci to think with. Other key loci are advertising and political messaging (ideology), also science and universities, to which I return in the book's afterword. In all these ventures, Singapore is a global soft-power player, looking to both the West and East. As first examples of sites of constant pivoting, looking both east and west, I draw upon Woon Tai Ho's satirical novel *Riot Green* (2013) and his commentary on the polymath painter, poet, and sculptor Tan Siew Hian, *To Paint a Smile* (2008).

For "knots," I use clinical psychologist Lydia Kwa's novel *Pulse* ([2010] 2014), and then follow out the theme of feminist and intercultural knots in a series of women-authored novels. I am looking there for a writing style analogous to Helene Cixous's notion of *écriture féminine*, which as I will explain below has different valences than "women's writing," ones that not only involve writing with the body, but retain the tensions and ambiguities of what dancer Steven Page calls "cultural fuels."

For "hinges," I use the evolution of the dance troupe led by Page, an evolution pivoting and navigating between tradition and avant-garde, "blak" and white Australia, rural and urban Aborigines. It is a particularly good exemplar of what I call a "hinge" in history: persistent slow change that only retrospectively seems dramatic and that remains unfinished, still swinging back and forth. Hinges are a counterpoint to the notion of "critical events," or even just "events," without the modifier "critical," as philosophers sometimes distill it in their singularizing fashion.[11] Critical events are more often markers than producers, moments of revelation of processes that have long been working relatively unobtrusively. One thinks of Karl Marx's notion of social revolutions that take a century to unfold, exploding in a moment when *anciens régimes* are swiftly swept away, and new constitutions confirm and give legal force to the social relations that have been changing for a long time.

While the Bangarra Dance Theatre provides a fulsome example of a hinge over time, chapter 1 suggests that Tan Pin Pin's documentary films can also illustrate such a hinge of history, as does chapter 2's juxtaposition of Sandi Tan's film *Shirkers* with her novel *The Black Isle*. I hope by the end of the book, especially with chapters 7 and 5 (for Indonesia), that the opening three chapters will show this kinetics as historical movement and not just moments in history. Indeed, throughout I am arguing that the novelists and filmmakers discussed are trying to set free *frozen historical narratives*, to bridge the gap between worn-out narratives and the weaving of more flexible new ones, incorporating ongoing changes. In Singapore, this desire is repeated over and over by artists. Many of them fall back into the trap that contesting a frozen narrative tends to reinscribe it. I try to deal with that puzzling dilemma especially in chapter 6. That chapter also contributes to the changing structures of feeling that chapters 2 and 3 foreground.

Dance, as noted above, often carries, reflects, and performatively changes the deep-play dilemmas in society in a largely nondiscursive medium. They emerge here from the margins especially in the post-afterword Exergue. While the afterword is about portals to the future, the post-afterword returns to hinges of history. As just said, Bangarra is a key example for me of how culture changes slowly, yet in retrospect dramatically, but yet always with more work to be done. I dub this, after Jacques Derrida, a *hinge* that slowly moves in one direction, and often back, before (perhaps, no guarantee) swinging further open. Hinges squeak and move back and forth, but also allow differences to manifest for negotiation. In Derrida's use, the hinge (*la brisure*) is an act of unfolding, a reawakening. It "enacts a recognition that . . . differing and articulating, is performative: to begin is to open; to open is to inaugurate; and to inaugurate is to create (again, anew)"

(Protevi 2005, ix). The work of the Bangarra Dance Theatre is an example worth thinking with back over this volume, even if, like Tarpaga's *Declassified Memory Fragment* from Burkina Faso (see Fischer 2023, 204), it is geographically a bit further afield in Australia and the Torres Strait. Some readers might insist on zombie concepts that would exclude Australia from this volume's centers of attention, but there are deep historical connections between the Malay world, the Melanesian one, and the Australian Aboriginal one. It is the conjunctural and historical geopolitics of the last four hundred years that has separated and continues to separate these places into different cultural spheres. Bangarra's engagement with intercultural relations, protocols of respect, and agency through art are in many respects parallel to those in Singapore and Indonesia (as well as the United States and its indigenous nations). In any case, as a methodological matter of ethnographic reinvigoration, this example of a hinge of history may perhaps prove to be a foreshadowing also of part of the story I want to tell in a future third volume on *Risky Theater and the Ethnography of Life*. That story is about the theater in Singapore and the slow but steady movement for gay rights, fuller intercultural recognition, and the remapping of structures of feeling in a fast-changing society.

Pivots have to do with geographical and topological mobilities, spaces of exchange, the shuttling of threads into new fabrics. This is the world of migrants, diasporas, émigrés, population shifts, cultural influences and exchanges. It is also the world of cultural fuel or tinder, and of art effects. In recent years it has also become (again) a term in global strategy, as in the United States pivoting from protecting oil in the Middle East to protecting sea lanes in Southeast and East Asia, making Singapore key in both versions of global visioning.[12] Singapore from the inside also sees itself as a pivot between East and West, playing a keystone role in the Association of Southeast Asian Nations, as well as readying its population for dealings with the West and China (asking citizens to be proficient in both Mandarin and English), and also forging an observer role in Arctic Circle diplomacy on which, as an economy dependent on logistics, it may have a future interest as Arctic sea lanes open.

Knots have to do with mental health, constructions of personhood, gender relations, pain and joy, with not so much nineteenth-century British utilitarian debates over individuals versus society, but rather with post-Freudian (Malinowskian, or Durkheimian) always already psychosocial beings operating within worlds of hinges and pivots.

PIVOTS: EAST AND WEST ART MARKETS/COMMISSIONS, ADVERTISING, SCIENCE, UNIVERSITIES

> Poor girl, Chinese in every aspect, yet she doesn't speak a word of her mother tongue. Not connected to her roots, her heritage. . . . Ah Poh has seen enough disconnected souls. When a strong wind blows, their illusive identities are swept away like fallen leaves.
>
> WOON TAI HO, *RIOT GREEN*

> The complexity that interests me here is not that of occult meanings, but rather that of the form itself and its power to evoke its non-visible parts, and convoke the act of looking, setting off an imaginative projection.
>
> CARLOS FAUSTO, *ART EFFECTS*

An obvious place to think about the pivoting between East and West, if you are not going to do finance or logistics, advertising or higher education, or science, might be the art markets. Each of these topics can be mirror worlds and pivot sites in which both actors and spectators can lose themselves.

A simple entry point might be Woon Tai Ho's satirical novel, *Riot Green* (2013), on the art market, and his commentary on the artist Tan Swie Hian, *To Paint a Smile* (2008). Woon Tai Ho has himself transitioned from being a founder of Channel News Asia to marketing consultant, along the way becoming an art collector, as well as a friend of Tan Swie Hian; both Woon Tai Ho and Tan Swie Hian grew up in the Singapore neighborhood of Geylang, where the latter still lives. *To Paint a Smile*, apart from its wonderful title, is a confection of observations loosely built around often astute engagements with the work of Tan Swie Hian, one of the polymath painters and poets of Singapore.[13] Among Tan Swie Hian's many honors, from both West and East, are being the third Asian to be named a correspondent of the French Academy of Fine Arts (after I. M. Pei and Kenzo Tange), as well as being invited to carve a portrait of the poet Qu Yuan (340–278 BCE) on the walls of the Three Gorges, and to carve the Heart Sutra on a twenty-story-high cliff above an 8-kilometer climb with calligraphic tributes to famous Eastern and Western figures along the path up.[14] The novel *Riot Green* resonates in part with Indonesian novelist Laksmi Pamuntjak's more intricate *Fall Baby* (2019), discussed in chapter 5, in its reflections on color, the art market, and the psychological struggles out of which striking art sometimes emerges. It also resonates with Lydia Kwa's more intricate use of both vernacular and classical Chinese cultural fuel in *Oracle Bone* (2017), discussed in chapter 3:

both draw upon the *Shan Hai Jing*, or *Guideways through Mountains and Seas*, a compilation from the Warring States period to the Western Han period, fourth century to first century BCE (see the translation and commentary by Strassberg [2002]).

Woon Tai Ho's books are time stamped: 2008 is the time of the global financial crisis that began with the US subprime mortgage collapse (a bubble created by efforts to create new "structured finance" mortgage-backed bonds intended to spread risk into disappearance). And 2013 is a time when Southeast Asian art suddenly began to shatter auction house prices: in 2011, Philippine artist Robert Ventura's *Greyground* sold for US$1.1 million, and Indonesian artists also began to pass the US$1 million mark in the years after 2008.

Riot Green is the story of a child prodigy painter, Melissa, who paints stunning green canvases in a lyrical, abstract style that express deep inner turmoil and family dysfunction. Her paintings break through and achieve new high auction prices. The color green she explains is not a primary color, and when it dominates primary colors it can take on a "rare, even mystical dimension . . . people seem to think the green paintings are more layered and powerful" (Woon 2013, 87). They are layered with many colors and shades of green. She paints them in a trance-like state during which she hums a Buddhist-like incantation. Among the most intense are the green canvases in which the green eyes of her cat are captured staring back.

Many of the painters mentioned in *Riot Green* are so-called practitioners of "lyrical abstraction," trained in China and then Paris (painters such as Zao Wou-ki and Chu Teh-Chun, both born in the early 1920s and both recently deceased); or they are of a younger generation, born in the 1950s and deeply affected by the psychological turmoil of the Cultural Revolution (such as Zhang Xiaogang and Wang Guangyi). These are all painters who are popular among foreign investors, notes Melissa's gallerist, who owns pieces of their work or represents them. While nothing more is said explicitly in the novel about their paintings, they are reference points for those who hover in and around the market.

Zhang Xiaogang, known for his "Bloodline: The Big Family" series, was inspired by photographs of his mother as a young vibrant woman, contrasting with the sickly schizophrenic woman she became. He has said, "For me, the Cultural Revolution is a psychological state, not a historical fact. It has a very strict connection with my childhood, and I think there are many things linking the psychology of the Chinese people today with the psychology of the Chinese people back then. We all live 'in a big family.'"[15] Although *Riot Green* is set in Singapore, not China, the dysfunctional family, and the distorting psychology of the market, that Melissa's painting reflects are similar. And similarly, Wang Guangyi is known for his cycle of works, "Great Criticism" (1990–2007), which combines Cultural Revolution propaganda images with advertising logos as two forms of brainwashing. He stopped the series when he felt his international success was compromising the original meaning of the work, advertising negating the meaning. I will return below briefly to advertising as another key pivot site, but here register the resonance with the work experiences of Woon Tai Ho (Channel News Asia, art market participation, and marketing consultancy).

The child prodigy painter, Melissa, is the object of psychological warfare among those who would control her painting destiny in a market that is heating up for young Asian painters. Hong Kong has just become the third Art Basel venue (in 2013) and Art Stage Singapore began in 2011 (lasting for the next decade as a global art fair with a Southeast Asian focus). The stock market collapse in 2009 allowed for money to move into gray markets of the art world, in which the novel's gallerist has successfully played, securing her collection (as has Woon Tai Ho himself) in Singapore's Free Port vaults—themselves marketed globally as a hyper-secure alternative to Switzerland (Woon 2013, 48). In the novel, Indonesian collector Kevin Gunawan (a nod perhaps to high-selling Indonesian painter Hendra Gunawan) visits an auction at the Regent Hotel in Singapore, musing that "auctions are still the best platform to determine the public worth of an artist" (171) in otherwise informal and loosely organized Southeast Asian markets. The mark of arrival in the top rank on the international stage in the first two decades of the twenty-first century was said to be an artist being able to command a US$1 million dollar sale, which a number of Indonesians had.[16]

> While Hong Kong may be the auction capital in Asia, Indonesia, the third largest country in Asia after China and India, has organized successful auctions for nearly two decades now. This follows the burst of young artists, particularly in Jogjakarta who have found an artistic language that departs from that of their Dutch colonial past. While modern masters like Affandi still rule, fresh images have emerged that spring from youthful abstract minds, influenced by prevalent trends from the West. Their Indonesian roots may still be present, the execution is clearly contemporary and unprecedentedly conceptual. (170)

The pressure on Melissa comes from both hidden family dynamics and "the senseless swordplay of hidden intent and conspiratorial jostling" in "the club of predators gyrating around Melissa" (141). Already at age twelve, Melissa had produced an oil painting of her mother, "a young girl's take on confusion, her precocious knowing of her dysfunctional family" (141). Only five years later would her father disclose that he was gay, allowing her to reassess what she has felt as danger coming from him, and allowing a reconfiguration of the family system dynamics of her mother and grandmother on one side, and her gallerist's efforts to align market forces on the other. As the latter puts it, "in the art world, good is not good enough . . . you have to be . . . manipulatively good" (165), or, differently expressed, "it's art, subjective and totally open to patronage or dismissal, support or neglect and it needs buzz, it's the auction house" (105).

The key scene in this strategic jostling of hidden intents—grandmother and mother trying to protect a vulnerable girl; gallerist, collectors, investors trying to align a market—is transposed into the language and forms of the world of spirits and ghosts, in which the non-English speaking (Hokkien-speaking) grandmother, the adult most protective of her granddaughter, is the most intuitive. A proxy battle is fought between a fortune-telling Taoist priest (using squares, calculations, and almanacs) consulted by the grandmother, and a computer- and Facebook-using immigrant from mainland China consulted by the gallerist. Each occult master extracts maximum payment utilizing their intuitions and guesses about the fears of the principals. In the end, it is the gallerist who has a nervous breakdown, trading places with Melissa, whose manipulated madness is lifted. It was important, the gallerist had admitted, to have a mysterious backstory about a mad genius girl so that the over-hyped high prices her paintings command, as a teenager, could have a future. One could engineer thereby a withdrawal from the market, and a return some years later, using the story of a volatile mad genius who could disappear again at any moment, thus generating another investment opportunity bubble.

It is fascinating that although Hong Kong is a modern rival to Singapore and receives most attention, Guangzhou and Fujian—from where the grandmother comes, as do many Singaporeans in previous generations—remain the focus of mystified nostalgia and charismatic forces. Rivalry with Hong Kong seems to overwrite the alternative universe of reality in which Singaporean and other Southeast Asian overseas Chinese money has been flowing back to villages and towns of Fujian, rebuilding temples, reigniting shamanistic practices (Dean and Zheng 2009, 2010). It also overwrites Shanghai (before Hong Kong) as the center of Chinese modernism in the 1920s and 1930s. As with advertising, this is in part a function of the dynamics of being in the pivot between East and West in a contemporary hinge of history.

Advertising is another arena in this pivoting field of seeing or losing the self in mirrored others. Jacques Lacan suggested that infants pass through a developmental stage of first recognizing themselves in a mirror as an objective whole apart from the mother—that is, misrecognizing themselves as whole, autonomous, omnipotent beings with desires that must be met (Lacan [1949] 2006; Johnston 2018). But more generally Lacan insisted it was not so much a developmental stage as a general process of self-misrecognition and alienation that can be manipulated by the disciplining and marketing industries—that is, by ideology and fantasy, both operating through desire or fear. Lee Weng Choy, drawing in part on the ideas of sociologist Chua Beng Huat (1995, 2017), notes that in official Singaporean rhetoric, "the frequent othering of the United States is symptomatic of what Chua describes as the anti-liberal democracy of the ruling People's Action Party," as if (now quoting Janadas Devan) "a young Singapore still in its mirror stage" (Lee Weng Choy 2001, 97). Key texts here could be any number of speeches by Lee Kuan Yew or his son Lee Hsien Loong. Lee Weng Choy chooses the 1994 National Day rally speech by then prime minister Goh Chok Tong in which America is described as declining due to losing its traditional values and adopting a liberalism in which all values are open to negotiation. For a short period, Singapore attempted to reinvent a tradition of Confucian Asian values as a counterpoint. What Lee Weng Choy finds fascinating is that this "ideological othering of America by Singapore's leaders may seem contradictory, since the United States is hardly a political, military, or economic threat but rather an important ally in all three regards" (Lee Weng Choy 2001, 97).[17] Writing at the turn of the twenty-first century, he uses "the term 'McNationalism' to designate the complex of tensions between nationalism and the forces of rationalization and globalization" (Lee Weng Choy 2001, 98); and in fact Singapore is ever more positioning itself as a hub for capital accumulation by multinational corporations, now both American and products of the growing state capitalism of mainland China. While Choy's examples of media campaigns from the mid-1990s are now dated—and have been subjected to wonderful ironic, analytic, and nostalgic poster exhibits of state and commercial advertising (held at Singapore's National Library)—his general account is well taken.

This pivoting tension is nowhere more coiled with pressure than in the restructuring of university education, caught between redoubling down on the production of engineers and designers to feed global multinational market competition on the one hand, and on the other an effort to rebuild a twenty-first-century humane society with more egalitarian stability and environmental sustainability.[18] The coiled tension is intensified and complicated by the drive to create a high-tech knowledge society drawing upon and competitive with a global pool of scientific personnel (Fischer 2013, 2018a). Singapore's drive to become a global arts city is partly driven by its educated middle classes, but also by its need to appeal to so-called foreign talent attracted to live and work in the city-state. See, for instance, the aspirationally titled *Art Cities of the Future* (Byrd et al. 2013) and *From Identity to Mondialisation* (TheatreWorks 2013).

Suppose you had an opportunity to create new universities in the middle world between East and West. What kind of vision for them would you design? Two such projects fell into my ethnographic vision during the decade between 2009 and 2020, at the oldest and newest flagship universities in Singapore. One was shaped by a humanistic STS (science, technology, and society) vision of dealing with big social issues on the intimate scale of cross-disciplinary teaching. I participated in that project by teaching a class on Biomedicine and Singapore Society with students whose backgrounds ranged from architecture and business to social work, bioengineering, law, sociology, and the visual arts. We used popular role-playing pedagogies, and produced final team projects on designing a multigenerational apartment complex, and a theater piece with video on negotiating end-of-life decision-making between hospital lawyers, doctors, finance administrators, and family members (Fischer 2018c). This was at Tembusu College, one of four new residential colleges of the National University of Singapore pioneering the breaking down of disciplinary silos in undergraduate education to give students a feel for working across disciplines on real-world issues. The other was helping coach a very different interdisciplinary model at the new Singapore University of Technology and Design (SUTD) built around the integration of engineering and architecture, with supplementary tracks in the humanities and social sciences and later biology and chemistry. Though both had connections with the Massachusetts Institute of Technology (MIT), the difference and tension between the two models might be signaled by two quotations. One is from Deputy Prime Minister Tharman Shanmugaratnam: "We are still a little too much of a hierarchy based on what happened to you at age 18, what scores you had, what qualifications you had, which course you could go to" (Chan 2013). The other is by the sitting prime minister, Lee Hsien Loong, at the official opening of SUTD on May 8, 2015:

> [In the first fifty years of independent Singapore, we] channeled people towards STEM, we invested in this. We made sure that our students received good education in maths and science in the primary and secondary school levels and in the post-secondary education whether in the ITE, Polytechnics or Universities. We weighted our whole education system heavily towards STEM. We strongly encouraged students to master STEM subjects, *rather than softer fields of study*. You may ask me which are the softer fields of study but I think I shall be polite today and leave it to you to imagine them. . . . At Silicon Valley, the parents are all scientists, mathematicians, IT engineers, married to mathematicians, scientists, IT engineers. Their children go and do mind expanding liberal arts. Nothing wrong with that but if everybody does that I think the balance has shifted and we have to maintain the right balance. . . . SUTD must ride this wave and champion science and technology. *Technology is in your name so you must live up to it*. (Lee Hsien Loong 2015)

You can imagine how this was heard by a faculty that had been hard at work trying to create a new interdisciplinary curriculum that included "the softer fields of study." A short time later, the president of MIT, Susan Hockfield, came to visit and gave a (somewhat obliviously) enthusiastic speech about how all new cutting-edge fields at MIT were built around the new biological sciences; SUTD had none of this.

These two quotations by Singaporean leaders are only minor signals in a much deeper and wider discussion of the proper directions for training and higher education, not only in Singapore. Exploring this is beyond the scope of this volume. I invoke them here only as part of the pivot situation of not only universities in Singapore but universities everywhere driven (perversely, many think) by international ratings based in Shanghai and London that can affect money flows and recruiting.[19] Constantly pivoting between West and East.

KNOTS: *ÉCRITURE FÉMININE*, WRITING, AND SEXUAL DIFFERENCE—THE ANTHROPOLOGICAL STAKES

> The pleasure that comes from pleasurable surroundings is
> not true pleasure.
> Only with the pleasure obtained in the midst of suffering
> Can one see the true movements of the mind.
>
> HUNG YING-MING, QUOTED BY KWA IN THE "SOJOURN" SECTION OF *SINUOUS*

> *one thousand and one nights*
> ceases to be a romantic notion
> when these tales of suffering keep me awake
> wondering what else is beneath
> frantic despair
>
> LYDIA KWA, FROM THE SECTION "UNSPOKEN" IN *SINUOUS*

Écriture féminine served me as an umbrella title for chapters 2 through 4 as the French seemed to resonate quite differently from the American "sexual difference and writing." Until it ran into disciplinary police. So I have used them both here and try to indicate how *écriture féminine* resonates for me in pushing, beyond the Euro-American canon, to novels from elsewhere (*écriture féminine otherwise or elsewhere* seemed too inelegant), which will require also some close reading, lest these novels get slotted simply into other quick-at-hand rubrics of women's writing in American reviewers' categories, without exploring what I think of as their ethnographic or para-ethnographic work—their situatedness geographically, culturally, socially, and in their historical horizons more fully. *Jouissance*, another French term, plays a role here. It means extreme pleasure, sexual orgasm, and the legal right to enjoy the use of something. For the psychoanalyst Jacques Lacan it was the split in desire between instinctual drive (need) and the demand for it to be satisfied by the Other, hence also more often than not an intersubjective mobility pursued in suspension, slippage, or transference.

Écriture féminine is often tightly bound to the work, writing style, and 1970s politics of Hélène Cixous, who coined the term her in her essays "The Laugh of the Medusa" (1976) and "Coming to Writing" (1977), though it is a style shared or overlapping with those of others, especially Clarice Lispector and Jacques Derrida; and developed in slightly different ways by Julia

Kristeva, Luce Irigaray, and Monique Wittig in France, but with affinities to such American literary feminists as Gloria Anzaldúa and Audre Lorde, and elaborations by such American feminist critics as Barbara Johnson, Gayatri Spivak, and Donna Haraway.[20] Laksmi Pamuntjak's essay "On Reading Woman" (2007) draws on Cixous, and much of her writing in essays, plays, as well as her novels, draws on these ideas as well.

Cixous's poetic writing attempts to show, and forge, how openness to the play of the gendered body, its unconscious and libido, can create differences between female and male writing and in the use of language and textuality: "Write yourself. Your body must be heard. Only then will the immense resources of the unconscious spring forth" (Cixous 1976, 880). Or: "*Je suis là où ça parle*," "I am there where it/id/the female unconscious speaks" (quoted in Jones 1981), sometimes in the "white ink" of the mother's milk (Cixous and Clement 1975, 94). Kristeva's version conceptualizes this as a *chora*, or prelinguistic signifying or "semiotic" with the mother, and a sexual pleasure (*jouissance*) that breaks the grammar of symbolic language (figured as male), disrupting rationality and order, and which is also explored in avant-garde experimental writing (James Joyce being a key example for her, as well as providing Jacques Lacan with an allied notion of *jouissance*). For Irigaray, this *parler femme*, "womanspeak," and women's *jouissance* originates in the polymorphous erogenous zones of the female body in contrast to male unitary phallic pleasure and linear thinking. Friedrich Kittler's version for an earlier period of women's writing—when mother's tongue was being overshadowed by father's tongue, the novel was coming into formation, looking back to that history through surrealism, symbolism, and structuralism—was *écriture féminine automatique* (Kittler 1992). Charles Baudelaire, in his short poem "Correspondances," neatly illustrated the poetic rhythm and personal prosody central to such writing, and, I will suggest, features in Lydia Kwa's novels as well as her poetry.

In all these speculations about *écriture féminine*, there is a weaving back and forth between essentializing woman (as difference) and the anti-essentialism inherent in the wild adventuresome, unboundedness of the unconscious, the libido, and openness to experience: "Her libido is cosmic" (Cixous 1976, 17). These theories merge sometimes uneasily with concerns about affects as socially created circuits that can be manipulated into repressive ideological instruments of capitalism, neoliberalism, biopolitics, and reproductive demands that constrain women and marginalize nonnormative gender identifications.

In efforts to clarify the political stakes, Barbara Johnson (1987, 2003; see also Damrosch 2020) shows how a purely rhetorical analysis of the insights and blindness of texts (undoing their own claims), such as those of Paul de Man, can erase gender, class, and race differences. But she further shows—in even such feminist novels as those of Nancy Friday's *My Mother/My Self* (1997) about women trying to gain independence from maternal figures, and Dorothy Dinnerstein's *The Mermaid and the Minotaur* (1976), showing that because parenting falls more on mothers, resentments do as well—that more complexities are involved than simple empowerment aspirations, and that, as with Mary Shelley's Frankenstein, the creation of mother-daughter relations can be complex "monstrous" knots. In Shelley's case there is a set of knots: Mary Shelley and her creation of Frankenstein, Frankenstein and his creation, Mary Shelley's relation to her own mother who died in birthing her, and Mary Shelley's own stillborn child (Shelley [1818] 2018).

Finding a political voice in such complexity is also the concern of Gayatri Spivak's analysis of Devi's story of Draupadi, in which Devi and Spivak, rather than identifying with Draupadi against patriarchy, both identify themselves with the police interrogator Senayak. "Whatever his [Senayak's] practice, in *theory* he respects the opposition. . . . Thus he understood them by (theoretically) becoming one of them. He hopes to write on all this in the future" (Spivak 1981a, 394). This is a position, Spivak suggests, like that of feminists in the First World. David Damrosch (2000) points out in his readings of Johnson and Spivak that in the *Critical Inquiry* special issue on "Writing and Sexual Difference" in which Spivak's "Draupadi" piece appeared, hers was the only essay with a non-Western focus. Spivak elsewhere calls for a stance in which "feminist alternative readings might well question the normative rigor of specialist mainstream scholarship through dramatization of the autobiographical vulnerability of their provenance" (Spivak 1981b). Donna Haraway makes such complexities and dialectics explicit, saying that she remains committed to three imperatives even though they may conflict, and when that happens one just has to "stay with the trouble": commitments to feminism, to democratic socialism, and to science (Haraway 2016).

The stakes for me, however, are not to harmonize the definitions, characteristics, theories, or positions like those above, but rather are ethnographic. Aside from descriptions of places, peoples, and time horizons, what do women writers and intellectuals have to say about the developments in the societies in which they are psychologically invested? How might they guide us in their emotional rhythms, para-linguistics, and behavioral scripts? Might they introduce us to the "heart of what's the matter," the semiotics of illness and health, to the vernacular gendered codes in times of war and conflict as well as in daily life (Good 1976; Good and Good 2013)? How can we use the creative writing of women about their lives and societies to paint, and understand, their societies not as essentialized cultures, but as changing, friction- and conflict-filled, worlds and social fields that often are counterpoints and deconstructions, if not contradictory to, or separated from male, official, or "normalized" (adhering to public norms) stories? Novelists are often para-ethnographers, particularly helpful when writing about their own societies with an eye for mapping worlds that lie athwart male worlds.

While the prelinguistic or the maternal is theorized as being an anchor point in *écriture féminine*, especially in the formula of the "m(other)" or the "not me within-me," which can include males,[21] a second important focus, genre, or topos is the *wise old woman* (Begum 2015, 71) who narrates, and provides a defiant counter to accusations of the female as hysterical. Or, as Cixous puts it, *écriture féminine* inverts the accusation of hysterical into a positive openness to the world rather than a pathology of not fitting into (male) constraints. In more technical terms, perhaps, the narrator turns the hysterical into hysteresis, the dependence of the state of a system on its history, on a lag between causes and consequences, and the memory that is retained despite the lag or delay.[22] Such memories in psychoanalysis (and reality) are open to distortions, displacements, "secondary revisions," but also, crucially, contain gaps, holes, and absences, particularly of traumatic events.[23]

Wise old women often are the truth-tellers who sift through the distortions, recovering connections that have been severed. Thus, accused sometimes of sorcery, of being witches or shamans, they are often marginalized in a constant dialectic of historical repression and recovery. On the other hand, wise old women are often lost to grandchildren through language changes, "listening through gaps for the occasional, recognizable word," from a poem whose very title is evocative of the ambivalent play of patriarchal and maternal, and between past and present, "Father:Mother:Tongue" (Kwa 1994b, 38).

Of technological note in these dialectics are the historical markers of writing (when do women's texts appear historically?) and when do cassette tape recorders become available (which, like letters and time capsules, may be hidden away and only come to light at a later time in a different context, interacting with Freud's *Nachträglichkeit*)? Writing can be a process of self-discovery, also an aide-mémoire, but texts, as often, lose orality's feedback and contexts, and frequently need interrogation, deconstruction, and situating. The novel might be seen as an attempt to incorporate rich contexts, but novels, too, provide the grounds for multiple readings and interpretations. The tape recorder, as a literary device in novels, often functions as a time capsule to be rediscovered at a later time, promising a "live" voice, often with a questioner who helps elicit and clarify the narrator's meaning, now lost in fading turns of phrase, allusions, idioms, and references. Text messaging is a newer device that begins to appear as a channel of intimacy, and as Lydia Kwa writes, "if a text message seems disembodied, it's only because the receiver knows little or nothing of the sender's facial expressions, the nuance revealed in the way someone uses his body" (Kwa [2010] 2014, 84).

HINGES: FREEING UP FROZEN HISTORICAL NARRATIVES

> Dance is a better *pedagogy* for the classroom than reading a text.
> JASMINE NG, JANUARY 19, 2020, INTERVIEW

> Dance is easy, compared to negotiating the cultural protocols.
> STEPHEN PAGE, IN *FIRESTARTER*

The documentary film *Firestarter: The Story of Bangarra Dance Theatre* (Blair and Minshin 2020)—*bangarra* means to make fire, or to ignite, in the Wiradjuri language—is about how this Aboriginal dance company is determined to teach Australians a different way of seeing their Aboriginal consociates, and newly recognized fellow citizens, by creating a fusion of authentic tradition, honest history, and creative modern dance. The film shows Prime Minister Kevin Rudd's 2008 apology to the Aborigines for settler colonialism. The film encourages white Australians to recognize alternative migration histories going back forty thousand years, as well as alternative ways of living on the land *with* the ecology, rather than against it, particularly now under conditions of climate change.[24] The aftermaths of the atomic bomb tests in Australia, recalled in one of Bangarra's dance performances, parallels Park Chan-kyong's film *Belated Bosal*, described in *Probing Arts* (Fischer 2023), which staged a funeral for the Buddha along with constant testing for radiation levels in the radioactive dark forest of our post-

Fukushima nuclear meltdown world. More recently there have been further parallel forms of the need for constant testing and monitoring in the coronavirus pandemic-stalled world of 2020–2022. In the Australian desert, radiation effects are marked on the land in glassy fused silicone embedded in the parched, cracked desert surface. The effects are also in humans and other mammals. They are in memories of white X-ray flashes that revealed one's bones. The flashes warned of proleptic dead men walking with hidden cancers.[25] Today, we have a few tests and sentinels for the changing external nature, habitat, or ecology within which we live. There is recognition that the Aborigines had some smart environmental management techniques for both agriculture on land and marine environments. There are monitoring tests for our internal nature, immune systems, microbiomes, and cell memories of past viral and bacterial agonistes. These constitute two of the *four natures* to which I have argued we should be paying attention (Fischer 2009, 114–58). Perhaps there will be further monitoring and tests for reconstructing our social bodies, for healing our structural inequities and disparities, not only at the level of aggregate socioeconomic statistics.

But, for now, novels, films, and dance are among our probing arts: probing our psychologies under different forms of governance, using different analytic monsters, myths, and ritual processes to map lines of stress and fracture. *At the Pivot of East and West* continues the discussion of *Probing Arts* (Fischer 2023) about the role of modern dance that can reignite the cultural fuel or tinder of generations of experience, and locate hinges of change—the hinges between different communities of common sense and sensibilities—attentive both to the sensoria and to the cultural logics, both to movement and to narrative.

Four claims made by Stephen Page in *Firestarter* (Blair and Minshin 2020) may serve more generally as methodological touchpoints for para-ethnographic social and cultural analysis of the novels and films in this volume.

First, "You can't tell the story of Aboriginal Australia without featuring Bangarra."[26] While this is a specific claim for Australia, I read it more generally as saying both that you cannot tell the history of a place without its central art forms and, further, that the arts are where historical hinges are often to be found most clearly articulated. This is somewhat different from older symbolic anthropology.[27] The historical hinge finds in the arts not a key paradigm or stable symbolic structure, but rather positionings betwixt and between larger complex contemporary worlds.

Second, the arts are a primary way that people are educated to accept others as having something interesting to share and teach, and to achieve acceptance. It is a claim I am making more generally for the role of the arts in changing general common sense and sensibilities in this volume, with films showing the state of conflicts, and novels working through details of lives and the ways in which choices are structured by historical circumstances. Conflicting norms of common sense constitute a politics both in the usual sense and in the sense of Michel Foucault and Jacques Rancière (or that of Marx, Weber, and Gramsci) of making some things more thinkable, or seeable, recognizing differences, and understanding dissensus as active politics.

The third claim is a warning for those who would describe, account for, or characterize others: "You don't define who I am, you don't get that, I'll define it in my language through my art."[28] This is the highest ethical standard and challenge in the writing of ethnography, intensely debated over the years. It is a methodological principle of respecting the local native point of view, allowing it (or them, in the plural) voice, allowing it on stage, and also getting it right. It is, as well, a postcolonial and de-colonial demand.

The fourth claim is about the situated form of knowledge that the arts and artists assert: "The thing we loved the most was creating, the thing we loved the most was our culture and feeling it through a contemporary expression."[29] As with all the dance forms in *Probing Arts* and in this volume, this is about the creation of a new language that is recognizable to carriers and maintainers of traditions, and simultaneously in conversation with all that is changing in the world. It is a warning against museumification, against not contextualizing, against not respecting the conditions of production. In *Probing Arts*, installations, painting, feminage, cut-outs, sculpture, performance, and dance were foregrounded (see Fischer 2023); in this volume, novels and film take front stage, including their staging of oral narratives, writing (hegemonic, minority, and gendered), and filmmaking (documentary, experimental).

Both volumes explore three kinds of critical cosmopolitanism. First, traveling cultural resources that take on additional, new, or different resonances in new settings (for example, the Chinese conceptual term *qui-shen*, which can mean "ghosts-spirits" but more abstractly "contractions-expansions," or "outreach-return," as discussed in relation to the work of Lydia Kwa in chapter 3). Second, appreciating different modalities of art effects and poetics (including such dance figures as the Indian *krauncha*, which names a bird but is also the conceptual origin of the arts in the *Ramayana*).[30] Third, traversing thresholds of political-economic systems that challenge and change, even transform, common sense.

The terrains of these hinges, cosmopolitanisms, and artistic probes are geographical places and regions, land- and seascapes, and today's electromechanical extensions (internet) and computational intensifications (geospatial intelligence) that are increasingly recognized as a "pivot between East and West," centered on, or intersecting in, Singapore but not contained within that one island (or set of islands). In simplest terms, Singapore is a meeting point of the Malay world with the Chinese, Indian, Melanesian, and Euro-American ones. Melanesian influences from the East already figured in the Malay worlds explored in *Probing Arts*, and they extend further into the worlds of Bangarra dance (incorporating the Torres Strait as well as mainland Australia). That China now has long leases on the port at Darwin in northern Australia and Hambantota in Sri Lanka only further brings the Chinese connections into these sea worlds beyond the old silk and spice roads, beyond merely art circulations.

Chapters:	FILMS	NOVELS	FILMS	NOVELS
	(documentary)	(historical)	(experimental)	(speculative)

The chapters in this volume explore the cultural tinder or fuels that give character and orientation to lives, even when ostensibly treated (by outsiders, by planners) as increasingly technocratic and without much need for the softer fields of study. And yet it is in the realm of the softer disciplines that fundamentalisms sometimes fester, unable to access the philosophical inclusiveness of their civilizational cultures. Such fundamentalisms may be religious, but they may also be impoverished rationalisms (for example, of engineering "solutions," not that we do not need good engineering where appropriate), drowned in localized certainties, deprived of the joys of discovery and wider perspectives that can unsettle prior knowledge (science and humanities). I am drawn to explorations of centuries' worth of exchanges, experiences, and knowledges of the habitats in which, and of the companion species—plants, animals, insects, birds, microbes—with which/whom we live. I write this volume during the ongoing coronavirus pandemic, which is rapidly expanding scientific knowledge of viruses, cross-species transmission, and immune systems, but also the politics and difficulties of organizing public health responses, with conflicts over centralized versus participatory, and efficient versus equitable governance. In *Probing Arts and Emergent*

Forms of Life, I argued that artists often work with parallel ethnographic instincts with those of anthropologists, frame their work as research-creating sites, work in labs and other scientific research facilities, and help us find access points for ground-truthing complex interactions in our emergent forms of life (see Fischer 2023). I continue that argument here.

In chapter 1 I explore the use of documentary film through the work of Tan Pin Pin to get below the surface of life and find "hinges of history," looking for the ways in which modes of "common sense" (or the *sensus communis*) are slowly shifting to accommodate multiple other changes from climate change, habitat transformation, internet and digital media (including hacks, infrastructural competitions, and geopolitical maneuvers); and the competition over governance and political-economy formations. Tan Pin Pin is one of Singapore's most distinguished documentary filmmakers, in part because her films often hit deep nerves, and yet over time become part of conventional understanding. She is an important figure in the arts community, and a close colleague of Jasmine Ng, who figures both here and in chapter 2. The controversy over Tan Pin Pin's film *To Singapore, with Love* (2013) is an indexical example of shifts in common sense. Tan Pin Pin's persistence in fighting for its role in the political education of the populace is one of many such struggles in the arts community that has steadily expanded public debate. Political education in this context is often the understanding that allowing older generations to talk about their experiences need not be upsetting to contemporary social peace, but on the contrary can be a way of strengthening the bonds across generational experiences and social diversity, of allowing people to listen to one another, and to build resilience and flexibility for dealing with new conflicts. *Singapore GaGa* (2005), another of Tan Pin Pin's films, is the most "ethnographic" in the conventional sense—that is, in footage of people and places, dialects and language usage, song and sounds—and includes two time capsules twenty-five years apart. The time capsules are distinctive time stamps not just in what they contain, but where they are set: in front of a nineteenth-century classical Palladian civic museum (once a library and museum); on the sidewalk outside an upscale twenty-first-century shopping mall. Her other films are equally ethnographic in helping to explore the common sense and structures of feeling of the place as they change. Her early film *Moving House* (2001) and the short *Gravedigger's Luck* (2003) explore the exhumation of graves to clear land for development.

The next four chapters form a quartet in pursuit of the phenomenology of women's worlds and *écriture féminine*. Chapter 2 deals with the work of the first member of the quartet, filmmaker and novelist Sandi Tan, who explores daemonic or charismatic figures in women's lives, representing three tropical or anti-colonial archive fevers: of autochthony; of warfare or tribute; and of rationalisms and their hauntologies. She rescores the emotional soundscapes of political history from the 1920s to the 2000s, and probes the ephemerality of archives and the documentary record. (Nota bene: I use "daemon" for a charismatic figure, "demon" for an evil one.) This chapter is in two main parts, one dedicated to a lost film, *Shirkers* (S. Tan 2018d), that is remade around the new center of loss, recovery, and psychodynamic mystery; the second is structured around musical movements that are also psychological reconfigurations of the main characters from striving immigrant, occupied subject, and the struggles and internecine battles to create national political independence, with countermelodies in Malay mystical minor keys. Much is recorded not on documentary or narrative film, but by the tape recorder of a now old woman who desires not to be erased by official histories. A new novel published just as I was finishing this book provides a smaller canvass of Asian immigrants (not Singaporeans) to California and Florida, with echoes of the comedic from the film *Shirkers* (the title itself is an echo: *Lurkers*), and with another daemon figure much like the teacher in *Shirkers*.

The second quartet member is clinical psychologist and novelist Lydia Kwa, the subject of chapter 3, who explores the psychodynamic knots of life (generational conflict of common sense; migrant efforts to escape parental superegos; immigrant efforts to write new life scripts); and the legacy cultural tinders available through rereading and reinterpreting the classical Chinese stories that still inhabit the literary and filmic imaginaries of Chinese culture and structures of feeling. Her four novels come in two parts inter-braided with her two books of poetry that extract minimalist elements of the novels like fine calligraphy. A fifth novel still being written will continue the cultural and psychological tinder from the past into the future through science fiction. Two of the novels are about migration (to Singapore, to Canada), and the frayed, but maintained, ties to points of origin. Two of the novels are exquisite reworkings of stories from the time of the Warring States, incorporating gender fluidities repressed under modern Christian influence. The "beastiary" genre *Guideways through Mountains and Seas* (*Shan Hai Jing*), together with the *zhiguai chuangi* (strange tale) genre, and the *I Ching* are all neatly woven into the two contemporary novels, while the historical novels play with gender fluidity and their psychosocial implications. The Forest of Illusions is partly from these Chinese traditions, while also a nod to Victor Turner's *The Forest of Symbols* (1967), which in turn comes from Charles Baudelaire's poem "Correspondances" (1857), and involves a quasi-Freudian understanding of strange tales and symbolic discourse as modes of dealing with psychodynamic problems and social dramas. The cultural fuel or tinder here is partly the fracturing of cultural knowledge through the generations. "I cannot remember a time I thought in Hokkien, it has always been English, the language of foreigners, of colonialism," Kwa says in a poem (Kwa 1994a). And it is partly a clinical psychologist's listening to the struggles of her clients, turning the gaze often back upon herself.

The third quartet position is inhabited by two writers, Jing-Jing Lee and Danielle Lim, with two short texts each, and which form the focus of chapter 4. Lee gives us a pair of finely worked miniature studies of housing displacements (from kampong or village to high-rise apartments, and from long occupied apartments to small senior housing). The longer of her two novellas is built around the reverberations across generations of secrets—a penetrating psychological account of a baby found after a Japanese massacre at the end of World War II, and who is adopted and kept by a woman whose own child had died, despite knowing that a father was desperately looking for the child. Lim gives us accounts of upsetting illness in the course of Singapore's history: leprosy in the period between the 1930s and 1950s, SARS in 2003, and schizophrenia and mental illness. Her work complements an earlier essay of mine on aging society (Fischer 2015), in which I draw upon Dr. Kwa Ee Heok's novelized account of treating elderly men at the Woodbridge Institute for Mental Illness, next door to the leprosy asylum where Lim's story is set. Lim's is a story of a young woman banished until a cure is found, and then released into a world that has partly moved on without her.

In chapter 5 I turn to the fourth quartet member, the Indonesian novelist Laksmi Pamuntjak, who in three novels accomplishes a trajectory across fifty-five years, paralleling the first quartet member Sandi Tan's *The Black Isle*, again exploring daemonic or charismatic figures in modern women's lives, the hauntologies created by anti-communist campaigns, Islamic fundamentalist demands, and bureaucratic infighting. Instead of music, painting provides a central aesthetic key. The first volume intertwines a love story from the *Mahabharata* (an account of war, paralleling the anti-communist struggles in Indonesia); the second continues the generational story with a daughter of the protagonist of the first volume, still sporting a name from the *Mahabharata*, but now focused on modernist art, both Indonesian and European; and the third substitutes for the *Mahabharata* two classics from the Perso-Islamic repertoire—Attar's *The Conference of the Birds* or *Manṭiq uṭ-Ṭayr* (hence in one English translation, "birdwoman") and al-Ghazali's *Book of Etiquette and [Moral] Reason* (*Kitab Adab al-Aql*), while satirizing Indonesian bureaucracy today (combining an anti-HIV/AIDS campaign with a road trip in search of the most delectable local foods in Indonesia). The charismatic figure around which Amba, the narrator of the novel of that name, subtitled *A Question of Red* (communism), is drawn, is an East German–trained Indonesian physician who ends up in the concentration camp on the island of Buru (Pamuntjak 2013). There are powerful scenes of the Bumi Tarung (a left-leaning artists' colony) made up mainly of graduates of the National Fine Arts Academy of Yogyakarta; the concentration camp holding 12,000 prisoners on Buru, the third largest of the Maluku Islands; and the journey by Amba and two ex-prisoners in search of the grave of her husband Bhisma. The sequel, *Fall Baby*, shifts focus to the daughter of Amba. The *Mahabharata* (except for the name of the daughter, and perhaps her fighting spirit) is replaced by a modern story of a group of women with shifting marital and sexual relationships. The centrality of a network of women suggests implicitly a possible rereading of the *Mahabharata*, in which the key figures are not the male warriors but the two central women, Dhraupadi and Gandhari, who foresee and attempt to repair the damage caused by their husbands (Fischer 2017b). In *Fall Baby*, the daughter, Siri, becomes a painter, dividing her life between Jakarta and Europe (Berlin, Madrid).

The novel shifts to a series of contemplations about portraiture and color: capturing complex emotions in painting, trying to paint from a photograph a father she has never met, and contemplating a series of famous Indonesian and European paintings as clues to her own artistic search. There is Djoko Pekik's *Tuan Tanah Kawin Muda* (an anti-colonial painting about unequal power relations) by one of the famous artists from the Bumi Tarung group described in *Amba*. There are Sindu Sudjojono's *Ibuku Menjahit* or "Mother sewing" (a portrait of his first wife Mia Bustam) and his *Malle Babbe*, after Frans Hals's painting of that name, used to contemplate how many faces of different ages can be seen in one painting. Pieter Bruegel the Elder's *Netherlandish Proverbs* substitutes for the *Mahabharata* as a resource for symbolism and the ways life plays out in contrast to normative social fictions. Above all, there is Matisse and his fauvist use of color, providing a lovely key to the use of greens and reds for a melancholy that Amba calls "blue" in her portrait, and Siri, her daughter, decides is a semantic usage from Amba's years of studying English and American poets' use of that word. She suggests that this semantic displacement "might have also cast a shadow over the other emotional range that was her native palette" (Pamuntjak 2013), that in a sense she no longer visualizes her emotion of melancholy like an Indonesian.

A third novel initially seems quite different, a kind of food travel book set in the midst of an avian flu pandemic (a satirical device for skewering bureaucratic infighting over control of vaccine production). But instead of the *Mahabharata*, the *Netherlandish Proverbs*, and Matisse, it uses two Perso-Islamic texts—Attar's *The Conference of the Birds* and al-Ghazali's *Book of Etiquette and [Moral] Reason*—for reflections on friendship, taste (common sense), and heaven on earth (food, sex, and differences). One of the ethnographic delights is that the narrator says she knows Attar through her Minangkabau grandmother (from the "West"—that is, the western part of Sumatra and Indonesia, and the Western influence from Persian and Arabic writing). The novel is a wonderful meditation on the ways in which food (pride in local cuisine) does and does not pay attention to political demarcations (most dishes have variants in other communities). The quest for the "heaven on earth" taste of regional foods is a quest just like that of the thirty birds in Attar's work who seek the legendary *Simorgh*, only to discover that wisdom and the *Simorgh* are located in their collective selves (*si-morgh* means "thirty birds" in Persian).

My interest, in part, is watching how deep cultural tinder is reignited and becomes a resource- and reference frame for living in the contemporary world, and how ethnic mixtures operate underneath, around, and in violation of categories, stereotypes, and politics, but also can be weaponized in illusory quests and battles that can do real damage. The social and cultural psychologies, affects and emotions, are brought out by novelists for inspection in complex knots.

Chapter 6 turns to filmmaker Daniel Hui, who returns to the dissociations and repressions of the official Singapore national narrative, and in his most recent film, with the almost overdetermined title *Demons*, turns directly to power dynamics (those of film director, charismatic leader, and dictator mirroring one another) and the limits to which a theatrical performance (theater state) can allow itself to push its actors (citizens). Hui's three films—*Eclipses* (2011), *Snakeskin* (2014), and *Demons* (2019b)—are each richly developed, with references to film histories as well as to contemporary Singaporean issues. There is a continuing concern with rewriting the history of Singapore around a charismatic male leader who reincarnates time and again, as if the society can neither get rid of such a figure nor recount its history except through him. The violence at the founding of states and corporations (as we have been taught by Walter Benjamin and Jacques Derrida) here is transfigured into the violence of what film can show or eclipse, and how it can profoundly affect what people know about their politics and history. Pamuntjak invokes the propaganda film (especially its music) shown every year in schools in Indonesia during the period of the Suharto regime to reinforce the president's official story of the violence at the founding of his New Order rule (as does Intan Paramaditha in the second of the chapter epigraphs, above). There is a moment in *Snakeskin* when the leader threatens to come back from the dead if the film is not edited in his preferred sequencing. As in Sandi Tan's *Shirkers,* this uses the device of being given reels of film in (or from) the past, and having to decide how to reconstruct the images into a legible montage or narrative.

In *Eclipses,* the making of the film is emotionally transfigured into a struggle over how to reenter society after depression. Daniel says the initial story line is a tribute to Roberto Rossellini's *Europa '51* (1954), and the return to society with an appreciation of its variety of social classes is a tribute to Dziga Vertov's *Man with a Movie Camera* (1929). These are both sociopolitical stories of emergence from war (World Wars I and II for Vertov and Rossellini, and the Cold War for Hui). *Europa '51* is about the repression of a saintly woman who is committed to an insane asylum rather than allow her to do philanthropy and community work among the poor. It prefigures the shadowy story in 1980s Singapore of Operation Spectrum in which a liberation theology effort of the Catholic Church to help the poor was repressed as a "Marxist conspiracy"—a story that appears through its exiles in Tan Pin Pin's *To Singapore, with Love. Eclipses* (a kind of study for *Snakeskin*) is also patterned on the filmmaker's own experience of depression and struggles to reenter society. In *Snakeskin,* these themes are expanded and focused on the film medium: both in the opening and a half hour into the film, film stock is literally put into a fire in order to kill the evil that it contains, a kind of echo of the evil in the figure of the charismatic Georges Cardona in Sandi Tan's *Shirkers.*

Among the important stories told in *Snakeskin* is the destruction of pre–World War II Malay cinema, a multiethnic industry in which, as famous lyricist Yusnor Elf puts it, the finance was Chinese, the technical talent (including directing) was Indian, and the aesthetics (and song) was Malay. Another important story in *Snakeskin* appears also in Sharlene Teo's novel

Ponti (a singleton first novel): the life of a now fading or deceased actress who lives on in the psychology of the next generation. A photograph of the actress in her prime is the object of a desire for animation and knowing what the earlier life was like. Aspects of this appear as well in Sandi Tan's *The Black Isle*, and Lydia Kwa's *Oracle Bone*: they both use the device of the wise old woman, the sorceress, the Cassandra.

Daniel Hui's third film *Demons*, inspired by Fyodor Dostoyevsky's *Demons* (in which a murder is used to create solidarity among the perpetrators), pushes power games of filmmaking even deeper into the realm of psychodrama. Hui claims to be obsessed with his contradictory positioning as both victim and privileged holder of power. As a gay cis-male living in a state where homosexuality is still illegal, he occupies a victim position vis-à-vis power holders; but as a film director, he is a privileged power holder able to make actresses do his bidding.

Chapter 7 continues the exploration of popular modern genres (road trips, horror films, ghost stories) with three novels published in 2017 that interrogate the meritocratic state and the Smart Nation (as Singapore now brands itself): a detective novel by Daren Goh (used to explore governance with the aid of artificial intelligence and psychopharmacology); a science-fiction novel by Kevin Martens Wong (used to explore Singapore's aspirations in biotechnology and to provide synthetic realist life to a lifeless tourist icon); and a mythic mashup of Greek and Chinese myths (used to protest racial disparities). All three pivot back and forth between East and West with interested watchers from across the world from China to Rwanda and Burundi (all places that have hired Singaporean design firms to aid in their own economic adventures). Its own efforts at constantly upgrading its "human capital" and learning in alliances with British, American, and Chinese universities is itself a fascinating example of such pivoting between East and West—SUTD, for example, established with the help of MIT, from almost the beginning established an exchange with Zhejiang University.

Daren Goh's novel *The HDB Murders* (2017) is in effect a rewriting of Michael Young's classic satire *The Rise of the Meritocracy* (1958), slightly updated with contemporary technologies from artificial intelligence to mood modulators (from beer to high-tech pharmacological biochemistry). The novel is a good reminder of newly independent Singapore's social democratic roots grounded in British Fabianism and post–World War II Labour Party planning for social reconstruction. It is thus also a good vehicle with which to think about the contemporary restructuring of the political economy that both Britain and Singapore are undergoing as each attempts to find its footing in the shifting sands of the post-twentieth-century world.

Kevin Martens Wong's novel, *Altered Straits* (2017a), reimagines the premodern history of the maritime Malay world of sea peoples and sultanates through the gamification of contemporary technological warfare, including future biological and genetic modifications. Outside the novel itself, Wong is a member of CoLang (the Institute on Collaborative Language Research), which tries to help communities preserve endangered languages, in his case Kristang, the Portuguese-based creole of his Eurasian ancestors.

There is a hint of this sort of linguistic project as well in Nuraliah Norasid's *The Gatekeeper* (2017), but Norasid's novel is a gesture in a different direction: that of game worlds that might eventually move into a video game or virtual reality space. Norasid tries to invent a language as part of her "worldmaking," and sprinkles it throughout the text to give readers a feel for what it might be like to enter an underground ghetto (literally as well as metaphorically), separated from the elite Chinese worlds above. It can be read both as a sharp criticism of class and ethnic discrimination as inequality grows in Singapore, and as a pivoting fusion or alternation between the Greek mythology of Medusa and the Chinese mythology of Madame White Snake. Perhaps the leading exponent of putting myths from East and West into juxtaposition and dialogue is Singapore-born, Boston-resident opera director Cerise Lim Jacobs, who has conceptualized, written, produced, and staged a three-opera cycle, the Ouroboros Trilogy—comprising *Naga* (2016), *Madame White Snake* (2010, 2016), and *Gilgamesh* (2016)—with Beijing-born, American composer Zhou Long and other composers, brilliantly putting Chinese and Western music into conversation. The myth or legend of Madame White Snake has been staged in ritual, opera, and film numerous times, and most recently and exuberantly by the Wild Rice theater company in Singapore as a musical called *Mama White Snake*, with lyrics by Alfian Sa'at and starring gender-bending Ivan Heng and Glen Goei as the "sister act" of Green Snake and White Snake, and set in a pharmakon-pharmacy, or poison-healing shop (Chan and Sa'at 2017). Lim Jacobs's opera company has since moved to activist productions on immigration, racism, and the separation of families. Her production *I Am a Dreamer Who No Longer Dreams: An Immigrant Story* (2019) stages the tension between Rosa, an undocumented Mexican small-business owner and community activist, who is jailed for a crime she did not commit (a fire set during a demonstration that kills a fireman)—and threatened with deportation and separation from her young American-born daughter—and Singa, her court-appointed attorney (and corporate lawyer), a green-card-holding ethnic Chinese woman from Indonesia who at the beginning of the opera has little sympathy for her client but as their stories unfold reveals that she has foregone having a child in order to maintain the model minority drive for success and the green card giving her legal residency in the United States. The knots of today's struggles to gain a better life in East and West are never more painful, and the jouissance of workable solutions and recognitions of one another never more important.[31]

And so we return to the four goals of this volume: locating engaging pedagogies; locating cultural resources/fuel; exploring media of conveyance (here, film and novels), and playing in the sandbox of three kinds of cosmopolitics (traveling resources; art effects and poetics); locating hinges of history, pivots of exchange, and trauma-slipping-and-releasing knots. Insofar as this introduction is a manifesto, its aim is to reclaim literary and filmic productions as worthy of full incorporation into anthropological accounts of contemporary culture. Once anthropologists privileged participant observations (what people actually do) over literary accounts—I well remember being chastised by an eminent member of an earlier generation for my effort to read Iranian short stories and films in an ethnographic context as an articulation of an intellectual class caught between its village roots and its European education, and as cultural critiques of Westernization and modernization (*Gharbzadegi* or "West-struckness"), landowner repression (feudalism or patrimonialism, respectively in Marxist or Weberian theorizing), and clerical conservatism (Fischer 1984; 2004, 151–221).[32] The rationale was that so many epic tales in Europe were manufactured out of nostalgia, or constructed for nation-building, or both, and did not reflect an acknowledgment of what Malinowski called mythic charters for action. It was to uncover those motives "for action," for legitimation of authority, and other purposes that anthropologists were called upon to evaluate, as stories were put into social action, told to specific audiences. In oral societies without, or with restrictive, literacy, this was an important methodological injunction: not taking literary, or even archival, accounts at face value; and observing how formulaic epic recitations are tailored to specific audiences, as well as how literary texts and paintings were modified to suit patrons' political interests. In literate societies of all sorts, we need a whole suite of methodological tools, and the dismissal of readings by anthropologists of arts and literature as somehow reductive can no longer be allowed to pass, any more than mere thematic or "content analysis" can be sufficient for anthropological readings. Indeed, as we move into virtual-reality worlds, artificial intelligence, and face-and-movement synthesis with generative adversarial networks, the need for critical tools increases, not only to distinguish manufactured images, truths, enhanced paranoid reasoning, and altered common sense; but ethnographically to track down how, why, by whom, when, and for what calculated and miscalculated purposes and effects.

In the afterword, I look to portals signaling, and opening into, the future: to universities pivoting in geopolitical space, to the Singapore underground mass rapid transportation system (MRT), the world's largest driverless system, with its stations marked by artworks by leading Singaporean artists, and to the peopling of technologies for worlds we want to live in.[33] Geographically as well as historically, I move (*à la* Tan Pin Pin's *Singapore GaGa*) across the urban landscape, first from arrival in Chinatown carrying the arts of calligraphy (and a mural by Tan Swie Hian); then to Tembusu College, the successful liberal arts, humanities, and science, technology, and society college, established in 2009—along with three other such colleges within the National University of Singapore, with a lively student body, public artworks, and intellectual forums on controversial issues; and third, to the relatively new Singapore University of Technology and Design, with a stunning series of fingerprints at its MRT portal that raise questions about encryption, information technologies, and identities in intriguing ways, not unlike Daren Goh's novel.[34]

In the post-afterword Exergue, I return to the Bangarra Dance Theatre to flesh out the discussion initiated above about historical hinges, the role of dance as a shaper of communal identity, and, importantly, a powerful example of change by people taking charge of intercultural positions so as to change the nature of interactions, to command respect, full recognition, and to do all this with a sense of humor as itself a device of inclusivity. The insistence on *cultural protocols* is gradually both a phrase and a practice that is disseminating from Australia, New Zealand, and Papua New Guinea to other parts of the world. It is good to have that recognition and not just "consent," for it to be a political project and not just an individual tacit or explicit assent. Bangarra, for me, at the moment, is one in a series that includes experiments in Indian dance such as those of Chandralekha, Kiran Kumar, Aravinth Kumarswamy, and Malika Sarabhai (in their very different ways), or of Oliver Tarpaga and Esther Baker-Tarpaga, and Edith Podesta.

The contemporary contexts that they register and shape are not stable or enduring but capture that ephemerality of longer and shorter durations, cycles, innovations, fusions, bricolage, and variations in the materiality of life, growth, and change, despite all constraints, reverses, and catastrophes.

For those who want quick refreshers on Singapore as a location, and on the post–World War II history of the region, two brief sets of reminders follow.

QUICK LOCATION REMINDERS

Close your eyes. Pretend you have never heard of Singapore.

Pretend you have not visited the fifth most-visited city in the world (according to Mastercard) with one of the perennially best-rated airports: 14 million tourists in 2017, 18.8 percent from China, 15 percent from Indonesia (Wong 2018). Pretend you have never availed yourself of the medical services that serve 200,000 foreigners a year. Pretend you have not heard of its six universities, two in the top five in Asia, and top fifty globally; or heard of its Biopolis, Fusionopolis, and Mediaopolis, funded by and overseen by the Agency for Science, Technology and Research, comprising a series of globally competitive institutes in biotechnology and engineering; or that it was the headquarters of the Human Genome Organization from 2007 to 2013, turning its mission toward exploring medical applications of genomics and systems biology; and helping build aspirations and genomic capabilities in countries beyond the initially scientifically dominant ones (see Fischer 2013).

Pretend you do not know that it is the world's second busiest port (after Shanghai) in shipping tonnage and the world's busiest transshipment port (transshipping a fifth of the world's shipping containers, half of the world's crude oil), that it is the world's biggest ship bunkering or refueling hub, among the world's top three export oil refining centers, the world's largest oil rig builder; and that its Maritime and Port Authority, in a joint venture with Turkey's Afken Holding, operates the international port at Mersin, Turkey. Pretend you do not know that the port (in 2021) used 1,250 self-driving trucks.

Pretend you do not know that Singapore is fast emerging not only as a financial center rivaling Hong Kong (with 200 banks' regional headquarters) but also as a fin-tech center (blockchain, cryptocurrency, and other digital trade technologies). Pretend you do not know that Apple built the Apple II computer in Singapore in 1981 or that the iMac was also built in Singapore, or that Singapore was, and is again, home to global computer chip foundries (Global Foundries, Micron); or that it is home to Lucasfilm's Sandcrawler building, one of the first buildings, along with a small Pixar building, to anchor Mediaopolis.

Pretend you know nothing of its ethnic diversity and its peoples' history of migration from South China, southern India, across the Malay world, Britain, and elsewhere; their multiple religious institutions—Hindu temples, Buddhist temples, Taoist shrines, *gudwardas*, mosques, synagogues, and churches; or the twenty-plus languages spoken—Teochew, Haka, Cantonese, English, Singlish, Tamil, Mandarin, Kristang, Bengali, Hindi, Tagalog, Burmese, Khmer, Thai, and more. Pretend you do not know the official national language is Malay; and that the three other official languages are English, Mandarin, and Tamil. Pretend that you have never seen the four-mile-long Thaipusam parade with hundreds of pilgrims, bodies pierced with hooks and spears, carrying huge *kavadi* on their heads, doing feats of ascetic devotion to Murugan, son of Shiva; that you have not seen the Monkey God trance-divinations, lion dances, or the Hungry Ghost festival traditions (burning hell money, making offerings to the ghosts, staging operas for the ghosts, and *Getai* or popular song performances). Pretend you have never heard of the Chettiars, the money-changers and financiers of South China operating from Singapore to Burma, who built one of Singapore's monumental temples. Pretend you have not seen the Chinese praying with their joss sticks in front of the Krishna temple next door to the Kwan Im Thong Hood Cho temple in natural syncretic devotion. Pretend you have not seen the day-long lines of Buddhists doing prostration, step forward, prostration on Vesak Day (the day of the Buddha's birth, enlightenment, and death) circumambulating the large Kong Meng San Phor Kark See temple and monastery.

Pretend you know nothing of Singapore's history in the Cold War (see below). Perhaps you are aware of the post–World War II efforts to build a new nation, and of Singapore's role as a temporary economic opportunity for guest workers from poorer economies around the region. But perhaps you are less aware of the cycles of economic change that have buffeted the working classes, destroyed Singapore's pre–World War II centrality to multicultural Malay cinema, deprivileged Chinese-medium education, privileged English, and encouraged Mandarin. These are all realignments as the global economy moves from artisanal manufacturing, family entrepreneurship, and state-guided capitalism (through two sovereign funds among other instruments) into the Industrial Revolution 4.0 (IR4.0) of automation through digitalization and artificial intelligence.

Open your eyes and ears. Look, listen *and*
Think about what and how film can reveal.

QUICK HISTORY REMINDERS

Pretend you know nothing of World War II in Southeast Asia or its aftermaths across the Malay Archipelago.

Close your eyes again. Pretend you cannot remember teenage life in the 1990s or imagine Asian immigrant lives in the United States in the 2010s. Pretend you do not know much about the past century of Asian and Southeast Asian history. Pretend you are not interested in ghost stories, or do not know much about shamans or *bomoh* (Malay healers); or about charisma, war, or trauma.

Pretend that you have not noticed the Southeast Asian world pivoting in a different way between East and West, with the steady expansion of China's Maritime Silk Road, notably the new Chinese ports in northern Australia (Darwin) and Sri Lanka (Hamanthota and Colombo's International Container Terminal); also the 24-square-kilometer new Smart Port City Project of Gwadar, in Baluchistan, Pakistan, to link to Xinjiang in western China; and plans for a deep-sea port and special economic zone in Kyaukpyu, Myanmar, with oil and natural gas pipelines to Kunming.

Pretend you are a little vague about World War II in Southeast Asia. Pretend you never heard of the dramatic drive by the Japanese forces down the Malay Peninsula using bicycle infantry to move through the rubber plantations; or the surprise attack on Singapore from the north from Johor, instead of from the south by sea, toward which the British cannon were pointed. Or the ground fighting by Malay, Indian, and Australian defense forces against the invaders.

Pretend you have forgotten the dramatic and near simultaneous Japanese attacks by air on Pearl Harbor, Manila, Singapore, Penang, Surabaya (on December 7, 8, and 11, 1941), and Darwin in Australia (two months later on February 19). Pretend you have forgotten that the British had pulled back most of their naval forces from Singapore, to defend the English Channel, the North Atlantic, and the Mediterranean; and that three days after Pearl Harbor, the HMS *Prince of Wales* and HMS *Repulse* were sunk off the east coast of Malaya, leaving little naval defense of Singapore. Pretend you have forgotten the British naval defeats off Palembang (southern Sumatra) on February 13–15, 1941, and in the Sea of Java and Sunda Strait between February 27 and March 1, leaving Java open to invasion, and meaning control of Java's food production, the world's fourth-largest oil-producing area, plus a huge pool of labor to be forced into service. (By January 1942, Japanese troops controlled parts of Sulawesi and Kalimantan; in February they encouraged Aceh (north Sumatra) to rebel against the Dutch, took Ambon, and landed in Timor.)

Pretend you have forgotten or repressed the ground campaigns: Japanese troops landed on Kota Bharu (northern Malaya) on December 8, 1941, began moving into Burma on December 12 (the capital Rangoon fell in March). After a few hours' battle on December 8, Thailand agreed to allow Japanese passage through its territory, then use of Thai railways and roads, its airfields and naval bases, and other facilities. Thailand then was forced to declare war on Britain and the United States, and sign a treaty of submission to Japan. Japan would station 150,000 troops in Thailand and build the Thai-Burma Death Railway with Asian labor (including Javanese) and Allied prisoners of war.

Pretend you have forgotten, or are too young to remember, that on February 14, 1941, Japanese troops entered the Alexandra Hospital in Singapore killing 300 patients, doctors, nurses, and patients by bayonet. General Yamashita had the responsible Japanese executed at the hospital. The next day, the British in Singapore surrendered to Yamashita. Then, from February 16 to March 2, the Japanese instituted "the Great Inspection" (*Daikensho*), or what the Chinese would call "the Purge" (*Sook Ching*), massacring between 25,000 and 50,000 Chinese men. The rationale was to get rid of sources of support for Chiang Kai-shek's Nationalist government, and all Chinese were suspect, having earlier provided financial support to China's resistance.

Perhaps you have forgotten that Lee Kuan Yew, the future long-serving prime minister of Singapore, having barely escaped the *Sook Ching*, and having survived, at first in the informal economy of petty trade in jewelry and other valuables, then worked for the Japanese occupation as an English translator (in the Cathay building, now a mall and multiplex cinema). In his memoirs he says he learned the most important lessons of his life in the three and a half years under Japanese occupation: that terror and brutality kept the crime rate low, made people behave as the Japanese wished, and even adjust to long-term prospects of Japanese rule (having their children educated in the new system's language, habits, and values). He admired Japanese organizational discipline, logistics, and administration; and after the war, he invited Japanese companies to return to Singapore to help build the economy.

Lee Kuan Yew derided faith in simplistic democracy. "Look at Malaysia or Indonesia. Is that the democracy and corruption you want?" was one of his retorts. Another was that governance by polling or plebiscite (echoing in this the French sociologist Émile Durkheim) is neither exercising leadership nor building the social institutions that true democracy requires (which was Durkheim's point). He derided ethno-nationalist polities such as Malaya was instituting. He derided the idea of the media as a fourth estate, seeing it as instead an important nation-building tool for explaining government policies. In Asian regional security affairs, he saw a need for a balance of powers: Japan's financial and economic power to complement the military and diplomatic power of the United States, with Singapore using trade and diplomacy as its primary tools, while also building a military defense force.

He came to deride the idea of the welfare state. Singapore is not a nanny state, he would say, while ensuring basic health care and housing for all (see Chua 1997, 2017). Japan was not Lee Kuan Yew's only education. He was trained in law at Cambridge, and absorbed the ideals of social democracy there and in London. Singapore has many of the trappings of European social democracy in its postwar housing policies, its basic health care provisions, and its efforts to ensure retirement funds. The People's Action Party was for a time (until 1976) a member of the Socialist International, an organization of social democratic parties.

Speaking of regional security and alliances, pretend you have forgotten the brave days of the April 1955 Bandung Conference for a Non-Aligned Movement, with twenty-nine new nations in attendance representing 54 percent of the world's population. Key organizers were President Sukarno of Indonesia and Jawaharlal Nehru of India, but also Mao Zedong and Zhou Enlai from China. Perhaps you have forgotten the guerrilla fighting by the anti-colonial communist Malayan National Liberation Army in Malaya to help hasten independence, and the British response (the Malayan Emergency), instituting "new villages" in which civilians were interned (a strategy that would be called "strategic hamlets" in the American Vietnam War). Perhaps you are too young to remember the battles over communism, socialism, and democratic constitutionalism in the formation of the new Singaporean state, whose legacies survived through the period of Lew Kuan Yew's rule in harsh security laws, and which remain visible in films such as *To Singapore, with Love* (see chapter 1) and videos of some of Charles Lim's *Sea States* (see Fischer 2023, ch. 4).

Perhaps you have forgotten or repressed the parallel struggles for independence and democracy in Indonesia, that the Japanese were initially welcomed by many as liberators from the Dutch, that many local officials and elites cooperated with the Japanese who in turn fostered and trained Indonesians to prepare for a future independence (under Japan's intended Co-Prosperity Sphere). Independence leader Sukarno was released from Dutch detention by the Japanese and worked with them to build popular support, in expectation that they would support independence, which he and Mohammad Hatta declared immediately upon Japan's surrender to the Allies in 1945. Meanwhile, the Japanese conscripted between four and ten million Indonesians for forced labor in Java, and another 200,000 to half a million were sent from Java as far as Burma and Siam (Thailand). Estimates are that four million people died due to famine and forced labor during the occupation. Sukarno led the resistance to Dutch recolonization, and tried unsuccessfully to lead resistance (armed confrontation) to British efforts to create the Federation of Malaysia, which he saw as a form of recolonization inimical to the consolidation of a new state of Indonesia, or to an independent, unified, single Malay state in Borneo. In attempting to balance domestic political factions, he advocated for a "guided democracy," which increasingly became allied with the rapidly growing Communist Party of Indonesia (PKI), in turn triggering the coup that overthrew him, the 1965 massacres, and the creation of Suharto's New Order dictatorship, which used the showing of a film every year in schools to inculcate its official story of how and why the coup and massacres happened.[35]

Finally, close your eyes and think about the formation of the map of Southeast Asia. Once upon a time, it was the guarded and patrolled sea lanes of the Hindu and Buddhist navigators from Majapahit and Srivijaya; and of the Bugis sea lords and the *orang laut* or "sea peoples" (see Fischer 2023). Later, it was divided between the British (based in Singapore) and the Dutch (in Batavia/Jakarta and Surabaya). After World War II, and with the wars in Korea and Vietnam, both the sea lanes and the Southeast Asian mainland came under American postwar protection. Today, China is systematically building a new Maritime Silk Road of state-of-the-art ports from Qindao (Tsingtao), Tianjin, Shanghai, Guangzhou, Shenzhen, Hong Kong, Xiamen, Nigbo, and Dalian, south to Darwin (on a 99 year lease), and west to Colombo, Hambantota (controlling equity and a 99 year lease), Kyaukpyu, Gwadar, Djibouti, Sokhna (Suez Canal) to Haifa (25 year management contract) and Piraeus (67 percent stake) and even Hamburg (35 percent stake). At the same time, a new overland Silk Road is being built across Central Asia, but also with hydroelectric dams and mining projects across Southeast Asia and down the Pacific to Papua New Guinea and Australia.

Open your mind's eye.

Think about what and how novels can reveal
what goes on behind the history outlines
alongside ethnographic investigations.

1

Oiled Hinges

Sounds and Silences in Documentary Films of Social Change

There are many more female documentary filmmakers than there are male filmmakers. . . . Comparing it with fiction filmmakers, you will find that there are probably more directors who are female (or minority) in the documentary field than there are in the fiction field. —TAN PIN PIN, "INTERVIEW WITH JULIA TAN AND YUKA KAMAMOTO"

We will probably be bringing [the] show about death and dying, *Both Sides Now* [first staged at] Khoo Teck Puat Hospital . . . to different neighborhoods. That's the good thing about art: it gives you a safe space to talk about topics that are typically taboo or unengaging. —JASMINE NG, "BEHIND THE CAMERA WITH JASMINE NG, FILM MAKER AND MENTOR"

This chapter is about the nature of documentary—and its relation to writing ethnography and ethnographic film—in an extended moment or hinge of social change, through a close reading of the films of a leading Singaporean documentary filmmaker, Tan Pin Pin. Her films both document and also contribute to a changing understanding of the constraints of the political, as the Cold War recedes and new global competitions place Singapore in a different relationship to its own narrated histories. Although I was well versed in the controversies surrounding her 2013 film *To Singapore, with Love*, in which she interviews political exiles still not allowed to return home, I first met her in 2020 at a screening of two of her other films, both of which struck me as remarkable para-ethnographic portraits. They became the germ and genesis of this chapter.

To Singapore, with Love (Tan Pin Pin 2013) looms larger than life because of its censored political history. It has become an ethnographically important social drama, which I will analyze as such together with a film made only two years later and which was treated more gently by the state: Jason Soo's documentary *1987: Untracing the Conspiracy* (2015) about Operation Spectrum, in which social workers associated with the Catholic Church's outreach work to the poor were accused of being Marxists out to overthrow the state. Quite apart from its politics, *To Singapore, with Love* is also part of an evolving experimentation with documentary film style, one that evolves along with changing modes of media reception (not just avant-garde production). Tan Pin Pin's films, I suggest, document a hinge of history that slowly accumulates social changes. In retrospect, such change is dramatic, in the same sense as the hinge of history documenting changes in race relations documented in *Firestarter: The Story of Bangarra Dance Theatre* (Blair and Minchin 2020), discussed in the post-afterword Exergue. More importantly, both Tan Pin Pin's documentaries and the theater-dances documented in *Firestarter* are active in spurring continuing change in social attitudes, in the *sensus communis*, and in their respective countries' relationship to their past.

Let me begin with that screening in 2020 in what seemed an unlikely place for a focus on invisibility, forgetting, the impossibility of knowing, unteachability, time to come, being gaga and in love—all things with which ethnography as well as film must struggle.

In 2020, at the new cinema in Singapore's National Archives, Tan Pin Pin's 2007 film *Invisible City*—or, as it is better titled in Chinese, *bei wang lu*, "in preparation for forgetting"—was screened together with the twelve-minute short *The Impossibility of Knowing* (2010). Outside, in the foyer, artist-collector Koh Ngauang How answered questions about his display of news clippings, photographs, books, and magazines chronicling the history of performance art in Singapore, an art form that had been banned from 1993 to 2003. *Invisible City* is about collecting—the decay, fragility, and ephemerality of collecting—as well as memory. There was a frisson of breaking old taboos in celebrating Koh's collection and Tan Pin Pin's films there in the National Archives. The ironies of the setting were noted by the locals, as if infiltrations of a monument of the state, the guardian of official history, by its most probing and creative constituent citizens were slowly being acknowledged.[1]

Tan Pin Pin, the director-producer of four feature-length documentary films—*Singapore GaGa* (2005), *Invisible City* (2007), *To Singapore, with Love* (2013), and *In Time to Come* (2017)—and executive producer of *Unteachable* (Yong 2019), as well as a dozen shorts, is also a leading organizational figure in Singapore's film community.[2] She has developed a distinctive style that explores how documentary evolves from photographic shots into montage and cinematic syntax, exploiting photography's mysterious abilities to evoke moods and stories beyond the frame, and cinematic syntax's associative narration, which does not depend on speech or dialogue. But in addition, and strikingly, she focuses attention on sound, silence, and song in four registers: first, the ambient sound that we normally do not notice (but that John Cage memorably framed in his *4'33"* and that Margaret Leng Tan performs in *Singapore GaGa*); second, two forms of broadcast voice: that of the state (in *The Impossibility of Knowing* and in *Singapore GaGa*'s metro scenes) versus individual and community voices (*Invisible City*, *To Singapore, with Love*); third, song repertoires (blues in *Singapore GaGa*, revolutionary songs of bygone youth, and the songs of a political exile in *To Singapore, with Love*); and fourth, the formal musical spacing and rhythm of film segments (*To Singapore, with Love*).

These modalities of her filmmaking differ from documentaries that capture events and try to narrate who did what and when. Instead, she says, "I am far more interested in our perception of the events than in the events themselves . . . In *Invisible City*, you get a sense of the memory of an event dissipating right before your eyes. The whole point of showing that is to question the very ground we stand on, to give you a sense of how tenuous memories are. . . . Because if you start questioning the basis of your beliefs, then you have to question everything" (Tan Pin Pin 2010, 275).

Her longtime script collaborator, Jasmine Ng, was present at the National Archives showing, and I discuss her work in chapter 2 along with Sandi Tan's *Shirkers*. Jasmine Ng's film *Eating Air* (Ng and Tong 1999)—an idiom for "having a good time" in Hokkien, a "kung-fu motorcycle love story" as it was promoted—is itself now a period piece documentary of the long-haired, motorcycle-riding, bored but exuberant youth of the late 1990s, using songs, attire, and gestures that are tags of a generational memory. One of its nicest touches is the use of black-ink kung fu comix panels for the fantasy world of the teenaged, working-class hero. The film has its own interesting trajectory in the dialectic of innovation and decay, forgetting and recovery. In 2008 it was delightfully novelized in pure sparring dialogue form by writer Ng Yi-Sheng; and in 2020 it was remastered in 4K HDR (high dynamic range) from negatives that Mocha Chai Laboratory tracked down after some twenty years.

Ng suggests, in reflecting upon *Eating Air* and *Shirkers*, that an interesting, if minor, film tradition in Singapore is fake documentary. This often can be a strategy to address state censorship, ideologically manufactured history, or doctored "archival" photographs. She associates its rise with that of local fantasy fiction at roughly the same time. Fake documentary is a set of forms, she suggests, "somewhat fitting for us, always taught to be suspicious of history." These forms often can "say a lot more about Singapore and how we control [our relation to the official or conventional truth]."[3] Perhaps Daniel Hui's *Snakeskin* (2014), discussed in chapter 3, qualifies in this way. It is a mannered effort to present Singaporean histories (and their destructions or deconstructions) as a kind of Möbius strip, perpetual set of repetitions, always different, always the same. Documentary and forms of quasi documentary, Jasmine Ng suggests, constitute a strategy of critique, especially in constrained circumstances of hegemonic control over the arts by government censorship, male norms and entitlement, or policies justified by invoking "conservative" community opinion. Ng has broad experience in production, advertising, and the film industry, including bringing film and theater into interactive local community settings for discussions about public policy and social issues (as referenced in the second epigraph above).[4]

The loss and recovery of film negatives (as with *Eating Air*) is not unusual. Inattention to archival preservation is an occupational hazard. Filmmakers tend to move on to the next project, allowing the remnants of old projects to be carelessly put in basements, closets, and other "temporary" places where they decay and become lost. It is a theme that Tan Pin Pin addresses in her film *Invisible City*, about collectors and the decay of their collections, as too does Sandi Tan in a different psychological key in *Shirkers* (see chapter 2).

The Impossibility of Knowing is composed of fixed long shots at seven crime and accident sites in their aftermaths of decay or overgrowth.[5] Each shot contains sounds of water—running, rushing, or dripping—and the chirping of a bird. There is no dialogue, only a dispassionate male voice-over, spoken in a mid-American broadcasting accent (by actor Lim Kay Tong), neither Singlish nor British. "With the limited information available concerning these events," the program notes say, "the film enquires into the possibility for spaces of trauma to transcend time and engender their own significance . . . [and] renders palpable the sorrow and unease that haunts even the most ubiquitous of places amidst Singapore's cityscape." This reading claims both forensic distance and an affect of unease. More precisely, the "punctum" of each series of shots at the seven places creates and captures something beyond the frame that the viewer's imagination is invited to complete or speculate with.[6] There are no people in these shots, only aftereffects and sounds (water, birds).

By contrast, in *Invisible City*, individual people are the focus and their juxtaposition constitutes a kind of stratigraphy of history along with their Sisyphus-like efforts to capture history before it disappears. Tan Pin Pin says, "Its kernel is the drive of certain people to collect."[7] The title beautifully encapsulates the film in a series of brushstrokes, the strokes overpainting one another. The white letters of the title appear and fade in both English and Chinese characters. Among the people Tan Pin Pin interviews and follows are Margaret Topley, an ethnographer of Cantonese life in Singapore (we do not see her, only hear her chattering in Cantonese in the Chinatown market); and Margaret Doggett, the photographer, whose book of photographs of Singapore, *Characters of Light* (Doggett 1957), has recently been reprinted and annotated. We see Doggett as a very old, bedridden character, who nonetheless answers the filmmaker's questions, and says that only when she became very old, when it was too late to return, did she ever regret not having gone back to England. There is a Japanese woman journalist who comes to interview Goh Run Wey, a former Malayan Communist Party member and songwriter, with his infirm old wife. The journalist is in Singapore to cover the visit of the Japanese emperor to Singapore, and there is video of his arrival in a white car. There is Ivan Polonin, a longtime Singapore-resident filmmaker, who has had brain surgery and has difficulty focusing on words, but is articulate enough to be interviewed, and irascible enough to repeat that no, he's giving his films not to the National Archives, but to his daughters. Tan Pin Pin interviews Chan Chow Tua (founder of Tangent, a civil society association that collects oral interviews), and a young archaeologist (who says that while he could excavate anywhere in the world, he has a local attachment that makes it more meaningful to excavate in Singapore).

In some ways, the most important figure interviewed in the film is Han Su Yuen, who holds up photographs of the 1956 police violence against Chinese high-school students who were demonstrating against the government.[8]

Such photos, he explains, were felt to be so dangerous that many of his friends' parents destroyed them rather than be caught with them; and he himself has never before dared to show them, but now, he says, maybe it is OK to have a record of them in the film, before he passes on. He is an advocate for the students, who, he says, history has mistreated as thugs, when it was the police who were violent. And while, yes, some were communists, they were essentially nonviolent, and essentially anti-colonialist. His advocacy culminates in a speech in The Pod at the top of the National Library building. He gets nods and applause when he insists: "History is made by winners and losers, not by winners alone. The Chinese students were losers but history is made by both, with the aspirations and passions of both, and had the Chinese students supported the government at the time, the British would have ruled us for much longer."

But later he is disappointed that his talk did not make the impression on people he had hoped it would: "It fell on deaf ears." He quotes Hegel defensively, "anything that exists has reason to exist," and the film ends with his cell phone ringing and interrupting him: his ringtone is Chopin's Minute Waltz or *Valse du petit chien* ("Waltz of the little dog").[9] Life moves on. There is, however, a second ending, with the students of the young archaeologist sifting dirt-encrusted remnants from a 1960s midden. One of them scrapes, two others measure a shard of a ceramic cup with the potter's mark, and another cleans a Coke bottle and reads off a code on its bottom, Yeo HIPNGS, as if it had been a valuable artisanal mark or museum accession number.

In the Q&A session, Tan Pin Pin remarked that both she and Koh Ngauang How (the newspaper collector) "see the present as if already past," thus a spur to collecting. She suspects that her own personal archive of films and materials will eventually be like Ivan Polonin's sanctum of old equipment balanced precariously on tables and shelves full of film canisters. Overall, she suggested, the film is about the decay of information, and thus that the atrophy of information (hard drives decay, and so on), along with the constant propagation of false information, means that everyone should always be doing their own fact finding.

The feature-length film *In Time to Come* (2017), on which Jasmine Ng was again a script consultant, continues the Sisyphean theme of trying to capture the passage of time, using mainly wide-angle shots, held still in long takes, as if they were each a "master shot," so that, Tan Pin Pin suggests, viewers might have the time to do their own derivative "cover shots" of particular parts of the shot, focusing in on details of their own choosing, finding meaning for themselves.[10] She says the film is about everyday rituals: kayakers paddle in the Kallang River basin; sprinklers water the grass by the National Stadium; families stroll and take selfies; crickets stridulate and birds sing; shop attendants stand at attention for the opening of the Kinokuniya Bookstore and bow to greet the first shoppers as the sound system says, "Good morning shoppers, we hope you have a good day!"; and schoolchildren sit cross-legged, each reading a book until a bell rings and they stand for flag-raising morning exercises, in front of a building that says, above the entrance, Kwan Im Thiong Hood Cho Temple Block.[11] For those familiar with Singapore, we have already geographically traveled from the stadium by the Kallang River into the arts and temple district of Waterloo Street, and on to the main shopping street of Orchard Road. Bells with red bows decorate the multiple floors of the Takashimaya shopping mall. A fire alarm sounds and the sound system directs all to "please evacuate, do not use the lifts." Dump trucks arrive and are hosed down by Tamil and Bangladeshi workmen; backhoes dig at a hill and fill dump trucks; tree branches are cut from tall cranes; and tree trunks are cut into logs with chain saws. Such are the morning rituals starting the day.

Conceptually bookending the film (albeit not literally at the beginning and end) are two time capsules, and the above sequence arguably is itself also a time capsule. A twenty-five-year-old large tin or aluminum cylinder is dug out from its underground burial place in front of the National Museum. Its contemporary bookend is on Orchard Road: a metal cube resting on one of its corners like a modernist geometric sculpture (or spinning top) being packed with items for the next twenty-five-year time capsule. The two time capsules traverse the horizons between aspirations of the classical neo-Palladian style National Museum (albeit now with a modernist glass addition at its back) and the head-spinning consumerism of the malls of Orchard Road, along with their flaneur-accommodating sidewalks.[12] Tamil or Bangladeshi workers in hard hats pound at the older cylinder, and tap open its cover. Inside are books, an old US SOS phone with its charger, and various other items. On Orchard Road, a welder at a worktable measures, polishes, and fits together pieces of the new cube, awaiting messages and objects for the future. A paper message is folded into a badminton birdie and wrapped in tissue paper. Gloved hands carefully wrap a white shirt with black-tie school uniform, and put extra crumpled tissue paper in the collar to keep it standing up.

Men with anti-mosquito fogging machines move across trees and lawns, by trash bins outside apartment buildings, through car parks, and down staircases. In the heat of the day, a "master shot" is taken from the then new (in 2013) six-lane Marina Coastal Expressway tunnel opening up toward the cranes of the Keppel container port and the financial district, with a lone guard in the tunnel, a tiny figure in the scene of the transforming cityscape (the vista already looks quite different in 2020).

And so, the details of city life accumulate across the hours of the day, culminating at night with people crossing Orchard Road as the traffic lights turn from red to green. In the evening glow we see a fancy dinner with Prime Minister Lee Hsien Loong at Marina Bay Sands, adjacent to the passageway of the newly opened Downtown Line of Singapore's subway, the MRT (Mass Rapid Transit system). Musicians carry music stands, trombones, and drums into the subway at Bukit Timah Road; and we are at the exit in the atrium of the Sim Lim electronics mall in Little India (all three named places—Marina Bay Sands, Bukit Timah, and Little India—are stations on the new Downtown Line traversing the city). It is a lovely mosaic of detail that can be appreciated for its rhythms and color, its pointillism of urban life. For Singaporeans, it has the pleasures of recognition, as well as of traversing space and diurnal time. In Tan Pin Pin's corpus of "documentation" it provides a historical horizon that will only increase in value as time passes.

The other two feature films in Tan Ping Ping's oeuvre are also her two most famous: *Singapore GaGa* (2005) does for sound what the other films do for vision, while *To Singapore, with Love* (2013) extends the personal portraitures of *Invisible City* and wraps them together with the struggles against forgetting in general, and of collective history in particular.

Singapore GaGa, Tan Pin Pin's first feature film, is a gem, from the title on. The word "gaga" has a double meaning. It can mean slightly crazy or silly, and also an infatuation or love beyond reason. Aside from being a constant play between sound and sight, the film also pays constant attention to the dialectic between order and life's disorderliness, exactly what gives Singapore its gaga attractiveness.[13] We begin with noisy National Day fireworks, a busker with an electric guitar (Melvyn Cedello) singing a blues in the Novena subway station, and a descent inside an airplane from Indonesia into Changi Airport, with views over nearby Malaysia. The blues, "Wasted Days and Wasted Nights," strikes a perfect note of the ambivalence about Singapore often expressed by those who travel or live abroad, yet remain passionately attached.[14] "Wasted Days and Wasted Nights" is about love, not negativity, and like gaga, it has a double meaning: of being wasted after a long night of carousing, as well as the effort invested in a desire that is (as yet) unfulfilled, and in the exuberance of life that overspills efforts at law and order. In the film, we descend over a sandbar with a tiny backhoe moving sand on it; "why should I keep loving you, when I know that you're not true, / why should I call your name when you're to blame for making me blue?" The tiny scene below, as seen from the airplane, might be the land reclamation chronicled in Charles Lim's video of the disappearance of Evil Island and other spots of shrines and historical settlements, now buried within the sand to create new land, an icon of the burying of the past (see Fischer 2023, 113–17). Singapore's massive land reclamation projects since independence have expanded the island by 59 square miles (from 224 to 281 square miles). As the plane lands and taxis on the tarmac, one sees a new airport terminal under construction. The stewardess's polished voice over the intercom, to which we will return in a subway intercom, smoothly repeats the comforting "Welcome to Singapore . . . To residents of Singapore, a warm welcome home." The screen goes black and the title appears.

This framing tactic, shifting focus back and forth from inside and outside and between sounds and visuals, is sharply dramatized in the middle of the film in a scene key to the movie as a whole. Constructed with calligraphic-like strokes, New York–based, Singaporean musician Margaret Leng Tan is seated absolutely still at her toy piano on the bare concrete floor of a void deck of an HDB apartment building.[15] Dressed in ink-black clothes, she bows, the formal ritual of a classical musician about to perform, or also like a calligrapher taking up a brush and holding it vertically before initiating the first down stroke. Like that stroke, she folds herself in one smooth motion to sit at the 52-centimeter-high toy piano. She sits, her back ramrod erect, left arm at a 45-degree angle with palm outstretched, finger tips just touching the keyboard, and right arm almost parallel, resting on her right thigh, the leg folded back so the femur rests horizontally along the ground. For four minutes and thirty-three seconds, she sits absolutely still. It is, one quickly realizes, the John Cage performance piece *4′33″*—but the initial effect is of disorientation, as if waiting for the ambient noises to subside so she can begin, and then realizing that the ambient noises *are* the composition, the point of the performance. People walk or shuffle by (in flip-flops or sandals), bicycles lean up against white-washed pillars and walls, figures wait for the elevator, go to the mailboxes. A swing or gate squeaks repeatedly, a (caged?) bird chirps, a child's voice sounds in the distance, a car passes somewhere behind, a siren is faintly audible, voices are muffled, the white noise of wind provides a kind of sonic backdrop, something drops, a car accelerates. The eye (camera) remains intensely focused on the seated figure at the toy piano, while the ears are attuned, ever more intently, to listen to the ambience.

Indeed, Leng Tan's posture is a calligraphic abstraction of an ear, a bit rounded in styling. The ear sits at attention, while the eye is stilled. At the breaking point of attention, she picks up the small clock she has placed on the piano, presses the stop button, and we see it register 4 minutes, 33 seconds. She unfolds, lifting her form as a calligraphy brush lifts from the canvass, stands erect, and bows.

If here the ear sits at attention, while the eye is stilled, in contrast eye- and ear-juggling happens in the MRT. We follow the antics of the wonderfully crazy, or just daft, unlicensed busker Gn Kok Lin, no longer young, an "uncle" in local parlance, bare legged in knee-length shorts pulled up high over his waist, shirt untucked in back. He is at first resting, sitting on the floor with his red-and-white striped tote bag, water bottle, little table, and framed picture of his performance. He stands up and, like a circus barker, gives a patter about his fame and uniqueness, as he affixes to a nearby white-tiled wall the black-and-white picture of himself performing. Announcing his act, he goes into his routine, playing "The Skaters' Waltz" on his harmonica, beating out the percussion with his red clogs while juggling two tennis balls with his left arm and hand. Commuters walk past hardly noticing him, though at one point in a cameo Jasmine Ng stops to watch, and later an older woman stops to ask suspiciously if he has a license, and a station official gestures at him to leave, which he does. As he walks slowly, bowlegged, up the stairs (next to people moving faster on the escalator), the film's visual pace also slows, and one has the feeling of vibrancy being sucked out of the space of the flow of commuters. The space is not unlike the dance and skating space that young people create in the Esplanade MRT passageway underneath a sign that says no dancing or skating. There are some amazing breakdance performances, lively dance routines with groups of self-organized teens, Indian girls practicing Bharatanatyam dance moves, ballroom dance practice, and vigorous youths performing acrobatics on their bicycles.

The play between ear and eye, vernacular and order, continues on the MRT itself. The doors of a train carriage are open, and we are allowed a moment to peer inside. A woman in white hijab stands next to a Chinese woman with uncovered hair, four men stand, a woman in a row of seated passengers reads a newspaper, a young man leans into the picture frame looking curiously back at the camera. Then the sounds begin: the two-tone signal (doors closing), the rapid beeping (leaving), and a woman announcer's clear voice ("Next stop: Tanjong Pagar"). Inside now, we observe a row of seated people, two children sleep on the laps of two women, framing a window behind them, black at first, reflecting the five passengers seated opposite, then passing apartment blocks and parks.

Then the screen, not just the window, goes dark, and we hear the announcer's voice discussing her articulation with another Singaporean, perhaps a trainee or a fellow passenger: "I don't go with the Singlish way of saying Lavénda. It's Lávender. Well, I did attend Raffles Girls' School and we had a principal at that time there, and she was a stickler for us speaking perfect English . . . The station Queenstown seems a bit muffled and I keep telling myself that is something I've got to redo." As the train emerges again into the light, and we see a high-rise passing by, the woman's voice continues but we do not see her. We only see the two children still sleeping on the two women's laps, symmetrically framing the view out the window. She continues: "I mean I want to be recognized by the industry but not by, you know, the passengers, the everyday passenger. No, there is no need to. It is good for them to know there is a voice that comes on again and tells them, gives them instructions." As the train approaches the station, her voice comes over the loudspeaker, "Your attention please. Eating or drinking is not allowed in the stations and trains. Thank you for keeping the stations and trains clean for the comfort of all passengers." The commuters need not listen to the routine instruction they hear all the time, and the children sleep on in comfort. One need not know all the cultural history of the Speak Proper English and Speak Proper Mandarin campaigns to understand the class distinctions ("I went to Raffles Girls' School"), and to catch the effort to erase the vernacular (Singlish and the non-Mandarin Chinese dialects) in struggles for upward mobility domestically and internationally (just as only a standard mid-Atlantic American English was allowed on national broadcast media in the United States until the late twentieth century, and *boyin qiang* in China).[16] For good measure, over the buzz of commuters as the doors open, we hear the sound of a harmonica, which plays through the film. The harmonica is alternatively vernacular (the busker Liang Yu Tao) and classical (the professional musician Yew Hong-Chow).

Here it is a sound bridge to a deeper play with sociolinguistics and ethnomusicology, and to the ambient sounds of a Sunday evening in the streets of Little India filled with young men, guest workers, sitting or standing around, amid destination calls by bus touts ("Kaki Bukit!," "Woodlands!").[17] The diffuse soundscape is evocative, like the childhood sounds that Margaret Leng Tan recalls in her interview segment in the film, and that, she says, the younger generation hardly has experienced but that she incorporates in her music. These are sounds of the *tok tok mee* (noodle) man, hitting a bamboo stick on a bamboo cylinder to announce his arrival, pushing his cart on wheels, and calling out "*tok tok mee*"; sounds of the scissor grinders, and sounds of the *karung guni* (gunny sack) men, rag-and-bone and newspaper collectors, blowing a horn and calling out "*karung guni*" as they made their rounds.

The camera looks all the way through a taxi's open windows on both sides of the vehicle, allowing the eye to continue enjoying the Little India street scene a little longer. Inside, the Chinese taxi driver tunes the car radio to a dialect (Hokkien) news station. The ear diverts us from the sight line to follow the sound. We enter into the radio broadcast studio shared by Hokkien, Hakka, Teochew, Fuzhou, and Cantonese radio news readers, each trying to preserve a fading language that the elder generation needs to stay informed, but the younger English- and Mandarin-speaking generations are in danger of erasing from everyday life. This tension parallels the Raffles Girls' School–educated announcer's English in the MRT erasing Singlish (albeit with declining success, as Singaporeans increasingly embrace Singlish as one of the several linguistic codes among which they switch in different contexts).

The harmonica returns, this time in the black-jacketed, elegant hands of the harmonica teacher, Yew Hong-Chow, and we get a lovely counterpoint exchange on pedagogy with another well-known musician, classical guitarist Alexander Abisheganaden.[18] Yew Hong-Chow has spent years teaching the harmonica in schools, and we get both some vintage black-and-white photos of an earlier era, of rows of Dunman High School students, each with harmonica, together with a wonderful present-day scene of exquisitely patient efforts to turn earnest cacophonous beginners into a respectable harmonica ensemble at Raffles College. Beginners who cannot tell the difference in pitch, Yew Hong-Chew says, can more easily learn music with the harmonica because it has a fixed pitch, like a piano. But despite his years of success teaching the harmonica in schools, he has never been approached by the Ministry of Education. At the Dunman High School assembly, he proudly recalls, he demonstrated the harmonica, and immediately five hundred students signed up to take classes. Abisheganaden holds up a recorder, the Ministry of Education's instrument of choice for beginning music classes. They felt, he says, "that every child has two hands and therefore they can use their fingers and blow and by movement of fingers they could get these notes." But even he, he says genially, would have trouble hitting the correct notes, because the air pressure has to be correctly gauged for each sound—you have to blow slower to get the low notes. The low C is the hardest, and when you blow just a bit hard you get the high octave, and if you blow too much you get the squeals children often make. This is because, he reflects, "our leaders were probably people who had their music education either in Europe or in England." Abisheganaden and Yew Hong-Chow laugh and play "Home on the Range," alternatingly and together on the harmonica and electric guitar.

The interplay of vernacular and refined continues with an interview with Margaret Leng Tan. She demonstrates the *tik tok mee* sound (hitting a bamboo stick on a bamboo cylinder), while playing her Schoenhut toy piano with her left hand. And then there is another kind of lively vernacular performer at the entrance to the Simei MRT station. Liang Yu Tao, a wheelchair-bound young woman, with lovely face and smile but only four teeth, sells packets of tissue at the entrance to the Simei MRT station, singing with a catchy beat, "Auntie, Uncle, brother, young lady, please buy my tissue paper, how much, one dollar, one dollar, hello, one dollar." Her other song is "Jesus is good to me." It makes her happy to sing, and she can forget her troubles. Good naturedly, after asking the filmmaker if she is Christian, responds to the answer ("I don't have a religion") with a come-on-over wave of her arm, "Come, believe in Jesus. Believing in Jesus is good for you." Sweetly reflexive, she adds, "Your filming affects my tissue sales. Your documentary will be on television and people are avoiding me because they don't want to be on television." The filmmaker offers, "I will stand further away." The young woman, head down, replies, "It's not bothering me," and then lifts her head to sing "one dollar, one dollar" as the camera focal distance is lengthened. Liang Yu Tao is a cheery soul despite her disability, and her song lingers in one's ear long after the film ends.

Threaded throughout the film are two recurring and rousing sonic scenes of ventriloquist Victor Khoo and his puppet Charlee entertaining screaming and clapping children; and the students of Madrasah Aljunied Al-Islamiah on their sports day, complete with pom-pom girls with red bandanas over their hijab, chanting for their respective teams ("We are the Blue House dedication, We strive for determination, We create a new sensation, Oh oh Blue House, thunder, thunder, thunderation!"); and singing in Malay the national anthem "Majulah Singapura" (lyrics and music by Zubir Said). The older generation is given a nod as well with a quartet of men celebrating their fifty-year school-leaving anniversary by singing, in Latin, "Gaudeamus igitur" ("we didn't quite know the meaning at the time, the implications—we just liked the rhythm").[19] More poignant are the scenes of Guo Ren Huey, an elderly gentleman who sings the old communist song "Red Blood" that he says he learned in a rural hideout:

> Who wants to be a slave?
> Who wants to be a workhorse?
> Our light will shine onto Europe.
> For peace, equality, and freedom,
> We will pay any price,
> we lay down our lives,
> our red-hot blood,
> like a river it will flow.

He recalls with a smile how he met his wife, now infirm, who walks or sits silently in their flat. The flat is furnished with rattan chairs, tables with dome-like plastic covers to keep the flies away, and a metal tray with pills and cups and glasses. He has known his wife since childhood in a village in China. She came first to Southeast Asia. When the Japanese invaded, he joined her to fight them. She taught the troops to sing and dance, but now with her dementia she has forgotten, though when he sings, she sometimes sings along. His song is not unlike the teenage kung fu fantasies in *Eating Air* (Ng and Tong 1999):

> China will not fall
> Watch our 800 warriors dash to battle
> Surrounded by guns and fire
> Surrounded by savage beasts
> Never will we surrender.

As he sings, she falls asleep. The generational passage is part of the point. The theme of Singapore's fifty years of nation-building is both a time of celebration (fireworks, fighter jets in formation, helicopters carrying the flag) and a new generation (the children cheering the puppet Charlee, who never ages though serving a father and son over fifty years of entertainment) coming to replace the generation of Gn Kok Lin (the harmonica-playing, juggling uncle), the Latin singing quartet of gentlemen, and the former communist fondly singing anthems of his past. The number fifty is repeated throughout and there is even a quick birthday party for a (fifty-year-old?) old lady (Singapore?) who is urged to make a wish as she blows out the last of the candles on her cake ("I wish I would be free from aches and pains") to the laughter of her middle-aged children (who do not know and do not want to hear of what struggles she might have gone through to get to this point). Even the John Cage *Suite for Toy Piano* (written in 1948, performed by Margaret Leng Tan at the Lincoln Center in New York in 1993) is a bit over fifty years old. The film ends again with a reprise of key moments of forgetting and remembering: the blues, "Wasted Days and Wasted Nights," of an unrequited love, often reciprocated with hardship or indifference; the slogans demanding doing things in orderly fashion for the good of the nation's survival ("respect and responsibility" is a slogan on the wall of a school above the little children screaming for Charlee); the claims of the public announcers about her use of language: not Singlish but Raffles Girls' School English; cheerleaders at the Madrasah Aljunied Al-Islamiah chanting about caring for the needy and elderly, and guiding the young; and the forgetting of the past (the wife of Guo Ren Huey).

In an important way, one might think of Goh Run Wey and Guo Ren Huey in *Singapore GaGa*, and Han Su Yuen in *Invisible City*, as sonic and visual bridges pointing toward *To Singapore, with Love*, whose title might in fact be a variant of *Singapore Gaga*.

To Singapore, with Love (2013) looms larger than life because of its censored political history. Entirely composed of interviews with only half a dozen to a dozen or so individuals (depending on how you count) aged between their sixties and eighties, exiles whose physical relation to Singapore is from the outside looking in, it is somewhat analogous to Charles Lim's portraits of the city from its watery edges (see Fischer 2023, ch. 4). Similarly, it presents an almost Rorschach-like surface with no explicit discussion of politics, no voice-over, no narration. There are only two brief intertitles, and a list at the end of the interviewees and which passports or travel document types they now hold.

The film is fascinating to analyze as an evolving experiment with documentary film style, and while I will try to analyze it as such, thanks to its banning it also has become an ethnographically important social drama, which needs to be dealt with, characterized, and acknowledged first. There are three phases to the social drama—perhaps, to use anthropologist Victor Turner's categories, ones of breach, liminality, and status mutation (Turner 1974): first, the ban on public showings of the film in Singapore; second, the debate about its viewability status and academic freedom at Yale-NUS (a college of the National University of Singapore in affiliation with Yale University in New Haven); and third, two years later, stung by the international reaction to the banning (technically a specially devised unique rating, NAR, or "not allowed for all ratings"), the allowing of a similar documentary film by Jason Soo, *1987: Untracing the Conspiracy* (2015), to be publicly shown. (Tan Pin Pin's film is now available on pay-for-view streaming on the Vimeo platform—except in Singapore.)

The interviewed exiles—marginalized from Singapore, albeit connected by letters, phone calls, internet and Skype, funerals, and family visitors—celebrate what friendship and familial ties they have preserved as they watch their families and their own bodies age; and in their different ways they try to pass on to the next generation not only histories, but aspirations for the future that were embedded in their lives, that otherwise are being erased by intent, entropy, or time. In a way, the film might have been titled simply "Friends." These are the generations electrified in their youth by anti-colonial struggles, independence, and the contests in forming new nations with new names, slogans, and power structures, and in the 1960s by the anti–Vietnam War and Civil Rights Movement in the United States, the student movement in Paris, and the Cultural Revolution in China.[20]

It was a paradoxical time of open electoral political contestation and of backstage maneuver, repression, and disappearances, as the People's Action Party (PAP) consolidated power. The key obsessions of the exiles and their friends are the two primary dead-of-night incarcerations of some 113 or 117 people in 1963 (Operation Coldstore) and some 29 in 1987 (Operation Spectrum) that precipitated exile and Gordian knots of implacable difference in history telling. For the exiles and their friends, the goal and function of Operation Coldstore was the decapitation of the Barisan Sosialis (Socialist

Front), which had split from the PAP over three demands: for the release of political prisoners interned because of independence struggles (and communist guerrilla struggles); over the terms of a merger with Malaya; and for the abolition of the Internal Security Commission (run in concert by the British, Singapore, and Malaya). The goal and function of Operation Spectrum, in turn, was the destruction of independent civil society institutions for the next two decades. Daniel Goh, a sociologist at NUS and now a member of parliament, argues persuasively that the social welfare efforts of the Catholic Church were seen to be infringing on the social welfare agenda that the new state wished to control (Goh 2010). Tan Wah Piow (one of the accused in the 1963 roundup), in a 2020 interview not in the film, described the atmosphere of his youth this way:

> When you lived in a place like Joo Chiat where there was a PAP branch just across [from] my house, in front of a temple. And behind that there was a Barisan Sosialis branch as well. And you see graffiti on the wall [with] the logo of Barisan and so on. And you occasionally hear of incidents of people being arrested and so on. Usually young people. When I was growing up with my brother, one of my brothers was from Chung Cheng high school. I was aware in my secondary school days that they were involved with some kind of boycott of classes and so on. And some people had to be on the run. (Tan Wah Piow 2020)

Singapore officials insist that the exiles could have returned if they foreswore their earlier allegiances (always coded as communist), just as had others. One might think of Goh Run Wey and Guo Ren Huey in *Singapore GaGa*, and Han Su Yuen in *Invisible City*. But the exiles feared the long detentions without trial that the detainees suffered, the physical and mental torture, the forced "ratting" on friends, the forced television confessions. On the PAP side, the continuing "red threat" was both real and a convenient tool, giving this politics a kind of "third rail" irrationality not unlike the McCarthy era in the United States.

The cultural politics surrounding the film became further inflamed when faculty and students at Yale University, halfway around the world, used the NAR rating as an excuse to agitate against their university's alliance with the Yale-NUS college on the grounds of abetting an authoritarian state and alleging lack of academic freedom. In fact, government officials said that watching the film in private or at universities was not forbidden. There were some private showings, and a group of 350 or so intellectuals and cultural workers went en masse to a screening in nearby Johor Bahru, Malaysia, and made their disagreement with the ban public. The student newspaper at Yale called up the then American president of Yale-NUS, Pericles Lewis, demanding to know if the film's rating violated the academic freedom that the college had pledged to protect in its agreement with Yale University. He reflexively said, no, there was no prohibition on showing the film at the college, and that he thought the film was being shown in classes. That hit the local press as a potential *cause célèbre* in constant negotiations over film censorship. Tan Pin Pin herself objected that she did not want a public confrontation as she was intent on appealing the NAR so that people in Singapore could have access to and discuss their own histories. The appeal failed. The government, all the way up to the prime minister, Lee Hsien Loong, defended the decision in terms that are available to watch on the internet, claiming that the film undermined national security (Lee Hsien Loong 2014).[21]

Today, one can no longer discuss *To Singapore, with Love* without also talking about Jason Soo's documentary about Operation Spectrum, *1987: Untracing the Conspiracy* (2015), which has been publicly screened in Singapore, importantly along with the launch of a book of reflections by those who were jailed, once again asserting they had done nothing wrong, and that the goals they had in those days remain valid today (Chng, Low, and Teo 2017). People seem agreed that the PAP learned from its experience with *To Singapore, with Love*, that banning only draws more attention and tarnishes Singapore's reputation more than allowing it to be shown. There is also a second lesson: that this history is part of an ongoing network of discourse in Singapore that everyone, at least in the older generations, knows about, not only intellectually but emotionally.

I was in the audience for both a screening of *1987: Untracing the Conspiracy* in 2017 at the Projector cinema and the discussion afterward with Vincent Chen and others. Chen was the lead person accused as the Singapore-based leader of the conspiracy allegedly led by Tan Wah Pioh in London, a key interviewee in Tan Pin Pin's *To Singapore, with Love*. Chen, during his incarceration, was named a prisoner of conscience by Amnesty International. Also in the audience was Nien Yuan Cheng, whose review of the event accords with my fieldnotes and memory. Cheng astutely captures both the body language and mood of the former detainees as they appear in the film: "Vincent Cheng repeatedly whips his forearm across the frame; Chew Kheng Chuan rises slightly in his seat, pumps his arms as if he were running in place, and slashes his palm across an imaginary face; and Low Yit

Leng maps the interrogation room with her fingers. These performative re-enactments evocatively tell the audience what they have been through more effectively than any verbal description" (Cheng 2017). She describes as "jovial" Chew Kheng Chuan's retelling of the night he was arrested and how he leisurely took a shower and put on a suit and tie while the police were banging on the door "just so that when they took his mug shot, he wouldn't look as 'deranged'—his word—as his fellow detainees" (Cheng 2017). It is, she notes, a powerful performance, one of many in which the detainees "subvert narratives of victimhood [and] show just how ridiculous the situation was [and thereby] redress the power imbalance between them and their detainers" (Cheng 2017). Vincent Cheng told us that to remain sane in solitary confinement he memorized a book on foot reflexology, and that after his release from three years of jail and a subsequent five years of house arrest he has become a traditional natural-medicine healer and yoga and wellness leader. Indeed, his demeanor was calm throughout, while remaining an adamant opponent of the misuse of the Internal Security Act, under which he and his colleagues were held for years without trial.

So, to turn now to a perhaps unusual, but interesting, analysis of the film along the lines of Vladimir Propp or Lévi-Strauss's structural-narrative models, in which there are two axes, one of characters and one of emplotment, composing film itself as a kind of musical form. If *Singapore GaGa* is a film of sounds, and *The Impossibility of Knowing* is about silences, *To Singapore, with Love* is a film of song. Its very title, of course, alludes to the 1967 film, title song, and earlier 1959 novel *To Sir, with Love* (Braithwaite 1959).[22] That autobiographical novel, by E. R. Braithwaite, a Guyanese immigrant to London, is about the love between a teacher and his working-class students. So too, *To Singapore, with Love* is a love song, an unfinished story, "our *riwayat kitab*," "our book of history or our story," as Francis Khoo sings in his song that concludes the film. Khoo is one of the four most vivid characters in the film. We experience him through photographs and two of his recorded songs in his own voice.[23] His songs function like the blues in *Invisible City*. And it is taken up publicly by the veteran ambassador Tommy Koh, addressing the "fourth generation" leadership of the country: "as long as the critics love Singapore," criticism should be welcomed. "The contestation of ideas is a necessary part of democracy" (quoted in G. Z. Tan 2019).

To Singapore, with Love is composed in twenty sequential clips, which I have numbered, that can be laid out like five four-beat bars on a music stave, arrayed like a rhythmic series of diamond patterns. Alternatively, this could be described as a Propp- or Lévi-Strauss-like matrix of character slots in vertical columns and syntactical relations horizontally. Each of the four speaking positions (or beats, or clips of interviews in places of exile) is either a person (Ho Juan Thai, Ang Swee Chai, Tan Wah Piow) or different exiles all speaking from Thailand or Malaysia. (Francis Khoo appears with or in the remembrance of Ang Swee Chai, his widow.)

HO JUAN THAI	ANG SWEE CHAI	THAILAND/ MALAYSIA	TAN WAH PIOW
1	2	3	4
	5		
6			7
		8	
	9		
10		11	
	12		
14		15 & 16	13
	17		18
19	20		

The opening bar, or line, introduces the four main character or protagonist slots; in emotional tonality they are descending notes. First, Ho Juan Thai, in London, addresses us as a happy, youthful, and domestic sixty-year-old, with two young children, cooking Singaporean food (sautéed *kuay teow*, noodles with prawns) at the stove in his kitchen and playing with the children in his garden. He arrived there, he says, thirty-five years ago, in July 1977. Second, in a slightly lower descending tone, Dr. Ang Swee Chai, a small, sharp woman and surgeon, sits on a chair on her tiled terrace, also in London, and talks about (and introduces us to) the very lively lawyer Francis Khoo, her late husband, whose ashes she has been allowed, using a one-time single-entry visa, to take back to Singapore. They too arrived in London thirty-five years ago, in 1977. The third descending tone comes from Thailand, where there is a funeral for Lim Boo and we meet three former Barisan Socialis leaders, one of whom will have his own funeral later in the film (in the fourth bar and second horizontal or syntactic line). The fourth upbeat, rising tone is Tan Wah Piow, who drives us in his Toyota to his townhouse in London, and takes us into the garden shed, in which architect friends (using CAD, computer-assisted design) have built tightly arranged storage spaces, from which he draws two small suitcases. These, he grins, were all that he brought with him when he fled Singapore; and in which, perhaps, if he can ever return, he will take all that he needs back again. He says he has been losing count of the years since he arrived in London, and performs the calculation for us to remind himself of the passage of time, but asserts that nonetheless in all endeavors in life one must keep trying: he is not giving up his advocacy for democracy in Singapore.

The syntax or sequence of the first bar introduces both the characters and the movement or plot of the film—from exile, through funerals and the fading of older generations, to continuing the unfinished business of life that includes the aspiration for democracy and against growing inequalities of wealth and opportunity. Like *To Sir, with Love*, Tan Pin Pin's film is a love letter to a learning process, and to the passing of a torch to a younger generation.

Amplifying the sequential structure is the counterpoint of the said and the unsaid. How could a film about exile, diaspora, generational experience, and hope be otherwise? These themes of dislocations, translations, and transmissions are evoked particularly in unguarded, painful moments—flashing up in an eyeblink, from below the surface of consciousness, or through the "face" that one tries to keep in place. There are allusions to framings that the film captures only in fragments—in clips.

It is as if multiple films (or narratives, accounts, or threads) intertwine loosely enough, so that silences, and slippages of face, like the puncta of photographs, reveal other ways of narrating the addictive games that societies and individuals play, over and over, to see if the scoring will result in different outcomes.[24] Five intertwined and overlapping narrative threads may be separated analytically: First, the *game of politics*, and how "players" and "pawns" can be silenced or moved off the board or field. Second, *character portraits*, and the *cultivation* of *emergent forms of life*: life courses, vocational and avocational detours, and the physical body and psychological development of *individuals* as they age into their senior years in places of exile and displacement. Third, *socialities and temporalities of diaspora*: the work of consociality or maintaining networks, connecting with family connections, and forging new friends, as people age and new generations appear; and as these contend with the workings of alienation and disjunction as frozen-in-place memories no longer match the places in the present.[25] Fourth, *anxieties of influence* in the work of history: not only time's erasures of history and Sisyphus-like efforts to prevent erasures, but more upsettingly narrative repetitions that generate a difference in reception across generations. And fifth, *Faustian bargains* either refused or accepted, in exchange for defining what counts as one's soul. None of these five narrative threads are fully developed. All are in various stages of curtain lifting, allowing one just a peek at what lies behind the curtain or below the surface. But they are staged in a dramatological, musical sequencing of interview fragments, returning to characters at different moments of the narrative arc.

The happy, "young" sixty-year-old Ho Juan Thai ("I'm sixty years old, do I look like a sixty-year-old man?"), who opens the film, has a smiling face, and he almost beguiles you into thinking he has come to terms with his middle-class life in London with his two young children, until he talks about how intensely he wanted his son to join the Singapore Armed Forces, how he tried to get the boy a Singaporean passport, and how for thirty-five years he has been trying to get his own passport back. He still travels on a political asylum travel document issued under the rules of the Geneva Convention. He speaks lightly of having built a new life, doing odd jobs in a hotel, translation work, returning to school, earning a living in information technology, which, unexpectedly, he finds quite interesting. There is the pain of having to visit his mother by having her come across the border causeway to Johor Bahru in Malaysia, or of celebrating family events by internet video link, but a punctum explodes when he talks, and reiterates, and stresses again, in a manic, almost irrational, rapid verbiage of desire, that he wants his son to be able to join the Singapore Armed Forces to defend the country. He had to escape Singapore in 1977 because "I know pretty well if I did not, it is only matter of time I will be put in, and not just put in—they are going to make you confess on television things that you've never done before." A newspaper photograph and caption tell us that he had been a candidate for parliament on the Workers' Party list. He was accused of being a Chinese chauvinist, code for advocating for Chinese-medium schooling or at least maintaining Chinese language(s) as equal to English in the public sphere, and for inciting violence (a catchall charge applied to almost all the detainees). There was nothing wrong, he points out, with what he advocated: "What I said, very simple, which I still believe even today: to be an important entrepot for Singapore's economic activities, we need to enhance the English language, but we shouldn't, while we are enhancing the English language, we should not forget to preserve our Malay language, our Tamil language, and our Chinese language." The accompanying headline of the *Straits Times* gives a different slant: "Hunt for beaten elections man Ho: Police want to question defeated Workers' Party candidate Ho for playing up 'gut issues' during the recent election campaign to incite 'violent chauvinistic reaction' among Chinese speaking population in Singapore." Chinese-medium schools had been sites of resistance to and demonstrations against British and later independent Singaporean government policies (including army conscription), but such charges were legacy anxieties rather than present dangers. Legacy anxieties also suddenly appear when, on his laptop screen, he watches and remotely participates in his mother's ninety-fifth birthday party, and people there tell Ho to "*stop filming*, they are uncomfortable being on camera." His mother comes to visit with him across the causeway in his Johor hotel, and he jokes that she has forgotten to bring him some of the two celebratory roasted pigs from her birthday party.

Dr. Ang Swee Chai and Francis Khoo are two of the three centerpiece characters (along with Tan Wah Piow) in the film. Through photographs and video and audiotape, as well as Swee Chai's telling, Francis Khoo is one of the most vivid characters in the film. There are photos of him as a boy, one of eleven siblings (all but one still in Singapore); as a defense lawyer for Tan Wah Piow, including a photo of three police officers taking notes as they questioned the latter, Francis looking on, on a warm day, both in short sleeves; another of him in a suit as a defense attorney; others of him with microphone in hand addressing students at a demonstration. There are pictures of Francis in London in exile, happily mixing with locals in a pub, beer in hand; seated astride a chair, hands on its back, with a table full of friends behind him, all posing for the camera; dressed up in a clown cape and oversized boots with a woman leaning over his shoulder with a rapier; and in a blue bomber-style jacket outside a cathedral in Yorkshire, where he went to support a soup kitchen for striking miners, bringing them cans of baked beans. And there are pictures of him playing music, and two recordings of songs he composed and sang in a quite lovely tenor, the first:

'Twas the fifteenth of February, the dead of the night,
they kept knocking and banging my door.
I slipped quietly away but the others could not,
and I know that I see them no more.
They had taken so many, how many I know not,
there's Maha, and Mike, and Samy,
and there's Jing Quee and others,
the brave and the tall,
and they're once more behind Changi wall.
Oh my dear bride, my dearest,
just two weeks we're wed,
please remember the vow that we made.
I have left my homeland for a place far away,
but I know I'll be back home someday.
Oh my people, my people, the ones that I love,
I will never see you again
till the storm clouds gather at break of the dawn
and Bunga Raya shall bloom in rain.

Swee Chai, his widow, describes herself as the one who never could feel quite at home in London, even though she requalified as a surgeon. She describes herself as miserable, while Francis was always ebullient and happy among new friends, locally in pubs, across England, and across the world. She adopts the Palestinian cause as a proxy identity, refugees who cannot go home. She works as a doctor and activist with Medical Aid for Palestinians in Gaza and London. She takes Francis's ashes back to Singapore and is able to meet up with her sister and Francis's two sisters there (they otherwise have weekly Skype calls on Saturday nights). And she visits other exiles at anniversaries of detentions and funerals (and to aid the filmmaker). In her telling, there are two emotional puncta, one for herself and one for Francis. For herself, she concedes that the most painful bit of torture that her Singaporean jailers inflicted was the warning that if she followed Francis into exile, she would become a nobody in England. She mourns the family life and prominence as a surgeon she might have achieved in Singapore, but she has the last word in the film: "Making a stand is expensive, supporting those who make a stand can be just as expensive. Personally. . . . Maybe there's an attitude that my generation did not fight hard enough to bring democracy and freedom to Singapore, but, I can tell you, some of us did, and we tried quite hard. Whether we fail or did not is not the point, but we did try."

The punctum for Francis, she discovered after his death, were letters he wrote to his parents and especially one to his mother responding to her lament that he is so far away, in which he uses the New Testament line "What profit a man if he acquires the whole world and lost his own soul?" (Matthew 16:26). He reminds his mother that she named him after St. Francis of Assisi, and writes, "I've lost a lot, I've lost you, I've lost my brothers and sisters, my career and so on, and here am I [we see a photo of him as a young man], a refugee, but, mum, I've got my soul." She phones him immediately: "Look, you do not come back and make confession and implicate your friends and put other people in jail. I'd be very ashamed of you, and if you come back, I will take a gun and I will shoot you, and then I'll go and shoot the chief of ISD [Internal Security Department]." Swee Chai laughs, saying this is "Peranakan language, very passionate." We see photos of Francis with his arm around his aged mother in a wheelchair. "It was only when I read his letter to his mother that I realized how much it affected him, you see. But he never let on. He would sing; he would write songs," and we see a photograph of him at a microphone, with backup musicians.

We meet Francis's former client and former president of the Singapore University Student Union, Tan Wah Piow, who got in trouble as a twenty-four-year-old for raising questions about detention without trial and illegal exploitation of workers by state-controlled unions. We meet him, a graying professorial type in his sixties, in the opening bar of the film, driving the filmmaker in his Toyota to his house in Shepherd's Bush, London. He asks the filmmaker, almost as a kind of bona fide, "So far has the Singapore Broadcasting, have they used your material?" She replies: "Yes, yes, I mean, I've only been banned once, for a short film." He introduces himself: "Well, I landed here on the 31st of June 1976, so that makes it thirty-six years, thirty-seven years. Have I got my maths right? I stopped counting—yeah, life everywhere is I guess the same: *you just have to keep trying*—my real challenge is not really in terms of livelihood; it is when and how I can get back to Singapore." This is unlikely since Singapore took away his citizenship and, as he explained in a recent interview: "Should I ever step foot in Singapore, I was told in no uncertain terms that I would go straight to prison and upon serving whatever sentence—and technically I found out I'm still under Internal Security Act—that was [for] 1987 [the so-called Marxist conspiracy which he was accused of masterminding from London with the help of Vincent Chen]. They would put me in prison and upon whatever period they feel like releasing me, I will be deported back to UK. So, I don't see the point" (Tan Wah Piow 2020).

He takes us to his garden shed, with its intricate shelving configured by architect friends and containing the two small suitcases. Seated in his garden, he reflects that he and his peers were supposed to be the *crème de la crème*; they were the future leaders of the new nation. "So theoretically I belong to that generation which should be the clones that Lee Kuan Yew wanted to see for the future of Singapore" (Tan Wah Piow 2020). But, he observes, the moment you started raising questions about detention without trial and the Internal Security Act, a British colonial legacy that continued in independent Singapore, things changed. "I remember the first time I raised the issue of detention without trial, I was the student leader. Toh Chin Chye [chancellor of the University of Singapore, and also chairman of the People's Action Party] was sharing the same stage. He went ballistic and was making strenuous criticism of what I said on stage." He recalls: "The matter that really got me and my colleagues at the Student Union in trouble [on-screen, we see the student undergraduate newspaper with the headline, 'The People's Struggle Shall Be Victory'] was when we started to identify a problem in Jurong Industrial Estate where workers were being retrenched, where workers were paid with vouchers issued by the trade union to buy things at the [union-owned] supermarket. That was absolutely illegal. [We see a demonstration and banner held aloft that reads 'Justice!']."

Son of a small shopkeeper—"people who do not get any benefits from the state and, well, they have a healthy, shall I say, healthy disbelief in the establishment" (Tan Wah Piow 2020)— Tan Wah Piow entered university as an architecture student. Elsewhere, he recalls that "I chose to do the longest course. The choice then was either medicine or architecture. I don't think medicine suits my temperament. Then I chose architecture because it was seven years" (Tan Wah Piow 2020). He was elected president of the University of Singapore's Student Union in 1974. In the film, we see a black-and-white photo of him on the lawn (called the Upper Quad in those days) of the university (today the Law School), holding a microphone, with students sitting around on the grass. As he mentioned above, "The matter that really got me and my colleagues at the Student Union in trouble was when we started to identify a problem in Jurong Industrial Estate . . . When we started raising concerns about that, our time was up, the whole system came down on us heavy."[26] There are photographs of an assembly of students on the university lawn, of men on the street in a circle around him, of him surrounded by police, of a *Straits Times* headline, "Breach of undertaking not to be involved in politics: six foreign students expelled." The lawn of the university is where many of the young future leaders of Singapore took their turn in debates and politics—richly described for the period between 1953 and 1971, the glory days of the famous University Socialist Club, where politics was vigorously debated (Loh et al. 2012). At these events, future ambassador Tommy Koh already played the role of diplomat between factions, and Lee Kuan Yew, known as Harry in those days, also played a role.

Tan Wah Piow today is an Oxford-educated lawyer. He did his law degree at Balliol College, hoping to practice in Singapore. Earlier, in England, he had worked in a publishing firm and started his own when he had his son (a turning point, as for Ho Juan Thai). It was at the time when printing technologies were changing and entry into the business was possible. In Singapore he had already intended to study law. As a university student there, he applied to switch from architecture to law, and was accepted by Tommy Koh, then dean of the Law School. But he was blocked by Toh Chin Chye, the chancellor of the University and chairman of the PAP, with whom he had several public meeting run-ins over detention without trial, and the workers' protest in Jurong.

We see his small law office, where he deals in "personal law, personal law dealing with human rights [asylum cases, refugee rights], dealing with criminal law, and all sorts of problems, which people find beyond their ability to cope." He has been winding down this practice, and in 2018 he "decided to put some of my thinking in art form, realizing that most people don't read" (Tan Wah Piow 2020). His passion is still his life project of advocacy for bringing democracy to Singapore. His office at home has shelves of books of the sort that anyone who lived through the 1960s has, such as William Hinton's iconic book *Fanshen*, and books on China, Indonesia, Malaysia, and Thailand. There are also numerous books on Singapore, including those of Lee Kuan Yew, about which he laughs, "I only refer to [them] for my research." There is his own earlier book, *Frame-Up: A Singapore Court on Trial* (Tan Wah Piow 1989); two copies of *Beyond the Blue Gate* by Teo Soh Lung (2008), a lawyer and another of the detainees; *Lee's Law: How Singapore Crushes Dissent* by Chris Lydgate (2004) on opposition politician J. B. Jeyaretnam; *Dark Clouds at Dawn* by Said Zahani (2001), another detainee who appears in *To Singapore, with Love*; C. V. Devan Nair's *Not by Wages Alone* (1982); *Public Housing in Singapore*, edited by Steven H. K.

Yeh (1975); *Governing Singapore*, by Raj Vasil (1984); and *That We May Dream Again*, a collection by Operation Spectrum detainees, edited by Fong Hoe Fang (2009).

We see his book launch in a small library for his book *Smokescreen and Mirrors: Tracing the "Marxist Conspiracy"* (Tan Wah Piow 2012). From the podium he says: "Those who voted in the PAP over the years, for the last fifty years, they could see their housing has improved from slums to high rise, they have seen themselves progress from being unemployed to being employed, their own position from being illiterate or with little education they're able to bring their children to university level. Now that we have achieved this very high level of economic development, who would still feel the need for high-level of political control?" He continues that if the issue of democracy in Singapore is no longer an issue, there is closure. But he thinks it is still unfinished business, and (in mock lawyerly idiom) "and I just don't like to close a file when we don't have it satisfactorily resolved."[27]

The exiles in the film who now live in Thailand or Malaysia provide counterpoint stories to those of the ones in London. They include two funerals—of Liu Bo and then of Lim Hock Siew—and a meeting with the former editor of an important Malay-language journal, Said Zahari. Zahari is now in a wheelchair and less interactive than in the past, such as in his earlier filmed interview with Martyn See (banned in Singapore, but available on the internet), where he is suave and articulate and even demonstrates the fluent Mandarin he learned from fellow prisoners. Even in his reduced condition, he still delivers one of the key lines in the film: "You see, the meaning of the struggle is to make the people, especially the younger generation, aware that our society today is not a free society . . . the struggle continues."[28]

There is the couple who live in Bangkok and now run a small storefront noodle factory, helping their son, who went to university in Vietnam, but returned to find no job. In their upstairs office a map of Southeast Asia hangs on the wall. They stay informed about Singapore and regional affairs. There is the couple who live in the mountains of Betong, Thailand ("safe from tanks and airplanes"), former guerrilla fighters in their youth who had expected to die in the jungle; who had left children behind they would not see for fifteen years; who fought for the British when the Japanese invaded; and who prepared for death when So Chin Peng, the longtime leader of the Malayan Communist Party, refused the demand to disarm and formally surrender after the peace treaty with Malaysia in which he had agreed to give up the armed struggle (but not disarm or surrender). There is a cello in the background, and they respond to the filmmaker's surprise by laconically saying there were many talented comrades. They show us two photographs, one of each of them standing in their uniforms with their rifles. They had thought to leave these photographs, if they were killed, as "memories" after their deaths. There is the couple who had been rank-and-file members of the PAP, and then the Barisan Sosialis. They were pushed out of Singapore in the cleansing of the nation of leftist forces, into the arms of the Malaysian communists, who they say were the only ones offering support to the refugees. They feel aggrieved that they were never recognized for their contributions to the fight for the independence of Singapore and Malaya (later Malaysia). They refuse to return to be interrogated and paraded for confessions on television, to rat on their colleagues, to abandon friendships and freedom of thought as conditions of return.

And finally, there is the rail-thin old man who has composed a written statement that he reads to the camera, sitting outside on a plastic chair in the dirt space of a street. It is a statement he wrote out in 2006, when he finally, "reluctantly and gratefully," took up Thai citizenship. Its content is a brief, dense pointillist set of detailed memories and marks of Singapore that constitute his formative identity, beginning with his smallpox vaccination scar on his left arm from colonial days, proceeding through war and independence:

> . . . where the Japanese drop their first bomb. On both sides of Temple Street lay bodies to be collected along with their stench. The white flags raised, we surrendered. The Japanese dogs leave, the British monkeys return, the Union Jack rises once again. In the old Kallang Airport, thousands cry "Merdeka!" ("Independence!"). Amidst the wind and rain we surged from self-governance to independence. All these things I've seen, the history that I witnessed! I still have so much to tell you, Singapore, oh Singapore, if only you knew how much your present and your future still preoccupy me every day. Written on the 25th May 2006. South Thailand, Hat Yai. Chan Sun Wing.

He nods at the camera, smiles, gets up from the plastic chair and walks away, carrying the chair with him.

2

Filmic Stutter, Taped Counter-Truths, and Musical Sutures

Knots of Recovery

As if an uncanny shadow of the fate of Jasmine Ng's film *Eating Air* (Ng and Tong 1999)—loss, recovery, new life—Sandi Tan's *Shirkers* went missing after filming wrapped in 1992, only to be recovered twenty years later, and was reconstructed as a new film, released in 2018 by Netflix, and awarded the 2018 Sundance award for best world cinema directing. This stutter in its career is amplified by the stuttering collage effect of having to reconstruct the story from original shots assembled together with historical photographs, recent interviews, and explorations about the mysteries of a film teacher and his three students (Sandi Tan, Jasmine Ng, and Sophia Siddique), who together tried to make a film in the early 1990s about the rapidly changing city of Singapore and teen fantasies about creating a maverick movie. The 1992 film has a "would have been" claim on being Singapore's first indie film and road movie, had it been edited and finished, although there are some earlier claimants, including ones in which her stepmother starred.[1] The original film was shot on 16mm, a favorite indie format in the early 1990s; the new version toggles back and forth among 16mm, Super 8, and grainy standard-definition video. The director of photography, Iris Ng, shot the contemporary scenes with a Sony FS7 digital camcorder, and reconstructed the older scenes with a Super 8 film camera. This makes for a further collaging effect. Film editor Lucas Celler used Adobe's program After Effects to convert images into .mov files "to render the static into the cinematic" (Celler 2018). He and Tan "worked side by side every day at an editing bay . . . selecting the right shots from the original *Shirkers* . . . Sandi and I are sound effect junkies so we spent a lot of time finding areas to incorporate sound effects" (Celler 2018).[2] The 16mm footage looks strange today; it feels like a time stamp of the indie films of the 1980s and 1990s. Yet, says Tan in an interview with Erik Luers, "the warmth and the color palette were so warm that it makes digital video look like shit" (Luers 2018). When they unwrapped the recovered 16mm film footage (in ten-minute segments) in 2015, Tan and her technicians were surprised at their pristine condition, but also at the many "weird coincidences" in her early filmmaking and that of others at the time, as if she had been tapping into a global subconscious. Viewing the footage was, she says, like finding "magical mysteries":

> When we were watching the 700 minutes of 16mm footage, my editor and I would become entranced. We didn't know what we were going to see! We'd take notes and make folders in Adobe Premiere. We made a long, several-hour string of these collected flying bits and cut and paste the bits we liked. . . . It's irresistible to compare how a place looked then and now, and so we did the before/after shot-matches thing. Singapore is so different from what it was twenty-five years ago. . . . My film is the stories people throw away. I really love to collect things, and I guess I'm a "collage person" as a result of doing fanzines. I'm not the kind of person who throws those kinds of things away. I love looking at leader tapes to find all the stuff that's really there. I want to find magical mysteries—secret clues within the footprints and fingerprints. (Luers 2018)

"I'm a 'collage person.'" Tan's novel, *The Black Isle* (2012a), which follows or precedes *Shirkers* (2018d)—written before the 2015 recovery of the 1992 film as an exorcism of the frustrations and disappointments of (not) making the original film in a timely fashion—is not done using collage in any conventional way. But, as I will argue, it too gestures at lost histories, only now partially available for recovery, and it brings together some film techniques together with popular ghost stories, Malay claims to priority to the land, tropes of the wise old woman who might be a witch, and a modern woman's refusal of patriarchal official stories. Indeed, it is visually so rich that there are hopes of turning it into a television series as well as a graphic novel. I will argue that it is also rich sonically and emotionally, drawing upon or playing off key film scores that Tan has identified in interviews:

> Very often, images come to me before words do. I wrote [*The Black Isle*] with several movie soundtracks on a loop, [significantly] including . . . *There Will Be Blood*, and . . . *The Talented Mr. Ripley*—and composed the whole thing as [a] kind of a movie of my wildest dreams . . . As if some fantasy amalgam of David Lynch, Alfonso Cuarón, and 1970s-era Francis Ford Coppola were directing *The Black Isle* in technicolor.[3]

These music compositions are never explicitly named in the novel, but I understand them as profoundly structuring the text, and as a kind of bridge between the official story of Singapore's nation-building and its more recent repositioning in the world, as Singapore struggles to devise a new official story for itself in the twenty-first century.

Claiming that her intent was "to write a novel about an Asian woman who's neither driven by grievance nor defined by marital or filial relationships," this chapter is the first of four chapters, a quartet, of explorations reading the works of women writers with an eye for the phenomenology and structural positioning of women's worlds in Singapore and Indonesia. Writing about subjectivity in the twenty-first century cannot be divorced from contested political histories. Or, to say it another more literary way, behind or alongside every ontology, a faddish word these days, or everyday ordinariness, including allegedly "conventional" gender roles, lies a hauntology. In Malay, *hantu* means ghost or specter; *haunter* in Old French (from German) means "home," one's haunt. A spirit or ghost haunts a house or recurs persistently in consciousness. At times, when the return or repetition detects a difference, the *heimlich*, "feeling at home," becomes *unheimlich* or "uncanny." It is these emotional differences that inhabit and create the sensing of ghosts, specters, or spirits, and that also help constitute subjectivity, the orienting immune system of the self, formed through relations with others. When the ghosts disappear, the self becomes disoriented, shadowless, insubstantial, without its parts, and pale, lacking the reflections of himself or herself in others, and thus unable to engage in the healthy interactions of living, drained of blood, and thus of life.

This is the message of two of the sorcerers in *The Black Isle*: the *bomoh*-Malay guru, the keeper of Malay repressed histories, lifestyles, and aspirations; and Cassandra, the keeper of alternative female perspectives (there are similar figures in different ways in the women-authored novels in the following chapters). Other alternative female perspectives, not necessarily calling on repressed histories, are also being made visible by Singaporean artists in various media such as Margaret Tan and Shirley Soh in their efforts to build collaborative civic action and human-scaled public art within the spaces of the Intelligent Island and Smart Nation.[4]

When the film *Shirkers* was reconstructed, the new film became a film about the film guru who entranced his young female students. I call him a daemonic figure, a charismatic, even obsessive figure into whose flame the young women were drawn. The novel *The Black Isle* was written before *Shirkers* was rediscovered, the author says, as an exorcism of sorts for the unmade film and its daemonic figure, but the novel has at least three other such male charismatic figures, each representing a different kind of obsession or tropical fever, around whom the female protagonist must navigate, and the narrator Cassandra herself becomes something of a daemon as well.

Treating *Shirkers* and *The Black Isle* together, there are four daemons whose passions are never exhausted, and around whom the female protagonist(s) must negotiate while protecting her sense of self. Georges Cardona is the art daemon in *Shirkers*. In *The Black Isle* there are three more: a Malay, or rather a sea peoples' *bomoh* (master of the spirits), called by his Chinese employer by a generic Muslim name that is oblivious to cultural, not just class, erasure; a Japanese commander who takes the protagonist as his trophy wife and cultural opponent through the hell of wartime brutality; and the key politician of a cleansed meritocratic postwar Singapore. I call these three the daemons of autochthony, of warfare, and of rationality; or one might call them tropical fevers: the *archive fever* and hauntology of spirituality located in old Malay thalassocracies; the *war fever* of tributary extraction, co-prosperity spheres, and national security states; and the *meritocracy fever* of out-of-control rationality. While these guru-daemons and fevers are male and patriarchal, the novel is constructed by its female author and old-woman narrator to imagine a woman protagonist "unlike the heroines of most Asian novels."[5] That too was the intention of the original film *Shirkers*: to create without barriers. It was a mood both of the times and of Sandi Tan's stage in life. But with age comes experience, and the novel's heroine significantly changes her name from Ling to Cassandra. She also becomes a daemon in her own right, marginalized by history, not a traditional *pontianak* (angry female ghost, usually avenging women who die in childbirth), but rather a once charismatic figure of female agency who works to outwit the historians and keepers of the archives from erasing her (there are shades here of Lydia Kwa's Empress Wu Zhao, discussed in chapter 3).

The daemons work as formal mythic features like Vladimir Propp's characters and standard plot moves (Propp [1928] 1968), or like Claude Lévi-Strauss's aporetic contradictions in the Oedipus myth (Lévi-Strauss 1955).[6] Like the musical-structural analysis of *To Singapore, with Love* in chapter 1, *The Black Isle* also has a musical understructure. The novel was written, the author says, while listening on a loop to the soundtracks of contemporary films. This was the key for me to read the emotional rhythms of the novel with these film soundtracks in mind. The result is, to my mind, one of the more successful of efforts to rewrite Singapore's twentieth-century history, one that does not simply recapitulate the official line of "the Singapore story"—the title of Lee Kwan Yew's autobiography, and phrase used by the marketing arms of the Singapore government to celebrate Singapore's rise "from Third World to First World nation in one generation." It does not present a different story of the seventy-year-long history, but details it with that wry spin that wise old women often use in their narrations to set history straight, or undercut official pretentions.

The wise old woman, sorceress, witch, ghost, or Cassandra figure in this novel is a trope that I try to look for throughout all of the quartet of novelists and their novels. One might say that *The Black Isle* utilizes mythic forms lightly, especially invoking the mystical knowledge of Malay sorcerers (*bomoh*) and Islamic mystical knowledge, while in chapter 7, Nuraliah Norasid will utilize a stronger mythopoesis. In any case, running throughout many of the novels is an acknowledgment that in variable degrees parts of the population avail themselves of the discourses of nonrational (mystical or irrational) forces in the world.

Sandi Tan's second novel appeared only after I had finished writing this volume. Its title, *Lurkers*, rhymes with *Shirkers* and deploys a similar warm, satirical tone. There are other continuities such as the importance of a daemon-teacher of questionable morality. It is focused on southern California and Florida, and its Asian immigrants are Korean rather than Singaporean (see S. Tan 2021). It gets a cameo appearance here (see also my appreciative review on the Amazon website).

FILMIC STUTTERING: REPLAYING THE PAST FOR CLUES

> Back then the thing I wanted more than anything was to make a movie but I never imagined it would end this way. Twenty-five years later I find myself on a strange backward journey, replaying the past for clues.
>
> SANDI TAN, IN *SHIRKERS*

So begins the soundtrack of Sandi Tan's remade film *Shirkers* (2018d). The original film, made by teenagers in the early 1990s under the spell of an American film instructor, is said to have disappeared, as did the teacher.[7] The canisters of film footage, without the soundtrack, reappeared years later, providing broken or diffracting mirrors into the past. The new film involves a three-fold displacement of reality: a project nagging for completion; a missing guru-teacher, hiding from his own incompletion traumas; and a disappearing and morphing city.

The film, for example, contains a number of photographic puncta.[8] One is of Sandi Tan's grandfather, standing in front of his beloved two-story villa in 1981, just before it was torn down in the name of urban renewal and modernization. The multistory building that replaced the villa would still flood in the rain, but would "no longer [run] milk chocolate muddy."[9] Sandi Tan lived with her grandparents because her parents' marriage was collapsing and the family was morphing, like everything else in Singapore, albeit under a facade of often rigid expectations that Sandi succeed in school and behave in public. "When we were growing up in the 1980s, the state and the family were constantly in your face. Singapore was so uptight . . . When Jasmine [Ng] and I were fourteen, we discovered unusual movies and unpopular music, and as weirdos we became best friends. We came from very different backgrounds . . . I was always expected to shine, which was exhausting. I needed a way out."

Of the film and its disappearance, Sandi's voice-over says, "I learned to pretend it never happened, which is of course impossible: *Shirkers* became a secret history shared by a small group of us, and it would haunt us and bond us, and tear us apart." Her friend Jasmine Ng and she bonded over doing "crazy things": showing up at school dressed as nurses, building shrines in Jasmine's room, reading *American Film* and *Film Comment* religiously.[10] To get to see the films they read about, Sandi "established a clandestine videotaping syndicate with my cousin Vicky in Florida just so I could watch [David Lynch's] *Blue Velvet* [1986]."[11] At age fourteen they wrote for Philip Cheah's *Big O*, an underground rock music zine. "He would make us tapes of Patti

Smith and the Velvet Underground and quiz us on them before he would let us go to their [boys] film society club." But their greatest feat was publishing their own zine, *Exploding Cat*, on the photocopiers at the National Library: "*Exploding Cat* was our attempt to catalogue everything that angered us, that made us laugh. . . . We received letters from New York, London, Paris, Jerusalem, even prisons in three different states.[12] Above all, it was a catalogue of us . . . our tiny island in the middle, the center of the world, charting our own destiny in 1989."

In 1991, Sandi and Jasmine and a third girl, Sophia Siddique, took a filmmaking class offered by Georges Cardona, "a man of unplaceable age and origin" who "projected himself" as "an American filmmaker."[13] They became his groupies. There is a photograph in the film of The Substation, where Cardona taught them filmmaking. The Substation was only founded in 1990 by the playwright Kuo Pao Kun as an experimental arts performance center at the heart of the arts scene. The film claims that Cardona's was the first film class to be offered in Singapore. Or if it was not the first, it was certainly a seductive offering for young women, trying to create a sense of empowerment. "My impression of Georges," says Sophia Siddique in the film, "was first of all his eyes; very metallic, almost icy blue. He spoke in very slow, calm, measured tones. And I just remember, even at that point, this kind of dissonance, you know, the eyes seemed so cold but his demeanor seemed so warm, and he had this ability that when he spoke to you, you felt that you were his sole focus." Cardona took them to shoot colorful Hindu festivals, talked about French New Wave films, and after class at nine or ten at night he would take them on "road trips" around the island. "We kept him out late even though we knew he had a wife and baby waiting for him at home. We went looking for ideas. . . . He picked us but he let us feel like we picked him." He invited Ng and Tan to join him on a road trip across the United States from Los Angeles to his hometown of New Orleans. Sandi seized the opportunity, not telling anyone because she feared how it would look traveling with a married man more than twice her age. A tentative pass occurred one night, and they both, then, pretended it never happened.

Enchantment was allowed to continue as they drove through the American South "with its moss and bugs and ghost stories" to New Orleans. Georges told stories of watching his elder brother bleeding to death when he was twelve, of Jayne Mansfield's decapitated head rolling over to his car in 1967, and of being the inspiration for the James Spader character in Steven Soderbergh's *Sex, Lies, and Videotape* (1989). "Whether his stories were actually true seemed beside the point," Sandi reminisces. "I loved his storytelling and how his stories made time, and place, and truth absolutely porous. I was suddenly staring at a puddle of blood in the living room in the sixties, I was two degrees away from Jayne Mansfield's head, three degrees from Steven Soderbergh." New Orleans was where Georges had studied film, where he had opened a film studio called Light House Media Center, and had started projects, never finished. They spoke of making a film together.

Sandi then returned to London where she was studying (while Sophia was studying in Los Angeles, and Jasmine in New York) and wrote a script about a road trip in a small country one could drive across in forty minutes, involving a teenage assassin, S, who shoots with her fingers, as she goes around the country like a grim reaper picking off characters in "games: toys in her imagination [that can] save the world in small numbers." It was high camp, a grrl-power-meets-noir crime story, shot guerrilla-style on the streets of Singapore in 1992.

Full of enthusiasm and drive, Sandi pressed on to shoot the film right away during the summer break of 1992. It was all improvisational. Auditions: "Okay, can you just imagine you are in a car right now and you are going around and like knocking all these old women down." They recruited Sandi's grandmother to play a nurse (she always wanted to be in a film), then a young cousin to play a crossing guard. They scoured the island for locations. Sandi says, "I made sure they found the shops and the old timey bakery that I loved because I knew they wouldn't be around for long." Sophia was the producer, using her contacts to get film and film equipment for free, and even managed to set up a meeting with a high-profile donor, at which point, she recalls, "Georges said to me, 'Okay, now you go into the kitchen, I'm going to take the meeting.' That was a very difficult moment for me. I did not believe in Georges but I believed in the film. Do I yell at Georges or is it better for me that I remain in the kitchen and have him secure the deal so the film could move forward? And I chose the film." After all, "we were trying to mount a feature film on the scantiest of practical knowledge. We had a production assistant who was fourteen years old. Georges talked Ronnie, a thirty-year-old first-time director of photography, into shooting the film for us."

It was part lark, part effort to show that Singapore could do independent film. Since the departure of the prewar film industry (the famous Shaw Brothers Studios, and the Cathay Studios), there had been little domestic film production, and they felt they could do better than *They Call Her Cleo-*

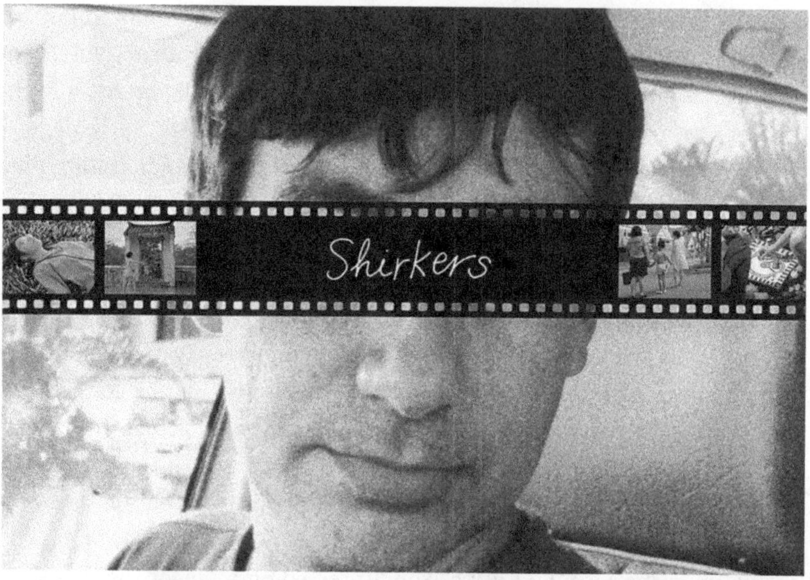

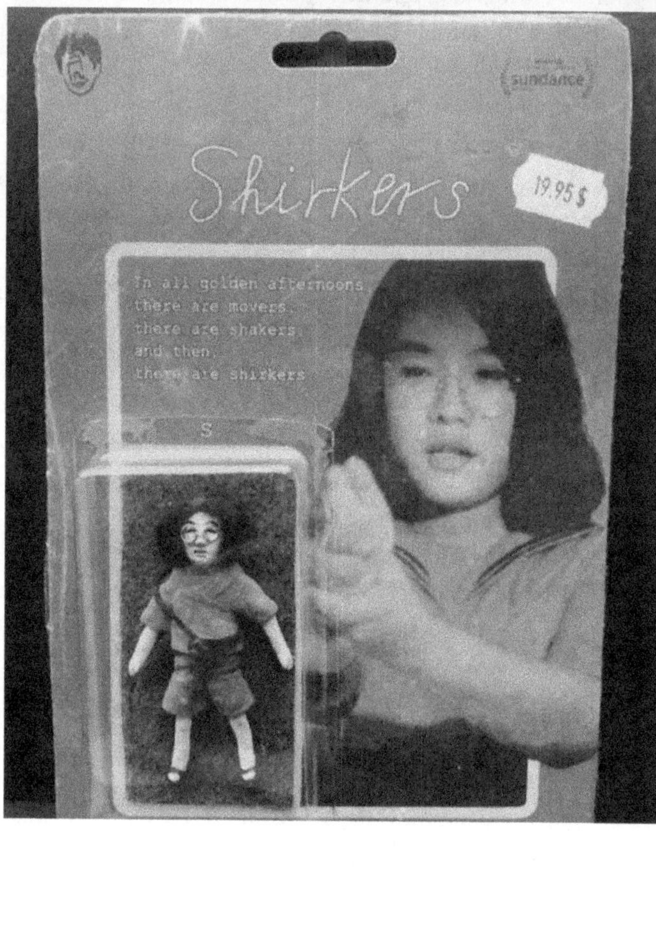

2.1 (*above*) Georges Cardona with filmstrip across his eyes, from a poster for *Shirkers*.

2.2 (*right*) Shooting with fingers, a poster for *Shirkers*.

patra Wong (Suarez 1978) or the film *Medium Rare* (Smith 1992).[14] Jasmine Ng would soon collaborate with Kelvin Tong to make the film *Eating Air* (1999), subsequently novelized by Ng Yi-Sheng (2008), more in line with *Shirkers*' camp style of capturing life around them. "Eating air" is the English translation of the Hokkien for joyride (*jiak hong*), particularly a motorcycle joyride. In Malay, it translates as *makan angin*, meaning, more sweetly, "to go for a short trip or holiday." So, the film was promoted as a "motorcycle kung-fu love story." There is a gang of teenagers who hang out in video arcades, ride their motorcycles, and fight other gangs; and there is a love story of Ah Boy and Ah Girl who naively plan to ride to the north (Malaysia) to escape the problems of Ah Boy's indebtedness to loan sharks. Ah Boy is a variant on the eponymous character of *Billy Liar* (Schlesinger 1963), daydreaming and fantasizing about being a kung fu warrior as escape from boredom.[15] The story is built around Ah Gu, who is ambitious to prove himself, loses his motorbike by defaulting on a loan, makes money again, and buys two motorcycles (one for Ah Boy), but in trying to sell drugs to repay his loans gets robbed by drug dealers, and then defaults on a motorcycle race for another loan shark. Joyrides and road trips, dreaming and performing—the themes of escape overlap with *Shirkers*.

Shirkers begins with a campy parody of films in Sandi Tan's head: protagonist S carrying old suitcase and camera, coming home to a suburban neighborhood with one-story houses, lawnmower sounds, clanging cutlery, whining puppies, and toy radios playing 1930s Shanghai show tunes (a mashup of Chinese, American, and Singaporean motifs). Rounding up her friend, TB, they go to "shoot" the piano teacher (shot with fingers, she falls over), with, no doubt, Truffaut's *Shoot the Piano Player* (1960) in mind.[16] Says Sandi: "Playing the teenage killer S back in 1992, I saw myself as a kind of Bruno S—that deranged non-actor in Werner Herzog's *The Enigma of Kaspar Hauser* [1974], a movie I loved, loved, loved. But, um, I'm not exactly sure that came across" (S. Tan 2018a). When TB gets too busy, S looks for a new sidekick and four more people "she likes enough to kill." Each person she meets she follows home, as if acting out a Jungian or Freudian motif of searching for an archetype or womb of attachment, origin, or explanation of character. She meets a "visibility inspector"—echoes of *An Inspector Calls*?—named Ravan and follows him home, where she picks up his young son Hario as a sidekick.[17] She and Hario wander around the island looking for more people to collect: they spot Cecilia, a nurse, and her giant dog Cherish, and follow them home where they collect Cecilia's daughter, Monster, an epileptic who loves to dance. They follow home a "funny dude" named Montana Ba, and "a mystery boy" whom S keeps encountering, "develops feelings for, and this means she has to kill him." They meet Albert, an inventor of sticky tape, who shows them his parodically massive new house, his wife Mimi, their son Robert, and their maids Hirchraro and Pacifica—a satirical look at Singapore's *nouveau riche* long before *Crazy Rich Asians* (Chu 2018). S and Robert go driving around the island: time is running out. S has three more people to take to the other world with her, though it is "not clear if this [other] world is heaven, hell, or a supermarket. So things happen, or maybe they don't, because maybe this whole thing was a dream after all, because, like, the plot was almost immaterial, it was a mood piece, it was, I don't know." For a quick mood accent, we hear performance sounds of a gamelan group, immediately playfully contradicted in tone by the next skit feature. "My script called for the largest dog in the country, and Sophie [Siddique] got hold of this giant wolfhound named Gigo, and she sneaked him into the supermarket when the manager's back was turned." Sophia adds, "I faked a seizure in order to draw crowds, so I was the crowd wrangler as well." Siddique and Tan borrowed some seniors from an old-folks home, and "returned them before they even knew what happened." All in all, "we captured some startling performances from friends and strangers."

The film critic Philip Cheah reflects in the remade film: "At that time I thought that *Shirkers* as it was proposed was incredible, it was way ahead of its time. This was a period when America was making some of these movies like [Dennis Hopper's] *Easy Rider* [1969]. To have something like *Shirkers* attempt to put Singapore on the map in a similar way was incredible." Responding to Sandi Tan's comment in the remade film that her acting in the original was terrible, too personal, and even childish, he replies that this was part of its power: "*Shirkers* is such a free film because you were very free yourself. It was such a joy that you were willing to experiment and express anything on your mind" in such an uptight period in Singapore. It was, in that sense, doing what *Easy Rider* had done.

But Georges's troubling role was beginning to manifest in ways that were not yet legible. In one of Sandi Tan's most visceral memories, after a long day of shooting, she asked Georges how the takes looked, and he nonchalantly replied that the camera had jammed at the first take. So they had nothing. She was furious, and they had to go back the next day and shoot it all over. Meanwhile, Ben Harrison was working on the soundtrack.[18] He had known Sandi and Jasmine from their work on *Exploding Cat* and *Big O* magazines, and in the 2018 film he recalls he had worked with minimal resources: "I guess I would have had just one tape, a lot of little doodles on guitar, electric flow backward stuff I think." But Georges intervened. "I remember my skin crawling, as I was ushered away from you guys at Newton Circus. What I wasn't expecting was Georges to take me aside, escort me to his car like some gangster meeting or policeman meeting an informer or something like that, straight out of the movies, and I thought, okay, he's going to listen to the tape and the stuff I have which I thought was odd because it was for you guys. But I didn't get that. He threatened me, sussing me out, to see if I had an agenda, telling me off, telling me don't take advantage of these guys, something like that. He also tells me that a far more professional and established musician was working on the sound track, which was news to me." Ben left the tape with Georges because he thought it was going to the girls, but Georges confiscated Ben's only tape and banned him from visiting the set.

Jasmine, sensing things were going wrong, started keeping notes. She reads from them on the soundtrack:

> Everything is bloody uncertain. Mr. C has no idea what he's doing, he has no idea how he's going to get the money. He claims he has a production manager who worked on *Apocalypse Now*. Who is that? I don't know. . . . How could we continue with this, when I was pointing all these things out? It was just you [Sandi] and Georges who wanted this to happen. So, at this point, you weren't paying attention to any of these progress reports. We were doing the legwork and you thought you were just going to wing it. You were obviously being an asshole. You've always been an asshole, just as much as you have the capacity to be really wonderful, you have as much capacity to be an asshole.

Sandi was obsessed and time was running out before they all had to leave Singapore and go back to school abroad: "So maybe I was an asshole, but I just wanted us to keep going, no matter what. There was no time to think." Cinema and reality began to interfere with each other as in a Buster Keaton train wreck.[19] "Georges was shooting us from a bridge overlooking the railroad track. I heard the train even before I heard his warning." And then with two weeks left to go they ran out of money: Georges said he just needed $10,000 or the production would have to be shut down.

> Sophia and I felt we'd come too far to let this happen. So, Georges drove us from ATM to ATM, and over the next few nights Sophia and I withdrew

> all of our savings. We never told a soul. After shooting wrapped, Sophie, Jasmine, and I were completely spent. But we had pulled off the impossible. We had made a movie. Sophie went back to LA, Jasmine went back to New York, I went back to England, leaving Georges in Singapore to process the seventy canisters of film and to tell us what the footage looked like. *None of us had seen a single frame* of what we had shot. And so, I waited and I waited and I waited, Christmas went by, New Years went by. Finally, a package arrived from Georges Cardona. [A tape with his voice:] Hope you are fine, hope you managed to open a bottle of wine, don't drink it all at one time, put on some music, piano, Chopin, Beethoven, very soothing, okay, that's it for now. I'll send you some stuff.

The school year ended. Summer began, when Jasmine had planned to edit the film. Sandi then received another enigmatic tape cassette from Georges as if it is he who has been put upon, as if the girls had telephoned him, disturbing him, and making fun of their questions about the progress on the film. That was the last they heard from him. He was gone, and so was *Shirkers*. Jasmine Ng says, "There was a piece of my spirit that died; all I was left with were those fuzzy memories of being on the set and just waiting; Georges took everything." And Sandi recalls one final incident:

> On the last day of the shoot, only Georges, Ronnie, and I were left. We drove out to a patch of land by the airport and built a very strange contraption. It was to make our young actor Romano fly. But there was no such flying scene in my script. How were we going to get rid of the harness and the rope? I asked Georges. Don't worry he said, there's computers. After the long hours trying to film that completely made-up scene, he popped open the camera by mistake, or maybe it wasn't by mistake, and there was no film in it.

Life goes on: the anger is buried, the film is gone, but the film addiction smolders. Twenty-five years later, Sandi wonders if Georges had been giving her a coded message only she would understand:

> There is a scene in my script where Hario discovers there is no film in S's camera. S tells him it doesn't matter because when you look through the hole and go click, it catches something or at least your mind catches something. You don't need film, just the action of doing that helps you remember. What was he trying to tell me? Film or no film, you must remember this? Was he role-playing as a director? Did he just view this en-

tire filmmaking venture as a psychological exercise? We were no longer magical kids who made a movie, we were just kids.

It all sounds like a variant of the daemonic director-actor power-plays of Daniel Hui's film *Demons* (2019b), discussed in chapter 6, and five years later, after *Shirker* wrapped, with yet another twist of the screw, a package arrived at Jasmine Ng's office with what seemed like videotapes from Georges Cardona. Excited, Jasmine, Sophia, and Sandi opened the package. These tapes had nothing on them. The young women were furious at the cruelty.

Life moves on. Sandi Tan attends film school at Columbia in New York. But the film keeps rewinding and nagging. "I know I was doing things backwards," she says:

> First, I made the movie, then I became a film critic [for the *Straits Times*], then I went to film school. But that's what happens when you no longer have a map. . . . But then it began to send me distress signals, and suddenly in my mid-thirties I found myself in Los Angeles of all places. I decided to turn to fiction, because to write a novel, I didn't have to wait for anyone, it's *just me and my ghosts*. My novel, *The Black Isle*, was the story of a young woman with extraordinary powers who falls under the influence of a charismatic but sinister man. *Writing it felt like an exorcism. But I would be wrong about that.* . . . On September 11, 2011, I received an email from a familiar name. It was Georges's wife; she said Georges was dead. She also told me she had found seventy cans of film labeled *Shirkers* and that they were all in perfect condition.

So now begins the rewind, the second film, and the passage through other people that Georges had also charmed into addiction to his persona, his stories, his dreams, his inabilities to finish anything, and still worse, his seeming inability to allow his protégés to finish anything, to be more successful than he was. The evil addiction passes through his widow, who never really knew what he was up to but funded him; it affects the novelist Grace Mazur and the filmmaker Stephen Tyler, both of whom were enrolled, entranced, and seduced by him in projects that went on and on but never came to pass.[20] They become, however, in the later-filmed sections of *Shirkers* not fellow victims but fellow detectives. Peeling back Georges Cardona layer by layer reminds Sandi Tan of Michelangelo Antonioni's *Blow-Up* (1966), when David Hemmings returns to the scene of the crime only to find nothing (the music track plays a bass saxophone), and she reflects on Georges's charm: "There is nothing there, but movies. There are characters he wanted to emulate [*the music track plays a jazz trumpet*] and there are characters he wanted to be, but the one who was closest to the one he really was was Nosferatu trying to become immortal by feeding on young people's dreams."

Sophia elaborates: "Georges Cardona had his own very bizarre love for *Shirkers*. I thought that when he absconded with all of the reels that they would be just strewn outside, the humidity would basically just eat up the film, and that would be it. But he loved those reels. We all fell in love with the film in different ways, and his was, I don't know, man, it was like necrophiliac." Sandi: "He might have loved our reels, but he threw all of the sound recordings away. He returned *Shirkers* to us as a mute." "When I saw the footage," Philip Cheah says, "I just thought that, gee-whiz, this film should have been finished. It would have been a rallying call that it is okay to try anything."

And Sophia reflects, "You know, *Shirkers* is like the ghost in between the lines of books, written in Singapore, on Singapore film history; and for me *Shirkers* has this very palpable absence." Sandi more pragmatically says: "There were so many surprises in this time capsule: the fashion choices of the era, Jasmine defiantly chewing gum, after gum was officially banned, and then there was the landscape, a Singapore I had let myself forget." Sophia finds her old notebooks with the film and marvels and laughs at her earlier self, showing analyses that foreshadow the film and English professor she would become, "breaking down the script for symbolism and metaphor and notions." She reads from her notes and directions: "the toys would be physical manifestations of her [S's] personality; they must reflect her (in all caps!); she's thinking mortality through the dreams."

Putting the film back together, or rather making a new film about the making of the earlier film, brought its own surprises. Sandi found a post-production house in Burbank, California, called Modern VideoFilm, that had worked on the Douglas Sirk films of the 1950s and Wes Anderson's *The Grand Budapest Hotel* (2014), a film about the 1930s, so she thought they would understand the palette she wanted. "Georges and I had shot the entire exteriors at the 'magic hour' (which in equatorial Singapore lasts only fifteen minutes, which is why the shoot took two and a half months, but also why it looks pretty fab[ulous], because he loved the work of the cinematographer Néstor Almendros who had worked on [Terrence Malick's] *Days of*

Heaven [1978].” She marvels: “Georges had wrapped every roll of film in black plastic before putting them in their own cans, so when Modern VideoFilm opened them up, they were shocked how pristine they were, it looked like it was shot yesterday. They did a transfer and a simple pass and that was that.”

In an interview, Sandi tries to be philosophical: “For the longest time I was trying to think of [this process] as an exorcism. I don’t think of him as a villain. . . . I was so angry at him for stealing my youth, and my dreams and my life. But I think of the things I got from him—the conversations about film, the French New Wave, and this feeling that it’s OK to be obsessed with movies. I got a love of storytelling from him and it never left me” (S. Tan 2018b). Replaying the past for clues, this film has an odd kind of staying power, made up of fragments and afterlives of youthful energy. The three obsessions—the fantasies of youth, of recovery of youth in adult reflection, and of turning recovery into resonant storytelling—depend upon “locat[ing] in the tenor of their settings the sources of their spell” (Geertz [1976] 1983, 120): of the young women determined to empower themselves in lives different from those of their parents; of a dreamy young man who tried to hide that he was unsuccessful in almost all his endeavors, while still managing to create magical worlds around himself, oblivious perhaps that he was being cruel in inflicting failure on others in the process of trying to redeem himself; and the Möbius strip–like infinities and twists and turns of life played out, backward and forward and laterally through allusions and jump cuts. After years of embarrassed, disabling, silence—not being able to talk about a film that had never been made, for which there was no proof that it had ever existed—Sandi is enabled to make a new film with bits of the old, and reexperience something of the grrl empowerment that she had felt during the making of the original film. The new film becomes a psychodrama about the ephemerality of Georges Cardona, the guru or daemon, who cast a spell not only over the three girls but also others he enticed into projects that never came to fruition. As Sandi repeats in one of the new segments of the film, she cannot bring herself to vilify him. He is still the best storyteller she has ever met, and he turned her teenage film infatuation into a taste of empowerment through filmmaking and storytelling.

The exorcism, if there ever be such, is not in the new film, but in *The Black Isle*. Again it is a trifecta: the richly peopled place, the creativity of storytelling, and the recovery of pasts that we dwell in whether we like it or not.

TAPES AND ERASURES: CATACOUSTICS IN *THE BLACK ISLE*

One writes with one's ears. It is absolutely essential.
HÉLÈNE CIXOUS, "THE LAUGH OF THE MEDUSA"

"My aim," Sandi Tan says in an interview, "was to write a novel about an Asian woman who's neither driven by grievance nor defined by marital or filial relationships. I felt that those were the types of Asian heroines found too often in novels, no matter the historical setting. And it's frustrated me, as a reader. I wanted to give my heroine the freedom to be her own person, to be complicated in a modern kind of way—and then see where a woman like that might take a story" (S. Tan 2012b). She might be thinking, among other examples, of Stella Kon's wildly popular monologue of the Peranakan matriarch, *Emily of Emerald Hill*, who starts as a poor girl married off into a rich Peranakan (Straits Chinese, mixed Chinese-Malay) family—as a fourteen-year-old wife to a widower's oldest son in an extended family with two wives of younger sons who are older than her; who ingratiates herself with her husband's parents, succeeds them as the iron-willed mistress of the house, but in the process alienates her children who are stifled by her controlling ways (Kon 1983).[21] Emily is a force of nature, making her way by dint of her wits and self-discipline, but constrained within a patriarchal world, and ends alone as the children move away. In contrast, Sandi Tan says, "The fun for me was throwing a passionate, unusual woman into the center" of the events of colonialism, World War II, independence, industrialization, "and figuring out how she—or indeed me, in her shoes—might pull through" (S. Tan 2012b). As a melodic tuning fork and temporal reference frame, she gave Cassandra, the lead character, the dates of Sandi's own grandmother, born in 1922, who had lived through the periods and ruptures depicted in the novel.[22]

And film remained as central as it had been in *Shirkers*:

> Very often, images come to me before words do. I wrote the book with several movie soundtracks on a loop—including Alexandre Desplat's *Birth*, Jonny Greenwood's *There Will Be Blood*, and Gabriel Yared's *The Talented Mr. Ripley*—and composed the whole thing as kind of a movie of my wildest dreams.... As if some fantasy amalgam of David Lynch, Alfonso Cuarón, and 1970s-era Francis Ford Coppola were directing *The Black Isle* as a technicolor film. (S. Tan 2012b)

As if on cue, Alfonso Cuarón released his own *Black Isle*, the film *Roma*, in black and white, six years after Sandi's novel, in 2018, the same year as the reconstructed *Shirkers*.[23]

The Black Isle is composed in three parts that I will call, according to their movie soundtracks: *Birth*, *There Will Be Blood*, and *The Talented Mr. Ripley*.

BIRTH: I, LING, BECOME CASSANDRA

Alexandre Desplat's track titles for the soundtrack of *Birth* (2004) are suggestive for *Black Isle*: "Day Out," "Mr. Reincarnation," "The Rendez-vous," "The Wedding," "Knights at Night," "Another Lifetime," "My Dead Husband," and "Elegy." Part I of *The Black Isle* is called "The Haunted," while part II is called the "The Haunter," although, I think, the latter should be pluralized. Desplat composed the music for *The Grand Budapest Hotel*, which figured above in Sandi Tan's account of the reincarnation and postproduction of *Shirkers*. He also composed the music for Ang Lee's film adaptation of Eileen Chang's *Lust, Caution* (Chang [1979] 2007b; A. Lee 2007), with its 1942 Shanghai tale, based on a true story, of a woman used in a honeypot sting to try to assassinate a collaborator with the Japanese occupation; as well as for Guillermo del Toro's *The Shape of Water* (2017), a tale of a mute custodian falling in love with a humanoid amphibian creature, in a way foreshadowing the octopus making love with a woman in *The Black Isle* and the merlions in Kevin Martens Wong's novel *Altered Straits* (2017a). So too, Jonny Greenwood's music for *There Will Be Blood* (2007), the movie about landmen strong-arming rights to oil patches, based on Upton Sinclair's novel *Oil!* (1927), seems appropriate to the *Black Isle*'s descent into the dark days of the Japanese occupation and competition for the Greater East Asia Co-Prosperity Sphere, not to mention Singapore's position in the oil industry. Gabriel Yared's music for *The Talented Mr. Ripley* (1999) seems similarly apt for the tales, in part II of *The Black Isle*, of charmers who escape condemnation for their darker deeds in the service of their ambitions and intelligence. The layering of these various allusions and histories hints at the cinematic feel of *The Black Isle*, the rich visuality of its prose, as well as its playfulness with genre forms.

Part I ("The Haunted") is composed of ten chapters or "music tracks" titled: "A Child's Hands," "A Child's Feet," "Doldrums," "Dirty Island," "Blood

Hill," "The Jungle," "Wonder World," "Limbo," "Where Have All My Ghosts Gone," and "The Serpent in the Garden." The titles, like music tracks, provide premonitions of the passage from Shanghai by ship through the tropical doldrums to crowded immigrant lives (on Blood Hill, subsequently called Bukit Merah or Red Hill), entwined with cemeteries, working in amusement parks, lives always in limbo, with evil always lurking. A short frame story surrounds several of the chapters, reminding one that this is a retrospective tale *told by an aging woman* in the shadows of society and of life. This retrospective tale braids back and forth between Chinese migrant narratives and Malay ones, between the *sea and land*, each haunting the other, hinting at the strange tales of the *Shan Hai Jing*, or *Guideways through Mountains and Seas* (translation and commentary by Richard Strassberg [2002]), but really more tales of the sea peoples of Fujian (coastal China) and the Malay world, each equally filled with shamanism, ghost stories, and other strange stories.[24]

The novel begins also with a cinema studies and anthropology joke. The old woman narrator tells us about two Flemish anthropologists—called Lucas Van Kets and Marjike Jodogne (actually Lucas Jodogne and Marijke Van Kets, the latter a friend of Sandi Tan, who wrote her dissertation on filmmaking at the University of Ghent)—who were writing about superstitions in modernizing Southeast Asia, and who had interviewed her. There is even a snapshot of her younger self picking up bones in a cemetery, "egregiously miscaptioned, 'Native girl practicing witchcraft'" (S. Tan 2012a, 4, 423), although, if published in 1974 as claimed, the native "girl" would have been then in her fifties. In any case, she says, the book has been kept in the Archive of Wartime Affairs, in a section on war crimes, but it has been removed from the shelves, the pages about the narrator ripped out, and the snapshot defaced with a *devil* face. Returning to her apartment, after finding the damaged book, the narrator's phone rings, a message is left on the answering machine by a professor who wants to hear her life story because in articles and books, in library after library, the narrator is always described as a key figure behind the scenes, yet all references to her story have been inked out or ripped out, as if she is being cut out of history. The professor is insistent, not only wanting her story but needing it (for reasons of psychological release that will eventually be revealed). The narrator slowly yields to this insistence, admitting, "All my life, people have tried to erase me . . . but I refuse to let them win" (11).

The story, in sum, is a mirror, slightly awry, of Singapore, refracting its history from different angles, from the 1930s to the present—a writing otherwise, an underside to "the Singapore story," capturing emotional moods of the changing historical horizons with page-turning intensity. The key haunter in the latter part of the novel is a near homonym of both Lee Kuan Yew, Singapore's longest-serving prime minister (1965–1990), and of Tan Kah Kee (1874–1961), the rubber tycoon–philanthropist and founder of schools from Singapore to Xiamen University in China. It is an inspired move to make this figure a love interest, one with negative blinders imposed by his ambitions—tracking closely the ambivalent feelings of Singaporeans toward the city-state. "He fed himself on the works of Han Fei, the Taoist philosopher (c. 250 BC) known for his cunning statecraft . . . [The leader must be] so still that he seems to dwell nowhere . . . I often found myself wishing [his] head had been filled with Machiavelli instead. It would have kept him much nicer" (418; see also 28).

The passage from Shanghai to Pulau Hitam (lit. "the black Isle," Sandi Tan's title) in the aged women's retrospective life history begins, as noted, with "A Child's Hands" and "A Child's Feet." In 1929, on their seventh birthday, the twins Li and Ling persuade their mother to allow them (think Alexandre Desplat) a "Day Out" in the park. There, an old man gets Li to strangle a badly injured kitten ("A Child's Hands"). Ling protests, but for Li it is a kind of male bonding test (he is only seven), and he has a desire and inkling that somehow it will get him freedom from his stifling family. He gets a butterscotch toffee in return from the old man, which will remain a talisman to him for the rest of his life, a reminder of what he will come to think of as a Faustian bargain, a cause of his misfortunes. Around the same time, in their middle-class home, primed by ghost stories told by the kitchen maids, Ling one night begins to see and talk to a ghost. In her description of the ghost, the two kitchen maids recognize their third sister, who drowned herself in the Hangpu River when a brother stole the life savings of one of them, and had tried to take Ling with her. The ghost returns and touches her feet ("A Child's Feet"), saying they will grow large and carry her away to freedom.

In 1929, the year of the stock market crash, Ling's father, a teacher, loses his job and his assets. He books passage for the twins and himself to try his luck with the Overseas Chinese in Pulau Hitam ("the Black Isle," or Singapore, named for being reputedly a former pirates' nest). He leaves his wife and a younger set of twins behind. The ship, named hopefully SS *Prosperity*, sails through the doldrums of the tropical "South sea" along the coastal lands called Nanyang. For a young girl, the ship is magical but also enigmatic, a semi-ghost ship, with the lower decks and steerage crammed with

Chinese migrants, while the upper decks are empty. The girl slips across the class division (as she will later again) and sees people in the upper-class decks others do not. She sees a girl her own age swimming in the upper-class pool, determines that it is Rachel, the dead daughter of Rosen, the Jewish ship's engineer. (Such odd and passing details of ethnicity occasionally reappear with the ghosts on the Black Isle.) She also meets a kindly, genteel, and multilingual Mr. Odell, carrying a cane carved with couples embracing (a symbol of the endless cycles of lust, life, and death, connecting generations). Odell treats her to a fancy meal, teaches her English, and entertains her with the Greek mythological tales of Perseus, Medusa, and the Minotaur, which are carved on the walls of the ship's dining room; and when she wonders if it is not cheating for heroes to have outside help (Perseus's special swords, shields, and flying sandals; Theseus's ball of string), Odell calls her "Pandora . . . a stubborn young girl who never wanted any help" (51). Ghosts are aids to the living that, at first, rationalist Ling thinks she can dispense with, but she later realizes they can change the fate of those around her. Odell is a double figure of civilizational learning and also a fading ghost of the world of the 1930s about to be upended. Odell tells her enigmatically that while he has high tea on the last Sunday of every month at the Metropole Hotel on the Black Isle with his wife, "there is no place on the Black Isle for someone like me . . . It's not like Shanghai over there. It's a jungle. People are less open-minded" (50).

Her male twin, Li, becomes seriously anemic on board, and their father takes a knife to slash Ling's palm to provide blood for the boy to drink to save his life. This motif will recur. They arrive in Singapore, the "Dirty Island"—the theme of being dirty and becoming clean, chaos becoming orderly, will become also a key important motif of modernizing Singapore. We get sketches of the crowded, impoverished Chinatown of the prewar period with ghosts everywhere: "everywhere . . . steps are taken to protect the past, the dead . . . street operas in Teochew and Cantonese to distract their ghost relatives from mischief, burnt hell money to support their netherworld spending," the placing of six-inch-high blocks in entryways "to prevent the unwelcome ones from gliding in" (68). There are *karung guni* (old clothes and odds-and-ends collectors), and, most disturbing, the ghosts of Samsui women (Chinese immigrant women who worked in construction), and Sago Lane "where the loneliest amahs and coolies went to die" (70). There is the surreal incident of a tiger in the midst of the chaos being intentionally hit by a car, getting up, glaring at the driver, and walking off nonchalantly (72).

The killing of the last tiger in Singapore is the subject of a legendary engraving, and this variant is a lovely figure of the clash of modernization.

There were, of course, better-to-do areas—Emerald Hill, where a free school for girls (St. Anne's, which Ling attends) has been built by rubber baron and Peranakan Ignatius Wee, whose family will figure prominently in the novel.[25] And Tanglewood, where his mansion is, and which is "the plushest of the colonial estates, shaded lanes with Scottish names—Inverness, Glencoe, Dalkeith—lined with large 'black and white' bungalows, black timber frames, zebra-striped verandah shades, blazing white walls . . . watered down Tudor effect" (80). These names still exist, and the novel is full of such landmarks that persist into the present.

The father takes on a job as a manager of a failing plantation, and we get a glimpse of demeaning labor relations on such enterprises in "the jungle." There are ghosts here as well, particularly around Blood Hill, said to be the burial ground for unwanted baby girls, and whose surrounding banana trees harbor *pontianak*s, the she-demon ghosts of women who die in childbirth.[26] The father is not up to the job, so Li and Ling come into their own as teenage managers trying desperately to maintain control, but eventually they retreat back to town, albeit not before Ling has found Li sleeping with a pretty plantation girl, possibly a *pontianak*, and the workers have torched the premises.

The narrator tape-records and labels these first six chapters "the early years, juvenilia." They set the themes of a novel that is and is not contained by the genre of ghost story, though there are ghosts everywhere, and ghost stories are a popular story form expressing emotions, trance experiences, and pasts (sometimes connecting with uncanny events in the present). The novel is and is not about a heroine with the freedom to be her own person, "neither driven by grievance nor defined by marital or filial relationships"—she has her grievances, and has to struggle against her parents' privileging of her brother, against expectations of a marriage to Daniel Wee, against a coercive concubine relationship with a Japanese officer, against an unrequited love affair with a soulmate, and against an unacknowledged place in the political history of the island. The novel is and is not a feminist counterstory to the erasure of women's stories (although this is a diegetic motivating premise); and it is not about the scapegoating of nonconforming women (not a mother, not married) in the figure of the witch or sorcerer, even if the traffic with ghosts and hauntings is ever present. As her mentor in *ilmu* (magic) reminds her, "They're not toys. Once we've called them up, we can try to make them obey but ultimately, they're just like people—it's up to them" (331). It is and is not a story merely about escape and freedom, albeit these slogan words are voiced throughout the story. It is a story of particular struggles, and maneuverings within the constraints of the historically possible.

The novel *is* structured to suggest the deep Malay traditions of the island and region that are and are *not immediately accessible to the Chinese* immigrants, and remain *unacknowledged by their Anglicized*, and hypereducated children steeped in the values of rapid social change, instrumentality, and meritocracy. The novel has a performative or enrolling quality for the reader as a compendium or treasury of similitudes and symbols, like Lydia Kwa's *Oracle Bone* (2017) and *The Walking Boy* ([2005] 2018), or like Michel Foucault's description of Renaissance texts (Foucault [1966] 1970). Things said in one place recur in others in different contexts or configurations, establishing *echoes* and a growing sense of an *idiom of a cultural landscape* and its interwoven cultural temporalities, ruptures, and repairs.

During the time Ling, Li, and their father spend on the plantation, the years 1934–1937 ("the Wonder Years"), the city has "reshaped" itself. The great amusement park, Wonder World, opened (one of several; see A. Lee 2015), a "social venue where different races could mingle" (S. Tan 2012a, 129), and where the father, aided by Li, eventually finds a marginal job. The family moves into the eighth floor of a new building in Chinatown, the word "eight" being a homonym for prosperity as is the number eight, but ironically the top floor is one favored by suicides, so it is also full of ghosts, especially those of prostitutes. Meanwhile, Ling finds a job with the Wee family, watching a dying wife sleep at night, haunted by a predecessor wife, who Ling finds out (by talking to the ghost) will not rest, and will not let the dying wife rest, until she gets her earrings back. Ling takes the earrings and buries them under some rose bushes, quieting both wives, but causing an uproar over the stolen earrings. She has cover, having taken up with the son of the family, Daniel Wee, under the benign gaze of his father, but to the enmity of Daniel's sister Violet. While burying the earrings, "digging like a dog" in the earth, she goes into trance and feels herself dancing with Mr. Odell from the SS *Prosperity*, and making a date to meet him at the Hotel Metropole. She keeps the date, and is surprised to find his wife there instead. Mrs. Odell throws her out, which the staff find encouraging progress, because Mrs. Odell is an inpatient at Woodbridge mental hospital, periodically released to have a day out with high tea in the fancy Metropole, but rarely does she say anything or react to anyone. In the commotion around the missing earrings, and a looming sense that war is on the horizon ("Limbo" and "Where Have All My Ghosts Gone"), relationships get rearranged. Agnes, the dog, coughs up the missing earrings; Mrs. Wee dies; Daniel gets his father to allow Ling to move into the house. Daniel and Ling have an engagement party, at which Kenneth Kee shows up, returned from Oxford, son of a fishmonger, but a childhood friend of Daniel Wee. His education has been supported by Ignatius Wee. He is a rival of Daniel, much the brighter and more ambitious of the two.

Issa (Ishak bin Shamsuddin), the Wees' Bugis chauffeur, also gradually emerges from the margins. Called bizarrely by the Islamic name for Jesus by his Chinese employers, he allows the slight to pass, saying it is at least better than being called "Ahmad," the generic name that Chinese use for their Muslim employees. These names betoken upper-class refusal to recognize the Muslim working class. Wee has a cross prominently displayed in the house. Issa drives Ling in the Wees' Bentley to the Metropole, and since he had witnessed her burying the earrings, he uses this secret as leverage to get her to acknowledge her powers of seeing ghosts, and to let him teach her how to use and control them.

Ling renames herself Cassandra (who saw things nobody else did, "my own private joke") to signal a rebirth: rebirth as a future Mrs. Wee cleansed of *dirty* immigrant Chinatown; as a Cassandra in the Greek mythic sense of intuiting (if not always understanding) the dangers to come; and as a shaman or *bomoh* whose powers do not always get the ghosts to follow her requests exactly. As Odell says, this Cassandra is also a Pandora. Daniel takes her to the family beach house, where they witness a surreal event: a giant octopus makes love to a naked Mrs. Nakamura, the wife of the lighthouse operator. Is this a sly reference to Alexandre Desplat again, to his soundtrack for *The Shape of Water* (Desplat 2017), a film in which a mute female custodian falls in love with an amphibian, reptilian monster imprisoned in a high-tech laboratory? Or is it a play upon the coming (octopus tentacles) of Japanese occupation under which Singapore will be named "Lighthouse Island" for its lighting the way to the Co-Prosperity Sphere, and for its infernal scientific laboratory to harvest fleas from rats to create plague?

Cassandra for a time remains resistant to Issa's invitations. He coaxes: "I know you are scared, but I can teach you how to take control [of the ghosts you see]. I come from many generations of *bomoh* [healers, shamans]. Medicine Men. Seers" (S. Tan 2012a, 194). But Cassandra recoils (like her mother, like the new modern class she is marrying into, and like the anthropologists searching for superstitions with which the novel opens): "Witch doctors. Black magic was the last thing I wanted to hear about. I led a *clean* life now" (194). Still, she appraises Issa: "his smooth brown face brought to mind a warrior from another time and place, maybe Tongan, maybe Māori. Or perhaps an indigenous tribe that preceded the rest of us invaders, exiles, and immigrants" (194). Finally, with the heightened fear of the Japanese attack, including the shock and repulsion of watching the British officers order the immolation of thoroughbred horses so that they do not fall into Japanese hands, Cassandra follows Issa to his father's gravesite. He tells her:

> You and I are links in an endless chain of ghosts. . . . They call my people the Badjao or Orang Laut—Sea Gypsies, the People of the Water. These names make us sound quaint, harmless, like simple people who spent their whole lives catching fish with their bare hands. But in the beginning, we had a title. We were the Royal Guards, the rajah's men. We were here for centuries before the rest of you came. We controlled the seas. We kept the peace by keeping the invaders out. . . . But then our kings became greedy. They let in the outsiders in exchange for gold and silk. . . . We were *warriors*. We kept the peace by claiming what was ours. If you don't draw lines, you give in and give in until there's nothing of yourself left. (210)

Issa's arms and torso are covered with tattoos, inscribed by his grandfather when Issa was twelve, using charcoal and tiger-bone dust: two black serpents on his pectorals, two black chrysanthemum rosettes below his shoulder blades, black thorny vines up his biceps—signs of both his Orang Laut warrior lineage and his magical prowess.

Issa tells her there are several ways of acquiring the use of *ilm* or *ilmu* (knowledge): book learning, esoteric and mystical knowledge, and magic. The way of his ancestors is "through study in which the seeker prays, fasts, and recites the Koran until he reaches a state of forgetfulness [and] eventually the magic descends on him" (213). But wanting something more powerful, Issa found "a different path, a path my forefathers warned me against" (213): to go on the night of a full moon to the grave of a murdered man. Issa's father was murdered, and it is at his grave on the Forbidden Hill (Bukit Larangan, called Fort Canning by the British, sacred due to the graves of Muslim rulers, a point of sovereignty claims) that Issa attempts, with the urgency of the coming war, to coach her, saying, "the Isle needs you, once all hell breaks loose, it will need as many of us as possible" (210). Cassandra, fearful and resistant, recoils instinctively: "Again with his sorcerer's pitch." But she follows his example and his instruction, "digging in the dirt, the loamy soil, graveyard meal," rubbing it all over herself, and allowing herself to enjoy its warmth. Issa gives her his *keris* [*sic*] (ceremonial dagger), and instructs her to paddle with it as if in a canoe until, suddenly, the *badi* will appear, a restless spirit always searching for a better home; almost always the *badi* is someone you know (214). You ask for a little targeted magic with which to achieve a limited goal, but then you should return the *badi* to a safe house inside a monitor lizard or a tree where it cannot do mischief. He also uses the *keris* to slash her arms above the elbow, saying, "fear collects you like an animal possessed," sharpens your senses (215).

Issa was thirteen when he had his first experience of the power of magic, and, inexperienced, he asked too much: for a lifetime of magic. In exchange, the *badi* demanded freedom, not being locked up in a safe house. Free roaming for ghosts can be dangerous to the living, including those to whom the gift of summoning them is given. Issa's first experience is an echo of seven-year-old Li, who much later, while imprisoned by the Japanese during the war, confesses to Cassandra: "Remember our seventh birthday? Remember the old man in the park? . . . I knew he would be there. Which was why I insisted on going to the park [his mother had objected]. The night before I prayed and begged to whoever or *whatever* was out there. To this day, I'm still not clear who or what I prayed to, but when I saw the old man, I knew he had heard me. I prayed for freedom. Escape" (285).

Cassandra's first efforts to paddle the canoe (also) end disastrously. She achieves the trance state and sees her *badi*, one of her younger twin sisters, but, terrified, she swings her oar at the apparition, tips the boat over, and sinks into a cold sea (the seas around Singapore are actually not cold, but body temperature). Issa grabs her, and, furious, sends her off to the car to wait for him while he quiets the ghosts. She tells herself, "in abandoning the ritual, I had lost my chance to master my own gift, to alter the cruel course of history . . . I would never be clean again" (220). They travel back across the Edinburgh Bridge (as if the bridge across Hades), a bridge constructed in Glasgow by convict labor in 1869, and shipped piece by piece to Singapore.

The cemetery is a place both of hermetic silence and of gatherings of ghosts of many ethnicities ("an obese Tamil woman . . . a skinny old Chinese man . . . a small European boy . . . a girl in a bridal gown . . . a Zoroastrian priest") and of ethnic scents ("temple incense, curry, jasmine, sweaty underarms, stale coffee breath, formaldehyde, tobacco and myrrh") (215). But at its center, Issa says, "every cemetery has a sacred heart, where no sound and no wind can enter" (215). That place in this cemetery is his father's grave. It is a prolepsis or echo of the Han Fei teaching that the leader must be so still that he seems to dwell nowhere, and of the imagery of the Malay theater state (*negara*), in which the center should seem still and eternal (Tambiah 1977; Geertz 1980).

The war approaches: dying jellyfish on the beach followed by swarms of flies, the thunderous noise of Japanese aircraft, the bombing of the British warships HMS *Crown Prince* and HMS *Resilience* (i.e., the historical HMS *Prince of Wales* and the HMS *Repulse*) caught in the harbor, the strafing of anyone moving in Chinatown. As the Japanese aircraft thunder in the sky, Cassandra has a moment of self-recognition: "This wasn't how I wanted to die, clinging to a rich man's son, my own adventure barely begun" (S. Tan 2012a, 225). Kenneth Kee is sent by Ignatius Wee to bring Daniel and Cassandra back from the beach house to the Wee mansion. Kee declines food, and is asked about his oddities, "you don't sweat, you don't eat, what are you?" He shrugs: "a ghost." In this case, to be a ghost is his quiet participation in the secret resistance and subversion of meetings that Ignatius Wee has been convening while pretending to collaborate with the Japanese. Kenneth tells Cassandra that he and Issa are heading for the jungle to fight the guerrilla war—"Officially we're Communists. Unofficially . . . we're survivors." They offer to take Cassandra along, but she is not yet ready. The Japanese begin rounding up Chinese men and taking them off to Queenstown Prison and Shahrbandar Prison, or to the beach to gun them down. As Cassandra returns from haggling for bits of meat from Fatty Wai's butcher shop, she sees a girl being raped by a group of young Japanese soldiers, and a group of Chinese men come to fight them off. As Cassandra tries to escape the scene, a tall man touches her waist—"'Miss, don't worry,' he cooed in English in an 'Oxonian accent,' saying, 'I'm not part of that fracas'" (257)—and he offers her a ride in his jeep. No, he has not learned his English in England, he learned it in Japan. He handcuffs her to himself, as they watch his men drag Ignatius Wee and his family from the house. Violet, Daniel's sister, screams that she'll hunt Cassandra down (a curse that in a way will come true), and Daniel too accuses her of betraying them. Sitting in a Japanese military jeep with the commander of the action, how could it appear otherwise?

THERE WILL BE BLOOD

The section of *The Black Isle* that covers the Japanese occupation of Singapore (1942–1945) takes on the feel of nightmare genres, and survivor strategies, of World War II through a series of literary allusions. There is, first, the noirish mood of World War II stories and films in both Europe and Asia, such as Eileen Chang's wartime stories *Love in a Fallen City* ([1943] 2007a) and *Lust/Caution* ([1979] 2007b), and their adaptations as films by Ang Lee (1984, 2007). These are stories with facades of cosmopolitan gentility, veiling deadly games of sexual and political treachery. Then there are horror genre films, Grimm-like folktales (such as that of Kiyohime) and ghost stories (told during the Oban festival) that play across enemy lines, sometimes heightening wartime xenophobia, at other times heightening concerns about the destruction of the environment. And third, *The Black Isle* incorporates powerful filmic sexploitation genres reminiscent of Nagisa Oshima's films, with their mixture of violence, sex, and sharp political criticism of the Japanese imperial state and treatment of others as toys and objects (e.g., Oshima's films of the late 1960s and 1970s), as well as the writer Yukio Mishima's nationalist celebration of samurai codes, ending in his famous ritual suicide (*seppuku*). After such intensity, the postwar return of British assertion, bluster, and imperial spectacle (anthems and ceremonies) carry little legitimacy. No civilized music ("The Quartet") can reimpose "European only" segregation, or overcome the abject failure of the British Empire to protect Singapore, a task Singapore will take upon itself.

This middle section of the novel, the first half of Part II, "The Haunters," begins with the arrival of the Japanese ("Turnip Heads") and with the failed attempts by Ignatius Wee and a few other members of the Chinese Chamber of Commerce to play at being double agents, conciliating the Japanese while trying to help the resistance. They are caught out, and Wee and his fellow conspirators are summarily shot, decapitated, and impaled atop the fence of the Wee mansion as examples. Adding even more indignity, Wee's head is put on the dog Agnes's body, and Agnes's head on Wee's body. Daniel Wee, the son and Cassandra's fiancée, becomes a pawn, toyed with by her Japanese captor, Taro, to control her. (In English taro is a root crop like the "turnip head" of the section title.)[27] Cassandra herself becomes a trophy "wife" for Taro, a Japanese Lieutenant Colonel, who moves into the Wee residence, and displays a genteel surface, but also a steely cruelness underneath. He is amused by the large cross on the wall in the sitting room, left by Wee in a lame effort to discomfort the Japanese.

Cassandra's own effort to deploy a spiritual defense also goes awry: while Taro is away, she goes into the garden and digs in the loamy earth where Agnes and Wee eventually were buried, to perform the rowing ritual to invite the ghosts to do her bidding, which she had half learned from Issa. She rows and prays, but the ritual goes awry. The ghoulish head of the dog Agnes appears on the torso of Ignatius Wee, its tongue glistening black.[28] Taro suddenly returns. Cassandra looks between Taro and the exhumed monster, "feverish about how the scene might play out" (S. Tan 2012a, 272), but the dog-man sprints away. "The experiment had been a complete failure. Instead of raising an army, I had let lose a monster" (272).

During the occupation, the old opium warehouse at the mouth of the river that "once housed trillions of pounds of Indian opium, cargo that turned civil servants into lords overnight and made Britain the wealthiest country in the world, has now become a Japanese 'scientific laboratory' for 'collecting fleas off rats with which to spread plague in China'" (275). Li is consigned to work there with minimal nutrition. Taro, as part of his emotional binding of Cassandra, has kept Li barely alive, giving in to her plea to give her brother a lighter "desk job," at a laboratory desk for delousing rats, and allows her to visit him. Like her father earlier, Cassandra slashes her arm and makes her brother drink her blood in order to restore some minimal vitality.

During Oban, the festival of the dead, Taro has his young soldiers tell a hundred ghost stories, blowing out a candle after each; when the last candle is blown out, in the dark, a ghost will appear. Taro dismisses most of the stories as crude or childish Chinese tales, but one, the story of Kiyohime, he translates for Cassandra. It foreshadows some of what is to come. Kiyohime is a famous Japanese beauty whose family inn hosts the monk, Anchin, of Dojo temple on the banks of the Hidaka River, on his annual pilgrimage to Kumano shrine. As she grows from a little girl to a woman, she falls for him and declares her love. He flees, crossing the flooding river, and tells the boatman not to let her follow. In her rage she transforms into a sea serpent and follows him. He hides under the metal bell of the temple, but she smells him, coils around the bell, belches fire, and melts the bell, fusing them together.[29] Does Taro tell the tale to Cassandra as an inversion of his relation to her, fused together for the duration of the war, but emotionally exploiting a monk-like detachment? When the Japanese surrender in 1945, after the stunning dropping of atom bombs on Hiroshima and then Nagasaki, Taro throws a final party at the

Wee's summer pavilion on the beach, and sets it ablaze with his men inside, intending Cassandra to die there as well. Plumbing the depths of wartime cruelty, chapter 12, "The Rat Brigade," reads like one of Nagisa Oshima's films: Taro sexually humiliates Cassandra in front of his superiors in a pornographic performance that gains him a promotion, and a second sakura (cherry blossom) on his lapel; when she retaliates, by kicking him in the balls and running at him with a samurai sword, he beats her senseless and tosses her into a pit with dead bodies both animal (including rodents) and human (including Daniel). He eventually complements her for surviving the ordeal.

With the return of the British—"The Quartet," "singing their anthems," reinstituting "Europeans only" at the Balmoral Hotel, "began again to hurry us in their insulting pidgin, 'chop chop'"—Cassandra finds a job at Woodbridge Hospital, the psychiatric hospital established in 1935. The Black Isle, Cassandra reflects, has long produced people needing such places: wives and daughters of colonials, hordes of overworked plantation workers. She finds her twin Li on the fourth floor.

There is a public ceremony to celebrate the return of the British on the Padang, the open playing field, then along the seashore, with a cricket club at each end, and municipal buildings facing the sea. The ceremony is in English only, and while Chinese and Malay resistance fighters are given medals, the attention is focused on the British themselves. Kenneth and Issa are among those given medals, each scarred by their ordeals in the jungle and caught by the Japanese. Issa's tattoos are gone, replaced by scars. Kenneth's tongue has been snipped in two; it is black and diseased, and he lisps (but will force himself with practice to eliminate this).[30] Issa says he excised his tattoos himself to prevent the Japanese from skinning him for them. As they leave the Padang to let the British celebrate by themselves, Cassandra tells them about the valuables the Wees had buried before the Japanese arrived, and they go to dig these up to finance a guerrilla resistance. This time Cassandra goes with them. It is 1948, and there is no jungle left, since the rubber plantations had expanded under the Japanese. These plantations were the island's biggest revenue source, and Kenneth was determined to destroy them. Kenneth grows into a leadership role, but also isolates himself, living monastically, as if an ascetic. Cassandra is disappointed both in feeling him slip away from her in intimacy, and in being relegated along with the other five women recruits to domestic tasks.

Later in 1951 Issa slips into the city to reconnoiter, returning to report on Chinese student boycotts and protests, and striking factory workers and bus drivers. Cassandra goes to Issa to ask for help in rousing the ghosts at Blood Hill, on the old Melmoth plantation where she and Li had worked as teenagers. She tells him of meeting a *pontianak* and devilish *bomoh* there, and he asks if she had been having her period at the time. Yes, she tells him. Blood and black magic are a dangerous mix. With his *keris* again she rows, and finds herself in a canoe. The *badi* that appears is Kenneth in his younger form as an Oxonian, who first demands to see her naked, then turns away. But in the meantime a hundred ghost girls have appeared and receive Cassandra's request for help. But they go wild ("The Night of the Burning Trees"), laying devastation to the plantations in fires that kill the caretakers of Melmoth, destroying British rubber plantations and those of the American tire companies, Goodyear and Firestone. Issa is devastated. Cassandra lashes out, "'Didn't you give them proper instructions?' 'I never expected . . . a woman's power . . . to be so . . .'" (339).

But as the British are slow to leave, Cassandra once again consults with Issa to try to use the powers of the ghosts to create restrained disruption, to give the already jittery British a little push, giving them reason and face to leave. She goes to meet Issa at a coffee shop on Kandahar Street, by the "white-walled" Sultan mosque.[31] "The colonials never came to these narrow, cobblestone streets, not even to gawk at the gold minarets and jade floor tiles of the celebrated old mosque. The lanes weren't wide enough for cars, and colonials didn't like being on foot in strange neighborhoods" (353).[32]

This time, with Kenneth's foreknowledge and advice of restraint, Cassandra and Issa return to Forbidden Hill (Bukit Larangan, today's Fort Canning), where Cassandra's first lesson with Issa had gone awry. Cassandra does the "Sufi," Arabic *zikr*, the repetition of the "names of the Muslim god, joined by names of the saints and magical forebears from Issa's Bugis ancestry" (357). Beautifully she relates, "specific emotions had to be attached to each cycle of names—joy in the glory of life, grief at the transience of life passion, humility as a seeker," done until they draw her into a trance (357). She is impatient for results, and soon goes by herself to "a Taoist mausoleum in Chinatown, packed with the cremated remains of lonesome amahs, and an overgrown field in Little India where Indian convict laborers had been thrown into mass graves" (359). She chants again. Strange happenings then occur over the following days:

> horses from both the Island and Kiwi [cricket] teams began bucking violently . . . a fortnight later, Cyril Cunning, the councilman who'd first sug-

> gested flattening Forbidden Hill, woke to find his eyes sewn shut with red Taoist thread. . . . The notoriously awful magistrate Alan Topper . . . [suffered the] slicing open [of] his lenses (eyes) . . . Naked Tamils vanished, bullets seemed to pass through their bodies. Entire squadrons of Gurkhas . . . resigned fearing for their lives . . . At the aquarium black kelp began moving [oddly], . . . lithe, demonic maenads all flowing black hair and naked flesh. . . . White eyes of the blind [sharks] . . . grew rigid and torpedoed toward the glass . . . breaking glass, rushing water frenzied sharks sampling the arm of one, the leg of another child. . . . The maenads standing in the empty tank, their grins told me everything. This was the high price exacted. (359–60)

Cassandra suffers exhaustion and nightmares, while Issa remains calm; "all riots burn themselves out. . . . Once they're sated, the spirits will eventually return to their graves" (362).

THE TALENTED MR. RIPLEY

The last portion of the book is devoted to the transformation of Singapore after the war and independence under Lee Kuan Yew, or as he was also known, Harry Lee and LKY: the clearance of the Red Hill slums where Li and their father lived during the war, the 1961 Bukit Ho Swee fire that helped spur land clearance and renewal, and Singapore's signature building of socialist-style housing estates under the Housing and Development Board (HDB). The political will to accomplish this is addressed through a focus on the daemons of rationality, and resistance to them. In the process, the love story between Cassandra and Kenneth is transmuted, and Cassandra "learns from the movies what it is to be a woman," caught between being a Lady Midnight—the fourth-century courtesan and poet lamenting the coming and goings of her lovers (405)—and a Li Ho, the Tang poet, "who wrote about demons, graveyards, and weeping statues" (405).[33] She finds herself being a sidekick to a man obsessed with Han Fei, the philosopher of statecraft who advocated for a leader who is "so still that he seems to dwell nowhere," and who for ceremonial, status, or other reasons marries Violet, the surviving daughter of the Wee family (418). This last, of course, is not true to the LKY story. The novel in this register is about the poetics of power, not LKY.

Change comes months after the Padang ceremony following the return of the British, but in May 1954 the civil service is opened up to non-British personnel, and Kenneth Kee is first in line. When his application is accepted, he and Cassandra celebrate with a night in room 13 of the once "European only" Balmoral Hotel. She studies "his future statesman's jawline" (364). True to the jawline, and tradition of ascetic revolutionaries, Kenneth takes a single-bedroom apartment, and Cassandra a separate flat on Clemenceau Avenue, not far away. They work and fight intensely over a new national flag for August 31, 1959, the first national day of independent Singapore. He objects to putting the Muslim crescent moon on it, and she has to remind him that he needs the Malay vote.

Kenneth observes that the citizens have become obsessed with the dead. Even the stodgy *Tribune* has begun carrying articles on ghosts (371).[34] Kenneth becomes obsessed with cleansing the island. He laughs when Cassandra reveals that she sees ghosts, and puts that together with Issa's claims to be the great grandson of a shaman, suggesting the two could collaborate: "There are people in this city who need to be scared into putting things right . . . If we could accelerate the process, I don't see why we shouldn't" (351). He suggests she set up a ghost-hunting business (374), and he'll feed her lucrative business. He says in one of those memorable lines (ones that LKY also was famous for, often slightly tinged with Chinese chauvinism, eugenics, and identification with the British), "I suppose our national outlook always tended Anglo-Chinese. We have both British indirection and Chinese cunning in our veins. It is a potent formula" (370). He becomes highly sought after to recommend geomancers to bless construction projects. The owner of Robinson's department store, the chief surgeon at Mount Alvernia Hospital, the president of the Green Spot bus company—all seek his recommendations, both for their own efficacy and for relations with him.[35] In his drive for cleanliness and ridding the isle of darkness, he orders experimental light bulbs from Hiroshima. "Could he not see that the lights turned the streets into paler, grayer—ghostlier—versions of themselves?" (387).

In elections for a post-independence prime minister, in an unseemly swipe, Cassandra says that "Kenneth's opponent, the incumbent PM, was a Eurasian millionaire drunk, put in place by the departing British" (403).[36] In contrast, Kenneth promised what everyone wanted: "peace, prosperity, prominence, and above all a new beginning" (404). That meant getting rid of all the ghosts. Cassandra is concerned about the destruction of cemeteries, and those inhabiting the slums, where ghosts are part of daily ritual life and community solidarity. On May 25, 1961, a massive fire broke out, destroying homes of some 16,000 people on Bukit Merah (Red Hill), named for its red soil and brickworks, where gambier had once been grown, and textile mills placed. The fire was suspicious, but for Kenneth it is an opportunity to raze 50 acres of prime land and build afresh low-cost, clean HDB apartment blocks that can be easily controlled by police, and the influence of local gangs be curtailed. The first housing estate, Tiong Bahru, had been developed by the Singapore Improvement Trust under the British. It remains behind Bukit Merah, where a Chinese cemetery had been, and where Kampong Tiong Bahru had had a fire in 1959, making 5,000 people homeless. The much larger informal township of Bukit Ho Swee carried in its name the history of Tay Ho Swee, an influential Chinese opium farmer, timber merchant, and ship owner, son of Tay Han Leong, the first opium and spirit dealer in Singapore. It would now be replaced with the Bukit Ho Swee Secondary School, which opened in 1967.

In quiet protest against this brutal urban renewal (the debate over who started the fires continues), Cassandra, Issa, and Zhang Ming ("Cricket") all resign from being aides in the prime minister's office. "Without his former comrades, the prime minister embarked on a building spree, like all the best dictators. To be fair, he built no monuments in his own honor. . . . It was his vanity that he should always appear humble, pragmatic, never vulgar. And so he erected apartments, schools, hospitals, and factories . . . making the entire island a testament to his caring" (416).

> His new idea was to turn the Isle into a base for foreign businesses—British and American petroleum refineries, Swiss banks, Japanese electronics firms. . . . I found most of Kenneth's plans admirable; they brought prosperity and stability to our country. What I objected to was the disinterment of graves in cemeteries for nothing nobler than golf courses and shopping centers. (416)

In 1972, Kenneth calls Cassandra to tell her he's located her younger twin sisters, long left behind in Shanghai. It seems like an excuse. She concludes he was sending her to see what a true totalitarian state looked like in contrast to what he was building (419).

In a wonderful image, Cassandra notes that Kenneth's desk was flanked by two framed pictures, a Jakarta slum and downtown Geneva. "Order . . . or chaos" (428):

> He kept the Isle clean and safe, well lit. He uprooted the jungles, vanquished the terrorists, and sucked dry the swamp. He gave everybody

> what all reasonable people wanted—honest work, affordable food, a roof over their head and the freedom to buy whatever they desired. (433)

But then strange things begin to happen: Thai construction workers begin to die, the new subway tunnels have ghosts of all ethnicities, a new tourist hotel collapses. Cassandra sends Kenneth to inspect for himself the damage tunneling through the Forbidden Hill has done.

SEGUE TO THE PRESENT AND FUTURE

I won't say how the novel concludes, but while Kenneth dies on October 31, 1990 (Halloween), LKY lived until 2015, and the story of Singapore's meritocracy continues, even as "Issa" and "Ahmad," those names of nonrecognition, continue their protest. The tape recordings that Ling/Cassandra makes of her life, and that she gives to the insistent "professor," pry open reflections on films, women's lives, the poetics of power, genre forms of storytelling, and the way hauntings undo presumed and ontological fixations or false claims about the fixed nature of reality. They force us to think anew, reconsider what we think we know, and prepare for a world of "unfinished becomings" (Biehl and Locke 2017) that require very different kinds of subjectivities than those of immediately past historical horizons. The communicative media of *Shirkers* and of *The Black Isle*—amateur and auteur film, oral knowledge, cinematic music, prose of varied intensities, and vernacular or oral knowledge—contest false claims about ontologies (just the way things are) and senses of time horizons and arrows of time (progress, reason). They force reflections on genres. They force reflections on narratives that may have outlived their utilities or justifications (nation-building, being besieged by surrounding enemies, a lack of resources requiring sacrifice). They repopulate seemingly sterile places of abstractions about mass living, providing dense histories of both resistances and emotional attachments. They reopen to inspection the many (rather than singular) trajectories that have led to the present state of things, or our current and temporary understandings of the present state of things.

3

White Ink, Family Systems, Forests of Illusion, and Aging

Knots of Passion

nothing thinks as clearly as the body

inside the bound a hidden code

for what torments us still
rope was a holy thing once
used to bind sacred objects
during the Jomon period
pottery shaped by the imprints of rope
on wet clay

as if she and I

were cast into Indra's Net
along with all other mothers and daughters
tossing innuendo
entangling intention
livid and loved
in the gasp and pause
—LYDIA KWA, *SINUOUS*

A fever which spread through my body, *delirium*. English, my adopted language, changing me out of one prison into another. . . . Mother's is not father's is not English is not mine. —LYDIA KWA, "FATHER:MOTHER:TONGUE"

L'homme y passe à travers des forêts de symboles
Qui l'observent avec des regards familiers.
—CHARLES BAUDELAIRE, "CORRESPONDANCES"

In this chapter we turn to a set of novels and poems that narrate ordinary lives of migrants in the twentieth century and extraordinary lives of concubines, nuns, and empresses. In genre terms they might be seen as dysfunctional family romances, plucky survival stories, and unrequited love stories among lesbians, gays, and hermaphrodites, albeit those are anachronistic terms. "Beings of third kinds" might be a better label for these individuals and their familiars, as they attend to rituals, possessions, and animal transformations; and as they attend to moral and psychological concerns outside conventional morality in the past and present. Our guide is a clinical psychologist, lesbian, and migrant from rapidly changing Singapore to Toronto and Vancouver, where she practices acupuncture as well as clinical psychology, and resorts for herself occasionally to herbal Traditional Chinese Medicine and the *I Ching*. She guides us through both historical horizons of past and present (and, in a novel to come, the future), as well as through our cultural educations of Anglo-Chinese and Toronto schools, Buddhist and Taoist imperial legacies, and immigration struggles around natal attachments versus having to live and guide parents in the contemporary world.

Attuned to psychoanalytical knots—the epigraph to her novel *Pulse* is from R. D. Laing's *Knots* (1970), a book of twisting aphoristic examples of psychological, cognitive, and emotional entanglements;[1] and the cover of her book depicts a fraying knot—Lydia Kwa's body of texts connect *écriture féminine* (or writing, gender, and sexual difference) and *écriture féminine otherwise* (of and beyond contemporary Euro-American feminist categories). It is unlikely that she has not read Helen Cixous, as her poems have references to Sigmund Freud, Mária Török and Nicolas Abraham, Carl Jung, Julia Kristeva, Cathy Caruthers, and other writers of psychoanalytic, deconstruction, and therapeutic literatures, as well as to Woodbridge Hospital in Singapore.[2] Lydia Kwa's novels—*This Place Called Absence* (2000), *Pulse* (2010, revised 2014), *The Walking Boy* (2005, revised 2018), *Oracle Bone* (2017), and *A Dream Wants Waking* (forthcoming)—and two books of poetry—*The Colors of Heroines* (1994a) and *Sinuous* (2013)—are about migrant transitions from China to Singapore to Canada. They are about the *jouissance* (ecstasy out of pain, implicitly or explicitly sexual) in lives bound by social change. They are about echoes of "secrets left behind / I cannot speak of" (Kwa 2013, 7). These "echoes" reverberate across at least four cultural horizons: the imperial court of an eighth-century empress of China; the early twentieth-century world of poor women who make their way from destitution in China to Singapore brothels, and with luck upward as second wives or businesswomen; the 1970s of post–World War II Singapore; and the 1990s and early 2000s of diasporic ties between Singapore and Canada.

SETTINGS

Lydia Kwa's novel *Pulse* ([2010] 2014) provides an entry point. It shuttles back and forth between, on the one hand, Singapore neighborhoods transformed by moving the coast, with "reclaimed land" or landfill, out into the sea, and building the first of a new generation of Housing and Development Board (HDB) flats on the new land (Marine Parade, built in the 1970s) near the older Peranakan (mixed Chinese-Malay) Katong section in which Lydia Kwa grew up in an apartment above her grandfather's Chinese traditional medicine shop that he named Cosmic Pulse; and on the other hand Chinese and other immigrant neighborhoods in Toronto and Vancouver. She leaves her biology graduate studies in Toronto for acupuncture after she experiences a transformative experience with acupuncture that dramatically quiets her anxieties. She also draws on her grandmother's use of an oracle booklet, a simplified version of the *I Ching*, to help divine or diagnose what she should do. She keeps track of her skin (eczema as a girl; shivers, sweat, blushes as an adult), of her blood (racing heart) and internal meridians (acupuncture), energy flow or *qi* (vital force, pulse); and thus of her libido connected to the world around her, her cosmic pulse. Toward the end of the novel, she reveals her participation in the therapeutic practice of *kinbaku*, the Japanese bondage tradition, involving tying up a partner so that the ropes leave marks on the body and the knots (often) align with acupuncture points.

"Pulse" of course refers to *jouissance* (sexual pleasure) as well as the forces of the cosmos, and the several flows of blood energy (*qi*)—hidden knots. Her earlier, first novel, *This Place Called Absence* (2000), is a kind of study for *Pulse*, but pairs the late twentieth-century emigration story of *Pulse* to Toronto and Vancouver with an early twentieth-century story of two girls sold from poverty in China into prostitution in Singapore. Both story lines, intertwined like knots, told in alternating first-person voices, probe for the psychological dynamics of absence from home, from parental figures, from love, from abilities to define oneself, and a finding of ways of coming to terms, which the publisher's blurb calls "enlightenment."[3]

A trilogy of later novels (two of which have appeared) explore a historically deep Chinese cultural armature or set of pragmatic and psychological resources that provide reanimation of identifications with the past, parallel to ones of escape to the West (or to future imaginaries)—escape into the past, to elsewhere, or into the future; escape from contemporary family strictures, gender roles, and from childhood disciplining. By being set in the ancient past, yet among stories that continue to reverberate in the popular culture of the present, they allow an expansion of consciousness beyond the constraints of the Cold War and the last few decades. They allow us to appreciate, as Cixous would say, "the openness to the play of the gendered body, its unconscious and libido, allowing the immense resources of the unconscious to spring forth" (Cixous 1976, 880). Or as Kristeva might put it, stressing the pain involved, it is in the dialectic between prelinguistic signifying or "semiotic" with the mother, and sexual pleasure (*jouissance*) that emerges from the pain of life, breaking the codes and grammars of symbolic convention. They also entangle contemporary icons of Chinese national symbols and carriers of political philosophy, from Xi Jinping's invocation of the ancient political philosopher Han Fei and the role of imperial rituals, to current historiographic reevaluations of the more recent Empress Dowager Cixi Taihou, who ruled China for almost fifty years until 1908, beginning as a low-ranking imperial consort, reviled as ruthless, but now credited for many modernizing reforms.

WHITE INK

Each character in Kwa's corpus is written in white ink. That is, while everyone has a mother, each character is shown to be fulfilling a mother's desire, using a maternal prophecy or skill, or driven by a maternal memory, each sufficiently interesting to at least catalog.[4] Nonetheless, while it is possible to read for these ever-present libidinal, maternal, and emotional explorations of women's writing, this alone is insufficient. Being a Chinese interior landscape with deep historical roots (not unlike Cixous's entanglement with her father, her Jewish Algerian, and German-language roots), Kwa's corpus needs to be read with a series of balancing elements in mind, not only with *yin-yang* (female-male) philosophy and cosmology in general, but also with at least three other key discursive registers or threads of meaning. These form psychological knots and physiological pulses of blood and energy. They are, first, psychologies formed in historically situated family systems; second, deep (transhistorical) cultural symbols and ghost names; and third, literary and philosophical traditions of meditations on beauty, art, aging, and imperfection.[5]

All of Lydia Kwa's novels can be read as philosophical texts in story form of clinical psychology family systems. Often these take the form of "yearning to be loved by one's enemy" (as in the complicated relations between servant or slave and mistress, or unrequited or miscommunicated paternal love). They take the form of struggling against hate and revenge, which can consume and turn one into a monster or demon.[6] They take the form of keeping narcissism and ego gratification in reasonable check. In the two earlier novels, *This Place Called Absence* and *Pulse*, this can take the form of conflicted feelings toward a once abusive father turned helpless old man who needs care. In both earlier and later novels, it can be a father "shamed" by having a daughter, hermaphrodite, or gay son, instead of a son in his imagined masculine or patrilineage-building image, leaving the child yearning and striving unrequitedly for his love. Throughout, Kwa teaches us Chinese terms, therapeutic approaches, the use of parables as therapeutic philosophies, and intertwines these with a clinical psychologist's or even psychoanalyst's eye for the tangles of interpersonal relations.

These provide, for an anthropologist, a rich palette of psychological semiotics of dis-ease and comfort (Good 1976) and gendered codes in daily and political life (Good and Good 2013). They provide an entwinement between deep Chinese Taoist, Buddhist, and Confucian idioms and twentieth-century psychodynamic ones, in which ghosts and phantoms translate one another. Ghosts—as in terrors, nightmares, and dealings with unresolved relations; phantoms—as in phantom limbs, Mária Török and Nicolas Abraham's psychic phantoms that come not from one's own traumas but from intergenerationally transmitted ones, Pierre Janet's work on dissociation and difficulties of narrating traumatic memories, and Carl Jung's *Ergriffenheit* (possession by deep transhistorical patterns or archetypes).[7] They challenge the arts of writing: what can be written and what is left between the lines, or hypostasized in folkloric, mythic, or figures of gods in the Chinese pantheon.

In the two later novels, *The Walking Boy* and *Oracle Bone*, the arche form of a tortured "enemy" is Gui (or Kui). "Gui" means poison. The homophone Kui Xing is a god of literature, a figure of our recognition of the need for dramatic conflict to work out what in this world we should do, and how we get entrapped by our relationships.[8] In the novel *Oracle Bone*, Gui is self-poisoned by hate and revenge. He is filled with resentments about his deformity and the way it has blocked positions and recognitions. The Taoist nun, Qilan ("strange orchid"), daughter of one of Gui's victims, determines the antidote is not to kill him but to release him from the fears and resentments that drive his aggression. The complexity of these emotional entanglements is captured in calligraphy and sculptures of Kui Xing, bent and hunchbacked, but full of vigor and life, right foot standing on a giant turtle (*ao*), left foot balancing a ladle, writing brush in hand (see figure 3.1). Kui Xing is the servant of the god of literature, Wen Chang, the figure to whom one prays for success in the imperial examinations. Appropriately for astral divination, Kui Xing is also the name of the "chief star" in the handle or ladle of the Big Dipper. In the novel, Gui is eventually exorcised and released, along with the human whose form he has possessed, Xie. Xie traded his soul to Gui in a Faustian bargain to allow his daughter, the nun Qilan, to live. Gui pursues his hidden intrigues while inhabiting Xie's form, and in this form seduces Wu Zhao, the empress. Gui's eventual release from his fears and resentments has a cascading effect, validating the nun's philosophy of not taking revenge but undoing the psychology that drives Gui.

The two novels *Oracle Bone* and *The Walking Boy* provide symbolic compendia and thus function much like, in anthropology, Victor Turner's *Forest of Symbols*, which not merely deciphered Ndembu philosophy, cosmology, and cultural semiotics, but was a call to take symbolism and ritual processes seriously (Turner 1967). Turner took the title, in turn, from Charles Baudelaire's poem, "Correspondances" (1857). In Kwa's novel, there is an analogous Forest of Illusions and a Wilderness of Meanings, the former in nature, the latter in the city. Like Turner's discussions with the Ndembu about their symbols, Lydia Kwa's trilogy delves into the symbolic resources of the *Shan Hai Jing*, or *Guideways through Mountains and Seas* (translation and commentary: Strassberg 2002), a compendium of 277 often mythical animals and mythic geographies, begun in the early period of the Warring States (476–221 BCE). She delves as well into the psychological resources of the

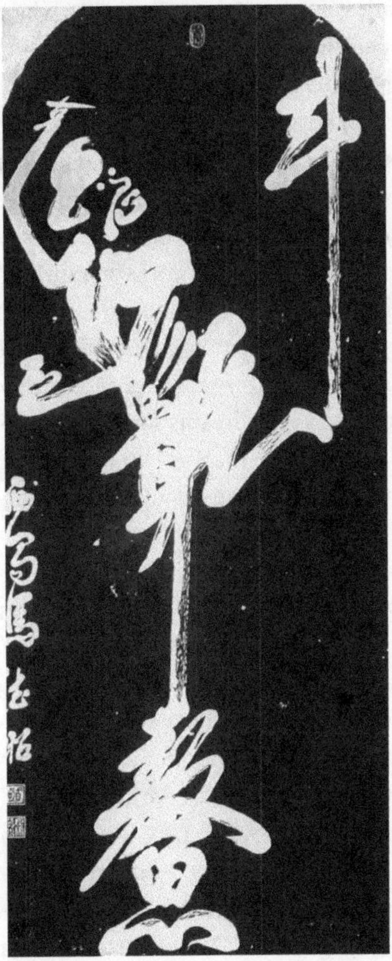

3.1 Kui Xing, servant of god of literature.

later genre of *zhiguai chuanqi* ("strange tales").[9] The names and marks of the characters often signal these connections: thus, the first radical of Qilan's name means "strange" (rather than merely "rare") orchid; and Ling has "dragon eyes" (eyes of different colors). The names can be read as mythological, but better as psychological—coming over time to signify in Kwa's texts the uniqueness and specialness of each person, whether patient, client, or confidant. In the projected third volume, *A Dream Wants Waking*, there will be a spin on post-Anthropocene and post-human futures, with genetic chimeras instead of animal transforms.[10]

The author, after all, is a clinical psychologist, and one can imagine her using such tales with clients (or at least in analyzing their stories) in the same way one uses Freud's family romance as a metaphorical story to which an analysand can abreact. Two large paintings or murals are described in *Oracle Bone*, depicting the bestiaries and other figures of the *Shan Hai Jing*. One of these paintings is in the empress's palace and provides a visualization for her of her visible and invisible empire. The other, its inverse, is in the mansion of Xie-Gu, providing a kind of sorcerer's guide to metamorphosis. These large paintings depict the interlocking and differential time scales of the mythic giant caterpillar which "counts five hundred years as one spring" as well as of small caterpillars that turn into short-lived butterflies. Both murals are figures or ladders of instruction that "certain phenomena exist that work according to other laws of time," that nature can transform, that there is an a-rational world of the intuitive, to which dreams sometimes provide cues and hints.[11] Therefore, one should "serve the Tao" and fit oneself into nature, rather than depend too much upon human calculations and efforts to control the volatile natures of humans and environments.

There is also an important tortoise's plastron (under shell) which is inscribed with the ancient ideograph of *yin* and *yang* (two *ren* or stick figures of persons, facing in opposite and inverted directions). This plastron is what becomes an oracle bone, a magic object sought by the empress in the hope that it can be used in an imperial cosmic ritual to seal her role as mediator between heaven and earth, and even provide her with immortality. The quest to find it is used by Gui to manipulate the empress. Like all spells and magic, as the Taoist nun Qilan explains to her new ward, Ling, the plastron cannot be used mechanically, but only with pure intent and righteous force (as also in martial arts that undo rather than kill opponents). This is a message that King Zhen of Eastern Qin failed to understand when he was shown the plastron and tried to misuse it. The philosopher Zou Yan had found the plastron while in a trance. He showed it to the king as a transcendental message that the king should rule according to tolerance and balance (*ying-yang*), rather than by Confucian rigidities. Zhen, however, was a legalist, who felt the population could only be ruled by fear. His reign ended quickly. That ending foreshadows one of the psychological causes of Empress Zhao's demise in the novel.

Yin and *yang* are components not only of everyone's nature, but they sometimes come in marked form physically: Baoshi, the walking boy of the novel's title, is a hermaphrodite; Buddha sculptures are androgynous; and the Hindu god Ardhanarishvara is a composite of Siva and Parvati. It is after that Hindu god that Ardhanari, the sculptor of buddhas in the Dunhuang caves on the Silk Road, is named; he is a lover of Harelip, a homosexual, a friend of transsexuals, and is particularly good at the sensual carving of androgynous buddhas.

The hidden meanings of names—"ghost writing, ghost names," as they are called in *This Place Called Absence* (Kwa 2000, 61)—are invoked in numerous places in the novels, as when the nun Qilan writes her own name in the dust, and asks Ling to write hers, so that they might know the meaning of each other's name, each name understood most clearly through its written characters to distinguish among spoken homophones of the different dialects spoken across China. Ling's mother has warned her never to tell anyone her true name, for then that person would have power over her, but Ling decides to trust Qilan. After writing their names in the dust, the names are blown away by a breeze, protecting the knowledge from others.[12] Similarly, the abbess Si, upon learning of Qilan's hybrid being (fox-spirit mother and scholar father), arranges for private accommodations so that Qilan can run free in the forest to hunt for fresh meat without being seen. Qilan uses her talents to teach Ling to run up walls and perform kung fu maneuvers that she will need in her future fight, a return match of retribution for the bandit who killed Ling's parents.

The hexagrams of the *I Ching*, and their numbers, structure the three parts of *Oracle Bone*: Part I is eighteen or *gu*, "poison"; part II is twenty-four or *fu*, "return"; and part III is sixty-four or *ji ji*, "completion." *Fu* is the summons to spirits and deities to return for an exorcism. It is the name of the magical script used by exorcists (*fangshi*, "methods scholars"). In the last section, "Completion" (*ji ji*), the monk Xuanzang completes his translations of the Buddhist texts (either the Heart Sutra, which becomes his special mantra, or the whole *Mahaprajnaparamita* (the sixteen talks on the perfection of wisdom by Shakyamuni Buddha) that he has brought from India, in violation of the law forbidding travel abroad. It brings to China transcendent wisdom that threatens to contest and absorb Taoism and Confucianism.[13] The lovers Ardhanari (bisexual) and Harelip (homosexual) are reunited after a thirty-year separation by Baoshi (hermaphrodite). And Empress Wu Zhao realizes that her ambitions of total control and immortality are in vain; and that she too must yield to the *shen tao*, the spirit of the way (which is also the ceremonial ascent, lined with mythological creatures, to the emperor's tomb).

These, and much other poetic and parable lore, are skillfully and seamlessly woven into the narration, so that one can read it naively as just a good popular story as one might watch a kung fu film, or one can follow the hints and clues as a rich tapestry of Chinese history and story.

BEAUTY, ART, AGING, AND IMPERFECTION

Another thread or register, particularly in *The Walking Boy*, is the meditation on beauty, art, aging, and imperfection, especially the way that, beginning in middle age, one reevaluates the desire for "idealized beauty and smoothness of contour" and comes to find "the marks and beauty of imperfections" as ways to awaken "the persistent spirit of overcoming chaotic onslaughts" (Kwa [2005] 2018, 267–68). The great Mogao Caves at Dunhuang provide an example of the contrast between a changing desert landscape and the art inside the caves created initially as images of perfection to outlast ephemeral weather and wind-blown sand dunes. But, with time, it is the marks of wear and tear, and other imperfections, on the great statues and murals that come to gain value as evidence of a greater persistence. We are told about the caves through the changing moods of the sculptor, Ardhanari, who is so skilled he can make his carved bodhisattvas seem to be alive. He decides to not fully repair statues that were used at the mouth of a cave to block ferocious sandstorms, saving the lives of the sculptors working inside.

Other marks of imperfection come to be signs of specialness. These include the tattoo branded violently onto the forehead of the Taoist nun Qilan by the empress to subjugate her. Only later does the court realize it is the back-to-back signs for *ren* (person), indicating both multiple perspectives and the *yin-yang* philosophy. It is the sign inscribed on the oracle bone. It is also associated with the form of Harelip's cleft palate, Baoshi's hermaphrodism, and Ling's "dragon eyes." The homosexual pairings of Qilan and Ling, and Harelip and Ardhanari, pose a reminder that even the past may have had more diversity than normative stories allow, and that recollection can become validating charter myths for the present.

ECHOES

In a lovely reading of Baudelaire's "Correspondances," Pascal Michon notes, "One of the most striking features of this poem is the spreading, dissemination, and return of the syllables that compose the title in the whole text," creating a "rhythmic experience of the subject [writer, listener, reader] in the language of the here and now" (Michon 2010). This *weaves* an "*écriture*" with "prolonged echoes" (*de longs échos*) from the past that "whispers through the correspondences," sometimes as a "shock" of recollections of, or differences from, an anterior life. In the last sentence, I combine Michon's words with his quotation of those of Walter Benjamin (especially "shock"). Michon wants to save Baudelaire from parts of Benjamin's reading. He wants to stress Baudelaire's personal prosody, an individual creativity, albeit one that can be shared, while Benjamin stresses a less individualist understanding, instead looking for the sociocultural dialectic between reanimating past utopian aspirations and criticizing violence in the history that creates the present. The idea of deeply personal symbols becoming public ones so as to become socially legible in (rather than being called) madness is much like the anthropologist Gananath Obeyesekere's reading of a new ecstatic religion constructed in Sri Lanka out of deeply personal symbols of trauma (Obeyesekere 1981). Obeyesekere's example is of lower-class urbanizing village migrants who are unable to fulfill family obligations such as returning home to grieve properly for their most intimate dead relatives. In psychological pain, they use ecstatic rituals (fire walking, hanging from hooks) to construct a language of possession that mixes Hindu and Buddhist public vocabularies, and that exacts what might be called a kind of *jouissance*.

Something missed by Michon, but taking on relevance in the context of Kwa's novels, is the couplet, cited above, in Baudelaire's "Correspondances":

> *L'homme y passe à travers des forêts de symboles*
> *Qui l'observent avec des regards familiers.*
>
> Humans pass through forests of symbols
> Which look at them with the eyes of familiars.

Familiers refers to the spirit world, not merely, as more secularized translations have it, "with kindred eyes."

Perhaps the four semiotic registers I have indicated might be rendered also in older Chinese terms, elaborated in *Pulse*, but present throughout as interactions of the trigrams of the *I Ching* grouped in three sets of four wooden chips each (twelve in all, like the zodiac), representing the human (white milk, family systems), heaven (forests of illusion), and earth (aging). I unpack some of these dense knots briefly in the four sections below.

ON CHANGING MODES OF STORYTELLING: CELL PHONE MESSAGING, TALK THERAPY, WRITING

> impssbl 2 expln 2 sme 1 who dsnt hve same need. crave a gre8er rush. nvr feels excting enuf. want > edge. Lookng 4 thse wh cn master fear, go bynd.
>
> LYDIA KWA, *PULSE*

> Aren't all stories true? To intuit the meanings of what is left unsaid.
>
> LYDIA KWA, *THIS PLACE CALLED ABSENCE*

> In every case, the storyteller has counsel for his readers. . . . After all, counsel is less an answer to a question than a proposal concerning the continuation of a story which is just unfolding.
>
> WALTER BENJAMIN, "THE STORY TELLER"

There are storytellers and storywriters. While there are many crossovers, they are not the same. There are translators, reciters, copyists, correctors, and memorizers (all part of Xuanzang's work on the Buddhist manuscripts he brought from India), but these are not writers of the stories. *Oracle Bone* has two primary writers; the empress and the imperial secretary. The empress dictates her version of the history of her rule to the imperial secretary who writes it down. What the secretary writes is a faithful recording, which the empress checks for accuracy. If the empress does not write her own history, she says, male historians later will write it differently, devaluing her. Maybe they will anyway. Both the empress and the secretary also write secret diaries and poems, their private versions, commentaries, backstories as it were. The empress hopes to give an account that will fortify other women attempting to operate in power worlds that men dominate, justifying her ruthlessness as necessary. The secretary tries to find her true self amid the contradictory imperatives under which she is forced to live: victim of the empress's murder of her father, a slave to the empress, allowed to live a life of luxury, albeit always reminded of her status. These diaries and poems are records of emotions as well as commentaries on events. Like dreams, visions, and nightmares, both the empress's diaries and the secretary's poems operate in response to the libido as well as reasoning or rationalizing; they are more fluid and open than the histories, yet they too follow and respond to literary conventions and social expectations. The secretary writes responses to the poetry of an earlier female poet, mimicking her style. One of these poems serves as a goodbye love token to her occasional lover, Abbess Ling.

Both empress and secretary are socially confined to the margins of public writing, much as Friedrich Kittler (1992) theorizes European women's writing around 1800, when the mother tongue was being converted by pedagogy into standardized national languages, and thence by 1900 into print technologies; or, as Marshall Berman (1982) similarly suggests, mother (and nanny) vernaculars and dialects were transformed into national languages (of Pushkin and Balzac). Both diaries and poems are secret and full of secrets that contain poisonous knowledge (Das 2000).

In "Father:Mother:Tongue," Kwa writes of another form of linguistic plurality and conversion to writing:

> My mother's tongue is Hakka, a high-pitched eruption of sounds. . . . Raised on the lower, sometimes sibilant, sometimes hazy register of my father's tongue [Hokkien], the meanings of hers were foreign, glimpsed almost as rarely as street accidents. Like those annual Chinese New Year visits with grandmother . . . listening through the gaps for the occasional, recognizable word. I never mastered father tongue, stumbling through tangled mazes in mind and mouth, the language trapped inside. . . . I cannot remember a time I thought in Hokkien, it has always been English, the language of foreigners, of colonialism.
>
> #
>
> Mother's is not father's is not English is not mine.
>
> #
>
> Going to school a temporary escape from the confusion of mother's and father's tongues razing the air with the fire of resentment and malice. A fever which spread through my body, *delirium*. English, my adopted language, charging me out of one prison, into another. (Kwa 1994b, 38–39)

Delirium, fantasy, dream, and nightmare go into the novels' fine calligraphic renderings of interior and exterior landscapes. The geographic landscapes of *Oracle Bone* and *The Walking Boy* extend from tea plantations and timber merchants in the east—transporting their tribute or tax payments along the Grand Canal and then by horse and cart—to the great city of Chang'an in the center, and westward across the northern edge of the Gobi desert to Dunhuang, with its great caves, repositories of Buddhist manuscripts, murals, and buddha statues. The city of Chang'an, the largest in the world at the time, is laid out in geometric quarters: to the west, the Foreign Quarter, with the western market and babble of languages; to the north, the palace; and to the east, the Vice Quarter (a mixture of mansions, brothels, and places of worship) and the eastern market.[14]

Insofar as the nuns in *Oracle Bone* write, it is with concerns for identifying which of several meanings in oral discourse the written characters identify (as in the exchange of names in writing of Qilan and Ling), and with the use of *fu*, the language of mystical symbols used by exorcists and diviners, where therapy and repair (or return to self) is more the point than mere meaning. The symbols on the oracle bone are selected by the empress as the brand (a physical writing) she has seared onto her secretary's forehead to perversely "repair" her rebelliousness or unruliness, to domesticate her with pain and visible disfigurement. In so doing, the empress fails to recognize the meaning of the symbols she has made so visible. She repeats the mistake of the king of Qin before her. Only much later would this archaic form of the *yin-yang* symbol be recognized by Ling, now an abbess, for whom the scar on the secretary's forehead is not a disfigurement, but to the contrary a sign of a world beyond the superficial.

Kwa's books straddle the sociological divide indexed by the rise of the novel. Novels, it is often said, come into being, replacing storytelling, fables, and epics, as societies urbanize, and as common parables become less useful for daily decision-making than the search for information tailored to the needs of each individualized person (Staël 1818; Benjamin [1936] 1969; Watt 1957).[15] Kwa's two earlier novels are about modernity, of living in two worlds, leaving one behind and entering another newly in the making (the world of clashing "Father:Mother:Tongue"). The two later novels delve back into the worlds of early Chinese empire formation in Chang'an (today's Xi'an) to recover the storytelling lore and parable wisdom that many "moderns" shucked as ignorance and superstition, but that now, in a twenty-first century interested in ecological connections, holistic healing, and ecumenical cosmologies, seem to hope might enculture perspectives for mitigating alienations of contemporary labor (whether in farming, or urban blue- and white-collar work). These perspectives now seem almost as powerful as Hong Kong movies, computer games, and graphic novels, as stimulation and resources for teaching new ways to look and see. Novels (along with film) are the nineteenth and twentieth centuries' mode of articulating and questioning how social change in one part of a social world has implications for other parts. Still composed by hand (or by typewriter or keyboard), novels provided accounts of learning about a world that will not stay still, but is constantly "urban renewed," destroying much of the old and requiring ever more information for living in the new: How much does it cost? Who does one talk to? What is the code?

Straddling this divide, mapping the meantime, women writers (bisexuals, lesbians, transgender, and so on), like the empress and secretary, document worlds that escape official histories, and that record and celebrate unruly passions. Kwa combines the wisdom of past storytelling with the information in the new. *Oracle Bone* begins with a counterpoint to scriptures and histories, with the wonderful figure of the "Imperfect One," an old woman storyteller with only a few teeth left, but loud and hypnotic bright tone of voice, holding forth in a narrow alley, in the light of a single kerosene lamp, with an audience seated around her: "'This is a fable, and hence spiced with all kinds of outrageous lies.' She cackled, and the audience applauded vigorously. 'Definitely not sanctioned by officials.' More clapping" (Kwa 2017a, 11). This is the first of twenty-one nights of storytelling, timed in the book by lunar half months and the annual ritual cycle. In the opening story, "The Unknown Wayfarer" (Baoshi, "the walking boy") is enchanted by the Imperfect One, observing, "Imperfections, especially in this new era of erasures, are rather quaint, yet subversive" (12). The Imperfect One pairs with Ardhanari's reflections about the Buddha statues marked and worn by sandstorms. Both contrast with images of smoothed-over official histories and icons of worship. Wu Zhao, the empress, and Wan'er, the imperial secretary, similarly provide subversions in their private poems and diaries. Wan'er's response poems to the poems of Cai Yan, the poet-musician of the second to third century CE, provide a mode of personal refection and self-assertion, but are also a gift and mode of communication to her lover, Abbess Ling. And the great murals of the *Shan Hai Jing* in the palace and the rogues' mansion are like the cloth paintings (Persian *pardeh*) that epic storytellers (Persian *naqqal*) use to develop the moral or pragmatic form of characters in their stories, as they customize stories for their audiences, often containing targeted criticisms and satire.

Walter Benjamin worried that the novel was an index of the rise of a middle class mediated by print technologies and increasingly distanced from abilities to tell the kinds of person-centered stories that could counsel people in their lives, in favor instead of abstracted information and bombardments of newspaper stories and news photos. It is a fear also expressed by contemporary Singaporean artist Zai Kuning (see Fischer 2023, 160–61). Kwa, among others, shows that this bifurcation need not be uncrossable. In a way, *Oracle Bone* and *The Walking Boy* provide a *pardeh* (cloth backdrop) to the counseling her narrator dispenses and seeks in *This Place Called Absence* and *Pulse*. They provide elements that still pulse through the blood of the narrator, a modern woman, a lesbian clinical psychologist in Canada. As Benjamin wrote, or Freud might have, and as Francis in *This Place Called Absence* echoes: "Counsel is less an answer to a question than a proposal concerning the continuation of a story which is just unfolding. To seek this counsel, one would first have to be able to tell the story" (Benjamin 1969, 86).

We are beginning to morph new twenty-first-century communication platforms (beyond newspaper, novel, and film): information compression, visualization technologies, shorthand prostheses (statistics, graphs, charts, animation, comix), virtual reality (computer-assisted visual environments), big data, and machine-learning algorithms, presented in "user-friendly," but nontransparent, formats, ever harder to submit to proof or accountability. It remains to be seen if these new platforms become hermetically self-referential, more and more distant from person-centered experience, as Walter Benjamin and Zai Kuning fear, or if they become tools of experience-rich counsel, self-critical thought, and artistic probes for living in the world.

THE THIRTY YEARS OF *ORACLE BONE* AND *THE WALKING BOY*

> Nothing remained unchanged but the clouds, and beneath these clouds, in a field of force of destructive torrents and explosions, was the tiny, fragile human body.
>
> WALTER BENJAMIN, "THE STORY TELLER"

Both *The Walking Boy* and *Oracle Bone* are populated with memories of mothers, mother figures, and m(others) or the "not me within me" that includes memories of fathers, conflicts in the nuclear family, or later violators and enemies, that remain unresolved into and often throughout life.[16] (As she writes elsewhere: "Dreaming double truths / my father, me / merged into one," Kwa 2013, 85). It is the struggle not to yield to the disempowerments of resentments, fear (or worse, hate). Repeatedly, the conflicts that Kwa deals with are the "persistent yearning to be loved by the one she should consider her enemy" (Kwa [2005] 2018, 155). *The Walking Boy* is dedicated to the author's mother, and the prologue opens with, "I am a poet and a woman acquainted with dilemmas" (15). The "prequel," *Oracle Bone*, appropriately and perhaps with punning intent, is dedicated to the "outcasts," punning on the casting of oracle bones and divination sticks, as well as building the story around a person with a harelip and one who is a hermaphrodite, both shamed and feeling outcast, but taken in by monks who themselves are nonconforming.

The two novels are set thirty years apart, during respectively the rise and the demise of Wu Zhao, who rises to become Empress Nǔ Huáng, no longer operating as the power behind the throne but openly ruling China from 670 to 705 CE. Her rise involves the ruthless sidelining and assassination of rivals, and her demise as she ages, likewise, is the result and intense focus of sexual and political court plots, not unlike those of classic Chinese novels such as *Dream of the Red Chamber*, or even the practical and psychological tricks of classic manuals of politics such as that of Han Fei. Controversial for her ruthlessness, historically Wu Zhao or Nǔ Huáng is also known for important reforms under the Tang dynasty, which saw its western capital, Chang'an, become the largest city in the world, and a cosmopolitan crossroads peopled by Hindus, Buddhists, Taoists, Zoroastrians, and Nestorian Christians, speakers of Turkish, Persian, Mongolian, Chinese, and other languages. Kwa is not the only one to have revived Wu Zhao's memory as an ambivalent feminist icon.[17] However, although a key player, Wu Zhao is not the center of the first two novels; rather, in *Oracle Bone* two other women (both Taoist and shamanistic nuns in a Buddhist-promoting empire), and in *The Walking Boy*, Harelip and the hermaphrodite Baoshi. Baoshi, the titular "walking boy," finds acceptance in a transgender community from India (Jogappas). (One wonders if Kwa might, in this vein, take on the more recent, also controversial Empress Dowager Cixi Taihou, who ruled China for forty-seven years at the end of the Qing Dynasty, from 1861 to 1908, or if in fact Wu Zhao is a stalking horse for Cixi Taihou in contemporary historiographic reevaluations.)

It is under Wu Zhao that the short-form genre of stories known as *zhiguai chuanqi* ("transmission of the strange") is said to have begun. *Oracle Bone* and *The Walking Boy* follow the genre in being ostensibly modeled on biographies in official histories, but with strange twists. They begin with information on the main characters, and while containing "anecdotes, jokes, legends, and tales involving mystical, fantastical or legendary elements," they often focus on characters' psychology, told in the round from different perspectives, often involving triangular relationships, and witty dialogue.[18] Kwa says the *chuanqi* were written by "male literati about strange creatures like ghosts, demons, and fox spirits . . . [who] were almost predominantly female and wicked"; and she says, "I'm attempting to subvert th[at] dominant narrative" (Kwa 2017b).[19] It seems that the genre itself was a form of satire and criticism of the worthies about whom the stories were written, but Kwa deepens, sharpens, and modernizes the psychology and gender relations.

Chuanqi is not the only genre being toyed with. One of the pleasures of Kwa's corpus is her effort to play, often subtly, with a number of conventional tropes and genres ranging from historical fiction to the forthcoming science-fiction experiment, *A Dream Wants Waking*, set in a twenty-third-century zoned city, Luòyáng, in which "the dream zone" contains our "chimeric creatures, ghosts, cast-off shadow selves" (Kwa 2020). In this work, there will be, she promises, "narrative references to *Oracle Bone* and *The Walking Boy*"; and the title is part of a couplet associated with the oracle bone (Kwa 2020). The oracle bone, an ancient divination tool, is but one of many diagnostic tools (often coded as magic) in her novels ranging from the body's skin (eczema as somatic trauma register, blushing, rope marks, distancing) to the body's blood and energy (pulse, acupuncture); to diaries and secret histories as messages to the future that cannot be disclosed in the diegetic present (Shangguan Wan'er, the female imperial secretary, records the Nǚ Huáng palace diaries with mixed feelings about her complicity with plotters against the empress, and writes her own commentary in secret poems). Couplets, poetry, and Buddhist sutras similarly function in polyvocal ways: "Words are merely sounds; they're nothing until one imparts meanings to them," says the monk Harelip to Walking Boy as he sets him on his journey and quest to bring back Harelip's lover, the sculptor Ardhanari, exiled from the capital to work on the Mogao caves near Dunhuang, carving statues for the thousand temples of Buddha (Kwa [2005] 2018, 57).

Wuxia (the martial-hero genre of novels and cinema) is another genre transformed. There is a major fight scene in *Oracle Bone* that Kwa choreographs to fit both *wuxia* and the woman-warrior trope. Kwa acknowledges, as several reviewers have noted, that the prose is cinematic, and she would not mind a film treatment of the two novels, but what she really wants are treatments of them as graphic novels (a genre that has developed heroes and villains with extra-human powers and pasts). In any case, she says of the male *wuxia* formula (the hero vows revenge and they go on a rampage), "I'm going to engage with this theme of revenge and see what I can do that's different" (Kwa 2017b). What is different is that the martial acrobatics and weaponized laser-like focus of projection of energy by the once orphaned girl Ling ("spirit, soul") against the killer of her father and rapist of her mother ends not with killing but humiliation of the bandit, and then sending him off to the Forest of Illusions to learn to liberate himself from his own murderous fears. Qilan also chooses, so as not to destroy herself with hate, not to kill the demon who possessed and destroyed her father, but return it to its natural place in the underworld.

Kwa elucidates in *Pulse*—in an elegant sparring discussion-debate between the narrator, a middle-aged lesbian acupuncturist, and a young gay man, son of her first female lover in Singapore—their very different *kinbaku* engagements with pain and trust. Each reveals traumatic childhood sexual abuse by their fathers. Through the therapeutic practice of *kinbaku*, each attempts to replace revenge, anger, shame, the inability to open up, and knots of trauma (caused by a loved other) with trust in another, in a partner who inflicts pain but only to rid the self of its debilitating effects. Slowly trust in others can be gradually rebuilt, and self-confidence and autonomy regained.

These feelings run through all four novels, and says Kwa, "Hopefully, these characters are struggling with things that many of us, in any time and place, can identify with. Not being loved, being abandoned, having one's loves and family taken away from us, anger, revenge, hatred, fear, lust for power—these are all themes that are there for all of us" (Kwa 2017b). Falardeau notes, "each character has a story arc that ultimately finds them questioning who they are and what they want versus what destiny has laid before them" (Falardeau 2020). Another reviewer says of *Oracle Bone*, "We are gifted, by the novel's conclusion, not only with a heroic narrative centered on two women, but a historical novel in which the course of a nation, a culture, a religion and an entire world are shaped by two women and a gay monk. To Kwa's considerable credit, readers are not alerted to the significance of this. Rather, the events of *Oracle Bone* unfold with the unspoken authority that this is how these events unfolded" (Wiersema 2017).

Actually, it is a bit more complicated. When Xuanzang, the monk who brought back the Heart Sutra and other manuscripts from India, dies, Harelip takes over and sends Baoshi to find Ardhanari, Harelip's former lover, to reestablish and repair their relationship. Baoshi, himself, as noted above, is a hermaphrodite whose father tried to pay Harelip and the monks to take him away, to protect the boy more from society's cruelty than from shame, but that does not lessen Baoshi's sense of abandonment. Ardhanari is a reference to the composite form of Shiva and Parvati (male and female) depicted as half male and half female, split down the middle, just as Baoshi has one plump breast and one flat, and both male and female genitals. It is with the Jogappas, the transgender community from India, that Baoshi finds a sense of community. The message is that the world is more fluid than Confucian or other normative categories would like, and that, as the plastron suggests, we should pay attention to the *shen tao* (the way of the spirit), adjusting ourselves to the forces and complexities of our natures and those of our coresidents in the world. The Heart Sutra and other sutras, brought as manuscripts to Dunhuang, translated by Xuanzang, written and copied by scribes, recited orally, memorized, and made into mantras, are long enduring. They are preserved orally and in the heart by combining writing, oral repetition, chanting, and melodic rhythm, often in congregation. And yet they take on altered meanings in different contexts. As Harelip teaches Baoshi, the word "boy" means what you make it mean, through the perlocutionary force of intentionality.

PLACES AND POWERS OF ABSENCE

> "Some things we try to tame aren't meant to be tamed."
> "And if we try . . ."
> "Violence is the consequence."
> I take another sip of my coffee. Violence within the body. Where has violence shown up in my life? I mean, I'm not the sort who acts out. Quite the contrary.
> LYDIA KWA, *THIS PLACE CALLED ABSENCE*

An *écriture féminine* with "prolonged echoes" (*de longs échos*) from the past that whisper through correspondences, and that physiologically provide heart rhythms or *qi* (energy) diagnosed through the taking of the pulse, sometimes treatable with acupuncture, weaves through the plots of both *This Place Called Absence* and *Pulse*. In some ways, *Pulse* is a rewriting of the Wu Lan story in *This Place Called Absence*, and it can be hard to keep the two novels apart for this reason. But *This Place Called Absence* has a second intertwined tale of two impoverished village girls from China who migrate to Singapore and become prostitutes, and find love in their lesbian relationship (it would not have been called that), both physical and emotional. One girl ends as a suicide, leaving a deep *absence* for the other, who eventually kills a cruel male brothel keeper, and is saved from the consequences by a gay man who arranges to marry her and slip her out of the country to Java. Wu Lan has access to these women's lives by researching prostitution in Singapore.[20] The publisher's blurb says she reads the women's journals, but they were illiterate, as one of them demonstrates by fetishizing and turning into a talisman the Chinese character that looked like a heart under a field, more meaningful to her as that than its combination meaning: contemplation. The three dots of the heart character "were the pebbles I threw up to Heaven. One falling behind, one landing too far ahead to grasp, and then . . . this last one . . . maybe I can catch this last one" (Kwa 2000, 127).

"Absence," of course, is one of the echoes woven through *This Place Called Absence*: the narrator wonders, "why is it *the absent ones* sometimes have a greater grip on us than the living?" (65); and how is it that the *pain felt through absence can be transmitted* to children, sometimes perversely through violence, recalling that already as a child she had "sensed that Grandmother Neo's absence grew larger than life for her son, so large that his pain about it filtered through to me?" (66); and, after her father's death, "all those years pretending not to mind his *absence*" (172). There is the narrator's *leave of absence* from her clinical psychology practice when she has "lost confidence in her abilities in helping people find a way past their powerlessness" (207). And there is her return to *this place of absence*, the Singapore she had left, doubling the loss of confidence and sense of place in her vocation to which she cannot so easily return. There is also the "something in me [that] feels the *absence* that goes with such a choice" (not to have children) (80), and more poignantly the "deep imprints of their loneliness, aware of some subtle inarticulable *absence*" felt by the daughter noticing her parents' bed having slept backs turned toward each other (148). More doublings of alienation appear: "where in front of me, a stranger talks. Stringing words together. Two strangers who sit across from each other in a small, soundproofed room. Face to face. Truth or lies?" (208). There is a mirroring between this space of therapy and the prostitutes' cubicles where they attend to men's bruised egos. There is another mirroring between the two prostitutes finding each other, and the serial lesbian relationships that the narrator goes through in her loneliness in Vancouver. The most developed of these is with Francis, who also has suffered a father's molestation, and who works out the resulting feelings in her paintings of women, one with teeth bared in a gesture of aggression (an epithet-like description used also for Qilan in *Oracle Bone* at two moments where aggression is shown).[21] Absence is also a position of power: the withdrawn, unseeable center that Han Fei, the legalist scholar, advocated for the emperor who could then rule by practical and psychological tricks, creating a panopticon of self-discipline among his subjects.

Power and class relations operate in these spaces as well. Patterson (2013) makes an interesting case that the prostitutes should be read as fetishized objects of rescue fantasies for the narrator, who is positioned uncomfortably as a middle aged (forty-eight-year-old) lesbian in what should be the utopian liberal space of Vancouver but which has many illiberal features. Patterson argues that the novel therefore should be read as satire, with the prostitutes as a gag. But the books the narrator reads in the library are well-recognized and peer-reviewed histories. Patterson suggests the narrator be read as a stock figure (the successful if unmoored immigrant) that sends up the self-promotion of Canada's tolerance. But Kwa is, of course, acutely aware of the repressive politics of tolerance, without allowing it to flatten the many other interesting things the novel weaves together. Her poem titled "base" (lowercase in the original) is about the incarceration in 1999 of 599 female migrants, arriving by boats from Fujian, in southeast China (Kwa 2013, 79–81). They were incarcerated in Vancouver's Burnaby Correctional Centre for Women. The poem wraps the hostility (newspaper headlines: Go Home!) with other histories ("large boats arrive on the shores of a foreign land / mythic echoes of conquest" and "I think about my ancestors / arriving in junks / on the shores of Sumatra and Singapore"); and with the stories migrants tell of violence in China as well as North America: "In over a decade since the arrival of the boats / a handful of migrants obtain / legitimate status / the rest, gone underground / working in restaurants in New York / or back to the Mainland"). Kwa is, after all, as well read as the theorists and critics: "tolerate, v. t. / to allow, without prohibiting / to permit / to recognize and respect / to put up with / endure / as in: medicine, to have tolerance for (substance/pathogen)." Another stanza lists the dark history of hatred in Canada.[22]

It is poetry (*shih*) as well as people's personal stories that help return the narrator Wu Lan to herself. Still thinking of the clinical consulting room, she says, "A torrent of words, like a seasonal monsoon, underneath which lies the deepest pain. Aren't all stories true? To intuit the meanings of what is left unsaid. I am Wu Lan, an exorcist of hidden demons. I am the discoverer of secrets. I stir fire into the bones of the dead. I prepare the dead for release" (Kwa 2000, 208). These words come as her farewell to the embalmed body of her father—"and whisper one last time, '*Goodbye Father*'" (208). It is after this farewell that she has her failure of confidence and takes a leave of absence from her role as a therapist.

Wu Lan? Her mother called her Lan-Lan, "precious one." It was the grandmother (Mah Mah) who named her Wu Lan, a name her mother resisted but her father delighted in. (Mah Mah gets a bit more elaboration in *Pulse*, where she helps Kong Kong, "grandfather," in the medicine store and runs a divination business in the back room. She gives the narrator her wooden *I Ching* divination chips when the narrator leaves for Canada. In *This Place Called Absence*, Mah Mah is a more distant, and vague, figure.) Wu? Her mother said it meant "one who helps others." Appropriate for a clinical psychologist. And later, enigmatically, her mother said the grandmother had named her after a dream in which a baby is drawn from a *deep well* with *fire* around it. ("Like water freed from a well / ungraspable," Kwa 2013, 72.) One day, long after, in Vancouver, having taken her leave of absence, and depressed, she wanders into a Buddhist temple and notices a banner with her name, Wu, on it, though she could not read the other characters. Asking a woman named Tze Cheng ("poetic greeting") for help, she draws her name on her palm. Tze Cheng asks if she knows what dragon eyes are (recall Ling is recognized as "dragon eyes" by the abbess Si and by the nun Qilan in *Oracle Bone*). Wu Lan does not. And then she asks if Wu Lan speaks a Chinese dialect. "Our family spoke mostly Hokkien at home with a few Malay phrases. I learned Mandarin as a second language at school. I know a bit of Cantonese . . . a mix" (Kwa 2000, 62). Ah, from Singapore or Malaysia! Tze Cheng pulls out a Mandarin book of reproductions of ancient paintings and finds a picture of a woman exorcist (*wu shi*) using a knife to cut the character for *fire* into the palm of a sick man, chasing out his demons.

Tze Cheng also gives her a book in English which "opens up to a *shih*." Titled *The Rain Is Not Controlled*, it is a meditation on injustices ("Why are the guiltless / Swallowed up in wide calamities?") and the narrator first thinks of her father's unhappy life: "Maybe he desperately needed a *wu shi*, someone to provide a scowl formidable enough to scare the illness out of him" (65). But then she reflects that the poem was written in a time of political upheaval (600 BCE, when the Chou Dynasty was losing its power) and in the time when language philosophy was flourishing (the "Hundred Schools"): "Maybe this *shih* was not merely about people expressing their powerlessness as victims. It could have been a way people spoke to each other in code, to spur themselves and others towards rebellion" (66). Her lover, Francis, later would gently suggest she seek help from a therapist, asking her if she thought she really helped her clients, to which she says she is unsure. Francis points out that Wu Lan always said about her clinical work that she could only help those who also helped themselves. It is the message of the *shih*. And it is untying the knots in the psyche, the knots that keep us from acting.

Before she meets Tze Cheng, on the spur of the moment, she goes into a Chinese medicine shop and consults a Chinese doctor, who says her problems are matters of spirit which have flown away, rather than physiology.

The father is one such knot. He is voiceless in the text; we know him through his daughter and his wife. While the mother Mahmee's grandfather established a family that did well, Wu Lan's father's side did not fare so well. Mahmee's grandfather came from China and became well-to-do, first with a shoe store and then a Chinese medicine store. Becoming well-to-do, he could marry a Peranakan from Java in an arranged marriage (when the girl was yet unborn, arriving to be married in Singapore aged seventeen). Mahmee's father took over the shop and hosted Japanese officers at the dinner table to keep his family safe under the Occupation. But Wu Lan's father's family suffered during that time, and Wu Lan's father, Yen, suffered real trauma, the affects of which grew more obsessive with time. The trauma, Wu Lan comes to think, was the loss of Yen's mother during the war. She had left her two boys with her brother for safety, and then died of cancer, so Yen never saw her again. Yen's brother was badly tortured by the Japanese. A family photo album has pictures of Yen as a happy young man, courting Mahmee, tossing baby Wu Lan into the air with delight, posing with son Michael; but then something went wrong. In an earlier time, he liked to sing the hymns he heard at a small neighborhood church, filling in words with his own inventions: "*What a friend we have in Jesus, all our screams and riffs to bear, what a privilege to bury everyone who hates our guts*" (4). But then he began collecting Daily Bread booklets, which his children joked was his "mad collection"; later, Wu Lan thinks, these might have been his "passport to sanity" as he descended into misery. He would come home frustrated from work, turn on the television, begin to drink and take pills to sleep, and occasionally engage Wu Lin in maudlin talk about his mother. He wasn't violent, "except once when he lost it with Michael." He and Mahmee drew apart and slept with their backs to each other. He for a time came into Wu Lan's bed, causing Wu Lan to withdraw, "evading anyone's attempts to understand me or my motives" (16). (In *Pulse*, this scene becomes much more intense and violent, when he discovers her in bed with another girl; also in *Pulse*, the relationship between father and gay son is more emotionally fraught: the son is not only gay, but refuses to use the name that the father gave him, Gabriel, preferring a Muslim name, Selim, with an "i" to emphasize an Arabic connection.) Wu Lan jokes that Father was a dragon (by the zodiac), Mahmee a pig, and they bred a snake (Wu Lan), and Michael was born in the year of the dog, and so the relation between Michael and father was the most troubled, Michael being the target of angry outbursts when the father came home, the mother handling it with indirection and phoning friends when the father was at work, and Wu Lan withdrew.

Mahmee has her own psychic knots, angers, and resentments. Her voice is distinctively Singlish as she worries, kvetches, and tries to give advice. For Wu Lan's forty-second birthday, Mahmee sends a pair of beautifully embroidered slippers that had belonged to her grandmother, never worn again after the Japanese occupied Singapore. The gift is not well received. But when Wu Lan asks her for stories about Mah Mah, who had named her, Mahmee's interior monologue goes, "Why? . . . better to forget, better to let go of the bitterness" (198). Mahmee resents Mah Mah having prevented her from studying and instead spoiling the son, who turned out to be a dissolute gambler.[23] She resents Yen, her husband, for committing suicide before retiring, and so spoiling plans for postretirement travel. And she is bewildered by Wu Lan for refusing to marry and then by her announcement that she is gay and has been living with a woman for thirteen years. After Mahmee has been disturbed at night by ghostly visitations by her husband, she is persuaded to see a medium during the Hungry Ghosts festival. The medium, rather generically, but with scalpel-sharp effect, asks, "Your [dead] husband give you problems?" (190). The medium goes into trance, growls, and responds when Mahmee asks the ghost, "Yen, why you still bother me?" And the ghost replies through the medium (also somewhat generically): "Not warm enough, feed me more spices; house needs television and music" (190). This is something she can happily do (it "made sense," as these were things he liked in life) and it allows her slowly to let go of her frustration and anger that he took his life, and had not waited until after retirement so that they could have traveled the world. She slowly also comes to terms with her frustration at her estranged daughter, who is not only a lesbian but has moved away. But as Yen's ghost stops troubling her, it begins to trouble the daughter.

Wu Lan decides to go back to Singapore for the birth of her brother's son. She has not been back since the death of the father, when she had felt no emotion and told herself she did not feel his absence. But when she returned to Vancouver from the funeral, her loss of confidence in her clinical psychology practice caused her to take a leave of absence, and the ghosts and guilt began to manifest. She is troubled by not having been there to take a phone call from her father just before he died. This occurred when she goes to the Buddhist temple and explored her name, and on a whim, she goes to a Chinese medicine store to get a skin salve she remembers from childhood. The store is resonant with memories of her grandfather's shop. She goes upstairs to visits a *sinseh* (Hokkien for Chinese doctor, or *yi sun* in Cantonese). He is actually from Tianjin, speaks Mandarin, but spent time in Hong Kong so also speaks Cantonese, and English with a bit of a British accent. Everywhere identities are mixed. He takes her pulse, asking if she sighs a lot and has been unhappy, finds heat in her heart and liver, and says that her *shen*, her spirit, is trapped and needs to be freed. He writes out an herbal prescription and tells her not to think too much (just as her mother has done).[24]

PULSE

> I yawn . . . this happens whenever I feel overcome by the tension of what's not being discussed. . . . The body communicates so eloquently. And I enjoy paying attention to that language.
>
> LYDIA KWA, *PULSE*

> Don't forget Cosmic Pulse. Don't forget the love between the both of you. Remember Godzilla's touch. And save yourself.
>
> LYDIA KWA, *PULSE*

If herbal Chinese medicine is important to *This Place Called Absence* (and for the prostitutes' stories as well), acupuncture becomes more central to the story development in *Pulse*. On the very first page, the narrator describes a "possession" coming upon her, set off by a registered letter from Singapore. Heart racing, she flexes her left elbow and finds the acupuncture point Heart 3 (*Saho Hai* or Lesser Sea), then on her right side, then on her wrists at Heart 7 (*Shen Men* or Spirit Gate), to bring down her anxiety. In this story, the father is aged, and he has moved into her Vancouver apartment; the mother is there too, and spends her time watching Cantonese serials. In graduate school, the narrator confesses to us, she used to listen to the vampire-inspired post-punk anthem "Bela Lugosi's Dead" by Bauhaus, and sing David Bowie's "Diamond Dogs," as reassurance against prolonged episodes of possession. She ran to a herbal shop to try acupuncture in those days, and felt "rising fire in the heart" as the first needle went to Heart 7. She left her graduate work crossing Drosophila flies to become an acupuncturist following her grandfather's footsteps. The letter she receives announces the suicide of Faridah's son, Selim, by hanging. The narrator's body reacts, and she takes her pulse, which shows signs of "shock, kidneys and adrenal glands most affected" (23). Faridah had been her lover in their youth, the one her father had found her in bed with. Faridah, a Muslim, later married a man whose designated ethnicity was Chinese but was really a Baba (mixed Chinese-Malay, Peranakan). Nausea threatens as she reads parts of Faridah's story. Stories take time to unfold: "It's imperative never to rush ahead. . . . All strategies in love and war advise us of this" (110). But it is not only her mother entranced by and crying at her soap operas, "lost in make-believe worlds" which allow one "to not see some of the awful things happening in [one's own] family" (46). The narrator says: "Somewhere, in another galactic system, all the feelings, all the memories that human beings across the ages couldn't accept or live with, are alive and thriving, never completely lost . . . churning in a black hole of immense proportions" (46).

In *Pulse* we get a slightly different version of the family from that in *This Place Called Absence*, but the topology of conflicts remains largely the same: Kong Kong came from Shanghai in 1932 after the Japanese bombing, adopted an English name (Conrad, after Joseph Conrad, whom he liked to quote in impeccable English, though otherwise he adopted a kind of Singlish), and married a fifteen-year-old daughter of a Malacca rubber tycoon. Mah Mah did divinations in the back of the medicine store, decoding trigrams with a Taoist book, *The Oracle*, a simplified version of the *I Ching*, and with twelve wooden chips with Chinese symbols, four for earth, four for heaven, four for humanity. Both grandparents believed in a cosmic pulse in the universe (Kong Kong named his shop Cosmic Pulse), but the narrator's mother warned her not to tell her father, who as a Christian thought this all the work of the devil. The narrator's name here is Natalie, given by her father because he liked listening to Nat King Cole singing Christian hymns. Now, in Vancouver, the narrator's parents go to a Christian church, where the people are from Hong Kong and the language is Cantonese (the narrator's Cantonese improves). The father has had a stroke and is fragile, and the narrator reflects that the man she once was afraid of is now gone. "Rage was a ghost that—upon discovering its diminished relevance to present circumstances—had to resign itself to eventually departing" (81). She now feels more sadness than rage, as he has become "inaccessible in an entirely different kind of way" ("What about *Shaolin Soccer*, Papa?" . . . He blinks twice, his code for 'yes'") (83). When she tells Faridah of her father's stroke, she is "surprised by the wavering in my voice . . . emotions choking me up . . . chest tightens . . . panicked . . . can hardly breathe. I take my pulses . . . my lung, spleen and kidney pulses are weak, . . . beads of sweat forming on my forehead and between my eyes" (135). A moment later: "'memories can hurt.' My chest tightens further as a dull pain spreads over it" (135). From Singapore, she calls her mother in Vancouver to ask if she regretted moving to Canada (in this version the family had moved together from Singapore in 1979; the present is thirty-two years later, 2012). "After a pause, 'All for better . . . don't like to think about past. Papa not happy living near my family . . . You not happy. Life there not suit you'" (141). Natalie hangs up, heart racing, feeling lost in a city she no longer recognizes, disoriented, "rankled by the harsh absences" (141). She pulls out her grandmother's divination booklet and wooden chips, but doesn't know what question to pose.

As she recounts growing up, another silence was about the war. Asking her teacher why nothing is on the syllabus about Hiroshima and Nagasaki, the teacher says many parents are still bitter about the Japanese occupation, and some lost relatives in Nanking. Another place of absence and silence. When the parents bought a television, she watched Godzilla and retreated to her bedroom quaking, breaking into a cold sweat, imagining being trampled by Godzilla, hiding under the bed (103). Faridah gives her a miniature plastic Godzilla as a token of love, pushing her up against the rough bark of a frangipani tree with deep pink flowers, and drops it in between her small breasts into her new Maidenform bra. The frangipani tree has double symbolic meaning. The deep pink, Naruse (2014, 231) suggests, could be vaginal, lesbian desire; but frangipani is also death, associated with cemeteries and *pontianak* spirits of women who die while giving birth, which in a way will be the fate of Faridah when her first born, Gabriel, is stillborn. Naruse points out in this erotic cluster that the idea of pulse may also be the "clitoral imagery" of orgasm. Her back on the rough bark of the tree produces a sensation Natalie will try to re-create with her lover Michelle in Vancouver, by pushing a rough hemp rope up Michelle's back, and then tying her in a *kinbaku* knot. The Godzilla toy becomes a talisman, something like the jade stone that Ling holds onto after her mother dies in *Oracle Bone*. Natalie forgets the Godzilla in Singapore, but Faridah returns it to her; and later it becomes a key referent in communication with Selim, who tells his mother "Remember Godzilla's touch" in his suicide note. Godzilla as the gift to Natalie is a story he had heard from Faridah when she was trying to comfort him as a child, after being molested by his father, and he connects Natalie with her grandfather's pulse taking diagnoses. Selim has grown up to be a policeman, but secretly practices *kinbaku*, wanting to experience the pain and pleasure of surrendering control. "Is a person who is bound / the obvious victim?" asks Kwa (2013, 52); or is the person who cannot allow herself to submit the one who is bound? Selim has identified Natalie by her handle, Cosmic Pulse, on a *kinbaku* online chat room. His own is Benkulen Bound, referencing the pride his mother's brother, Osman, had in their lineage descended from Munshi Abdullah, the tutor of and translator for Stamford Raffles, and more importantly the author of the *Hikyat Abdullah*, part autobiography, part history of the Malay Peninsula. Bencoolen was the British East India port on the southwest coast of Sumatra from 1685 to 1824 that Stamford Raffles governed before Singapore.[25]

Selim's story involves thus another family of mixed heritages and unfulfilled expectations and desires. His father Adam saw him as a replacement for the first child named Gabriel who had died, and he was determined to call this son Gabriel as well. Having a gay son who wanted to identify with his Muslim side also did not fit expectations, and knowing of Faridah's love affair with Natalie, Adam worries his daughter will go to Canada where gay marriage is legal. He drinks and complains that he is lonely and has no one to talk to. Selim, who despairs that his father does not love him for himself but only as a replacement, asks if God will punish someone who hates his own father. He also leaves a suicide message on his cell phone for Philip, his lover, stating that he can no longer live with the unrequited love for a father who cannot love him back.

The cell phone goes missing before the police arrive. "Somehow," Philip tells the narrator, it "must have gotten lost in the river," becoming another of the river's secrets. Or as Kwa puts it in *Sinuous*: "Like water freed from a well / ungraspable" (Kwa 2013, 72).

CONCLUSION: KNOTS OF PASSION, OF COMMUNICATION, OF ABSENCE, AND OF KNOWLEDGE

> I kept myself fueled listening to "Bela Lugosi's Dead" as I carefully crossed Drosophila flies . . . I heard the refrain of "Undead, undead, undead" echo through my loneliness. . . . a few thousand years between Lao Tzu and David Bowie, Taoism and punk rock, but it wasn't hard for me to imagine the old sage dressed in black in a goth music video, singing those lines.
>
> LYDIA KWA, *PULSE*

Although this chapter is the headliner for psychological and psychodynamic knots, it also partakes of this book's investigations into hinges of history, and pivots between East and West. The current hinge of history for the

Sinophone world, whether mainland or overseas Chinese, is one of swinging back and forth among what remains of still strong cultural threads and modernist-futurist aspirations, seeking relief from the double binds and psychological knots of both. From a Singapore point of view, it is relief from the constraints of the Cold War ideologies signaled with the death of Lee Kuan Yew; and the rise of anxieties about new geopolitical conflicts over the South China Sea between East and West. This is the historical era in which Lydia Kwa's novels are written, and which they reflect, interrogate, and refract into new forms for the future. Kwa's narrator in *This Place Called Absence* and *Pulse* is of the sandwich Singapore generation, between that facing West for education and aspiration, and that of the stressed meritocracy anxious about the competition from mainland Chinese meritocracies. The rise of China renews China's force of attraction, particularly through the pull of popular old Chinese stories that need to be unfrozen from simple *wuxia* or kung fu or red-lantern gender relations. This unfreezing operates through psychodynamic insights and new gender sensibilities, while also retrieving and redeeming some of the marginalized old ones repressed in modern times. Kwa's stories, in this sense, perform para-ethnographic work not just of mundane migrant stories, but of the much more difficult to access interior landscapes of the mind.

These stories explore the psychodynamic knots of life (generational conflicts over common sense; migrants' efforts to escape parental superegos and material constraints; immigrant efforts to write new life scripts); and what I have been calling the legacy *cultural tinders* available if one tries actively to recast the classical Chinese (and Christian) stories that still inhabit literary and filmic imaginaries and structures of feeling. The cultural fuel or tinder here is partly the fracturing of cultural knowledge through the generations. "I cannot remember a time I thought in Hokkien, it has always been English, the language of foreigners, of colonialism" Kwa says in a poem (Kwa 1994b). And it is partly a clinical psychologist's listening to the struggles of her clients, turning the gaze often back upon herself: "I turn from textbook theories / toward listening to strangers in my office / their mute underworlds / articulating / through speech and body" (Kwa 2013, 27).

Kwa plays in the sandbox (a fiduciary metaphor for experimenting with new business practices and technologies such as cryptographic currencies or driverless cars) of three kinds of cosmopolitics: traveling resources in theory; art effects and poetics in writing; locating hinges of history, pivots of exchange, and trauma-slipping-and-releasing knots of the past and present.

4 Miniatures

Small Kindnesses across Poisonous Knowledges

I still talk to him because it was easier to do that than to stop. If it is something you have done for sixty years, more than half your life, you would find it difficult to stop. —JING-JING LEE, *IF I COULD TELL YOU*

Grief is a strange phenomenon, a very strange thing indeed. . . . Even if I've managed to untie my knots, I can't reach in to help Mum untie hers. —DANIELLE LIM, *THE SOUND OF SCH*

They are moving me out, you know, into another neighborhood. They keep saying it will be a. What. An upgrade. The building will be for people like me—old ones who have nobody, no children, or children who don't want them. —JING-JING LEE, *IF I COULD TELL YOU*

I received a few messages as a result of the notices I put up. None of them have led me to finding my family but almost all of them have led me to kindness. . . . I am sorry that you've lost people too. I cannot imagine how hard it was for you to tell me this and I wish you all the best for your future. —JING-JING LEE, *HOW WE DISAPPEARED*

Meaning can only be found in that flow, in that moving forward. —DANIELLE LIM, *THE SOUND OF SCH*

My father used to say that the most powerful stirrings are the rhythms we cannot see . . . elusive, unseen, like a poem that can never be read. —DANIELLE LIM, *TRAFALGAR SUNRISE*

This chapter turns from documentary film, epic-scale national stories, and archives of available prosthetic tales to miniatures and close-ups of mended and patched lives, focusing on threads of kindness across poisonous knowledges. Poisonous knowledge is a term I take from the anthropologist Veena Das (2000). She writes of women who not only underwent trauma during Partition, when India and Pakistan were established as separate nation-states, but who cannot really speak of what happened or who did what to them, lest those bits of knowledge further tear apart the families in which they found shelter, often accepting subordinate or marginal positions. Fear of the unspeakable can be socially powerful or equally psychologically powerful in what Das calls "ordinary life," as in Jing-Jing Lee's accounts of stigma, silences, and repressions that return in other forms (obsessive quirks, letters unsent, white lies), and in Danielle Lim's accounts of illnesses that have ravaged families across the years, whether leprosy and tuberculosis in the 1940s, viral pandemics today (SARS in 2003; COVID-19 for three years since 2019) and schizophrenia and mental illness; and in her book of short stories about difficulties of expressing emotions that result in torn marriages and other "ordinary" discontents and fissures related to the competitions, pressures, and double-bind imperatives of the Singapore economy.

The forms of writing discussed in this chapter—novellas, short stories, crafted memoirs—occupy worlds betwixt and between fiction and real lives. They are based on ethnographic inquiry, personal experience, and close observation, much like the ethnographic work of anthropologists. It is the backstories that I often find most fascinating in thinking about narrations of ordinary people, creative writers, and ethnographers. Ethnographies, too, are more than just collections of fact glued together with theory. They can have philosophical and therapeutic ambitions or implications. The best ethnographies can spark generations-long discussions and debates about the organization and meaning of life beyond the local worlds they describe. Those local worlds, in their rich specificity (the Trobriand kula ring, falling Azande granaries, and so on), inversely, become the very elements or tokens of these discussions. They are invoked for similarity and difference, and their descriptive features are not just local color but, in their contextual complexity, generative (exchange theory; modes of rationality; risk and hazard). So, too, well-crafted creative writing based on "true" stories.

The writing of miniatures (as painting analogues) or close-ups (as film analogues) depends upon glances and the mobility of perspective. Persian miniature paintings, as anthropologist Nahal Naficy (2007) points out, are often divided into two views, and very often have figures peeking out from behind bushes or rocks, expressing surprise with a hand to their mouth, or otherwise instilling a sense of hidden activity to which one needs to pay attention and try to decipher. Similarly in cinema, master shots, according to Francis Ford Coppola (2017), are establishing scenes held for long enough, within which the viewer can focus on whatever details their eye catches, and the camera then can pick out what to zoom in on. Jing-Jing Lee's two short novels sketch emotional features of Singapore's postwar development: of 1945 (the end of World War II followed by the Malayan Emergency and insurgency) with children lost and replaced; of 1980s urban renewal (with children moved from kampongs to high-rise apartments; and of the 2000s, as elders are moved again from apartments to small senior studio apartments. Danielle Lim's novel and memoir present complicating emotional features of public health crises over the same period surrounding leprosy (Hansen's disease) lasting until 1968, SARS in 2003, and nervous breakdown and schizophrenia from 1961 to 1994. The suffering (in Buddhist terms) or struggles (in Marxist ones) and coping (in Aquarian New Age ones) are of three generations: the impoverished, dialect-speaking, immigrant generation; the working-class, upwardly mobile, education-driven second generation; and an English-educated third generation, whose successful children will become the current fourth generation, comfortable on the international stage.

CLOSE-UPS: KNOTS OF SILENCE IN THREE GENERATIONS OF DISPLACEMENTS

If Sandi Tan's *The Black Isle* (2012a) is a big "technicolor" panorama and "master shot" novel (see chapter 2), Jing-Jing Lee's novels *If I Could Tell You* (2013) and *How We Disappeared* (2018) are miniatures and close-ups of the psychology of silences in the intimate lives of survivors of World War II and the Cold War and the difficulties of expressing emotions in their families. In this, they overlap to some extent with a novella by the psychiatrist Kua Ee Heok about a group of aging men who come to a day center run by the Woodbridge Hospital and Institute for Mental Health, and who eventually (after a suicide attempt of one of their members) learn that talking about their war experiences is therapeutic for them, their families, and their generational age-mates, thanks to speaking on a radio program (Kua 2007; see also Fischer 2015). In Jing-Jing Lee's novels, the primary narrators are, instead, women, two of whom are former comfort women, whose lives are intertwined in ways we (and they) only discover at the end.

Much of the psychosocial interest is not merely in blockages to narration, but in the ways in which people deal in small kindnesses with people who are psychologically damaged in their deep interiors, who do not have ways to recognize themselves as generationally sharing these traumas, and who thus suffer alone. These are people who feel parts of their pasts to be unspeakable and likely to spark further interpersonal damage if spoken (poisonous knowledge), yet otherwise live more or less normal lives shadowed and infiltrated by their silenced experiences (their descent into ordinary lives). "Never, never tell anyone, not even your husband," the mother of Wang Di (unkindly named "to hope for a brother") tells her after the war, referring to her life in a Japanese brothel (Lee 2018, 4, 279). And, indeed, when her gentle husband (who has his own traumas) attempts to get her to talk, her body revolts, freezing, eyes widening, vomiting. Fear is visceral.

The husband dies. A young emergency doctor attempts unsuccessful chest compressions on the husband, attempting to splice the life back together as with a sputtering film strip. The husband had not wanted to move into the new Flats for Old Folks. He had said he would rather die; "elderly people living with other useless elderly people, what a foolish idea" (92). Even before he dies, Wang Di takes to collecting cardboard boxes, soda cans, and various small items. This obsession has to do with her inability to tell her older husband about her time as a comfort woman. It is a kind of acting out, a neurophysical obsessive compulsion, from the time in the brothel where women kept candy wrappings and other tiny colorful objects, fragmented possessions. She cannot tell him, even though he knows. He had even pinned up prompts on the wall, pictures of Lee Kuan Yew shaking hands with the Japanese prime minister, and pictures of two Korean former comfort women, one of whom she fantasized was a colleague from the brothels.

In the end, it is to a grandson's *tape recorder* that the old woman tells her story. And more: it is *only* to the grandson she can tell it. She cannot tell it to oral history, professional interviewers. Her husband had voluntarily gone to the National Archives, to record for the public record his wartime experiences. He did this after she had *refused* to listen to his wartime stories. It was as if he had to tell them to someone, and if she would not hear them, then he would tell them to a public memory repository. He had encouraged her, saying, "what the unsaid did to people ate them from the inside." But he understood, everyone must do it in his or her own way, in their own time.

Jing-Jing Lee's earlier *If I Could Tell You*, a kind of study for the later novel, with many of the same characters, and the same attention to the ways in which people cannot open up, is structured around a different trauma in the lives of Singaporeans, not the current displacement into buildings with single apartments for seniors, but the earlier displacement from kampongs into high-rise apartment blocks. The setting is Block 206 on Red Hill. Red Hill is a landmark residential area (one that figures prominently also in Sandi Tan's *The Black Isle*), once an area of gambier and pepper plantations, then waste land, then cemeteries up on the hills and rubbish dumps down in the swamps, then brickworks and industrial factories surrounded by squatter settlements. Before and immediately after World War II it was the slum area in which Cassandra's brother and father lived (in *The Black Isle*), where two infamous fires, in 1961 and 1963, burned down the slums so that the land could be used for new housing.[1] It was where Samsui women (single, immigrant women laborers, mainly from Fujian, famed for their hard labor in construction work) are now among the eldest residents. The first public housing (Red Hill Close) was put up by the colonial government in 1955, and over the next five decades public housing, of varied building typologies, was added. In the 2000s, as the population aged, there was considerable debate about building separate public housing for seniors versus reconfiguring buildings to be more senior- and family-friendly. This is something also partly captured in Danielle Lim's short story "Leo's Home" (2020), about a well-intentioned planner, who in his forties was tasked with constructing ten large-scale, modern, nursing buildings over three years; and who finds himself in a wheelchair in his sixties, living in one, and trying to reconcile this with what he had imagined as a younger, fully abled planner (Lim 2020, 123–35; see also Fischer 2015, 2017a, 2017b). Jing-Jing Lee captures something of this current moment of the growing "silver tsunami," while Lim looks ahead to its massive growth.

The name Red Hill alludes to the red laterite soil and sticky clay from which bricks were made, but also to a popular legend and political parable about a sultan who had a boy killed out of jealousy. The boy had come up with a defense against human-eating swordfish that were attacking the city. The parable is about leaders and elites who get hysterical when credit or alternative agendas are accorded to anyone but them. When the boy was executed, the hill ran red with blood, staining it into memory. The parable remains as relevant today as ever. The Red Hill residential estate has gone through several upgrades, requiring involuntary moves: Flats for Old Folks in 1974, upgrades in the 1990s, and slated for redevelopment in 2011 (Chong et al. 2013a).[2]

The advantage of focusing on characters in a single building, with only two plot events (moving elsewhere, and a man committing suicide by jumping from an upper floor) is that each character speaks or thinks in his or her own voice, so that one gets multiple perspectives on each event, and a sense of the building as an environment, not always a community, but a place where people are aware of one another. To a young boy, Auntie Cardboard is just an old lady wildly gesticulating to the Bangladeshi worker cleaning up around the stain of the dead man's blood, warning him not to touch the food offerings at the impromptu shrine. Both Auntie Cardboard and the Bangladeshi man have their own thoughts about the other, and they do not match or connect across linguistic barriers. A short story by Dora Tan (2012) does something similar with seven different voices in one family remembering life in Red Hill: their memories are quite different, and one gets a sense of quite different moments in the life cycle of a housing estate from new to old and decaying.

In *How We Disappeared*, there is a central section on the Japanese occupation as violent as that in Sandi Tan's *The Black Isle*. There is something of redemption when a grandchild manages to reconnect the linkages among his father's two mothers and his biological grandfather's two wives. It is a story of a lost child, saved from a massacre by a woman who took the child as a replacement for another child, her own, whom she had lost in the war. She could not give up the new child, despite feeling guilt and trying to write repeatedly (but never sending the letter) to the father who had desperately searched for his child. Secrets are deep and entangled in hard-to-face, yet obsessed-over, histories. Sometimes when the secrets are released, they are received with relief and gratitude, rather than reigniting conflict and pain. In a way, this resonates with the *kinbaku* exercises in Lydia Kwa's novel *Pulse*, with pain, fear, and learning to trust again.

DIGNITY, CARE, AND THE SOCIAL BURDENS OF LEPROSY, SARS, AND SCHIZOPHRENIA

Danielle Lim's novel *Trafalgar Sunrise* (2018) and her earlier memoir *The Sound of Sch* (2014) take on the mental health landscape and what she calls the "three brothers" of the most feared diseases—leprosy (the eldest brother), tuberculosis (the second brother), and mental illness (the most recent to gain public attention for its burden on society). In *Trafalgar Sunrise*, leprosy as a social scourge, cause for quarantine, and stigma born of fear is succeeded by the SARS pandemic in 2003, the narrator-nurse having been cured of leprosy and now caring for cancer patients during the SARS panic. Tuberculosis is replaced by SARS as the airborne droplet disease of concern, and viral infection succeeds bacterial infections, not that bacterial infections are no longer of concern, and indeed we are treated to an episode of MRSA (methicillin-resistant *Staphylococcus aureus*, which is difficult to treat and often acquired in hospitals) and thus the feared coming crisis of antimicrobial resistance, in which our antibiotics will become increasingly ineffective. In pandemics, public health, medicine, and pharmacology are overwhelmed with urgent searches for cures, emergency mitigation regulations, and the stress of living under constant uncertainty and biological terror that one's neighbors or fellow citizens or fellow patients and even health-care workers might infect one. Under these conditions we are guided through women's worlds as caretakers: two girls looking out for each other in the Trafalgar leper home and their lives afterward; a nurse in a cancer ward during the SARS epidemic; and a daughter-mother pair in *The Sound of Sch*, caring for the mother's schizophrenic brother. The two books centrally explore the "white ink" longing for lost daughters and mothers.

Trafalgar Sunrise is a story of the SARS pandemic (of 2003) haunted by the leprosy story of a cancer nurse, a reminder of the parallels of uncertainty, quarantine, and stigma. The narrator, who later becomes a nurse, is torn away as a thirteen-year-old from her father, a "humble physician who came all the way from a distant land in search of a better life, only to have his wife and daughter taken from him" (D. Lim 2018, 172). There is "a terrible sadness in his eyes . . . as he nodded to me" as she is taken away to the leprosy asylum, giving her as a keepsake his wife's (her deceased mother's) wedding ring. After she is cured in 1968, she goes home: "My father still lived in the small shophouse in Chinatown above the Chinese medicine shop where he worked," taking people's pulses, prescribing herbal medicines (73). The mother committed suicide four years after being raped by a Japanese soldier, one year after Grace, as she would come to be called, was born. At Trafalgar, she bonds with a slightly older girl, Alice, who becomes pregnant by Henry, a male teacher and patient (there is a school in the compound that takes patients through O-Level exams), whose leprosy advances painfully, wasting his muscles. Alice is persuaded to give up the child for adoption to a family in Perth, Australia, for fear, she is told, that the child otherwise will become infected. Alice finds a source of pain medications for Henry, but he needs more and more until he overdoses, leaving Alice with a second deep sense of loss and guilt. When we meet Alice in the SARS story, she is in the terminal stages of cancer, and Grace supervises her care as she goes into a hospice. The hospice is run by Franciscan nuns, as was Trafalgar, tucked away "in the far reaches of Yio Chu Kang," on the land of a former rubber plantation, beside Woodbridge Hospital and the Institute for Mental Health. Woodbridge is referred to above in Kua Ee Heok's novella (Kua 2007), as well as in Lydia Kwa's *Sinuous* (2013), and it is where the narrator's uncle in *The Sound of Sch* is taken.

By the time of SARS in 2003, both Alice and Grace have new families. They revel in the miracle of their cures and ability to lead normal lives; yet they are guarded in what they feel able to reveal. The chapters of *Trafalgar Sunrise* move back and forth between on the one hand the "ethnographic present" of the SARS crisis experienced both in a cancer ward and in the nurse's home; and, on the other, the fear in lives that survived with poisonous knowledge and deep fears of telling, living with the memories and the stigma of leprosy. The fears of the SARS crisis are told as they intensify—the masking and personal protective equipment (PPE), washing, disinfecting, and other protocols gradually increase until no visitors are allowed in the hospital, even to visit the dying. A taxi driver tells her a wet market (Pasir Panjang Wholesale Market) has been identified as a source of infections and has been closed (a true event), and notes other places taxi drivers have been warned about. Feeling worried for him, guilt for taking a taxi, and for possibly increasing his risk, she suddenly asks him to let her out, and begins walking despite the impossible distance she has to travel. But he stops, gets out, and opens the door, saying in Singlish, "What to do?" She cannot walk that far, he says, and he says he will take her. It is one of many such kindnesses across lines of fear; although there are also stories of taxis which refuse to pick up nurses and doctors for fear of infection.[3] Her granddaughter runs up to greet her, throwing her head against the nurse's uniform. In a panic, she goes to shower, admonishes her son to instruct the child not to hug grandma when she is in uniform, and says that perhaps they should not meet until SARS is brought under control.

An earlier fright was not so benign. Her firstborn, a one-year-old, develops a rash on his stomach. In a panic, she insists they must take him to the doctor for a skin test. The husband is bewildered: Skin test for what? It is just a rash. Consumed with fear, and maternal protectiveness, she tells him what she has tried to tell him several times earlier, but never could work up the courage to do so: that she has had leprosy. It was such a rash that caused her teacher in grade school to refer her to the doctor and her sudden removal to Trafalgar. The marriage nearly implodes.

In their new families, Grace has a daughter, a son, and a granddaughter. The daughter follows in the footsteps of her nurse mother and doctor grandfather: she is a clinical-trial analyst in San Francisco. Alice also has a now grown daughter, Karen. As Alice's health declines, her thoughts turn more insistently, if tentatively, toward her first daughter, Wei Ming, now called Helena, living in Perth: Would she want to hear from her birth mother or not want her life upset? Grace contacts Helena, who after a tense debate with her husband, decides she must see her birth mother, despite the deepening SARS crisis in Singapore—it is not clear that visitors will be allowed into hospitals desperately trying to keep the virus out. In the meantime, Karen has prodded Auntie Grace about the cure for leprosy, which Grace remembers as dapsone and then a multi-drug treatment. They wonder who had discovered the treatment.

This quest for knowledge of the cure for leprosy, as understood by ordinary people, continues uncannily throughout most of the novel, shadowing the real time multiple and conflicting claims made by scientists for credit for discovering a cure. At issue, as frequently in science and medicine, are time frames and what counts as novelty or a breakthrough.[4] The lingering stigma makes it hard to ask for clarification. With some trepidation, Grace casually asks a doctor, but he only vaguely knows the drugs to give, since it no longer represents a concern; doctors do not see leprosy cases anymore. He does not know who discovered the therapy, and when he asks Grace why she is interested, she deflects the question, "Oh, a friend asked." She then asks a French Franciscan nun at the hospice, who says she is not sure, maybe a German, but, being French, she thinks the Pasteur Institute in Paris. Grace takes this with a grain of salt, given the rivalry between France and Germany. Karen does some research and finds it is Gerhard Domagk, working for Bayer, who was given a Nobel Prize for it, but was forced by the Nazi government to decline the prize. (It turns out the discovery of the treatment is more complicated, and others were involved, but the novelistic point is that such things are subject to claims and counterclaims, and it depends on what degree of specificity is required.)[5]

The stigma of mental illness and schizophrenia is perhaps even more daunting, and in combination, Danielle Lim's first novel and memoir are efforts to show how disease burdens, and their concomitant care, are widely distributed in a population, something often harder to see through statistical categories of differential diagnostics and social correlations (that is, disease causation rather than the social burden of illness). The title, *The Sound of Sch*, is the sound both of a broom sweeping up leaves and of rubber slippers or flip-flops sliding along the floor. It is also, of course, the first sound of schizophrenia, an ill-defined illness category, that once was categorially applied to persons for life (madman), but which has come to be recognized as more often episodic relapses that often can be controlled with medication. It is, in Lim's prosody, a philosophical query: "Can a life weave along the same notes and yet come to play forth different sounds? . . . Perhaps each of our lives has its own sound, meandering alone amidst other sounds, and sometimes, another sound comes along mirroring the first, moving in tandem, nudging the first along. Music? Who cares to listen? Well, you never know" (Lim 2014, 13). Although a memoir, *The Sound of Sch* is written in novelistic form, with dialogue and a first-person narrator in the present tense, who begins as a child and evolves into a young woman, a scholar at Oxford University. The voice of a child is a vehicle for explaining the world, the ethnographic attitude of needing things explained in local cultural idiom, and it too evolves as the text adds layers of knowledge as it proceeds, so that one is more richly informed toward the end. Like *Trafalgar Sunrise*, this is a third-generation story, of the children and grandchildren of immigrants rising from the working class and lower middle class to be university educated.

This is achingly clear through both the lifelines of the immigrant grandparent generation and the difficult lives of Seng, the young man of great promise who becomes mentally ill, and his sister Ah Chu, who gives up her own scholarly promise to care for him and her arthritic mother. Ah Chu is eventually rewarded by both of her daughters going to Oxford. Language, again, is a marker of social position. The grandparents speak only Hokkien. The grandfather came from Fujian aged forty-five, leaving behind a wife and son, and remarries in Singapore at age sixty-five. The grandmother is tiny and hunched over from a life of being a water carrier and then a washer woman, and so suffers increasingly painful rheumatoid arthritis. Ah Chu's husband Ah Lim (aka Steve), is Peranakan and speaks only English and Malay. Seng speaks Mandarin, Hokkien, and some English. A top student, he was admitted to Nanyang (Nantu) University (today Nanyang Technological University), but declined to go so that the family could afford to send his younger sister, Chu, to the prestigious, English-medium, Raffles

Girls' School, where she proved to be a top student. We do not know what precipitated Seng's illness, but early on his girlfriend breaks up with him, and he sinks into depression. Various biological causes are also speculated about: that having an older father correlates with children's schizophrenia; that viruses in pregnant women (influenza, rubella) can have that effect on the fetus, a reaction of the mother's immune system. Seng wanders, talks to himself, spends long periods just sitting and smoking and reading the newspaper. There is a "cacophony inside his mind, silence outside" (Lim 2014). Complaints by neighbors cause the police to take him to Woodbridge Hospital, where the psychiatrist tells Seng's mother he has schizophrenia. "What?" she says, not understanding. He begins to repeat the name of the mental illness but stops himself, "That's sch . . . never mind" (24), and continues that they have caught the mental breakdown early and it can be treated and probably cured. "Sch" becomes a sonic refrain in the novel. The mother is terrified of electricity going through Seng's brain and insists on taking him home "A.M.A., against medical advice" (26). She takes him to a series of *bomoh*, healers (first Thai, then Malay, and finally a Chinese medium who diagnoses seven spirits possessing him, and has them go to seven different cemeteries with offerings). Nothing works. Seng gets worse, and, when he relapses, has to be taken repeatedly to Woodbridge. He is never violent, just wanders, gets lost, begins to limp, walks hunched and tilted to one side, and his teeth begin to fall out. Chu manages to find him a job sweeping around the Police Academy grounds, a job which he manages to keep for many years, until a new and younger supervisor fires him after many incidents of just wandering off, sometimes getting lost. Seng's mother later has second thoughts, as a friend's son who received ECT subsequently led a normal life, but given her life experience, how could she know? "Sch" is the repetitive sound of Seng's sweeping, a sound the narrator-niece often hears in her mind when she thinks of Seng.

Chu gradually takes over watching over Seng from her mother, while also raising two children and caring for her husband, a teacher whose salary is not much. We watch the stress on her build: migraines, an overdose of migraine pills, a fight with her husband that causes her to leave for a day or two, clinical depression for which she is given amitriptyline (139). Seng gets hit by a car, is hospitalized, and our young narrator, Seng's niece, watches her mother stroke Seng's gray hair: "As I watch the two of them, I wonder at how intertwined their lives have been, and yet how lonely each of them must have felt. It's as if they're connected in a place deep within . . . But what's this connection, is it the brother-sister bond? Is it the human bond of suffering? Is it the bond of helplessness at what life throws at you?" (146). Seng's injuries are said to be superficial and dismissed as nothing, but his stomach bloats and in the middle of the night they determine he has a punctured bladder and needs emergency surgery, which goes well, but then he gets MRSA and they begin giving him larger and larger doses of antibiotics. He keeps throwing up and pulls out the needles from the drip, and Chu begins to berate him for not being compliant. But then she stops and thinks maybe in fact the antibiotics are making him sick. Though the ward doctors dismiss this idea, the surgeon orders the antibiotics taken off and he quickly recovers. It is not only finding cures for epidemics that is arduous, but also ordinary hospital problems.

We also watch the husband (a good deal more briefly) and the grandmother become more stressed. The husband lets off stress by drinking with his buddies and losing money gambling, which in turn leads to fights with his wife. In an amusing resolution, the children are given pet guinea pigs, which also provide him with play and comfort. But grandma does not have it so easy as her arthritis becomes more and more painful, and she worries about Seng (who now lives with her) and Chu (for whom she feels she is an increasing burden). She tries to commit suicide by drinking detergent, and then successfully jumps from the twenty-fourth floor of her apartment building to her death. Both of these scenes (husband and wife bickering and fighting over drinking and gambling and money; suicide from high-rise buildings) are Singapore tropes, but whatever their frequency, the stresses are quite real. The primary stresses on the women of the family are exquisitely detailed (and it is not all gloom, for there are also moments of joy and pleasure). And part of the richness of the text are the observations of Lin, the narrator, on her own need to create a space for herself amid all these family dynamics. In commenting on the difficulty of sleeping in the top bunk of a bed where her grandmother lies in the bottom bunk groaning all night in arthritic pain, Lin lays out a key psychological *knot*:

> Half the time, I feel sad and sorry for her but the other half of the time I feel sad and sorry for myself because it's really hard to sleep with your grandma moaning in the bed just below you. You feel helpless, you get frustrated and then you feel guilty for getting frustrated and then you get more frustrated because you can't do anything about any of this—you can't relieve her pain, you can't stop your own frustration and then you

can't ignore your own guilt—and who can sleep with all that going on inside them? (125)

CONCLUSION: THE POWERS OF SMALL KINDNESSES

> There's nothing special, nothing extraordinary about the characters. But there's a lot of beauty, pain and also healing that goes on which we don't see, and I think we don't recognize enough.
>
> DANIELLE LIM

> The small things that we do for each other every day are what give us our dignity.
>
> ELDERLY RWANDAN WOMAN

Children are like mediators in the binary oppositions of Claude Lévi-Strauss's structuralism: they are *thirds* between mother and father, or between clan totems, that allow life to reassemble and continue. Lydia Kwa's narrator jokes: "Father was a Dragon, Mahmee a Pig. And they bred a Snake in me, while Michael was born in the Year of the Dog. Which could explain why . . . Michael was often the target of Father's scathing outbursts, whereas Mahmee knew how to handle Father with her indirect strategies" (Kwa 2000, 16). Nowhere is this mediating role more poignant than in the story of Kevin in Jing-Jing Lee's *How We Disappeared* (2018), to whom his grandmother finally told her story, but only to him and his tape recorder, not to the professional interviewers at the National Archives. Nowhere is the story more painful and then affirming of the human spirit than when Kevin's father responds so gracefully to the woman who abducted his son, acknowledging her lifetime of guilt, but also loving care. Knots of passion indeed.

In all these stories of conflict and pain, I take comfort in the kindnesses that people are able to afford others across deep divides, their own troubles, and the limits of their own worlds. Both Jing-Jing Lee's and Danielle Lim's stories resonate for me with others that I have discussed elsewhere (Fischer 2015). In that work I draw upon Kua Ee Heok's novelized account of treating elderly men at the Woodbridge Institute for Mental Illness (Kua 2007), next door to the leprosy asylum about which Danielle Lim writes, as well as stories based upon quasi-ethnographic interviews with elders in nursing homes written up by creative writers. They were told to "go interview people in these homes, experience a little of what these places are like. Then use your skills to write." The results, like those here, are often profound. If poorly done, they could be primarily sentimental, but in the vise of history, they often provide moral exemplars of what in a philosophical register Emmanuel Levinas dubs the ethical call of "the face of the other." Danielle Lim says, "During this pandemic and with the climate crisis and so on, I think it's really important for us to be more attentive to changes, especially the unseen changes which take place in the mind" (quoted in Ho 2021). This is part of the joint project of psychosocial medical anthropology and narrative writing.

Auntie Cardboard (Wang Di) is one of those unforgettable neighborhood characters, just a "character" to some, but whose backstory opens up personal and societal histories, if we care to inquire, and if they choose to open up and tell them. She is not the only cardboard collector we see in our comings and goings. Each embodies a different story, but their lives at the same time are social hieroglyphs of living across horizons of history and social change that we can choose to ignore or engage with.

I am reminded of Aalyia Sadruddin's ethnographic account of elderly women in Rwanda, trying to live lives as fully and joyfully as they can after the 1994 genocide, in a "country of holes" (*igihugu cy'imyobo*)—holes in their families, communities, and networks (Sadruddin 2020a, 2020b, 2022). They create new intentional families, organize groups in their homes, churches, and "dialogue groups" (*amatsinda*) as "vibrant spaces for storytelling, reflection, prayer and intergenerational exchange" (Sadruddin 2020b, 2022). They make preparations for death in tidying up their clothing, homes, and gardens, while they insist on enjoying life in public in ways that had not been possible during the waves of mass violence (*imvururu*) in their earlier lives. They provide for one another, and allow one another to provide for them, including the intimate, emotional "care of small things" (*utuntu duto*) such as bathing, toileting, feeding, and dressing. This intimate care of small things, Sadruddin points out, is the most difficult form of care to perform "due to the affective investments and physical energy it requires" (Sadruddin 2020a). Such intimate care exposes the women's vulnerabilities to themselves and to one another, but the care and respect for these vulnerabilities, they explain, is "inextricably linked to their personal and collective dignity" (Sadruddin 2020b, 83).

This is no small thing.[6]

5

Blue Widow with Green Stripes

Pivots in Widening Horizons

But every so often something happens on this island that is so singular and so irreducible, that folks don't know how to talk about it other than in whispers. — LAKSMI PAMUNTJAK, *AMBA: A QUESTION OF RED*

In addition to being a Surah Yassin whiz, Kemala also knew her Mahabharata inside out. She was the perfect Indonesian specimen, Hindu name, devout Muslim, slightly Chinese face, and pale complexion, had a sister who had just eloped with a Jew, knew her Ramas from her Rawanas, and was totally Malay myth-kind-of-laid-back. — LAKSMI PAMUNTJAK, *FALL BABY*

Katong before 1939 was a place for the poor, the middle class, and the rich. For the poor, it often meant the fishing and farming villages along and to the east of Kallang River, where, in the 1830s, the Sultan sent aides to "colonize" the area, attracting in the process Malays from the adjacent lands of the then Dutch-controlled Indonesia. — LAKSMI PAMUNTJAK, "EATING AND DIFFERENCE"

This chapter—the fourth of the quartet of chapters on perspectives, accounts, storytelling, and the writing of recent and contemporary history by women novelists—deals with three pivots of social change: first, between political enthusiasm and state repression, partly registered in family and local histories, partly in buried letters, whispers, and the uncanny; second, between two very different generations of women's "common sense," partly registered in paintings, short stories, and novels; and third, between bureaucratic governance and localisms in health care, class, and taste—registered in food (taste), etiquette (morals), and aesthetics (taste), but also in society's responses to public health (pandemics and mental health). These three pivots are parts of a gathering momentum toward a larger movement or hinge of history in the making, one that uneasily balances democratic decentralization and diversity in the world's largest archipelago nation. It is a nation with the world's largest Muslim population (87 percent majority), historically inflected by Hinduism and Buddhism, and constitutionally committed to recognizing five world religions, while subordinating other belief systems, older folk religious practices, and negotiating everyday amalgams of beliefs (*kejawen, abangan*), a question also of red (*abangan,* the Javanese word for "red").[1]

In her three novels to date—*Amba: A Question of Red* (2014a, originally published in 2013); *Aruna* (2014b), or *The Birdwoman's Palate* (2018a); and *Fall Baby* (2019)—Laksmi Pamuntjak traces a trajectory across seventy-odd years of Indonesian history (in a way paralleling Casandra in Sandi Tan's *The Black Isle*, herself in *Shirkers*, and a next generation in *Lurkers*, discussed in chapter 2). Like Tan, Pamuntjak also invokes daemonic or charismatic figures in modern women's lives, and the hauntologies created by Cold War anti-communist campaigns, but also Islamic fundamentalist demands, bureaucratic infighting, and local particularisms. Like Lydia Kwa's use of the *Shan Hai Jing* (*Guideways through Mountains and Seas*), the *I Ching*, and other Chinese classics, Pamuntjak uses the *Mahabharata*, *The Book of Centhini*, and the *Wedhatama* as cultural tinder, amid more recent references from Rosa Luxemburg and Bertolt Brecht to Philip Larkin, Sylvia Plath, and the painters Djoko Pekik and Sindu Sudjojono.[2]

As noted in chapter 2, Sandi Tan says in *The Black Isle* that she wanted "to give my heroine the freedom to be her own person, to be complicated in a modern kind of way—and then see where a woman like that might take a story." So too, in *Amba*, Pamuntjak has the father of the female titular character give her an unusual name. He is a school principal, a *priyayi* descended from the administrative elite of the Yogyakarta court, "a very moderate man" (I hear Gilbert and Sullivan), committed to his locality, the small town of Kadipura at the foot of Mount Merapi (59). And "yet every so often people dare choose a culturally unpopular name for their offspring . . . because they may have a different take on mythology's influence in human lives, or they are prepared to challenge the notion that a name makes a person" (Pamuntjak 2014a, 20).[3] He explains to his daughter that while her sisters are bewitchingly beautiful, she is the only who can stop a war. Bewitching is a repeating leitmotif in the novel both psychological and magical. The reference is to the war of the Kauravas and Pandavas in the *Mahabharata*; magic and bewitching are semantic, generic, and metaphoric shifters operating to shunt between ordinary life and the world of myth. We all know luminous individuals who walk among us, luminous men, and women so beautiful it is undecidable if beauty is a virtue or a curse.

The portrait Pamuntjak draws of Amba's father Sudarminto, a school principal, and his wife, a former singer (*pesindens*) of a shadow puppet (wayang) troupe, articulates the lifestyle and views of a class that is rapidly being passed by in the rapid changes that came with World War II, Japanese occupation, the war for independence against the Dutch, the new independent nation, and increasing tensions between nationalists, Islamicists, and communists that broke apart President Sukarno's efforts at a unifying slogan of *nasionalisme*, *agama*, *kumunisme* (nationalism, religion, communism) and led to the bloody calamity of 1965 and its very long aftermath. It is the eldest of their three daughters (princesses in the *Mahabharata*), Amba, who will feel the full brunt of the changes, and pose the question whether mythology's apocalyptic conclusions can be altered, "as though it never occurred to anybody there might have been another way, an outcome less brutal and more merciful, a solution that didn't so inextricably intertwine their fates like the red and white of the Indonesian flag—so heavy, so weighted with destiny" (2).

Amba, winner of the 2016 LiBeraturpreis at the Frankfurt Book Fair and other accolades, is perhaps the most ambitious of Pamuntjak's three novels, insofar as it is an intervention in accounts of the still fraught political territory since the 1965 massacres, a national trauma and critical "event," "so singular and so irreducible, that folks don't know how to talk about it other than in whispers" (7).[4] Or they "cannot utter the acronym for the Indonesian Communist Party—PKI—without flinching, without feeling obliged to show disgust" (26). Or perhaps they can only talk about it as folklore or mythology. The use of mythology from the *Mahabharata*, *The Book of Centhini*, and the *Wedhatama* provides some protection perhaps (though the tactic did not help Salman Rushdie with *Satanic Verses*). Nuniek, Amba's mother, at one point says the *Mahabharata* is, "after all, hypothetical, half myth; for hadn't the gods decided to suspend all disbelief for the sake of a good story?" (82).

Hypothetical, good story, novelistic mode of critical thinking.

Nuniek is described as a beauty, once a self-assertive *pesindens* (who often *de facto* ran the wayang shows), and now a woman who knows when to stop bickering with her husband, not pushing him too far. She wants Amba married and opposes Amba's wish to go to university, for fear it will reduce her marriage chances, even though her own maternal lineage is one of strong "white ink," Nuniek's own mother having been head cook at the Surakarta royal court.[5] But the father supports Amba's university ambitions. After eighteen years of marriage, the ex-singer and royal head cook's daughter Nuniek secretly breaks out, selling homemade desserts to a local *warang* (street eatery) to earn her own money, and to her husband's dismay, is attracted to Gerwani, the communist-linked women's movement. Indeed, in the early 1960s, behind the screen of Pamuntjak's novel, female wayang troupe singers in Central Java such as Nuniek overshadowed male puppet masters and narrators (*dhalang*), and were targeted by anti-communist forces, who accused them of propagating communist ideas, while at the same time many communists saw them as feudal remnants (Eickhoff et al. 2017a). So while Nuniek in the novel remains apart from the coming violent storm, her history as one of these singers, *pesindens* and *dhalangs*, and Amba's observations of her struggles for independent opinions within her marriage, as well as her moves to manipulate marriage arrangements for Amba, are parts of larger emerging sociopolitical conflicts and generational gender rearrangements. *Dhalang* (Javanese, or *dalang* in Malay) is also a political metaphor: puppet master, an operator pulling the strings behind the screen. The PKI was accused of being the puppet masters behind the murder of six army generals on September 30, 1965, providing a justification for the institution of General Suharto's New Order dictatorship that ousted President Sukarno, and for the unleashing of the military and US-supported anti-communist hysteria and resulting massacres. Puppet master links also semiotically to other shadow and magic dealings. Indeed, in at least one case, a woman *dhalang* in Semarang was said to have been buried alive because she could not be killed by bullets due to her magic powers (Eickhoff et al. 2017a, 538–39). Hidden powers, magic, shamans, and bewitchment by beauty are all leitmotifs in the weaving of Pamuntjak's novel, and also figure in many ethnographies of Indonesia since they operate as hypostases or the heightening of interpersonal dynamics, theatrics, and shorthand explanations in ordinary life and in the haunting dynamics of trauma.[6]

The Book of Centhini, an early nineteenth-century compilation commissioned by a ruler of Surakarta in Central Java and published in 1814, "isn't only one of Indonesia's oldest manuscripts. It is also an encyclopedia of life filled with poems, song and prophecies. What's more, it is named after a maid. Yes, a maid, a woman low on the pecking order, but one who held all the wisdom of the world," and who, while not supposed to express opinions or judgments, does so (Pamuntjak 2014a, 56). It is a book with an important filial charge for Amba, a book her father discusses with her after he finds out she has been reading it, probably, he surmises, including the (sexual) parts she should not as an eleven-year-old. Framed as journeys around Java, collecting wisdom and lore, it is also framed as commentary on the four goals and stages of life: *artha* (seeking meaning, being a student), *kama* (desire, being a householder), *dharma* (duty and merit, being a forest dweller), and *moksa* (liberation or freedom from the cycles of life and death, being a renunciator or *sanyasi*). The stories of meeting various seekers of these goals contain many *suluk* (mystical teachings), but Centhini, as a young maid and maiden, is well placed with her beautiful young mistress to observe the ways of desire and eroticism, and *The Book of Centhini* is thus sometimes called the *Kama Sutra* of Java. When Amba's schoolteacher father would try to tell his students about this Javanese manuscript, he would pause, as he had "learned to skirt the brink of the allowable," and would recite a different poem. But at night, "as if in an opium-induced trance, his thoughts would travel with Prince Jayengraga on his sexual escapades. . . . [He] would linger on the vision of Jayengraga bedding three women in one night" (57). Amba, as a precocious, book-loving eleven-year-old, takes all this in, and bonds with her father, becoming his companion in discussing this and other texts.

The *Wedhatama* is a nineteenth-century mystical poem by a later ruler of Surakarta on the journey to God. It describes types of worship, or more accurately the stages of understanding on the path to God from physical worship (*raga*), through reason (*cipta*) and spiritual alertness (*jiwa*), all the way to essence (*rasa*).[7] The poem is particularly valued as it is "considered a successful discourse of harmony among traditional Javanese principles and Islamic principles" (Indhiarti et al. 2017). For Amba's father in the novel, the *Wedhatama* contains prophecies that the Javanese will be ruled by whites (Dutch) and yellows (Japanese), but the foreigners' rule will fall and the world will revert to harmony. It is a long view, with psychological comfort in a stormy world, but whose consonance among the levels of understanding do not prevent Amba's father's irritation at "instant preachers" who reprimand Amba for not reading the Qur'an or himself for not going to

Friday prayers, with dark warnings that God will not protect him from the communists' knives. He sees the sudden influx of "instant preachers" as due to the growth of new populations in small-town Java, upsetting established patterns of life. They arrive, it seems to him, on a wave of mobilized Islam in the form of the Muhammadiyah and Nahdul Islam movements that gained momentum in the 1950s.

Pamuntjak's novel *Fall Baby* (2019) is a sequel to *Amba*. Amba's daughter Srikandi, called Siri (Sirikanda in the *Mahabharata*), is an independent painter and conceptual artist who only late in life learns about her biological father, Bhisma, who died on the island of Buru after living in the concentration camp there and experiencing the spillover of the fighting between Christians and Muslims in the Maluku Islands. She has to recalibrate what she thought she knew about her German social father and her mother, with whom she has a fraught relationship. She grows up amid a group of strong modern women with shifting marital and sexual relationships, a counterimage to the masculine groups of men in the *Mahabharata* and in the 1965 patriarchal genocide in Indonesia. Her world is modernist art, both Indonesian and European, and she lives as much in Europe as Jakarta, involved (sequentially) with men from Madrid and Berlin. The key referents here are not so much texts—though both the *Mahabharata* and *The Book of Centhini* remain important, the one regarding her relation to her father, the other the joys and frustrations of sexuality—but paintings: Pieter Bruegel the Elder's *Netherlandish Proverbs* (1559), Matisse's fauvist *Portrait of Madame Matisse* or *The Green Line* (1905) and *Blue Nude with Rope* (1952), and paintings by two of Indonesia's most important modern artists, Djoko Pekik's *Tuan Tanah Kawin Muda*, "Old landlord marries a young woman" (1964), and Sindu Sudjojono's *Ibuku Menjahit*, "Mother sewing" (1935).

In a third novel, *The Birdwoman's Palate* (2018a), Aruna (yet another name from the *Mahabharata*) is an epidemiologist working for the Indonesian Ministry of Health. She is sent out to investigate outbreaks of avian flu and possible human infection in various parts of the archipelago, and takes along three friends on a foodie road trip to find the most heavenly taste in local foods, while satirizing the Indonesian bureaucracy. Here again the master narrative, despite Aruna's name, is not the *Mahabharata* but two Iranian classics, the mystical philosophical poem by Farid ud-Din, Attar of Nishapur, *The Conference of the Birds*, based on the Qur'anic verse 27:16, in which Suleiman and Dawud learn the language of the birds, and the philo-

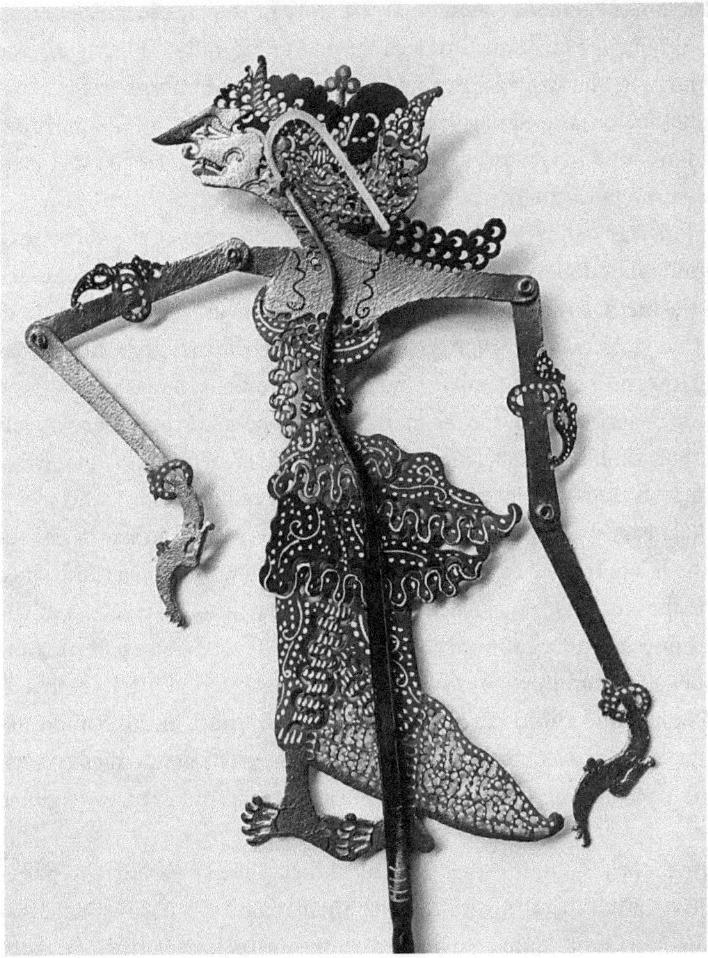

5.1 Shrikandi wayang. Courtesy of Suprihono and Entang Wiharso.

sophical text on hospitality by al-Ghazali, the *Kitab Adab al-Aql* ("Book of moral reason").[8] These come to Pamuntjak, she says, through her Minangkabau (Sumatran) grandmother, thus from the West both geographically and metaphorically from beyond India. The Indonesian title of the novel, *Aruna dan Lidahnya* (Pamuntjak 2014b), translates as "Aruna and her tongue," but in English it has been published as *The Birdwoman's Palate* (Pamuntjak 2018a). By combining an avian flu (birdwoman) panic with an earlier anti-HIV/AIDS campaign, and combining forensic epidemiology with a road trip in search of the most delectable local foods (palate, tongue, tastes), the novel becomes a version of the story of the mystical bird of wisdom, the Simorgh. The name Simorgh is Persian, literally "thirty" (*si*) and "bird" (*morgh*). Thirty birds on a journey to find the Simorgh realize that collectively they *are* the Simorgh, and that their quest to find the most delectable food found in the most local of places is a fantasy, since most local foods are variants of foods elsewhere, and all together constitute the genius of Indonesian culinary arts (Pamuntjak is well known as the author of a popular guide to Indonesian food, now in its fifth edition; Pamuntjak 2010).

Taking a further metaphor from Iran, the Persian miniature-style of painting that puts two scenes or perspectives horizontally together across a dividing line, or from the similar cinematic movement of master shot and close-up, as described above in Francis Ford Coppola's terms, these novels hold together, simultaneously, mythical or philosophical master shots, while the local action close-ups interrogate present-day realist dramas and melodramas. The realist or down-to-earth serial contents are, in historical sequence: the era in Indonesia after the 1955 Bandung Conference (and Third World nonalignment enthusiasm); its replacement, the destruction of the world's second largest communist party, and hysterical massacre of some million alleged communists in 1965; the Reformasi period after the resignation of Suharto in 1998; the Muslim-Christian conflict in the Maluku Islands from 1999 to 2002; and avian flu and subsequent pandemics (SARS, COVID-19), each of which spread across the archipelago and also were global phenomena.

Despite the mythological or classical philosophical overlay, the page-turning drive of the three novels lies with their realist dramas (or melodramas) in the stories of Amba, Siri, and Aruna. In *Amba* it is the love story involving Amba and Bhisma carried on surreptitiously, and then Amba's search for Bhisma, lost to the Buru concentration camp. In *Fall Baby*, it is the capturing in a painting of the face of Siri's biological father (Bhisma), about whom she has only heard as an adult, and the belated recognition through a painting of the emotional history of a mother. The psychological conflicts in *Fall Baby* are similar to those in Lydia Kwa's *Pulse*, moving now back and forth between Europe and Jakarta, drawing in global culture, and also parallel to the emotion portraits in the artworks of Entang Wiharso (see Fischer 2023, ch. 3).[9] In *The Birdwoman's Palate* it is Aruna's story, the dual search for evidence of deaths from a pandemic and a quest for the most exquisite of tastes in places outside the capital city. At the same time it is the skewering of the micro-politics of the bureaucracy (with real effects on vaccine development) and assessing restaurant business models.

The three novels illustrate a generational shift of common sense from the era of the Cold War—which was cold mainly to the superpowers but hot in many proxy wars in Southeast Asia, as elsewhere in the postcolonial and neocolonial world—to newer contexts of life in Southeast Asia as a pivot between East and West registered as education systems, corporations, advertising (including much of social media), and arts communities internationalized across, as much as between, East and West. This theme is satirized broadly in Hwee Tan's satirical novel *Mammon, Inc.* (2001), which Narumi Naruse (2014) reads as a "coming of career" (rather than coming of age) critique of the Singaporean state's effort to turn its next generation of citizens into bearers of neoliberal subjectivities, made "world-ready" for "plug and play" in the transnational worlds of multinational corporations operating in and through Singapore. This is also the world of *Fall Baby*, with Siri's gallerist and a local politician competing to manage and control her art; similar, as well, to the struggle over the young artist in Woon Tai-Ho's *Riot Green* (2013), discussed in the introduction. It is also the world of Aruna's discussions with her restaurateur friend about Jakarta's restaurant scene in *The Birdwoman's Palate*.

The shift in common sense is the framing of life from a question of red (politics) to a question of green (aesthetics, class, taste, gender, and perhaps even tiny hints of ecology), and finding real joy and passion even in a blue world. Bhisma in *Amba* is color-blind and cannot tell red from green; Amba in *Fall Baby* says she is a Blue Widow, but Siri thinks that is because Amba's years of immersion in English and American poets had taught her "to read the color blue the Anglo Saxon way" (serenity, poise, loss, grief), forgetting the "other emotional range that was her native palette: the terrific teal they say blazes from behind misty mountains, the deepest indigo of the horizon they say can only be caught at choice hours, the curious cyan they say emanates from certain men and women of myth" (Pamuntjak 2019, 317). She looks again at the painting of her mother's face on the wall, "so like how I saw her but had never realized I'd seen her: green bleeding into red, copperish, turning into fire; the blue but the faintest ruse. . . . Why do you need to be so sad, Ibu (mother), when you're so clearly red, so clearly glowing? But secrets are like colors; look closely and they tell a thousand stories" (2019, 38).

THE QUESTION OF RED: IS IT NOT TRUE THAT ALL STORIES EXIST TO BE WRITTEN ANEW?

> Yet every so often people dare choose a culturally unpopular name for their offspring. They do so because they may have a different take on mythology's influence in human lives, or they are prepared to challenge the notion that a name makes a person . . . For is it not true that all stories exist to be written anew?
>
> I grew up with red, you see. . . . I learned at school, of course, that red meant one thing . . . But I never bought it. . . . At home as a child, I grew up with the most glorious shades of red. Ruby, scarlet, vermilion, puce, carmine, claret, burgundy, crimson, magenta, damask, garnet, maroon.
>
> But over the years I have felt increasingly ashamed—and I cannot stress this enough—for not being able to go it alone, for not being able to rewrite my story without involving a man. I am telling you this because I want you to know that my daughter . . . was the one who opened my eyes to what I could be, given half the chance.
>
> Here, in Buru, things, as in a long twilight, are never black or white. It is a place of perpetual gray, which makes it a better place than the Buru that exists in the collective imagination, and certainly better than the other prisons I've been to.
>
> LAKSMI PAMUNTJAK, *AMBA: A QUESTION OF RED*

The question of red is, of course, the suppression of leftist forces in Java, Bali, Sumatra, Borneo (and by extension Singapore and Malaysia) and the fate of democracy, decentralization, secular (or inclusive) governance, and the open society's public sphere. Using an aesthetically pleasing variation on, or contemporary retelling of, the story of Bhisma and Amba in the *Mahabharata*, Laksmi Pamuntjak's novel *Amba: A Question of Red* (2014a) tracks the suspicions, secrets, and evasions people use to protect themselves from the explosive rages that wracked Indonesia in 1965 and that people fear will return even today.[10] Indeed the story of Bhisma and Amba/Srikandi is a cross-generational one, and Pamuntjak's sequel *Fall Baby* (2019) continues the story, foregrounding the art scenes of the two eras, as well as tracing the rise of the contemporary political Islamicist scene, mirroring them with Islamist movements in the 1960s. *Amba* is an ill-starred love story that crosses class, religious, and ideological lines. The love of Bhisma and Amba is enduring but, like the story in the *Mahabharata*, also tragic. Bhisma in the novel is an East German-trained physician raised in Menteng, the elite neighborhood of Jakarta (designed as Jakarta's first garden city neighborhood, and in which Barak Obama would live as a child for a time). Bhisma is a left-leaning fan of Rosa Luxemburg and Bertolt Brecht, who works in a small East Java hospital, and is rounded up by the anti-communist pro-Suharto forces and sent to the concentration camp on the island of Buru. Amba is a small-town girl from Central Java who makes it to Gadjah Mada University in Yogyakarta to study English, which allows her to work as a translator and meet Bhisma, although she is already betrothed to Silwa. In the *Mahabharata*, Amba is spurned by two men and is remembered as vengeful, and in her reincarnated form as Srikanda, she kills Bhisma, or he lets her do so. In *Amba*, Bhisma has a vision of a small girl killing him. In the sequel, *Fall Baby*, Amba and Bhisma's daughter, Siri (Sirikanda or Srikanda), a conceptual artist, will live in Berlin but return to a Jakarta uneasily torn between Islamists and those like her who attempt to negotiate freer lives. Like her mother, but differently, Siri is on an interminable quest for Bhisma, her father. Her face resembles his more than her mother's, a troubled Narcissus-Echo metaphor, as she tries to find her footing between East and West.

Amba, as a matter of narrative strategy, is a fascinating exercise. At one level, it tweaks a mythological story, while at the same time showing how real histories upend and work through emotional lives that use myths to think with. The play across genres and metaphors mirrors how traditional tales suffuse, and are referenced in, Indonesian daily lives, and not unlike how today's Indonesian wayang (puppet) masters use what they call *realis* (realism)—non-wayang elements absorbed into wayang from film and television, which are part of today's Indonesian reality or realism (Mrazek 2019). Pamuntjak acknowledges such multiple forms of interpenetration of realities (instead of only traditional spirit or mythic worlds) in occasional lines such as the bursting in of the giant shaman, Manalisa, "as if on cue in some third-rate TV sitcom" (Pamuntjak 2014a, 31). Or another example from the novel: while her words seared him, the look she gave was rather "like the look on the face of an actress realizing that her rival had remembered the line she herself had forgotten" (326). Or again: "It stunned her, quietly, to feel this vital and unspooled, like a character out of a wayang story appearing on a blank screen, entering an epic poem whose story was not yet decided by the puppet master" (113). But it is more than genre or metaphor play. It also stages a cultural transition, a hinge of history, from a time when the war between a world informed by the *Mahabharata* in small-town Central and East Java and one informed by Cold War polarization (a question of red) are succeeded by a different, neoliberal and cosmopolitan, global politics. The latter will be the world of Siri (Srikandi), daughter of Amba, the narrator-heroine of *Fall Baby*, as well as Aruna in the competitive, bureaucratized world of *The Birdwoman's Palate* (2018a). In *Amba*, Amba's father is a *priyayi*, a small-town Javanese aristocrat descended from the administrative layer of the royal court in Yogyakarta, preferring to immerse himself in the tales of the *Mahabharata*, the poetry of the *Wedhatama*, and *The Book of Centhini*, resisting the rise of Islamic fundamentalism. It is his daughter, Amba, who will suffer the agonies of these transitions. He and she ponder the mysteries of how the living can speak with the dead, and he tells her: "Know that in the world I know, the dead do not sleep. They exist in the same sphere as human beings. Remember while reincarnation may be a pillar of Hinduism and Buddhism, it is not known in Islam. Yet, we in Java live with both. We are Javanese because we are both" (Pamuntjak 2014a, 64).

Part of the pleasure of the text is to watch the acrobatic play between descriptions of Bhisma and Amba as undecidedly mythic or just the heightened perceptions of people in love. Describing a lover easily takes on hyperbolic tones, as does a work-gang leader's memory of a man who had saved his life by chopping off the head of a snake lying on his foot. As the epithet-like descriptions accumulate, the reader can wonder when the tightrope acrobatics will collapse into disappointing mere myth or comic melodrama. The longer, however, the delicate balancing works, the longer realist accounts of history are allowed their play of contending and unresolved forces (both social and political). The delicate balancing provides space for reflection and (cultural, postcolonial, and theoretical) critique. Pamuntjak provides, in her acknowledgments and notes, sources for her historical detailing and for some of the poetic lines she quotes in the text. While Pamuntjak openly shares with the reader a metafictional, even joking, consciousness, it is with a light touch that stimulates thinking about not only genre but also the arts, and especially painting (and, I would add, the miniature), also wayang shadow plays, the use of colors, and the theatricality of everyday life. Especially important in such theatricality is the unconscious interpersonal signaling of emotion that the characters try to read in each other. These signalings are like those that the sociologist Erving Goffman elaborated (in *The Presentation of Self in Everyday Life*, 1956), Berger and Luckmann popularized (in *The Social Construction of Reality*, 1966), for the American and European everyday.[11] Clifford Geertz enriched the analysis with contrasts grounded in Javanese and Balinese efforts to maintain a nonemotional public face (Geertz 1966).

Veena Das further complicated them, as does Pamuntjak in *Amba* and *Fall Baby*, in the management of poisonous knowledge's descent into the ordinary in the aftermath of critical events in forms of dreams, traumatic somatizations and psychodynamic acting out (Das 2000).

Pamuntjak explores all these registers through four different choreographies of courtship by respectively Salwa, Bhisma, Adalhard Eilers, and Samuel—"what all men in thrall to a woman do: he began, quietly but actively, to court" (Pamuntjak 2014a, 311). Salwa displays Javanese decorum, reserve, and deference to duty, but, in the end, says Amba, "He's certainly not the Salwa of the wayang. This Salwa is a deeply human and ethical man" (402). Bhisma's courtship is that of a demi-god or luminous individual. It also involves the physician's ability to employ dissociation (learned in dissection exercises in medical school). He displays impulsive intense love, but also cerebral remoteness at moments of involvement in the medical care of political comrades. He seems to have the powers to vanish and later to die, at his own will. Eilers settles for the warmth of family life, knowing he is a replacement placeholder, and yet, like Amba's father, his genuine fathering of Siri provides a literary wealth, a cultural palette of German books and poetry.[12] Samuel's courtship style is submission to the love object, and providing aid to her in navigating the hidden powerbrokers on Buru.

Amba comprises six books and nineteen chapters. The books alternate between 1965 and 2006. There is first a short retelling of the *Mahabharata* story of three princesses (story variant 1). There are many variations on the tale, but Pamuntjak tells it this way: Amba is pledged in marriage to King Salwa, but in a flash of blinding light, Bhisma abducts her and her twin younger sisters Ambika and Ambalika (who will become the grandmothers of the Kauravas and the Pandavas, the great rival clans of the *Mahabharata*). Salwa sends an army to retrieve Amba, but is defeated by Bhisma. Amba meanwhile falls in love with her captor, but becomes overwhelmed by the depth of her passion, and asks to be returned to her rightful husband, Salwa. Bhisma concedes to this demand. But Salwa, feeling dishonored, refuses to take her back. She then tries to return to Bhisma to save her own honor, not knowing that, long before, out of filial piety to his father, he had taken a vow of celibacy, for which sacrificial good deed he had been granted invincibility in battle and the right to determine how and when he would die. Bhisma, albeit grief-stricken, also turns her away. Abandoned by two men, Amba's heart turns to stone and revenge. She is reborn as Srikandi, a wife of Arjuna (or in the Indian version as a male warrior Sikhandin who once had been a woman). Riding in Arjuna's chariot at the great battle of Kurusetra between the Kauravas and Pandavas, Srikandi's beauty stops Bhisma: he allows her arrows to penetrate and kill him.[13] These are the great themes of love, grief, promise, honor, and consequences unfolding in unforeseen ways across time.

But Pamuntjak highlights two other themes, asking first whether there could be a less brutal and more merciful solution "that didn't so inextricably intertwine their fates like the *red and white of the Indonesian flag*—so heavy, so weighted with destiny" (Pamuntjak 2014a, 2). Second, she notes that while Amba/Srikandi's martial prowess would seem to make for a feminist role model, "this is not what happens. The name Amba, far from being heroic, still reminds folks of the worst of all fallen women, a woman twice spurned" (3).

And yet, Pamuntjak tells us, "every so often people dare choose a culturally unpopular name for their offspring. They do so because they may have a different take on mythology's influence in human lives, or they are prepared to challenge the notion that a name makes a person. . . . For is it not true that all stories exist to be written anew?" (3).

So, story variant 2: in book I, Pamuntjak recounts the story of Amba and Bhisma retrospectively until the 1965 massacres. Bhisma is already long dead, and Amba (not unlike Centhini's mistress), having learned that his grave was on Buru, goes in search of it with the aid of two former political prisoners, who do not let on they might have known each other. The prison has long been cleared away, though its legacies linger in people's minds, or as Pamuntjak puts it, "theatrics of concealment go many ways" (24), or again, "people are used to asking questions without receiving answers. And turning the other way" (7). A former prisoner says Buru is "like a festering wound, there will always be bad luck here" (275). The story, as told in book I, is superficially framed as a local assault case, but also more mysteriously as if the local social order is tentatively and fragilely held together ritually by sacrifices, shamanism, colors, and ceremonies that all mediate the animist realities of an island shrouded in layers of political pasts and unspeakable legacies.

Amba and another woman, Mukaburung ("bird face"), are in the Weapo Hospital, the latter having stabbed Amba and then herself when she found Amba hugging the grave of Bhisma, and felt Amba had no right to hug the grave of her, Mukaburung's, husband. In establishing the facts of this event, it emerges that Mukaburung was given in marriage by her adoptive father, the *mauweng* or headman and shaman of the local village, in gratitude for the many services of healing and community-building that Bhisma had rendered. It further emerges that Mukaburung is the niece of the great shaman Manalisa, a man "so bulky and tall and enfolding, like a wild, overgrown tree . . . over whose soot-black naked torso hangs an imposing stone-and-feather necklace, and whose back-strapped spear is rusty with blood" (31), with a face that is "a riot of slash and burn" (31). He is the real (shamanic) master of Buru. The doctor in the hospital, a Javanese who "knows about many shades of wordlessness" (11), speculates that Amba's presence on the island is perhaps a *nituro*, a dead soul who haunts the coast in search of a lost lover or daughter. Metaphorically, he is not far off. As Amba comes to consciousness in the hospital after her stabbing, she begins to demand to see her husband who she says is in a bed at the other end of the hall. She demands also the return of a photo of a small girl she had been clutching. Told that Bhisma is dead, she laments, "so I am married to a dead man." Recovering from the attack, Amba seems herself near death, her hands yellow and jaundiced, her skin mottled with tracery of "bestial blues and reds and greens" (12). She has a quiet ruthlessness, "startling eyes, a mother's eyes," and a mouth "vulnerable and guarded" (8). Mukaburung says that Bhisma had never touched her. He had said that he loved another woman, and needed to stay true to her. The stabbing was done for love, not from hate. The doctor speculates that Mukaburung has stabbed herself as a rite of purification, though it might be that her father ordered her to do it as a way of trying to protect her from being arrested. She is, nevertheless, taken to the police station, where she is to be charged for assault on the direct order of the police chief—that is, without any legal proceeding. But Manalisa storms in "as if on cue in some third-rate TV sitcom" (31), and orders the woman released. His word rules over any secular or corrupt powers of the police or army. Amba is invited to an annual memorial ceremony for Bhisma's many good deeds in the local community. Bhisma is venerated, it is clear, as a luminous "wise man," on a par with Manalisa, who calls Bhisma his brother and tells stories of their deep bonding. Manalisa had watched from the forest as Bhisma was the only prisoner allowed to move about freely in the camp tending to patients, and to Manalisa's surprise in 1979, when the last batch of prisoners left, he saw that Bhisma was not among them. "Manalisa finally conceded he'd met his match. His brother had left the island, and he had done so through magic" (37). Manalisa laughs. Two or three years later he meets Bhisma "sitting on a huge rock, like this, like an ancient sage. Obviously, he was trying to look like me, ha, ha, ha" (37).

Manalisa shows Amba the meranti tree at the base of which Bhisma had buried twenty-two bamboo tubes with letters to his wife. When Manalisa had asked why Bhisma had not left with the others, Bhisma said he had no home to go to, he could not go home without bringing shame to his family; and the woman he loved would only be able to live in peace if she thought he had died. Bhisma and Manalisa had continued to swap stories, and Manalisa showed Bhisma many secret graves and related the stories behind each (as if to keep their spirits alive, to keep the land animated with their presence). At one point, earlier on when Manalisa was still observing Bhisma from a distance, he overheard Bhisma ask what color a bird was that flew by. When told it was red and green, Bhisma nodded and sighed; it had seemed one color to him. Thus did Manalisa learn that Bhisma was color-blind, and that he must have developed an instinctive camouflage, "an arsenal of deception: phrases, remarks, bogus histories," to avoid "being found out, on the verge of making the wrong call at any time" (35). This would have been a challenge, it is noted later in the novel, when he was in medical school, where he had to learn to use his other senses in dissection and learning to be a surgeon.

In the semiotics of Pamuntjak's novels, reds and greens (and secondarily, if no less important, blues) are central, recurrent motifs, as are birds. Amba is called the self-willed bird in one chapter title, and also the "free-willed bird" (52). Birds are freedom, and as Manalisa says, "we are inferior to birds, and the birds know that" (35). But in Indonesian, bird (*burung*) is also slang for penis, symbol of desire, not always under the control of conventional rules, morals, or reason. Mukaburung, one of the arresting officers cruelly says, must have been given her name by some *tapol* (political prisoner), implying she might have been a comfort woman (*jugun ianfu*) brought from Java to service Japanese soldiers (later in the novel we learn that she had fled from an abusive husband higher in the mountains, and had been given protection by the village headman who adopted her and then gave her in marriage to Bhisma). Mukaburung, the bird-faced woman, is caught, and released. She is fiercely loyal to Bhisma, but she, like the villagers, acknowledges Amba's priority and suffering. Amba in turn demands the police release Mukaburung, something the police only concede at Manalisa's intervention.

Manalisa asked Bhisma once why he did not spell his name the Indonesian way with an "o" at the end, and Bhisma says this is the name his mother gave him, telling him never to let people spell it with an "o." It is a bit of white ink legacy (see chapter 3), parallel to the naming of Amba: stories exist to be written anew.

Amba, somewhat like Mukaburung and somewhat like her *Mahabharata* namesake, is a bewitching beauty. Both words are leitmotifs throughout. Beauty, Amba decides when she watches how easily her more beautiful twin sisters make their way in life, is also a trap. She has a different kind of beauty, a luminosity when she is engaged, and an intelligence that bewitches her father. Bewitching is what she seems to do to all the men she engages with. It is again a semantic shifter allowing one to think about the magic at play in shamanic beliefs and in myth, or it can equally refer to Amba's physicality and her way of being in the world. She is a Helen of Troy figure.[14] She arrives on Buru with the help of two former political prisoners, one a close friend of Bhisma (Zulfikar Hamsa), the other a somewhat younger man (Samuel), an Ambonese who grew up as a child on Buru, but is the son of people from south Maluku who had fought with the Dutch to hold on to Indonesia, and is described as "vaguely Melanesian" (9). Now forty-eight, he is bewitched and besotted by Amba, whom he meets on the boat to Ambon and Buru, and he becomes her companion until she gives him the slip so she can search for Bhisma's grave alone, with the help of two local policemen with connections. Amba gently parts with Samuel, urging him to give up jealousy, and confiding, "jealousy is what did me in," then "false pride, the woman warrior thing, thinking that I didn't need his love" (43). Now she knows, having looked at Bhisma's letters, what really happened the day they were separated in Yogyakarta in October 1965, and that Bhisma had loved her. Samuel wants to know "how it all began, the story of Amba and Bhisma" (45).

And so, the retelling of the story begins again, this time not from after the fact, but in the beginning, between 1956 and 1965 (story variant 3). Book II is the longest in the novel, with ten chapters. The mythic overlay is relatively light, but Bhisma is often described by the love-struck Amba as like a tall, handsome god, with luminous eyes and skin, and commanding presence, though there are times when she tries to figure out if he is just a man who might have other loves (including his underground work as a surgeon for leftist militants) and might leave her. Later she describes him as having the weight of the earth, wind, and fire, and the deepest waters. There is, as well, a Salwa in her life, a Salwani Munir, a young man her parents think would make a perfect match. The characters are all aware of the irony of their names, and joke and comment about the degree to which their lives are not those of the myth, and they need not always worry how their actions do or do not follow it.

Still, their names are often useful in playful talk, and as psychoanalytic-like templates to measure the dynamics of their interpersonal conflicts and dramas, an Amba-Bhisma complex perhaps, analogous to Freud's Oedipus-Electra complexes. Amba gains admission to Gadjah Mada University in Yogyakarta, where she studies English and falls in love with hermeneutics, ambiguity, and literary theory. Salwa is two years ahead of her, training to become a teacher. She begins to fall in love with him. But he goes off to a job as head of teacher training at Airlangga University in Surabaya on the north coast of East Java. He does not press for marriage, understanding her drive to get her degree first. But he begins to wear on her: too nice, too understanding, too helpful to others, and unresponsive to her sexual invitations. The novel provides some psychological background to his character: he has parents who belong to different Islamic movements and constantly fight over obligations, duties, and loyalties, so he finds comfort in the warmth of Amba's parents and home. But without being overly ritually minded, he seems more Islamic conservative than *abangan* (syncretic). Still, her first reactions to being told by her parents that there was a Salwani she was supposed to meet take on an uncanny echo: "The big joke—about Princess Amba . . . abducted, along with her twin sisters, by the great, powerful warrior Bhisma, with whom she—ha ha ha—fell in love . . . who was not only chucked out like a diseased cow by her fiancé for having brought dishonor upon him, but also then refused by her abductor, because he loved something else more than he loved her? Something he called duty—really!—which in his case involved remaining—mother of all bullshit—chaste" (81). She had made peace with her name, viewing the story of Salwa and Bhisma as "nothing more than preparation for her mission in life: kicking good men into their manhood and burying the useless ones under a hail of her superlethal arrows" (82). And her mother pooh-poohs the myth by saying, after all, there is no Bhisma around.

Meanwhile, Indonesia under Sukarno is drifting into closer alliance with the communists, and violence is breaking out in many places between tenant farmers and the Peasants Front of Indonesia (Barisan Tani Indonesia, BTI) supported by the youth arm of the communist party. In Yogyakarta Amba learns from an old Chinese woman that rural Chinese traders have been forced out and into the cities, something vigorously opposed by the PKI. Ford Foundation scholarships to the US are cut, the Indonesia Foreign Ministry says no Indonesian will go to America to study, and representatives of the US Information Agency and the Peace Corps leave. Amba's English classes are shuttered. She applies and is accepted to be an English translator of medical texts for a doctor in a small town in East Java. There is trouble there too—labor conflicts at a sugar mill. Pamuntjak writes in good epic and aphoristic fashion: "History had knocked on the door. Soon it wasn't content being a guest in the living room; it also wanted to snuggle in bed with you" (104).

The chapter on her travel to East Java comes with not exactly a warning, but an instructional verse, from *The Book of Centhini* (sometimes called the Indonesian *Kama Sutra*, invoked by Pamuntjak in several of her writings, and especially when she invokes Javanese sexuality): "On certain days you have to avoid heading east because it will bring you ill fortune. You can still head east, but you might do so after going westward first" (111). How pragmatic. How *abangan*. The doctor there turns out to be named Bhisma, surname Rashad. He is not Javanese; his father is Minangkabau from the west coast of Sumatra; his mother is from a noble family in Central Java, and who took to Minangkabau matrilineal power with alacrity. There is immediate combustible chemistry between Bhisma and Amba, and initially as a distancing feint, he jokes about their names, but he is bewitched, smitten. He charms her with tales of his life in Menteng, Leiden, and Leipzig, does not probe into her life, is voracious in his love making, and as besotted with her as she with him. She is puzzled that he periodically disappears. Sometimes he comes back with an injured patient. He repeats often enough to puzzle her, and we readers pay attention (it is also in italics), "I know something about responsibility. Just don't ask me about politics" (131). This is sensible for someone working underground, but again there is that faint echo of the Bhisma in the *Mahabharata* and the latter's sense of duty, which keeps him from providing Amba with shelter and respectability after Salwa's defeat.

Chapter 7 of book II is called "Precipice." The precipice is three-fold: the precipice of head-over-heels love between two unmarried people in an Islamically conservative place; the political precipice before skirmishes become calamities; and the precipice before their personal calamity of separation.

The push over the precipice comes like a volcanic eruption the morning after September 30, 1965. Six generals have been killed, one escaped. There is an urgent call for Bhisma to come to Yogyakarta to perform surgery. At 9:00 p.m., a two-star general on the radio says he has taken charge. "It was as if some ghostly wind had rushed in and just as quickly rushed out" (143). Stunned, the head of the hospital comments how strange that General Nasution, "apparently the assassins' main target and their only escapee, had joined Suharto in the [radio] studio yet had neither spoken nor assumed control of the Army himself" even though he was more senior than Suharto (143).[15] In Yogyakarta, Bhisma somewhat awkwardly takes Amba to Bumi Tarung, a hangout of leftist artists, mostly graduates of the Yogyakarta Institute of Fine Arts, just across the street. He comments, "The thing about people who speak for Communism is that very often they don't know their Marx and their Marxism. . . . In the end, Marxism, as with all the other isms, is upheld as an encouragement for people to seek this, well, purity. Those who believe they have found it become absolutists forcing it onto others . . . more like a fundamentalist sect than a secularist program for social change" (196).

Amba responds that she had grown up with a gentle kind of religion, "But suddenly the community changed" (196)—a sentence I have heard from an Iranian friend from a small town in Iran, who had to flee as a young teenager during the Iranian Islamic Revolution. There is a memorial service for the leftist leader on whom Bhisma had operated and tried to save. Amba wears a red blouse, which pleases the leftists. Another beauty shows up also in a red blouse, and Amba is immediately jealous of the woman's familiar way of talking with Bhisma. Suddenly, panic sets in. The meeting is surrounded by heavily armed forces. A bomb goes off. Bhisma pushes Amba to the floor, saying there is always a second bomb. The second bomb shatters everything and produces dense smoke. Someone grabs Amba's arm and leads her out. She loses track of Bhisma. He had fled following a woman in a red blouse, but it turns out the blouse was green. His color blindness had misled him.

Book III goes by quickly. It is a transition before we return to the ghosts and hauntings of Buru. One chapter is called "The Third Man," and there is a return to the theme of the last chapter in book II, "Vanishings," of which there are at least four described for Bhisma, three for Amba, and one for Zulfikar. Bhisma vanishes repeatedly from the hospital in East Java to tend to wounded colleagues. He vanishes from Amba's life more definitively following the Yogyakarta bombing at the Res Publica University (aptly named, and a real place, albeit in Jakarta, not Yogyakarta).[16] He vanishes on Buru from Manalisa's surveillance, only to reappear, a sign of magic powers like Manalisa's own. Finally, he vanishes when he allows himself to be killed. Amba chooses to vanish from Central Java (where she is in political danger), from her fiancée Salwa, and from her father. Zulfikar, the former political prisoner, who first accompanies Amba to Buru, also vanishes for a time. Vanishings are not endings but can have sequelae in resurrection, the world of spirits, or letters that explain what happened. The two short chapters are replete with color metaphors, mystical references, dream or nightmare worlds, paintings and textual refrains from *The Book of Centhini*. I will repeat some of these refrains in their contexts, but they can be abstracted as several philosophical orientations from the letter that Amba writes to her father (256–58):

> "You taught me not to color my world only black and white. Not to pass judgment too easily" (258). "Black can be the color of light, . . . vanishing can be the sign of resurrection" (258). "To journey is to enter Deep Contemplation," quoting the 136th song of *The Book of Centhini*, in which Lady Tambangraras sets off to find her husband and writes to her parents of her decision. "For me love could not be duty. I only knew . . . a love that fuses the sensual and the spiritual, each fortifying the other. . . . That meant loving a thousand colors" (257). Like black, like blue, "green too can be many shades with many meanings: the cyan of her sorrows, the viridian of her jubilations" (250). (Clauses slightly reordered)

After the bombings and loss of Bhisma, "her heart sick with sorrow, Amba started having vivid dreams. Maudlin, abusive nightmares with baby burning witches and gods with deformed cocks" (237). She has dreams about her father reading the *Mahabharata*, and once a dream, like a Persian miniature painting, in which she is peering around a tree, eavesdropping on Bhisma and Salva, who do not fight as in the *Mahabharata* but sit under a banyan tree talking about great revolutions and ideas to transform the world (237). She dreams of using her arrows to kill Salwa and then herself, allowing "the warrior-healer," Bhisma, to continue healing. In the nightmare she hears Bhisma saying he must leave her so she will have a future, then groaning, and falling to earth. She realizes she is pregnant. She finds a teacher of English who has not left the city, a German-born, Princeton-trained economist, attached to Gadjah Mada University, Adalhard Eilers.[17] To him she tells her story. He is the third man. He offers marriage and support for raising the child in Jakarta, and comfort, knowing he can never replace Bhisma in her heart. She writes to Salwa to say goodbye, and to her father to explain, and to announce his granddaughter. The idea of the third man could be a literary reference to another postwar, corruption-ridden, and divided city—

Vienna, in the novella and film written by Graham Greene (Reed 1949). But more structurally and aphoristically, Pamuntjak writes: "when a woman wavers between two men—the one she didn't get and the one who didn't get her—she usually encounters a third" (Pamuntjak 2014a, 238).

If the nightmares are like noirish Persian miniatures (with peeping from a distance at horror scenes), for the goodbye letters she finds support in the 136th song of *The Book of Centhini*, where Centhini writes to her parents that she is setting off on a journey to enter deep contemplation, while her mistress Lady Tambangraras sets off to search for her husband. Amba reminds her father that it was he who pointed out to her the manner in which Centhini *vanished* on the wedding night of Tambangraras and Amongraga: "It was your belief that it was in tribute to that vanishing that the Javanese bestowed her name to *The Book of Centhini*. It is you who taught me that vanishing can be the sign of resurrection, as black can be the color of light. You taught me not to pass judgment too easily. You taught me not to color my world only black and white" (258). Colors return. Particular ones. Adalhard Eilers becomes the one "who knew the cyan of her sorrows, the viridian of her jubilations . . . that everything about her tended toward green" (250). He too is bewitched by her. Amba later describes her infant daughter as having "liquid green eyes" (335).

Book IV: the return to Buru. Upon receiving an anonymous message that Bhisma is dead, Amba finds a former prisoner, Zulfikar Hamsa, a former friend of Bhisma, who is willing to guide her back to the island to search for his grave. Along the way Samuel (who had been a boy at the time the prisoners arrived on Buru) attaches himself to her. Although "you can't help but talk history on an island like this" (275), the island is wrapped in secrets, and under surveillance by both the army and police intelligence. The stigma of having been a political prisoner (*tapol*) is strong, although those who stayed on the island were given land and continued to transform it into productive rice paddies and a green place. Samuel, looking vaguely Melanesian, says his family was "typical Ambonese Protestant" who spoke Dutch and served in the Dutch army during the Japanese invasion. He is also part Chinese, and during battles between Christians and Muslims, he chose to fight "with other fifth-generation Chinese Muslim families" against their Christian neighbors (269). When the short-lived, pro-Dutch, South Maluku Republic was crushed by the newly independent Indonesia, he and his family were resettled in Holland, but he was sent back to Buru to live with an uncle who ran an oil depot for the state oil company. He watched as the prisoners were brought to the island and forced to build their barracks and transform the island into paddy fields.

Three notes of myth inhabit this retelling of the historical story: Bhisma's extra-human powers and emotional, sometimes clinical, affect; his self-preservation abilities, which would allow him to choose his own moment of death; and the names that former prisoners give to two eras, that of their imprisonment, the Tapol Era, and that of their release and resettlement, the Transmigration Era. Rukamanda, now an old man, tells Amba and Samuel that he remembers Bhisma from his work gang, and particularly the day that Bhisma chopped off the head of the snake. Bhisma had the strength of a dozen men, never expressed pain when beaten, and his "essence was that kind of wisdom, at once impulsive and measured" (309–10).

Bhisma, too, in one of his letters to Amba comments in surprise that he feels no pain when beaten or injured. It is as if a god descends into humanity forgetting that he is a god. Rukmanda puts it this way: "He'd do this kind of stupid, surprising, artless thing one moment and the next he'd exercise the utmost control. Everyone cleared the way when he walked because they all saw the light that emanated from him, and they never doubted his intentions were just" (310). Rukmanda, who now lives isolated on top of a hill remote from everyone else and affects shamanic powers, knew from the day of the snake that Bhisma "would be the one to receive his powers. His were neither the powers to perform magic, nor were they the powers to heal, to kill, to vanish at will. They were the powers of self-preservation" (310). And just to make sure the mythic is registered, Rukmanda says, "Once I conferred those powers no one would be able to touch Bhisma, alter his physical self, or harm him without his consent. He'd be able to choose the moment of his death" (310). Amba asks if Bhisma in fact managed to choose his moment of death, and in more realist temper, Rukmanda says, "My own powers do not extend to knowing such things" (310). But he tells Amba that Buru is full of spirits, and good spirits will lead her to Bhisma's grave.

When they locate the grave, the letters that Bhisma buried under the meranti tree, protected in bamboo tubes, provide an account of the "missing years" when Amba had no word of whether he was dead or alive. Pamuntjak has collected accounts from the writings of the celebrated writer Pramoedya Ananta Toer, and memoirs and letters of others imprisoned on Buru, to give a vivid picture of Bhisma's time there as a physician able to move among the barracks. This allows Bhisma (and her) to comment on the ironies of imprisoned Marxists who haven't read Marx, and their incarceration as alleged communists while it is their jailers who put them in a centralized commune system. Bhisma writes of following the woman in a red blouse on the day of the bombing in Yogyakarta, only to be confronted by her telling him that she is wearing green not red (though earlier Amba remembers she was wearing maroon): his color blindness misled him to follow the wrong woman. He also writes that Salwa had found him when he was first imprisoned in the Salemba penitentiary in Jakarta, before being transferred to the prison on Nusakambangan Island and then to Buru Island. It eventually dawns on Amba that it must have been Salwa who kept track of Bhisma and sent her the anonymous message about his death, as always trying to be dutiful in not disturbing social relations, in this case not telling her about Bhisma, while her new husband Adalhard was still alive.

Among the details of life in the concentration camp, Bhisma mentions the eating of *kelabang* (crab-like spiders or centipedes) and other insects for their protein.[18] When it touches fire, the *kelabang*, he notes, releases a bluish substance, which gives those who eat them debilitating diarrhea (363). It is one of a number of items in the novel that seem innocuous or sweet but can be lethal, like the nightshade in the title of the novel's opening chapter, the description of Bhisma's face as "lovely and lethal" (137); both Amba and Siri are variously described as beautiful, vengeful, and vulnerable (334); attention is repeatedly paid to Amba's eyes (fiery) and mouth (vulnerable and guarded) and bluish lips. Blue, like red and green, can take on various hues: in the small town hospital in Kediri, East Java, as she contemplates the ward for patients with serious injuries, "a flash of light . . . refracted through the landscape, infusing it with sadness; strangely it was blue" (119). There is the sea's "blue like you have never seen" and the pearly blue sky in which Bhisma sees Amba crying.

The closing chapters of books V and VI end with the dream premonitions that Bhisma, Amba, and Siri have had and how reality actually worked out; and with the setting up, through a gallery show, of the sequel *Fall Baby*, about the next generation and the career as a painter of the now forty-year-old conceptual artist, Siri. She has some of each of her parents' features (her father's and her face are like Echo and Narcissus) and character (both are beautiful, vulnerable, and vengeful), but will chart an independent way. Amba recalls that when Siri was an infant, one day a shaft of light fell on her face. "As I watched, the two faces flickered, half female, half male, so absolute was the transformation" (335). It is a nod to the Srikandi and Srikanda (male and female) of the various variants of her *Mahabharata* story. Amba has a dream of Bhisma's death, "a red dream, the color he was blind to—the color of his blood, the color from which our daughter sprang" (388). Bhisma reports a dream of the little girl, a cocky eight-year-old, with a tilt of her chin like Amba's, who in an otherworldly streaming light from an outside window, says, "'You really think I'm going to do it?' . . . 'I don't know what you mean,' I told her. The little girl laughed. 'But I think you do'" (376). A realization washes over him: this is the assassin Amba has sent. "And in the dream I laughed and said to myself, 'Amba, you crazy, cheeky, wonderful woman. Only you would have thought of sending me a little girl'" (377). As Amba says in a letter to Samuel, "My daughter, Siri—Srikandi—is not just beautiful: she is both vengeful and vulnerable. Those two qualities . . . are interchangeable. She can be self-righteous and full of herself, but also surly, diffident, sometimes completely done in by her own insecurity" (334). Like mother, like daughter, yet different. In Bhisma's dream the girl says petulantly she does not want to talk about her mother, but then does so, concluding, "I never wanted that sorrow . . . I have my own life to live." "So what will you do?" Bhisma asks in the dream. "I will become an artist. I want to explore the disconnect between word and matter" (378).

FALL BABY: A BIT MORE GREEN

> The facts are not enough, they will never give me more than information.
>
> LAKSMI PAMUNTJAK, *FALL BABY*

In the sequel, *Fall Baby* (2019), Pamuntjak begins to explore new social psychological territory after the fall of Suharto, albeit without escaping the shadow of the events told in *Amba*. "Amba" is literally "mother" in Sanskrit, so the two novels are mother and child. Like Pamuntjak herself, who was adopted and only learned of this late in life, Siri only learns of her birth father (Bhisma) well into adulthood, after the death of her husband Riaz and her adoption of his daughter Amalia, so continuing adoption stories. As a painter, Siri's quest is capturing complex emotions in paintings—the "deathless love song," a goal of meaningful paintings beyond the razzle dazzle of the art world.[19] In particular, the deathless love song is her multiple attempts to paint from a photograph the face of a father she has never seen, looking always to capture in the painting the correct light that will make him come to life. "I want him to emanate the light. *For that, I need more fic-*

tions. The facts are not enough, they will never give me more than information" (85, emphasis added). She meditates on light and color as she views other emotionally striking paintings, including one of her mother (*The Blue Widow*), Munch's *The Sick Child*, Frans Hals's *Malle Babbe* (1633–1635), Pieter Bruegel the Elder's *Netherlandish Proverbs* (1559), Sindu Sudjojono's *Ibuku Menjahit* or "Mother sewing" (1935) a portrait of his first wife Mia Bustam, and Djoko Pekik's *Tuan Tanah Kawin Muda* (1964). All are crucial to the story. The last is a psychological centerpiece of the story, the portrait of an unequal power relationship (not unlike Daniel Hui's film *Demons*, discussed in chapter 6). The title of Pekik's painting means "old goat (literally, 'the landowner') marries a young girl," both an age and feudal referent. It is a famous painting from 1964, made just before the anti-communist massacres of 1965, a statement against unequal feudal social relationships. Djoko Pekik was the best known of the communist artists of that period, and in the earlier novel, *Amba*, is introduced to a group of these artists associated with the Lembaga Kebudayaan Rakyat (Institute for the People's Culture, known popularly by the acronym LEKA).[20] She just misses seeing Djoko Pekik himself in Yogyakarta during the urban fighting when one of his sculptures was torn down by anti-communists.

Siri is shown a photograph of her mother and Bhisma standing next to this painting. Amalia, thinking of a current family issue, says the painting could portray the situation of a mother out of wedlock made pregnant by an older man, though Amba reacts strongly against this reading. Aged thirty, Amalia is no innocent and repeatedly operates according to her own lights, although the threat of exposure of her relations is a political issue operating according to old gender and honor rules. For Amba, Bhisma is her "deathless love song," contributing, in Siri's estimation, to the difficult relationship both between mother and daughter, and to the fact that Amba could never fully love the man who married her, Adalhard Eilers, who raised Siri to love music and German literature. It is this painting and its community of artists that connects mother and daughter, for it is Amba who takes Siri as a young girl to meet Sindu Sudjojono and other artists with whom Amba continues to have friendships, but who are not part of Adalhard's circle (a repetition of Amba's mother's emotional connection to her earlier life as a wayang singer, separate from her husband's nationalist preferences). Sudjojono blows smoke in Siri's face the way elders did to children in those days and shows her a poem on love that makes her blush.

Adalhard has the painter Ibra do a portrait of Amba and it hangs in their bedroom. Amba insists on calling it *The Blue Widow*, but Siri doesn't see her as blue, rather more like Munch's red and green version of *The Sick Child*:

> Nowadays, it's the red and green of her I let myself swim in, the way the painter Ibra saw my mother in the turbulent sixties. . . . And then it came: the voice in my ear, coming from a warmth within me that I couldn't place. "Give her more green if it is the colors of the grave that you're after. To get that sad tinge on flesh, that curious rotten ginger, you need more green mixed with rouge." It almost didn't matter who the voice belonged to; it might have been Ibra speaking to me from the grave, it might have been the ghost of Munch, watching over the sick child, aging before her time. . . . After I'd said goodbye to *my deathless love*, I wandered around the exhibition for a while. (43, emphasis added)

She recalls "looking one last time at [her] mother's face on the wall, so like how I saw her but had never realized I'd seen her: green bleeding into red, copperish, turning into fire; the blue but the faintest ruse. . . . Why do you need to be so sad, Ibu (mother), when you're so clearly red, so clearly glowing? But secrets are like colors; look closely and they tell a thousand stories" (38).

Sudjojono's *Malle Babbe* (after Frans Hals's 1633 painting of that name) and *Ibuku Menjahit* are both occasions for contemplating how faces might be seen as they age (in the one case by Siri and the other by Amba). How many faces at different ages can be seen in one painting, Siri asks herself as she contemplates these two paintings. She uncannily feels her own shadow following her into the Gemäldegalerie in Berlin, taking on faces at different ages. It is the shadow of her search for how to capture her dead father. *Ibuku Menjahit* is also a moment for thinking about how a painter treats both his wives quite differently, even if, as Amba says, he loves them both.

Pieter Bruegel the Elder's *Netherlandish Proverbs* (*Nederlandse Spreekwoorden*, and also known as *Flemish Proverbs*, *The Blue Cloak*, and *The Topsy Turvy World*) is of interest to Siri for its bright blues, reds, and white, as she thinks through her recurring dream of Bhisma's death, face down in a pool of blood, but as if painted in red and white. When she turns Bhisma over in her dream, the face she sees is her own. Red and white are the colors of flower petals put on graves, collected by urchin boys for sale and recycling among other mourners. Of Bhisma, Siri asks on the very first page of the novel, "What had it looked like, his death? What was its color?," and reflects, "He was color blind, you see. He might have seen it, the red of his life seeping away, but splattered on his murderer's cloth it might have looked like something else" (ix). *Netherlandish Proverbs* is also a key to much of the novel's symbolism and plays upon the kind of actual life that underlies normative fictions, not just the blue (a color of cheating folly in sixteenth-century Holland) and other colors, but the proverbs that are literalized as images. One proverb, "One shears sheep, the other shears pigs" (one has all the advantages, the other has none), reminds her of the jealousies between herself and her schoolgirl friend, Dara, and the intense psychological and often physical love between them that is sustained over the years. Another, "He who has spilt his porridge cannot scrape it up again" (don't cry over spilt milk), is the fierce determination of her four mothers when Amalia (Siri's stepdaughter, who is taken in by the sisters Dara and Rumita) becomes pregnant by Arif, Dara and Rumita's brother. "Two dogs over one bone seldom agree" (to argue uselessly over a single point) is the motif of endless debates among the women in the novel.

But there is a subtler and more important clue to the novel's painterly quest. Matisse provides clues to painterly color effects. His *Blue Nude with Rope* (1952) in the Berggruen Museum is "supposed to sound the bluest note," but Siri sees "not blue but a hue of black . . . the blue of my mother on Ibra's painting" (94). Matisse's *Woman with a Hat* pulls together the repeated refrain of greens and reds creating effects of psychological blue, death, and Bhisma's color blindness. It's a portrait of Matisse's wife, Amélie, which he showed at the Salon d'Automne in 1905. Amalia is the name of Siri's stepdaughter, a fall (autumn) baby of the novel's title. Matisse's *Woman with a Hat* has all the characteristics of Ibra's portrait of Amba ("more green"); and indeed Matisse's second portrait of his wife, *The Green Stripe* (1905), has an explicit green stripe down her face in an attempt to produce light, shadow, and volume in a new way that would lead to cubism: "it isn't about getting the hue right, it was about acknowledging its effect" (317). Later in the novel, struggling to enliven her nine portraits of Bhisma, Siri tries a Picasso-style exercise (86).[21]

That Amba insisted she was "the blue widow," Siri eventually concludes, might have been because her years of reading English and American poets had taught her "to read the color blue the Anglo-Saxon way: as serenity and poise, loss and grief. It might have also cast a shadow over the other emotional range that was her native palette: the terrific real they say blazes from behind misty mountains, the deepest indigo of the horizon they say can only be caught at choice hours, the curious cyan they say emanates from certain men and women of myth" (317).

It is in Siri's quest for the deathless song and deathless love that she senses something about the missing emotional answers to her restless life (moving from lover to lover, from Jakarta to London, to Madrid, to Berlin). The fierce emotional economy of care and women's lives in post-Suharto Indonesia, analogous to the different styles of courtship in *Amba*, represent a multi-stringed second great instrument of the novel. Here, none of the adult female characters live in normative Islamic relationships. They are a group of women with shifting marital and sexual relationships. Amalia, Amba's granddaughter and Siri's stepdaughter, for instance, is described as fatherless but having four mothers (a birth mother she calls Mama; an adoptive mother she calls Ibu; Dara, whom she calls by an honorific and is a childhood and close friend of Siri, who adopts her; and Dara's sister Rumita). Siri has a never-ending, on-and-off, psychological and physical relationship with her childhood schoolmate Dara, in addition to her male lovers and husbands (of which there are three), and a strained relationship with her stepdaughter Amalia. Dara has a marriage of convenience with Mahdi, who lives in Bandung, while she lives in Jakarta with her sister Rumita and is an activist for women's and human rights. Dara and Rumita take in Amalia for a time as a member of their three-women household, and at the end of the novel, Amalia and Siri live with Amba in another three-woman household, with Siri's German husband who comes and goes from Berlin. These multifaceted relationships are all intense, and much of the novel details the other meaning of "fall baby": their fallings in and out of love (*jatuh cinta*), and their falling into illnesses (*jatuh sakit*) and dis-eases of emotional ups and downs.

These intensities extend into the art world in Siri's tumultuous relationships with her dealers, sponsors, curators, and gallerists (most of whom are women). The intensity of the plot develops around the politics of Amalia's pregnancy and Siri's artwork. A seventy-year-old right-wing operative claims to have pictures of Amalia and Arif (the father of her child, a married man with other children) which he threatens to use to force Siri to cancel what is advertised to be a major taboo-breaking show, to be sponsored by a rich Chinese-Indonesian businessman. The latter wants to sponsor the show as a blow in the struggles against censorship, the oppression of women, and fundamentalism. (The Christian-Chinese mayor of Jakarta, Basuki Tjahaja Purnama, previously popularly known affectionately as Ahok, was sentenced in 2017 to jail on trumped-up charges of blasphemy against the Qur'an, threatening also his ally, Indonesia's president, Joko Widodo. When he emerged from his ordeal in jail, to distance himself from the mob pillorying, he dropped the name Ahok.)

The novel contains a series of contemplations about portraiture and color: capturing complex emotions in painting, trying to paint from a photograph the father Siri has never met, and contemplating a series of famous Indonesian and European paintings as clues to her own artistic search. Above all, there is Matisse and his fauvist use of color, providing a lovely key to the use of greens and reds for a melancholy that Amba calls "blue" in her portrait, and Siri, her daughter, decides is a semantic displacement that "might have also cast a shadow over the other emotional range that was her native palette" (317), so that in a sense she no longer visualizes her emotion of melancholy like an Indonesian.

5.2 Shrikandi wayang with camera.

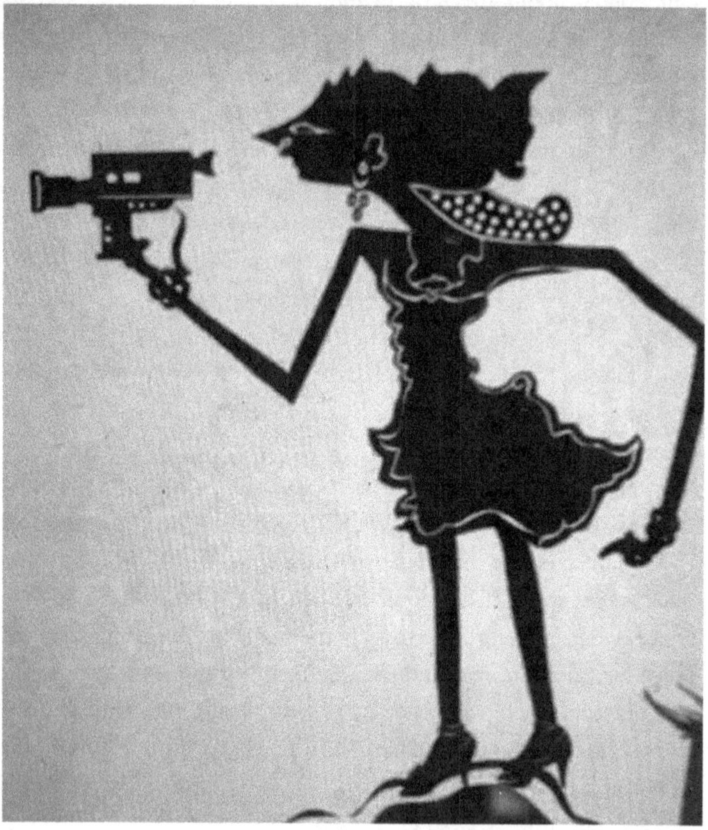

BIRDWOMAN AND THE TAWNY REDS OF DAWN

In her novel *The Birdwoman's Palate* (2018a), Pamuntjak shifts gears from blood red and grief blue (or green-red) to the tawny reds of dawn, and from the *Mahabharata* and Matisse to birdsong, food, and the wisdom of friendship, hospitality, and collaboration in Attar and al-Ghazali. *The Birdwoman's Palate* operates (as to some degree does *Fall Baby*) in a quite different world than the hangover histories of the twentieth century. It is written as a satire of bureaucracy, consultancies, the celebrity commodification of everything, food writing, sex, beauty, avian influenza panics and the money and corruption to be made from them. Pamuntjak, in another of her several lives, is the author of the best-selling *Jakarta Good Food Guide*, and also runs a Jakarta bookstore, while splitting her time between Berlin and the Indonesian capital. One way to read *The Birdwoman's Palate* is as a *road trip* and local cuisine-cum-travel guide for Java, Maluku, Sumatra, and Kalimantan in search of delectable food. A film has been made from the book, and its producer and screenwriter are hopeful it will help both the tourism and local film industry gain attention abroad.[22] The novel is also satirical chick lit, full of continual commentary on relationships, dress, and seeing other women as rivals, and gender as a battlefield of uncontrollable stratagems. Along the way it has notes on political and religious conflict: the killings of Shi'ites by Sunnis in Madura; the aftermath of the Aceh conflict and tsunami; the continuing control of territory in southern Sumatra by the Pancasila Youth—"in name defenders of our national ideology; in reality, government sanctioned thugs," whose guardhouse in the middle of the road "is plastered with face of their leader, Yapto S., a face the whole world has now seen, most likely without his knowledge, thanks to *The Act of Killing*" (Pamuntjak 2018a, 220).[23] It has some miniature portraits of the cities and towns visited, and it has a real-life epidemiology premise: the effort to determine if there has been an avian flu outbreak and what vaccine policy should be adopted.[24]

The novel opens in November 2012, only two months after the September detection of a novel coronavirus (nCoV is still the term used from that period in the novel), though later we will come to know it as MERS (Middle East respiratory syndrome). The threat in the wake of SARS in 2003 and avian flu in 2005 led to biosafety measures being put in place, especially in South Korea, Singapore, and Taiwan, which in 2020/21 would prove, initially at least, to have the most effective public health controls against the pandemic of COVID-19. The avian flu of 2005 in particular panicked not only Southeast Asia but the world at large.[25] So, the premise has a realist basis, as does the novel's speculations about producing vaccines locally in epidemic or pandemic emergencies (which Indonesia has the capacity to do, and does, for a number of vaccines).

It is not incidental that Aruna, aside from being a woman's name, the female form of Arun, is Sanskrit for "the rising sun" or "dawn light," and thus is the red or tawny color of the dawning sun. She is the charioteer of the Sun-God (Surya), a female avatar of the charioteer Arunidevi in the *Ramayana*. In the novel, Aruna is nicknamed "Run"—both as one always on the move, fluttering with her friends, and as paint "running" on the canvas, diffusing and modifying all around it. Color here works like the green stripe in Matisse's painting of his wife Amélie—as a fauvist reorganization of the canvas of perception and emotion. It is a dawning of perception, an intuition of and driving desire for delights of taste and of carnal drives, which are the objects of the quests in the novel, but a dawning in the end that satisfaction, not to mention enlightenment or understanding, is to be found by cultivating and maintaining relationships. Aruna is a single, thirty-five-year-old epidemiologist tasked with tracking bird flu (hence "Birdwoman" in the English translation) working for OneWorld, an NGO, on contract to the Ministry of Social Wellness, called So We Fit for short, but as her friend the rock-star chef Bono (born Johannes) says, "You're not really an outbreak expert. You're a person who finds joy in doing whatever, as long as it involves food" (27).[26]

OneWorld, of course, is a recent funding slogan (OneHealth) in the world of global health, aspiring to foster the health of not just human beings but also animals, plants, microorganisms, and the biosphere that make life possible and sustainable. One of the four friends on the road trip, Farish, and even more his friend Toba, represent this aspiration most fully, trying to be vegetarian or at least not eat meat or pork. Toba, from Lake Toba in Sumatra, grew up on the land and works with an organization to save four charismatic keystone species in Sumatra: elephant, tiger, rhinoceros, and orangutan. His father taught him to appreciate the dawn, name the colors of the rainbow, and protect the land. Toba accompanies the friends to Parapat, on the shore of Lake Toba, where they seek a taste of *naniura*, the local fish specialty, once the food reserved for kings, and now made for birthday parties and the wedding ritual when the groom feeds the bride.[27] The raw fish (best is black carp) is put in a mixture of lime and spices and sits for twenty-four hours to give it its heavenly taste.

By two-thirds of the way through the novel (by the time we get to Lake Toba), the satire begins to accumulate more density and gravitas, as the initial premise of the threat of an avian flu epidemic falls away, and we are on to more serious matters of art and philosophy. The road trip to check out reports of avian flu cases on which Aruna ("Run") is sent involves visiting eight cities in seven days (a typically impossible, bureaucratic deadline): Surabaya, Bangkalan, Palembang, Medan, Banda Aceh, Pontianak, Singkawang, and Mataram. Aruna invites along three friends: the aforementioned Bono (previously in public relations advertising, with experience as a chef in New York), Nadezhda (food writer, socialite, one of the ten most glamorous women in Jakarta), and Farish (fellow consultant, veterinarian, and with good network connections such that he knows he need not fight for position and that he will never fall out of a job; also a potential competitor, and a former and potential love interest). If they are relatively homogeneous in class position, they are different in ethnic background, and food triggers different memories: one is pure Minangkabau (Farish), one is Balinese-Minangkabau (Aruna), another is Chinese-Surabayan-Madurese (Bono), and the fourth is French-Sundanese-Acehnese (Nadezhda) (177).

The chase for avian flu takes us to local hospitals and local motives for claiming, or acquiescing in, reports of an avian flu case. In two cases the hospital is bribed to give cover for one of the Jakarta ministry's bids for control over potential vaccine production by claiming an active threat; in another case, a thirty-five-year-old single woman wants to be transferred from a small town to Indonesia's second largest city (Surabaya) as an escape from her constricted life; in yet another case (in Palembang) a widower who wants the state to cover his recurrent medical costs has bribed a nurse to put avian flu on his medical record; and in still another case there is a new hospital in Aceh with fancy new equipment but no patients (the equipment stays locked up as it is too expensive to use in other parts of the hospital), while in a clinic destroyed by the 2004 tsunami on the west coast of Aceh two nurses struggle to cope without facilities or resources. At the national level, Aruna is on her way to being fired for determining that there are no cases, and another consultant is being sent to finish her trip, although the ministerial agency that hired her has in the meantime been audited and is itself on its way to being dissolved.

But by this time we are onto more important matters and "Birdwoman" is no longer just a light, dismissive epithet for a forensic bird epidemiologist, but a reference to the famous Persian poem *Manṭiq uṭ-Ṭayr*, or *The Conference of the Birds*, by Attar of Nishapur (Farid ud-Din), which Aruna recalls being a favorite of her grandmother, "a Minangkabau woman who spent her whole life steeped in the pictographic Arabic and Minangkabau writing of her culture" (310). The title, *Mantiq ut-Tayr*, as noted above, is from the Qur'an 27:16, where Suleiman and Dawud (King Solomon and King David) are taught the language of the birds. Some thirty birds come to set out on a pilgrimage to seek the wisdom and transcendental beauty of the Simorgh, and after traveling across seven valleys of diversion from their goal, they come to understand that the Simorgh is to be found in themselves as a collective community of conversation, perspectives, and experiences (Persian, *si*, "thirty" + *morgh*, "bird"—hence Simorgh). Aruna reflects, "Only now do I realize what the last stanza of that long poem means, that there are things so beautiful and so impossible to fathom that no human being, not even a poet, can penetrate them" (310).

The illusory quest for a transcendent object is parodied, or maybe only analogized, in the pleasure-seeking quest of the four companions on their culinary road trip in search of the most exquisite tastes, "what folks mean by heaven on earth" or "a taste of heaven" (166, 2). They are led on by celebrity hype and recommendations as well as their own enthusiasms. There are parallel quests for sex and love (led on by ideas of beauty, most easily deployed by Nadezhda, with whom Aruna compares herself as popcorn with champagne), and indeed for the detective story or forensic effort of looking for the avian flu. Already the avian flu incidence is suspicious as each city has only one case. And gradually Aruna figures out that she is being sent on a wild goose chase (the pun of goose and avian flu is apt) as part of in-fighting between governmental ministries and agencies to control the production of vaccines. So the quest for the avian flu outbreak is a series of "valleys" of misdirection, money-driven bureaucratic corruption, and government propaganda about vaccines and the money that can be made from their production. By the end of the novel, Aruna reflects that "at the beginning of 2014, Indonesia officially became a producer and exporter of . . . seven vaccines being developed nationwide—for tuberculosis, hepatitis B and C, rotavirus, HIV, hemorrhagic dengue fever, and avian influenza," but by then she has become more concerned with setting her human relationships right rather than the rivalries in the public health and vaccine sector: "let's just be eating buddies" (340).

In her essay "Eating and Difference," Pamuntjak reflects: "It struck me that somewhere between polished virtuosity and timid competence, global chic and convivial naïve, might just be where real cuisine lies; with its privilege of texture and contingency—of self-contradiction, of trial and error—it has no other direction but to grow, ever outward, all the time." And in the same essay: "For what is really at play is not just the law of scarcity, but also the metaphysics of taste. In some cases, traditional cuisines are always definable in terms of a few staples and seasonings which are readily available in their places of origin; in turn, they leak into collective tastes and inform palates already saturated in memories of them, rendering indifference to other flavors" (Pamuntjak 2005).

Some of the best parts of the novel are the series of some fifteen dreams, riddles, and reflections upon the memory work that composes food knowledge. "Behind a stone, there lurks a prawn; like water on a taro leaf—the first means someone has a hidden motive, the second someone keeps changing his opinion" (Pamuntjak 2018a, 301). The high-jinks tone of the novel is set in the opening pages with a raucous dream in which Koh Copin, the Chinese King of Noodles, is shot and falls head-first into his soup, and his wife is urged by the dreamer, Aruna, to cross the street and take vengeance by shooting the rival King of Noodles, Malay-Muslim Awat; and, then, somehow (it is a dream) Koh turns up in Tokyo as the chef of a high-end Japanese restaurant, serving food that is like a "taste of heaven" (2–3). It is a miniature for the book: already we have a rivalry between questionably distinguishable ethnic and regional foods, showing that the search for distinction is all too often illusory; or rather, the pleasure in eating is the quest itself and the company. Borrowing and modifying foods is ubiquitous, defying all politics of boundary making; and yet, of course, places are distinctive and have their local pride in cuisine and their local food-origin stories. Even so, Aruna reflects, they are not really making new discoveries as they travel: "in this age of technology, of information galore, . . . we are talking about something already discovered . . . so that all that remains for us to do is sharpen our personal perceptions" (276). Moreover, harking back to the theme of affects as something other than language, cognition, or rational evaluation, "What's the use of language if we already have this conference, this gathering—four people who are for one brief moment, happy?" (310).

Bono, in the second of the fourteen or so dreams that Aruna has, articulates his technique of identifying the spicing and tastes in a dish: "One nibble and my mind begins parsing out each distinct sensation: sweet, spicy, salty, sticky, the spices, the fibers. I assign them adjectives, I assign them colors, I weave each sensation into a swell of verbal music until each and every aspect of the dish has been translated into a magician's litany that binds us all under its spell" (22). This is a counter to her initial impression in the dream that he is stuttering in front of his father who is testing his abilities to discern the ingredients of a hot bowl of *botok pakis* (fiddlehead soup). The father leaves in disgust, and Bono says (still in the dream), calmly and without a stutter, that he has no fear of the father, but that he "didn't want him to think we were alike, because that would mean that he was someone worthy of respect, of emulation. And that would mean I had lost. It would mean Mother had lost" (22).

A more organic process of memory comes from Aruna's mother. Aruna feared as a girl that she would never be able to remember all her mother's recipes. Her mother points to her head and says, "This is where it is—the best database humankind has to offer. Our minds. Our memories. . . . Someday you'll have a thousand recipes stored in your brain. . . . Trust me. You'll be happy—because you'll never be hungry" (239).[28] "And thus we each play our parts, falling into each other's lives. And not a single person knows why or for how long" (Pamuntjak 2019, 222). *The Birdwoman's Palate* (read together with her "Eating and Difference" essay and "Living with Difference" keynote speech) uses the satirical form of a road trip and cuisine tour of Java, Sumatra, and Kalimantan to advocate for the ways in which the small things in life belie the oppositional divisions and categories of national and ethnic boundaries (Pamuntjak 2005, 2015b, 2017b). In "Eating and Difference" she discusses cuisine in Singapore and Jakarta, the latter for which she has produced a food guide, and the former where she went to secondary school, and so writes of that city's changes with the same intimacy and affection as she does of Jakarta.

So too, the quest for the new avian flu outbreak is a series of "valleys" of misdirection, money-driven bureaucratic corruption, and propaganda of at least two sorts: government propaganda about vaccines and the money that can be made from their production; and celebrity hype about food and sex and the transcendent experiences of "what folks mean by heaven on earth" or "a taste of heaven" (Pamuntjak 2018a, 166, 2).

One of the ethnographic delights of *The Birdwoman's Palate* is that the narrator says she knows Attar through her Minangkabau grandmother from the "West"—that is, the western part of Sumatra and of Indonesia, and the Western influence from Persian and Arabic writing. The book is a wonderful meditation on the ways in which food (and pride in local food) does and does not pay attention to political demarcations (most dishes have variants in other communities). The quest for the "heaven on earth" taste of regional foods is a quest just like that of the thirty birds in Attar who seek the legendary Simorgh, only to discover that wisdom and the Simorgh are located in their collective selves.

CONCLUSION

> There is a sense that Goenawan's use of *wayang* stories ("Kunthi's Coitus," "Before the Immolation of Sita," "Bedtime Story"), Javanese texts and songs ("Pariksit," "Asmaradana"), and Greek legends ("Oedipus") is also part of this mental travel, where memory, forgetting, history; pain, faith and irony can meet and have their dance. They are but podiums from which he could turn his observer's eye on how many daily things—the cycle of seasons, lust, laughter—escape mortality, when you only stop to look.
> LAKSMI PAMUNTJAK, "THE POETRY OF GOENAWAN MOHAMMAD"

> History is like a long, twisted joke. You never know when the punch line will come.
> LAKSMI PAMUNTJAK, *AMBA*

> History is not always on your side, but for the most part it knows its place.
> LAKSMI PAMUNTJAK, *AMBA*

This chapter has invoked three novels by Laksmi Pamuntjak as the fourth of a quartet of para-ethnographic meditations on storytelling, and the writing of recent and contemporary social history, social psychology, and politics by women novelists with attention to things below the usual historical surface to changing modes of common sense, hauntologies (as opposed to ontologies), and shifting abilities to make alternative accounts and perspectives visible and hearable. Like Sandi Tan's first novel, Pamuntjak's first novel traces a twentieth-century history spilling into the twenty-first century, which arguably is a qualitatively different world, one with different common understandings of power, gender, ethnic, linguistic, and generational relations, including new pressures and opportunities for dealing with postcolonial continuities and ruptures. The device of an older or even not so old woman writing her account of history, partly to make sense of events to herself, partly to pass on a different history than the official story, is again present in Amba's letters, as it is in Sandi Tan's *The Black Isle* (2012a) and in Jing-Jing Lee's *How We Disappeared* (2018). Like Lydia Kwa's novels, Pamuntjak pays close attention to interpersonal relations, the white ink of maternal legacies for daughters and sons, and the rich textual cultural tinders that have dispersed through everyday thought, and pragmatic philosophy. Like Jing-Jing Lee and Danielle Lim, Pamuntjak also paints the miniature and intimate scales of intensely interacting small groups, be they patriarchal legacies in courtship and warfare patterns in the 1960s or the matrifocal groups she charts in today's Jakarta. Among the concerns with power, gender, and breaking the chains of historical repetitions (psychic and otherwise) are those of bureaucracy, meritocracy, and ethnic biopolitics, issues that will be dealt with further in the next two chapters.

The emerging transnational milieux of the generation of Srikandi/Sirikandi and Aruna is further amplified in Intan Paramaditha's first novel *Wandering* (2021), in which Jakarta is but one of many global settings and landscapes of urban reference. Stylistically, this novel is an inventive play upon the "choose your own adventure," trialed first in children's books, and later in hypertext digital experiments. But thematically, the novel amplifies Pamuntjak's concerns with generational analysis, especially of the "wild child" generation after the fall of Suharto, in search of new artistic languages truer to the detachments from traditional moral and mythic formulations, sometimes routed through the languages of deconstruction and de-colonial feminism, as well as through local conflicts—for instance, in West Papua—in which Javanese and Indonesian nationalism is the framework calling forth demands for decolonization, alongside resistance to transnational political mining economies that destroy ecologies and locally controlled ways of life.[29]

More linguistically nuanced, one of Pamuntjak's many sources of inspiration is the writer Goenawan Mohamad, of whom she writes: Goenawan "has rejuvenated the Indonesian language—sound, rhythm and balance are continually held to experimentation, metaphor is richly mined, and the language of the penumbra—the shaded area between past and present, personal and universal, distance and intimacy—is given a new lease on life, supplanting bureaucratese and Indonesianized English by innovative use of rarely used synonyms, especially Malay and Javanese," and she is "struck by the number of words whose ambiguity inspires deeper concentration" (Pamuntjak 2004).

As I have suggested with the first of the above section epigraphs, this aspiration is one toward which Pamuntjak's own writing aspires, even through her own and an Indonesianist colleague's translations into English and German. It is an ethnographic aspiration as well, to engage the nuances that make the world more meaningful, enjoyable, and shareable (as well as understandable and actionable)—something I have called the ethnographer's jeweler's eye, or, in a more interactional register, following Derrida and Levinas, paying attention to the face and the ear of the other, especially as enlivened in the creolized linguistic carnivals of James Joyce's *Finnegans Wake* and Salman Rushdie's *Midnight's Children*, and in Hélène Cixous's capacious gendered yet fluid sensibility of *écriture féminine*. As suggested in chapter 4, care in small things is often no small thing, especially in dealing with others in the post-trauma societies in which most of us live.

6

Filmic Obsessive Repetitions, Dissociations, and Power Relations

Still later, there came along a movie too. (There always has to be a movie, Nina says, in sympathy.) A good old anti-communist propaganda movie. And by good, I mean it was effective. Folks who saw the film came to believe in evil. They knew what it looked like. History. Its patterns and its fate. In the beginning many of the good guys, the virtuous, god-fearing guys were killed, and it was the bad guys, those Commies, who killed them; but eventually, the remaining good guys rose from the ashes and defeated Evil. That was all of history, all they needed to learn. And then there was the music. *That* music. The one that lived in the head, crawled beneath the skin. —LAKSMI PAMUNTJAK, *FALL BABY*

In this chapter, we turn to three films by Singaporean director Daniel Hui that experiment in the space between documentary film of the sort we looked at in chapter 1, and the fictive documentary we looked at in the first part of chapter 2. Hui's films *Eclipses* (2011) and *Snakeskin* (2014) are efforts, as in Sandi Tan's novel, *The Black Isle* (2012a), to deal with the authoritarian repetitions in the stories that Singaporeans narrate about their histories, be they of princes and sultans, or post-independence meritocracy involving a leader-figure, questioning whether even in the future such patterns can be disrupted. The third film, *Demons* (2019b), is a horror film (or so the filmmaker thinks of its genre) and is a return to the obsessions with daemons that can be found in Tan's *The Black Isle*. Gender is again a subtext, this time not the power of independent women, but rather the dilemmas of gay males, and even more the ethics of using power itself. Here there are resonances with Lydia Kwa's novels, especially her exploration of gender fluidity in the past in her later novels, but also in the present in *Pulse*. As with Laksmi Pamuntjak, there is also a constant questioning of artistic form, including the labor of filmmaking, the transparency (or not) of film artifice, and the social dynamics of the director's power beyond what any given actor is comfortable with. The theatricality, in the sense of Erving Goffman (1956), is ratcheted up to psychodynamic levels, pushing the boundaries of what people can accept—boundaries like those in Japanese ***kinbaku*** explored by Kwa in *Pulse* (see chapter 3).

At the premiere of Daniel Hui's *Eclipses* at the twenty-fourth Singapore International Film Festival in September 2011, the moderator of the Q&A session asked Hui how and why he shot on 16mm film when "it is an outdated technology in the independent filmmaking scene," and it must have been not so easy to do in Singapore. It must have been something like the experience of Sandi Tan, Georges Cardona, Jasmine Ng, and Sophia Siddique in shooting *Shirkers*, both in the 1990s and in reconstructing the film's 10-minute takes (chapter 2). Noting that 16mm projectors were no longer easily available in Singapore, Hui told the audience that they, in fact, had only watched an HD digital projection of the film footage. He then went on to issue a kind of personal credo, which holds for his film *Snakeskin* as well:

> The process of shooting on film is completely different because you are working with film and you are always loading film. Your takes can't be longer than 10 minutes. I like the process of working on film. I think it is the best format to shoot documentaries. I think that is the reason why Frederick Wiseman still shoots on 16[mm], because when you have a digital camera, the camera is always there, right, you just turn it on, and people forget about the camera. But on film, the film camera is so big and so noisy that nobody will ever forget that it is there. But it does give you a really good advantage because you are always working. You always feel like you are working. And you are always loading film, and checking the light and measuring light, and all that. And the subjects will [notice]. Because a lot of times I am shooting people working, and I am doing my work. It is a form of labor too. And I think they get used to my presence being there working side by side. And they don't ever forget that the cam-

> era is there. But it is kind of like a different relationship with the camera. Does that make sense? It is not a fly-on-the-wall kind of scene.[1]

Not a fly-on-the-wall relationship, but a form of labor, side by side with the people in the film who are working too; and not secret, in part because of the bulk and sound, and in part because Hui is committed to a kind of truth-telling, exposing how his films are constructed. It is a different kind of relationship that he wants to recapture, one not unlike those of Dziga Vertov and Sergei Eisenstein, who made films in the days when montage was new, and then when "sound was always throwing you out of the movies—the Russian movies, the Soviet movies, even Hollywood movies at the time. There is a lot of craft in sound. I have respect for people who work in sound especially, because I think the craft in Hollywood now is sound not the image" (Hui 2016). He argues:

> I think cinema has lost its opportunity to teach us things, to help us see things, you know? When cinema began, that is what cinema was about, to help to see things we could never see before, and now cinema is about seeing things we have already seen millions of times before. I'm not interested in seeing things that I already know; I want to see things that I don't know. . . . We don't see anymore. In films these days everything is edited to present one point of view and a lot of times they . . . they don't want us to be aware that we are watching a film. But it is important to be aware that we are watching a film, because we need to be aware that we are seeing and listening all the time. That's how we think, that's how we feel. (Hui 2016)

Implied in this credo is that there is no single or all-seeing point of view, and that film should make the techniques, construction, and perhaps financing, part of the conversation about how films interact with different audiences (something like the discussions in anthropology and ethnographic writing in the 1980s about incorporating many voices, a polyphony of perspectives, cadences, and articulations).

GRIEF, DEPRESSION, REPRESSIVE CONTROL, AND REINCARNATION

One tactic for constantly revealing this multiplicity is Hui's fusing of two or more films together, overlaying the soundscapes from each, and keeping the sound disjunctive from what is seen. *Eclipses* (2011)—what is eclipsed by what?—for instance, was meant originally to be a remake of Roberto Rossellini's *Europa '51* (1951), which in a way was also Vel Ng's (the lead actress of *Eclipses*) diegetic story; but it is also Hui's own story of coming back from depression after the death of a close mentor and friend. These are all stories about grief, depression, and coming back into society. But they are also stories about labor, surveillance, and control by the state. When it became uncertain that Vel Ng's scheduling would allow her to participate, although the film stock had already been purchased, Hui began thinking more about Vertov's *Man with a Movie Camera* (1929), and how to do similar portraits of people in different social classes, beginning with people around Hui himself, and then expanding outward to other people. When Vel Ng did arrange to come back into the project, Hui decided to mash the two film ideas together: "If I could just mash those two films together, maybe people could have something to compare the two films. So that's what I did, and the second part was basically I wanted to shoot people around me, so literally I'm Vel who is rediscovering society, which is really my story too" (Hui 2011).

Rossellini's *Europa '51* is a neorealist film set after World War II. An upper-class woman is deeply depressed after her son's suicide, but she is gradually brought out of it. Her cousin takes her to see the "other Rome," the Rome of the poor. She engages with a series of people and tries to help them. Her husband thinks her obsession a mental illness and has her committed. A review board decides that her helping people on her own is dangerous for fragile postwar society and denies her request for release. The people she has helped stand outside her cell and pray to her as their patron saint. Rossellini's "source image," or idea was of St. Francis of Assisi. Rossellini said he wanted to create a saint for postwar Italy and see what happens to the character (not unlike Sandi Tan wanting to put a modern agentive woman in Singapore in *The Black Isle* to see how she might fare in different historical horizons over the past few decades). A more direct parallel in Singaporean history might be Operation Spectrum and the jailing of twenty-two members of a small Catholic social justice movement in 1987 (see also chapter 1). The social activists were said to be a "Marxist conspiracy" trying to subvert the existing system of government and to seize power in Singapore using the Catholic Church and its religious organizations as fronts. How fragile was the postwar government, caught between the great powers in the Cold War, that it needed to stage such demonstrations of absolute control (see Goh 2010)?[2] For Daniel Hui, the parallel with Rossellini begins more personally. As mentioned above, he was devastated and went into deep depression when his close friend and mentor passed away. Rossellini and Vertov provide two ways of showing the reemergence from turning inward in grief to becoming reengaged with other people.

Hui's depression came with disillusionment and loss of confidence about filmmaking. Hui worried about film as being too manipulative. And so, the other part of Hui's credo was to show the labor that is usually effaced in films, and to attempt to adhere to a particular kind of truth-telling that eschews prettifying and hiding the mechanics. Coming out of his grief, Hui says:

> As time passed, I began to see the struggles of the people around me and through that I began to come out of my hermetic world to interact with the world at large. And so, I wanted to replicate that experience in cinema. I started out with a fictional story about a woman losing her husband, and gradually pulled back to show the real lives of the people around her. I wanted to create a film where there are *no supporting characters*, each person, each landscape is important. (quoted in Sindie n.d.)

The second half of the film, Hui says, eclipses the first half:

> It is about [those] who are eclipsed in Singapore, and what we want to see and what we don't see. I think in movies especially we never see labor these days, we don't ever see work. I mean we do see a certain type of work and it is always police work, and not even real police work. I think it is important to actually see people work because it is what we do two thirds of our lives.[3]

As Vel Ng in the film comes out of her self-absorption and depression, she comes to realize that she is connected to everyone in society, and that is how the film spins itself into a second film (the Vertov-style film).

The woman's voice in the opening of *Eclipses* sets up the theme of doubling and of the Chinese *ying-yang* sense of everything coming in balancing pairs, also between interiority and exteriority:

> As everybody knows we never see the sun in our dreams [*the screen shows sun shining through greenery*], even though we are often aware of a light that is far more luminous, objects and bodies have a radiance all their own. [*We see an apartment block that reappears in* Snakeskin. *A young man sings to himself in Hindi, as a woman listens*].

She continues:

> One day I realize we are all double. [*A Chinese woman's face; a Chinese man's face.*] I feel two women within me. In every person there is a spectator and an actor, someone who speaks and someone who replies. [*A hospital ward; lively recorder music.*] Who knows whether at some point these spirits do not part ways. Both are bound to the same body, but perhaps one is destined for happiness, the other is destined for eternal suffering.

MULTIPLES

If there are two films mashed together in *Eclipses*, in *Snakeskin* there are more than two, maybe as many as seven, one for each of the characters ("no supporting characters"). The film won the prestigious Yamagata Prize and a number of other awards. The title, *Snakeskin* (2014), can mean many different things. Most obviously it is the shedding of the old skin and growing of a new one, yet the snake remains the same, a metaphor of the reincarnating political leader, each attempting to remake the city-state, but the structure remaining always the same patriarchal, quasi-authoritarian, obedience-demanding, macro-political formation. Hui suggests that the snake can also be a metaphor of fluidity, or the shape-shifting images and sounds in a film (although mistakenly he asserts that snakes have no bones: they are vertebrates, just very flexible). *Snakeskin* is more directly about the endeavor of filming, what it eclipses and what it can show about history, propaganda, and its own ambivalent complicities.

Fire

Snakeskin begins darkly with two epigraphs: "No more water but fire next time," and "The dark night has given me the eyes of darkness, but I use them to search for the light." At the same time, we see a fire taking hold. The first quote, from James Baldwin's book *The Fire Next Time*, comes from an African American spiritual, "Mary, don't you weep. God gave Noah the rainbow sign. No more water, *the fire next time*." The latter, the short poem "A Generation," is by the poet Gu Cheng, who experienced Mao's Cultural Revolution, became an internationally known modernist poet, suffered from depression, and killed his wife and himself at the age of thirty-seven in New Zealand. The fire is from Kent Chan's short video, *Watching Eclipses* (2011), which documents the audience watching Hui's first film, *Eclipses*. That is, the fire of *Eclipses* begins *Snakeskin*.

Fire is regenerative, burning the old, constructing the new, destroying memories in the fires of time, but fire is also involved in cooking, culture creation. Fire can be used anywhere; it is repetitive, always the same elemental fire—although as we are beginning to learn from wildfires the dynamics of fire can differ dramatically (Petryna 2020). Looking into fire one might see into the depths of time, or the movement of time. An image of smoking follows. Smoking is destructive, addictive, narcotic, but claimed by its users as momentarily creative, sharpening the wits, and is often associated with work, coffee, sex. A male voice says it is the same fire we can use to burn down history. He enigmatically says that "he" gave "me" rolls of film shot in 2014, back "when people still used film" (a repetition again of *Shirkers*).

This opening of *Snakeskin* resonates with *Shirkers* in the idea of film, memory, and history being destroyed and having to be reconstructed. As in *Shirkers*, there is a wish to destroy the film, the refusal of that wish, and the sense that there is something evil registered in the film (think of Jean Baudrillard's [1984] "The Evil Demon of Images"). The man in *Shirkers* is Georges Cardona; here it is a cult leader from 2066, but also Lee Kuan Yew (LKY) the long-serving prime minister of Singapore. LKY died in 2015 shortly after *Snakeskin* was made, and in his will he asked that his house be destroyed after his death, lest it become a shrine, a place of remembrance or locus of inquiry.[4] Destroying it would incidentally also destroy other eclipsed histories of its previous owners, including a nutmeg plantation owned briefly by a Scotsman, a Dutch builder of the house itself, and the Jewish merchant-philanthropist Sir Manasseh Meyer.[5] For Sandi Tan, the "something evil" in *Shirkers* is located in Georges Cardona's perverse charismatic charm mixed with a compulsion to destroy the work of others, even when the creation is partly his own and so he cannot really bear to destroy it; and hence the film he helped make and then hid ultimately survived, to be reconstructed in fragments and later explanations. For Daniel Hui, the something evil is at the origin of sovereignty, of control, and ambivalently of being empowered to direct others. It is the demon that is not unlike that which bedevils Cardona.

Lights follow. The lights of contemporary Singapore at night: first an icon of capitalism, the DBS bank tower with the bank's acronym in neon against the dark sky. Originally the Development Bank of Singapore, DBS is iconic of changes in Singapore—a local development bank that grew into a multinational regional financial services corporation, the largest bank by assets in Southeast Asia, headed since 2009 by India-born Piyush Gupta.[6] The shot of DBS is followed by the illuminated trapezoidal tower atop Millennium Walk, designed by the Belgian company Magic Monkey; and then lights on the new South Beach Towers (where Google and Facebook had sumptuous offices in the 2010s). The dramatic colored lighting of the bridges and buildings of the Central Business District and Civic Center are also signs of a post-LKY Singapore feeling its way from nation-state to global node, training its citizens to become bearers of neoliberal subjectivities, "world ready" for "plug and play" in multinational corporate worlds (Naruse 2014).

After the lights comes a trumpet trill with white writing on a black background: San Francisco, 2 June 2066. It announces the history of a beginning, the beginning of a history. But it is a Freudian or Derridean beginning, suggesting that at the origin of every sovereignty, of every business empire, there is a criminal act. Before we get there, the traveling shots of the camera show lighted nighttime streets lined with eateries (Singapore's famous hawker centers, storefront restaurants, and fruit stands with piles of rambutans, mangoes, and durians). Karaoke lounges leak sounds of trumpets, cymbals, and jazz. The male voice of the diegetic filmmaker ruminates, "As I looked at the images [he gave me] on my computer [*people walking by*], I wondered, 'Who are these people? what is the right order for them?'"

Although the press pitched the film as science fiction from the future, from 2066, the only future visually evoked is repetitions from repressed pasts, and the noirish everyday life of ordinary struggles of little businesses and their customers.

But now in two segments of *Snakeskin* we are introduced to the destruction of the Malay film industry in Singapore, and the question of what would history have been like had this not happened. Singapore once was the regional hub for the Malay film industry, P. Ramlee was the industry's iconic figure, and Yusnor Ef its prolific songwriter, whom we will meet shortly. As we watch three older men, one with a large drooping mustache, another with a backwards baseball cap, sitting on chairs in a ramshackle tarp-covered open area, amid randomly placed potted plants, an Indian voice recounts the frequent formula about that early film industry: "Financial part come out from the Chinese, but the technical part from India, mostly the director, the soundman, cameraman, the beginning all come from India; the beautiful part the artistic part, actor, actress, even script writer, mostly Malay." They are sitting in the shuttered old Shaw Brothers production studio complex at 8 Jalan Ampas Road. It was a multicultural enterprise, such as Singapore longs to re-create, or wistfully asserts that it still is.

Despite the political separation of Singapore from Malaysia, why this undoing? After all, the theater world still operates back and forth between Kuala Lumpur and Singapore, albeit on the smaller scale of the working theater world, not the mass market of the earlier big-screen or Broadway musicals. A lively exchange with theater directors in Hong Kong, Beijing, and Taiwan also exists, and international big-stage productions come to town. But film is harder to sustain, partly because it remains bureaucratically under the aegis of the Infocomm Media Development Authority, which tries to apply business plans, looking for returns on investment, a mismatch of income goals and cultural form. Many argue that film would do better under the more appropriate Ministry of Culture, Community and Youth, but while this Ministry is better culturally matched, it has fewer funds to grow even small but increasingly expensive film productions. Perhaps nostalgia for the older multicultural Singapore-Malay films conflicted (as Sandy Tan suggests indirectly in her account of struggles over newly independent Singapore's flag in *The Black Isle*) with a national identity imperative that the old form was not likely to deliver, and that keeps national film industries across Southeast Asia small. But Hui is focused on the destruction that actually happened, not the potentials of what might have happened.

An Indian interviewee in the film speaks of working as a security guard at the Cathay studio on East Coast Road, and how the directors who spoke Punjabi would stop and speak to him, causing him to daydream about one day himself telling stories on screen. The centerpiece of such reflections is a wonderful interview with famed screenwriter and lyricist (with over 250 songs to his credit), the octogenarian Mohammad Noor bin Mohammad Yusof. Known as Yusnor Ef, a name he was given by P. Ramlee in 1959, he is the founder, and still president, of Perkamus, the Association of Malay Singers, Composers and Professional Musicians. Rail-thin, he still runs a production house in Kuala Lumpur, and says he is writing a history of Malay cinema. He is also a 2011 Singapore Cultural Medallion awardee, one of the highest honors Singapore gives to cultural figures. Hands behind his back, he looks at a high-rise tower under construction, and points out the difference between "multicultural" or "multiracial" then and now:

> Some, they create the story, they want to show the multiracial. . . . Now you create the multiracial story in the film by propaganda, like that.

> Like propaganda, you know? But those days [it came] naturally in the storyline. We can feel the Malay and Chinese and Indian also together in those days. It is not like this one [today, which] must be multi-racial, or you must put Malay, or you must put Chinese inside, you know? No, no, no. Automatically, naturally they come.

As he talks the camera follows his gaze from a reflecting pool up the side of the high-rise condo tower. The camera focuses on Tamils doing construction work, grounds-keeping, window washing. "You see? That's why the story mostly is life in the kampong. Between the family problem, husband and wife problem, children problem, how the Malay give too much face to the children." Yusnor Ef points up at the tower to underscore his point about the obsessive nostalgia for something called the "kampong spirit," which has become also a planning slogan for designing new high-rise housing estates.

The filmmaker is less sanguine. At 33 minutes into the film, he says: "Memories flicker and fade. Only the fire remains the same. [*White light of projector.*] If this is my story now, how do I start telling it? [*Blue bulb in the projector barrel.*] Maybe I have to first free myself of him. Free myself of the things he's told me, of the things he's made me believe. Can I use the master's tools to dismantle the master's house? Let us go back to this image." The image shifts from the blue bulb to the fire catching hold.

> When I see it, I don't think of creation at all. All I see is destruction. No more water but fire next time. I can only think of it as the thing that consumed all of us, my family and my friends, and it will consume everyone in the future. Just like history, which will consume all of us alike. He only wanted us to remember the legacy of the Chinese people who according to him built Singapore. That meant erasing the Malay culture that came before the Chinese. He *especially detested the Malay film industry* [emphasis added]. The radically egalitarian society these films dreamed of. The defiant antiauthoritarianism during British colonial rule. The description of the Malay community's struggle to define itself, a struggle that I as a Chinese person will never be able to understand. He was envious of that struggle. He could never accept the idea in these films that the different races could live together as brothers. He needed us to believe that the different races lived in constant tension, *that even the smallest spark can start a fire* [emphasis added].

As film strips are fed into the fire, we are transported to a theater and see a Chinese girl with her head on the shoulder of a Malay boy. A Caucasian man's face, a Chinese woman's face, and then a second Caucasian man who looks down and then up with concentration. Are they working on a film-editing deck? Later we discover that these are videos from Kent Chan's *Watching Eclipses*, now repurposed for *Snakeskin*. They are the only scenes of video footage in what is otherwise a 16mm film.

Spirited Away

The second segment or second film of *Snakeskin* is initially narrated by a female voice, and like *Shirkers*, it begins as a story of teenage rebellion against parental, social, and religious taboos or proprieties, with a nostalgic sense that once such strictures were not so repressive, that there had once been a freer time. Time has become regressive rather than progressive, seeming to foreclose a future of self-discovery and empowerment. In *Shirkers*, the image of America—of *Blue Velvet* smuggled in from Florida, Georges Cardona's stories of New Orleans—plays this role of a freer world. In *Snakeskin* it is the discovery among the narrator's mother's things of a still from an old Cathay movie of a young woman: Could it be her mother? Did something bad happen to turn her into a religious prude and to make her condemn film as evil?

There is the suspicion that something evil lies at the heart of film in the films of both Daniel Hui and Sandi Tan. The idea resonates with a recent novel, Sharlene Teo's *Ponti* (2016), in which a femme fatale from popular 1970s horror films about *pontianak*s (ghosts of women who die in childbirth) lives on beyond her expiration date, like a dysfunctional myth no longer in touch with the living world. Both the female narrator in *Snakeskin* and the narrator of *Ponti* try to come to terms with once famous actress mothers, women who are no longer functional in the world. It is almost as if all three—Hui, Tan, and Teo—were working from the same cultural templates regarding film, mythic tropes, and the past.

In *Snakeskin* the female narrator deals with her mother's rules, and a too early sexual encounter, by dissociating, or in film terms, a jump cut. The visuals that accompany the narration are of walking along Stamford Road toward the high-rise, circular Swissôtel building (once the tallest tower in town, with a restaurant on top with a magnificent view). When she was fifteen (the same age as Sandi Tan in *Shirkers*), she complains her religious mother did not let her hang out with a Malay girlfriend (whom she called with a generic pejorative "Mina") or with boys even if they were Chinese, although those boys turned her off by exhibiting racism toward her Malay friends. She began rebelling and hanging out with older white men, but got freaked out by a sexually aggressive Australian. She dissociated. Suddenly she was in San Francisco with her father. Like the San Francisco 2066 sign we saw earlier, this is a fantasy of freedom, the one elsewhere, the other in a future time, neither facing the diegetic reality.

There is then a jump cut. Although we are listening to the narrator talking about being in San Francisco, what we see on screen is the inside of a train on the Green Line of Singapore's Mass Rapid Transit system. "Last stop Joo Koon" flashes on the digital readout. A male voice takes over, asserting that he sees mute fear in everyone, desperation, and despair. The passengers (uncharacteristically) are silent and not on their mobile phones. Three of them are reading sheaves of papers: lecturers perhaps preparing for class at Nanyang Technological University, just beyond Joo Koon station. The narrator returns to the concerns of the opening segment of the film: "He said he'd come after me from the grave if I went against his wishes. Will he do to me what he did to so many others while he was alive?" This is, despite Hui's disavowals, a Singaporean discourse about LKY and the repressions of the 1980s.

The subway train comes up to the surface in the sunlight (the film is being developed against "his" dark wishes). We see people taking pictures at Marina Bay from the Esplanade, near Helix Bridge, looking toward the soaring boat platform floating on the three hotel towers of the Marina Bay Sands Hotel, with the convention center and casino below. No casino, LKY swore, would ever be built in Singapore, but his son, Lee Hsien Loong, who succeeded him as prime minister, thought otherwise. It is hard, the narrator admits, to separate the man (LKY) from the myths he tells as history. A close-up follows of the Merlion statue spouting water into the Marina Bay basin. Then there is a black screen with a list of myths from the official Singapore story.

Among the stories that follow is one of a man running away from the Japanese police during the occupation, when Chinese men were rounded up and massacred, many on Changi beach, others elsewhere. The man ran, and only came back years later. He was suspected of having joined the guerrillas after the war, and was imprisoned. Somewhat bizarrely, the narrator asks if he had not run away might he have managed to live a normal life. The jarring question is perhaps intended to remind people of the unpalatable choices and severe consequences that they can face during times of extremity; and the unpalatable choices they face if they wanted to return after fighting in the jungle: public disavowal of previous beliefs, perhaps also with a jail term (chapter 1). It is one of many historical traumas that lives on under the surface.

Max the Cat

Suddenly we switch to the point of view of the Other: cat, Japanese soldier, and Chinese student activist. We see a cat; we hear purring which gets louder. The film "runs out," and we see a black screen, and the cat narrates, "Before I was a soldier, I was a cat." This is followed by a list of events of the war (World War II) as the cat's purring continues. At first the narration is about being a student in the Chinese-medium Chung Cheng High School amid demonstrations against being recruited into an army to defend the British government, at a time when Chinese-medium–educated students felt growing discrimination, not given the privileges of their peers educated in English-medium schools. Arrests and disappearances. This is now juxtaposed with visuals of the Padang (the open space in the city center often used for communal events and cricket, known as the *meidan* in the Persian-speaking world and India) and cranes over the new National Gallery (the former municipality and court buildings) with Norman Foster's saucer-shaped Supreme Court building behind. As the story of the arrests and disappearances of students is narrated, we see three young men sitting on the grass of the Pandang, the former court building behind. The tail of the cat appears, the fur and ear come into view, the screen goes black, and the cat muses, "It's funny that I could fly when I was alive, because I can't do much of that when I am a cat."

We have been treated to a double time-travel fantasy. One fantasy is in search of a mother's past as perhaps a famous film actress. Another fantasy is a dissociation, blocking out life with a mother in Singapore, and instead being with an absent father in San Francisco enjoying his wished-for protection.

DEMONS AND THE SOURCE OF NIGHTMARE

> I like the idea of the whirlpool most of all, the idea of looking at the water from above. Of staring down at the surface, and being sucked into it. The quicksand effect. . . . It's the magnetic pull . . . the vicious circle, the idea of history recycled and there being no way out. . . . I want to stay with the water, how it washes everything, including the past, away.
>
> LAKSMI PAMUNTJAK, *FALL BABY*

We live simultaneously in multiple, multimedia worlds: dreamworlds in film, identity quests in picaresque novels, speculative futures in detective rationalizations of our puzzling worlds. "A question of place" (Fischer et al. 1967) haunts the simplifying models we make for ourselves, just as the geoid of the earth itself is lumpy, only approximated by the useful geodetic ellipsoids that model and map it, yet make GPS and space travel possible (Fischer 2005). Place is hardly ever autochthonous or fixed, but composed through circulations, precipitates, borrowings, and legacies from multiple elsewheres and other times.

In the epigraph to this chapter, the film about evil to which Laksmi Pamuntjak refers is Suharto's New Order propaganda docudrama *Pengkhianatan G30S/PKI*, "Treachery of the September 30 Movement/PKI" (Noer 1984), mandated to be shown in schools and on state television every year from 1984 to 1998. The exaggerated violence in the film convinced many that communists were evil. Only after the fall of Suharto was there any room in public to question the propaganda of the New Order. Three films began the process. Anthropologist Robert Lemelson's *Forty Years of Silence* (2009) provides a series of powerful case studies of individuals and families who suffered torture, incarceration, ostracism, and dealing with post-traumatic distortions of the worlds around them. It is among the best examples of documentary filmmaking, useful both as a historical record but also for mental health case studies of survivors of violent destruction. Joshua Oppenheimer's *The Act of Killing* (2012) began as an invitation by an international union to give filmmaking tutorials to plantation workers in Sumatra, dying from exposure to pesticides, who wanted to make a film about their efforts to form a union (Emont 2015). The Belgian company that owned the plantation hired the paramilitary organization Pancasila Youth to terrorize them, and succeeded in derailing the original film. But workers told Oppenheimer that such groups had killed their parents and grandparents for unionizing in 1965, and he began interviewing the older generation until stopped by the army. The locals encouraged him to continue to make a film and suggested he interview the Pancasila, who continued to be proud of their anti-communism, and were willing to reenact their violence and intimidations. In a sequel, *The Look of Silence* (2014), Oppenheimer interviews an optometrist whose older brother was murdered, and he talks about how he continues to live in a society that has yet to come to terms with the killings of 1965. Though banned in Indonesia, the films were seen, and many credit them with opening up public discussion.

Playing with the fire of our passions, as Clifford Geertz wrote of the cockfight in Bali, is a *fort/da* fascination, a daemon or fever that does not let go, a "deep play" (Geertz 1972). Some films similarly act as critical modes of *fort/da* attempts at mastery and freedom, and horror films are often credited with this function.

Daniel Hui takes on this territory directly in his film *Demons* (2019b), in this case in an exorcism of sexual violence and trauma that takes place in the power relations between a director and his lead actress. It is both a trauma that, in interviews, he hints he has suffered, and a nightmare that he himself, as director, could inflict on others. Staged as a kind of queering of the horror film genre, the violence in the film is psychological. By coincidence, as it was being edited, the case of film producer Harvey Weinstein in Hollywood blew up, setting off the #MeToo movement, mirroring the story in the film (it is of course an old image of the casting couch). The setup is similar: a young actress who wants to land a role, and the director who pushes her to do things beyond her comfort zone, ostensibly helping her to grow as an actress. The director in the film, played by veteran actor Glen Goel, is called Daniel to make clear the "autobiographical" anxiety of director Daniel Hui. In this case the actress, Yang Yanxuan, is a close friend of Daniel Hui and helped work out the idea and script, so the cast became a close-knit group that knew how far to push one another and when to stop. Still, Hui says, "It is a very personal story for me: I wanted to portray a lot of my feelings of anxiety and depression, and you know the best genre for that is horror because it is a very physical genre . . . a nightmarish movie" (Hui 2019c; also in Hui 2019a).

It is the anxiety he feels as a director (he points to a scene in the film which was funny when they were doing it, but upon reflection made him feel uncomfortable), but also, he says:

> What I was trying to do is to depict the emotion I feel while I'm in Singapore. . . . I think everyone living in Singapore can feel it. To me, it represents some kind of madness which gets under everyone's skin, so people feel very angry, but they don't know where to direct this anger. To me, it is a permanent state of madness, so I wanted to show his feeling on screen, that how the whole movie started. . . . There is this rage and you feel it everywhere. . . . It comes out very violent psychologically, it's not a physical violence. (Hui 2019a)

Hui explains these feelings as a function of living in a society where conforming is a very important part of daily life, such that you also feel like your body or your thoughts are not completely yours. "So you always have to change yourself in order to function in society or in order for society to function" (Hui 2019a). One inspiration for the film, Hui says, was Dostoyevsky's novel *Demons* ([1871] 2008) because it is about a group of people who commit a murder in order to stay together, and he "was interested in this idea of how in order for every unit to function there has to be a hidden violence or a foundation of violence" (Hui 2019a). The violence becomes something the victim internalizes: we end up doing to ourselves what society is doing to us. There is a splitting so that one feels oneself a double, not in control. With close-ups, mirroring, and other techniques, he says his intention was to make the audience uncomfortable, and to make the body strange. "From the point of view of someone who has been through trauma, your body becomes very foreign to you, and that is something that I definitely wanted to put on screen" (Hui 2019a). His understanding of trauma, he says,

> is that we split into two, you know, we become. The person who existed before the trauma does not exist anymore and, we, it is hard to even remember that person. But that is the person or persona that continues living in the world, the person that people perceive you as. But internally you are not the same person. So, how to resolve these two people? . . . So, for me, the metaphor, not really metaphor, but the image of the double in the film is a literal manifestation of the so-called demon. (Hui 2019a)

Moreover, the victim and abuser become parts of one another; in a sense they fuse, an image he also creates with colors and lighting to superimpose the faces of his two actors, one in red and one in blue.

Hui admits to liking and being very influenced by grade-B horror films. He loves the way that things in those films do not make sense, that things are there seemingly just for the shock value, but that the image can affect you physically. Moreover, "narratively I am very interested in how things don't make sense, because it is a way of 'jamming' logic, and I feel we need to jam logic in order to produce new logic" (Hui 2019a). The film ends campily with what he thinks of as a cannibalistic exorcism, eating the other (of oneself) in order to fully incorporate, assimilate, and perhaps overcome it. The campiness and overacting are intentionally "hysterical," as in nineteenth-century uses of hysteria to pathologize and control women as scapegoats for society's strictures. Though the film as it developed became more and more personal, about his own demons, in the end the collaboration turned, he hopes, into a group exorcism about collective demons (Hui, quoted in Young 2019). In response to an interviewer's question of whether he thinks of it as a particularly queer way of filmmaking (the relationships in the film include a gay director abusing an actress whose brother is racially different from herself), he says yes, and points out that while being a "gay cis-male" in Singapore (where homosexuality is still illegal) puts him in the position of victimhood, he still lives in a position of privilege as a director with the power to (unintentionally) inflict pain and harm on others, and that is the source of nightmare.

CONCLUSION

Daniel Hui's experimental films dissociate, become multiple, and stage gendered psychodramas of political leadership and film directing. They address gender issues of both traditional male-female dominance and the middle world of gay life in a disciplinary state that outlaws homosexuality. Hui claims to be obsessed with his contradictory positioning as both victim and privileged holder of power. As a gay cis-male living in a state where homosexuality is still illegal, he occupies a victim position vis-à-vis power holders; but as a film director, he is a privileged power holder, able to make actresses do his bidding. Insofar as sovereignty is founded in an original violence (that establishes the rules), the writing of history is also at stake. Hui provides an account of repetitions of the patriarchal order from thirteenth-century Malay founders (Sang Nila Utma or Sri Tri Buana), to fifteenth-century Malacca and Johor sultans with Islamic names but Hindu-Buddhist sacred regalia, to nineteenth-century British re-founders (Sir Stamford Raffles and William Farquhar), and to the twentieth-century post-independence Anglo-Chinese-inflected leader, Lee Kuan Yew (see also Fischer 2023, ch. 6). The bonds of practice, myth, and desire are hard to break, and Hui casts post-independence Singapore as a disturbing psychodynamic repetition, one that in the contemporary world propagates a certain masochistic dissociation.

Hui's contribution to the discussion as to whether history can be written otherwise is to inquire whether the film medium can probe, and perhaps cause viewers to think about, the psychological limits to which a theatrical performance (or theater state, *negara*) can allow itself to push its actors (citizens, subjects). His three films draw upon many references to film histories, most notably to films that stage new modes of perception (both visually, as in the work of Vertov and Eisenstein, and in terms of the creative use of sound), that question social justice and social harmony after traumatic disruption (Rossellini), that recall pre–World War II multicultural labor environments and regional audiences of Malay cinema, and that recall the failed promises of past and present. Of relevance to the latter is Chris Marker's *A Grin without a Cat* (1977), which Hui transposes from Marker's commentary on disillusionment with the promises of 1968, socialism, and Third Worldism, to reflections on the Chinese student movements and war trauma in Singapore, caught in the vise of the Cold War, and whose legacy is more horror film than Alice in Wonderland.

7

Meritocracy Blues, Chimeras, and Analytic Monsters

Three modes of Smart Nation. Whether or not it is easier to conjure the past, it is certainly a different form of exercise to figure out the present and near future. Perhaps this is why architectural drawings and models, gaming screens, economic models, statistical charts, and planning documents seem (and are intended to be) bloodless and abstract, with at best notational, standardized, if customizable, avatars or iconic stick figures for human or other inhabitants.[1] Daren Goh's novel *The HDB Murders* (2017) is one of a set of new speculative fictions about Singapore's present and near future with a predictive artificial intelligence (AI) machine, tied to biopolitical and economic growth calculations, at the center of its mysteries. Kevin Martens Wong's *Altered Straits* (2017a) provides a more science-fiction mythos—mixed with ancient mythic figures—and speculative near future for the naval might of Singapore from 1823 to 2047, while also using genetic and tissue engineering, neural networks and AI clouds to explore the multiplicities of language, genders, and temporalities that are often made invisible, or seemingly impossible, by official histories, bureaucracies, and psychological pressure. Nuraliah Norasid's *The Gatekeeper* (2017), in yet a third mode, deploys legends of East and West (China and Greece) to generate an *écriture féminine* or women's writing as double counternarrative to reform both traditional gender messaging and minority marginalization.[2]

Its use of what I call analytic monsters allies it with *Altered Straits* as well as the dystopia of an inegalitarian meritocracy, less polite than that of *The HDB Murders*. Analytic monsters are figures for the processes that outrun earlier paradigms. They are like wildfires that take on a new kind of plume physics quite different from forest fires of the past. They are like a "primitive within" or zombie (or Count Dracula) within that was a carrier of a glorious past, but now lives on unnaturally in the present, out of phase and dysfunctionally with reality.[3]

Detective stories, science fiction, and reinvented myths are different modes of deciphering the strangeness of the present, and working out that strangeness by plumbing the rationalities and technologies of the present for their potentials of (rational) absurdity and (technological) self-destruction. Wong reenvisions Singapore as it could have been and could become, creating a double or triple time horizon in which we in the present are metaphorically trapped, as if part of a future "anthronaut" (Wong's name for a new hybrid form of human, nautical, or astronautical defense forces) mission to rescue from the past cultural resources for survival. He reenvisions old naval wars, especially those involving the Sultanate of Sulu as well as Aceh, Makassar, and the British, but in a world in which the British were defeated and expelled from Singapore, leaving the sultans Abu Bakr and Ibrahim in charge. And he projects a future global war with both an alienated hive mind called Concordance and the ancient world serpent, the antaboga (Sanskrit: *ananta*, "endless"; *boga*, "food, possession, wealth")—the one expands by consuming neural networks of humans and other sentient beings, the other expands by consuming all that plus all material objects and waste products, sinking finally into the sea.[4]

Both *The HDB Murders* and *Altered Straits* describe the present in slightly surreal or paranoid terms as extensions of current technology and institutions. Both novels reflect upon present-day government codes of military training to absorb pain, and to become "polite, consummate media professionals, tight lipped and closely watched" (Wong 2017a, 24).[5] Both novels incorporate the essential use of AIs that gradually morph into hive minds for governance. *Altered Straits* invokes today's familiar, actually existing Agency for Science, Technology and Research (known as A*STAR), Singapore Technologies Engineering, the city-state's Mass Rapid Transit system (MRT), the highway tunnel infrastructures, the drive to expand hydroponic agriculture, and Singapore's cyber and satellite capacities. But in addition, *Altered Straits* explores genetic and biomodifications. It posits a backstory for Singapore's mascot, the Merlion, designed by the tourist board. In the novel it is a bioengineered sea creature with enhanced echolocation, superheated air-bubble-shooting weapons, and genetic or graft pair-bonding that twins (or triplicates) each merlion with a human officer in the defense forces. Bonded also with other merlion siblings, it is part of a fragile gestalt with enhanced warfare capacities, but also fragilities, such as unbearable grief when a merlion's twinned human is killed or lost (and the grieving, disabled merlion has to be killed by its merlion kin). *Altered Straits* also invokes physics speculations—time travel, parallel universes, and Alcubierre warp drives—and so crosses the boundaries into genres of video gaming, militarized dystopic science fiction, and fantasy.[6] Nonetheless, *Altered Straits* opens spaces for rethinking the myths of Singaporean historical and psychological identity, both historically and as consequences of ego anxieties and bureaucratic and military discipline—not unlike visual artist Charles Lim and the Candy Factory video that I have analyzed elsewhere (see Fischer 2023, ch. 2).

The HDB Murders, by contrast, sticks more closely to the immediate technological anxieties produced by the administrative protocols and educational planning strategies for a high-IQ, elite-led society. Its narrative and sociological horizons intertwine Max Weber's iron cage of rationality and bureaucracy, British Fabian and Labour Party utopian socialist planning, and the post–World War II notion of meritocracy (including such biopolitical psychological measures as Hans Eysenck's advocacy of IQ tests).[7] The sociologist and social worker Michael Young satirized this set of imaginaries for postwar England in his classic book *The Rise of the Meritocracy* (1958). Singapore's People's Action Party, once part of the international social democratic movement, embodies these imaginaries about order and wealth amid fear of the economic fragility of a small state and regional frenemies. Similar imaginaries have currency in China: Deng Xiaoping's visit to Singapore in 1978, and his comment that China should follow the Singapore model, is memorialized in the bust placed along the Singapore River in front of the Asian Civilizations Museum. Xi Jinping's programs, in part, continue these imaginaries, inflected by rapidly expanding technologies of integrated, AI-enhanced surveillance.

Indeed, Daren Goh's satire reads uncannily, if unsurprisingly, like a continuation or instantiation of Michael Young's. After all, much of Singapore's policy, legal, and penal frameworks stem from British and colonial foundations. Goh's and Young's books overlap, mirror, and diffract one another in a double sense. First, temporally, Young writes as if from the double time horizon of 1958 and 2034, encompassing, as it were, the present time horizon in which Goh's novel is set, leading to questions not only about how logics of 1958 have unfolded into the present, but also how the logics of smart-city technologies are being integrated in both Britain and Singapore. Second, both societies are anxiously focused on the reform of education to create an elite leadership, the biopolitics of repeated educational testing, and emotion management—what since the 1970s has come to be called the neoliberal need for individualized self-responsibility in upgrading skills (human capital) and productivity in a world of international competition—and skepticism toward democracy as appropriate for the management of complex societies.[8]

Goh's *The HDB Murders* sticks to Singapore's worries about its fragile economy, its drive to be guided by the best and the brightest, to have a productive and educated public satisfied with material wealth and conditions of life, living in what Singaporeans sometimes refer to as their gilded cage. The novel integrates into these concerns the developing technologies of AI, gaming, real-time sensing, mapping, face recognition, and other "smart-city" infrastructures (including so-called Virtual Singapore), and, *sotto voce*, smart drugs, metaphorized and misrecognized as programming, data mining, and nightmares.

Virtual Singapore, for instance, is a real project, described by Singapore's National Research Foundation and the Prime Minister's Office as:

> a dynamic three-dimensional (3D) city model and collaborative data platform, including the 3D maps of Singapore. When completed, Virtual Singapore will be the authoritative 3D digital platform intended for use by the public, private, people and research sectors. It will enable users from different sectors to develop sophisticated tools and applications for test-bedding concepts and services, planning and decision-making, and research on technologies to solve emerging and complex challenges for Singapore. (SNRF 2019)[9]

Similarly, the Smart City or Smart Nation branding is but the latest of a sequence of Singapore's branding campaigns (Intelligent Island was the immediate predecessor) as computerized digital technologies remake the infrastructure.

These two novels are part of a larger florescence of recent techno-science fiction writings, much in short story form, and which sometimes overlap, as do Wong's *Altered Straits* and Norasid's *The Gatekeeper*, with a more mythic mode. A few examples will suggest the terrain: the stories of Shelley Bryant (2021), the Centipede Collective (2021), and Justin Ker (2021) are interesting examples. Each of these is to be found in the collection *Fish Eats Lion* (Lundberg 2021), the title, working in the mythic mode, alluding to the Merlion, the mascot of Singapore. Other stories in that collection are in the more mythopoetic mode of *The Gatekeeper*, with more or less serious undertones, such as that of Ng Yi Sheng (2021), which does for the national flower of Singapore (*Papilionanthe* Miss Joaquim, one of Singapore's first hybrid orchids) what the volume as a whole, and *Altered Straits*, does for the Merlion. The orchid, previously known as *Vanda* Miss Joaquim, was hybridized in 1899 by a Singaporean Armenian, Ashkhen Hovakimian (Agnes Joaquim). Ng's story makes the new hybrid an out-of-control growth that takes over the Raffles Hotel with Queen Victoria inside, and converts the queen into a patron of anti-colonial movements, spreading globally as Singaporean sailors also smuggled Joaquim around the world (a kind of internal coup like the British education system would become for anti-colonial leaders). The orchid has imitative effects on other plants: Tsar Nicolas II dies with mango roots shooting through him, President McKinley and Maria Christina, regent of Spain, are killed by bougainvillea.

Shelley Bryant's story "Rewrites" (2021) involves a synthetic biology scheme to restore corals and create new ecosystems that nicely satirizes several of Singapore's large-scale engineering projects, including building out and up from the seabed (described in Fischer 2023), which ends badly, and, in a conceptually weak or unelaborated ending (it is only a short story) is bought for repurposing by a foreign superpower military strategist who points out, since it is completely synthetic, no bioweapons treaty has been violated. Somewhat more inventive and hilarious, if macabre, is the story "Energy" by the Centipede Collective (2021), also known as Brandon Chew and Olivia Lee, and formerly as the Pen and Eye. This projects trends in energy shortage, disposal of the dead, artificial protein production (by the Center for Holistic Meat Progenesis, or CHoMP), Post-Promethean Power or P3, and a Closed Loop Regenerative Humanity Action Board (ReHAB). Some of the dead may be reanimated, albeit as servant bots or avatars. All these schemes of closed-loop energy conservation interact. Already the dead are no longer buried in cemeteries but incinerated, their ashes placed in columbaria (that look, the story says, like Singapore's high-rise apartment buildings). Soon, the story speculates, Singaporeans will be encouraged to spread the ashes at sea, but first the bodies can be burned in a novel process to produce more energy than is consumed (as "NecOil"), just as "NuWater" (recycled used water) is already purified for drinking, contributing not only to energy self-sufficiency but a new export industry. The acronyms—creating them is a favorite Singaporean game—are often brilliant, the best perhaps being the SiMURgh Flock of Ideas Conference.[10] Justin Ker's closed-loop story "0100110101000101010001101010011110101001001011001" (2021) picks up on a tradition of speculation around digital media's uncanny ability to construct (out of past emails and videos) a machine-learning, increasingly accurate, voice-and-video reconstruction of a person, such that a widow might find comfort in continually talking to her husband on her "memory phone." After all, much of human conversation involves mirroring the utterance of the other person. The narrator breaks into the police station to watch the passive surveillance cameras, and has a fantasy of splicing together into one video all the videos of herself walking past CCTV cameras so as to get some insight into what she was doing with her life.

These are all short takes. But three novels involve longer takes on the issues of meritocracy, chimeras (in the biological and bioengineering sense), and analytic monsters.

SMART NATION: GOING BY THE BOOK AND ACCELERATING LIFE AND STAMINA WITH THE PHARMAKON

In Daren Goh's novel *The HDB Murders* (2017), the city-state is a place in which cabinet ministers are recruited among top scholars. For instance, Lim Chiu Kua, the senior executive minister who reports to the prime minister, graduated from Oxford University's PPE (Philosophy, Politics, and Economics) program at the age of eighteen, and was immediately drafted into the top ranks of government, on track to be the next prime minister, to the envy of other ambitious ministers.[11] In Michael Young's satire *The Rise of the Meritocracy* it is "philosophy and administration as well as in the two S's of science and sociology" (Young 1958, 18). In Goh's novel, science and sociology are thematized through constant mathematical calculation, logical reasoning, and management by using the media of social responsiveness or feedback.[12] It is a place where cabinet and lower-ranking ministers can write intellectually rigorous reports on the growing usage of mobile phones, identity theft, and blackmail on social media, but cannot write their own Facebook posts because the government owns and operates all public officials' social media accounts to make sure all public statements are consistent across ministries.

Senior Executive Minister (SEM) Lim delegates a new young minister, Chew Bee Hong, an emerging technologies enthusiast, to head a task force to inquire into a double crime wave, one involving burglaries (household goods, designer dresses, limited-edition sneakers), the other an ongoing series of unsolvable suicide-like deaths or murders—bodies falling off, or being pushed off, the tops of Singapore's Housing Development Board (HDB) high-rise public apartment blocks.[13] The consumer goods, stolen and fenced abroad, on the one hand, are a distraction, since Singaporeans are wealthy enough to replace the material objects easily. But on the other hand, the burglaries have consequential psychological effects. People become defensive and distrustful. They lock their doors as they never did before, and clutch their bags in front of their bodies when walking in public. Given that elections are coming, this psychological mood is not good for public morale nor for faith in the competence of government. People increasingly hire foreign help (bodyguards, extra nannies) as protection. This in turn drives up population pressure on public services, higher household living costs, and higher taxes on foreign workers (which the government ineffectively uses to dampen demand). Higher taxes and labor costs force citizens to work harder to be able to pay for their life styles, adding to general stress levels in society. The wave of mysterious suicides or murders, and the inability of the police to solve them, adds to the unease, as does cyber taunting by a mysterious hacker, using the handle awkwardboi58. The hacker uploads his taunts on social media to the internet, where they circulate for all to see. These include uploading police body camera feeds (amplifying the visibility of the deaths and the lack of explanations by the police), as well as feeds from the ubiquitous public surveillance cameras around the city used both to improve services and maintain public safety and order.

With elections only two months away, all the government protagonists are in a pressure-cooker situation to solve the deaths and crimes. To deal with the stress, the new minister, Chew Bee Hong, finds himself having a few drinks in a bar called Bojangles. He recognizes this as troubling, an early warning sign, since "Ministers were expected to be upright and above reproach which meant no alcohol" (Goh 2017, 24). The prime minister and SEM Lim keep reminding their personnel that management of domestic opinion about the competence of the government is of the utmost importance lest the fragile economy fail. This pressure, and Chew's inability to make headway in solving the deaths, becomes so intense that sitting in the bar watching the National Day parade, Chew suddenly takes his beer mug and hurls it at the television, shattering the mug.

Afterward, he replays in his head the eruption of anger that overcame him, and is frightened by the intensity of that anger, not knowing where it came from. Out of control is not ministerial behavior. His performance anxiety intensifies and his affect shifts from being grateful for opportunities to prove himself, to a persistent and "irrepressible worry he might fail again" (95). Chew comes from a humble background; his parents are food-stall owners. The youngest member of the eighteen-person cabinet, he often experiences imposter syndrome, the feeling that he is a fraud. He hides behind a mask of humility, afraid to reveal what he does not know. When his opinion is sought on policy, he answers in generalities or enigmatically repeats the terms of the question with a slightly different inflection (providing an Eliza-like therapeutic sense to the questioners that they have been answered).[14] This facade of humility attracts others to seek out his opinions even more. "Chew had entered politics for the same reason most did: to be respected, to be part of the elite, to make a difference in the world, though mostly it was the million-dollar salaries" (25). Million-dollar salaries are meant to make ministers incorruptible, to allow them to live up to, and fully devote themselves to, their jobs in public service.

Responses to the two crime waves take on parodic but true Singaporean forms: poster campaigns and expert committees. For the burglaries, SEM Lim orders that complete sets of six huge posters be posted in every lift lobby and on all available public walls. Poster campaigns have a long history in Singapore: "leaders of this country are constantly telling everyone what to do: speak better English, speak better Chinese, have more children, conserve water, save money . . . there's no end. They say this is for a better life, but their measure is the national GDP. It's almost like the GDP and citizens are interchangeable. Happier citizens? Easy. Higher GDP. But people can only take so much" (166).[15] In this case, the posters promote values of community, alertness, and cooperation, and threaten caning for anyone caught vandalizing them. A million-dollar prize is announced, for which citizens must create videos online to propagate the same public service message. The winner is feted at a public ceremony in the middle of Singapore's prime shopping street, Orchard Road, pausing the shopping for a few hours, but then, as the lights go off and darkness comes, there is an uneasy shifting in the crowd, and people clutch their bags more tightly.

To counter awkwardboi58, Chew convenes a task force of students from the best universities who know about social media, since "the right people couldn't be found in government." In parodic exaggeration of Singapore's meritocratic behavioral training and entrained instincts, Chew crowdsources the names of students, each having to be nominated by at least ten professors.[16] But their solutions of building data sets and running simulations are far too slow to keep up with awkwardboi58. Chew is demoted to CEO of the Building and Construction Authority (HDB!), and given a consolation medal. At first the job is easy and mindless, but soon he gets pressure from SEM Lim to answer why it is that the public housing he now oversees is where so many deaths occur.

In desperation Chew calls upon his best friend from his schooldays, one Tan Boon Tat, who is now the country's Internal Security Head of Intelligence. Tan is suspicious of all higher-level officials, and maintains an attachment to his schoolboy passions: heavy metal music, comics conventions, Rihanna, Star Wars. These were the things Chew and he had bonded over in school. Are they signs of failed maturation? Neither Tan nor Chew seems to have a love life or family, and Tan is unable to respond to come-ons by beautiful young women at the comics convention. Chew keeps a confidence-exuding toy soldier on his desk, and Tan has Star Wars wallpaper on his cell phone. They pore over the statistics of the deaths, and two mysterious correlations emerge: after each death there is a period of no crime for two weeks; after the completion of new public housing, there is a death. In a panic, Chew writes an evidence-based report defending his Building and Construction Authority (and buildings) from any complicity. In a slight bureaucratic adjustment, he recalculates the times between building completions and deaths: not from the date of occupation, but from the earlier date of purchase. When awkwardboi58 becomes one of the mysterious deaths, they lose a presumed suspect. They begin to have animistic or Durkheimian thoughts that the city is killing its citizens. Durkheim would look for fractures and pressure points in the social structure as places where suicides are likely to occur (the science and sociology of Michael Young's satire). Durkheim, of course, was a master of pointing out the ambiguities between determining if a death was suicide or homicide.

When Chew blurts out (over an encrypted chat) his animistic hypothesis to SEM Lim, the reaction is typical: What are the metrics? If it cannot be measured, it cannot be improved. More importantly, afterward Chew is stunned not by Lim's response, but by his own words: "He'd been in a trance, where—against his will—his thoughts had gone on autopilot, and he had babbled every first thing that came to mind" (139).

The city is replete with intelligence officers, surveillance cameras, and sensor networks. Store counter staff, taxi drivers, construction workers, food-stall operators, all wear microphones and body sensors that send location data feeds in real time to information hubs and analysts. Bus drivers with cameras in their glasses collect data on commuters, and there are officers embedded in religious organizations' highest ranks. Freddy, the Bojangles bartender, turns out to be also a field agent, and like each of the others has only limited knowledge of the larger network of which he is a part.

Videos captured by citizens as well as those captured by surveillance cameras often go viral, creating a kind of ocean-like communal peace-keeping, as in the case of a fight on an subway train between a middle-aged immigrant and a teen wearing an "immigrants go home" T-shirt. People on the train encircle the older man, and won't let him move, until police rush in and take him away. Everyone sits down and takes out their mobile phones and acts as if nothing has happened. It is as if ocean waves wash aside debris and close behind, leaving no trace. The pervasiveness of surveillance does not make things necessarily any more transparent since one never knows who is an informer, or where cameras are hidden, or who is integrating what information to what purpose. A fight in Bojangles between Freddy and Abe is captured on customer mobile phones; they are incomplete, not recording the scene after Freddy drags Abe outside behind the bar and away from mobile phone cameras; but there are also steady feeds from hidden cameras out there, unbeknownst to Freddy.

A subplot that gradually becomes important is the regulation of illegal immigration. The government has been paying a contractor to import, under cover, at least twenty thousand immigrants a month to keep up the population needed for economic growth. This has been going on for forty years. It, too, is a pressure cooker for the supplier who makes good money but is always having to find twenty thousand new immigrants who are required to have an IQ of 140 ("genius" level!), and stay in the city-state for twenty years. It looks like "human trafficking" from countries where life circumstances are terrible, using freight containers aboard ships, with the migrants tied up and their mouths taped shut. The contractor dies and passes the business on to his son, Abe, who would rather play World of Warcraft. Freddy is Abe's contact for deliveries of the immigrants. Freddy is caught between his law enforcement job, and his instructions from above not to look into the work of

Abe's company, Cornucopia. Abe, under intense pressure to fulfill the contract, comes to Freddy for advice and help. Freddy unsympathetically views him as an entitled rich boy who always wants others to do his job. That Abe has been trying to play a tough mafia type does not endear him to Freddy. They yell and shout. The rage overflows and Freddy attacks Abe with brutal force (captured on the hidden video cameras). Freddy is appalled at himself: "He had lost himself for a few moments. That was all it had [taken] to push him down this path that he could never leave" (140). Overcome with guilt, he also calculates that he cannot tell Chew or Tan; Tan and he have long been wary of each other, and Chew, after all, is a minister with ambitions.

Aside from this form of undercover immigration, there is also open recruitment, especially from China. Deputy Police Superintendent Wang Zi Yang, for instance, was recruited the day he graduated from a top Chinese university with degrees in statistical probability, Bayesian inference, and R programming. He was brought to Singapore, given a job and housing, and given a contract he could not really read (English still being a new language for him), but which later he finds out is a ten-year, non-negotiable commitment as an investigative officer, a job in the police station with the highest work load that no Singaporean wanted to do. It is he who figures out that there is a higher governance authority, above the prime minister, that there is a "meta-search engine," or a "metacognitive algorithm discovery platform," or an artificial intelligence platform that "began as a simulated version of the world we live in, collecting credit card information, text messages, emails" and that over time became so effective that predictive capabilities were incorporated, allowing the identification of unproductive individuals (239). It also identifies whenever a citizen's Central Provident Fund (for retirement, housing, health care) contains exactly $161,000. It turns out, Wang observes, that each of the mystery deaths is of someone with exactly this amount in their account.

But this AI system, called Modafi, seems to be more interesting yet. Modafinil is one of today's most popular nootropic or smart drugs, used especially by Silicon Valley techies and Wall Street financial whiz kids. In the United States it is marketed under the name Provigil, and was FDA approved in 1998 for narcolepsy—that is, for staying awake. It is used by several armed forces for missions involving sleep deprivation. It is said to heighten concentration, and especially visual acuity, and reduce anxiety, the very qualities required for the steady, unflappable, highly rational state of affect that is de rigueur for the administrative elite in the city-state. Modafi is the AI program that can sift through surveillance footage and identify persons needing optimization, behavior modification, or elimination. It is an equilibrium-finding algorithm that keeps the biopolitical balance between GDP and population levels. Still experimental, it requires some human input by people undergoing behavioral modification to make them function as beta-testing gamers, who sit at computer interfaces tracking people in the streets who are identified by Modafi as "players," as objects in continual need of rebalance.[17]

The logic is that those selected by Modafi as players invariably are people who are failing the nation. Chew himself becomes one of these, and since he becomes enraged at the time of his selection by the "infallible" Modafi, it becomes clear to his erstwhile teammates that his earlier outbursts of rage, as well as his own doubts created by his failures to solve intractable problems—in some cases, deliberately constructed to frustrate, as in the highly classified folder he is entrusted with that only contains public information from the newspapers—already had been indicators that he was indeed not sufficiently up to citizen or ministerial standards of conduct. He is aggrieved, feeling that he has tried to protect his fellow citizens, as well as the country, in good faith. But he is accused by the system (by the prime minister, by SEM Lim, and by Modafi) as not recognizing that the good of the nation is a higher calling than merely the good of its citizens. This is a position he refuses.

But it turns out the good of the nation may not be the ultimate goal of the governance system. The system has been optimized for efficiency and flow of information, as Deputy Superintendent Wong explains:

> As you know Singapore has the most liberal surveillance policy in the world. It lets us monitor anyone in the country without consequences. No questions asked. Mobile phones, emails, video calls, Google searches, text messages. Anything passing through the country's network. . . . Because of this, many countries . . . use us as an information hub. Through us, they can access all the activity that passes through the undersea fiber optic cables that run below us, which lets them run whatever clandestine operations they want. We're a search engine for everything that passes through us. . . . The search engine is modafi. Modafi is meta. It is everything. (190)[18]

There is one final image in *The HDB Murders* that perhaps provides a metaphor for the intensities of becoming and for the idea that life is more than survival. Exhausted, Chew turns on the television and watches *Shark Week* on Discovery Channel. A marine biologist is in a glass cage to observe a great white shark. The shark attacks, cracking the glass, cutting the diver's hand, the blood further enticing the shark to break through the glass. Shipmates barely have time to pull the cage to safety. The diver's reacts by saying, "That was fucking awesome . . . I nearly died today. It was awesome" (173). "As [the television show] plays on, Chew fell into the blackness of his subconscious mind, and slept" (173). Playing with the fire of our passions, as Clifford Geertz wrote of the cockfight in Bali, is a *fort/da* fascination, a "deep play" that works in the everyday as much as in the spectacular (Geertz 1972). It is part of reading the coffee grounds of our futures, and keeping us down to earth in the interplay of actually existing taboos, conventions, and boundaries. These passions and logics are handled in two different ways in *Altered Straits* and *The Gatekeeper*.

RESCUED BY FOLKLORE: CHIMERAS AND SAVING ENDANGERED LANGUAGES

> We're only sending animals back that would occupy ecological niches without causing ecosystem wide havoc, and at the same time would satisfy some of the myths and legends that already existed in various cultures around the world.
>
> KEVIN MARTENS WONG, *ALTERED STRAITS*

Kevin Martens Wong's novel *Altered Straits* (2017a) brilliantly creates a backstory for, and creolization of, Singapore Tourism Board's Merlion, the advertising logo for the island, that as a white sculpture also sits on the banks of Marina Bay, spitting out a steady stream of water into the bay, and, at times, becoming the screen, coat, or skin on which is projected a light show of rainbow colors in changing patterns. The Merlion is often the subject of local jokes about its artificiality. A cartoon once showed it plaintively asking Indonesia's Garuda why the Garuda gets respect but the Merlion does not. Even the ubiquitous images of sharks and crocodiles in Surabaya get more respect, rooted in the very name (*sura*, "shark"; *baya*, "crocodile"). The answer many Singaporeans give is that there is no real history for the Merlion, that it is just a recent invention like the brand names that Singapore gives itself (Garden City, Renaissance Island, Intelligent Island, Smart Nation). Wong gives it a history and turns it into a conceptual platform for Singapore's multiple histories. Fittingly, *Altered Straits* does not have the singular Merlion, but many merlions. The merlions of *Altered Straits*—and the queering of *straight* history of the three maritime *straits* surrounding Singapore (Johor, Singapore, Malacca)—are an inversion, mythopoetically, of the legend or fable of the attack of the swordfishes: merlions defend rather than attack Singapore. In the legend, swordfishes used their sword-like bills to kill fishermen and to aggressively chase them, even onto the shore. A boy suggested building a fence of banana stems. The swordfish impaled themselves on the sturdy fence, and thus they could be killed. And so the island was protected. The sultan of the time feared that the heroic cleverness of the boy was a threat to his own standing, and ordered the boy killed. But when the sultan's soldiers arrived, the boy's grandmother (another old lady with shamanic or *bomoh* powers—see chapter 2) waved them off, and all they found was a pool of blood that ran down the hill, staining it red. Ever since, the area has been known as Bukit Merah (Red Hill). The "boy-king" makes cameo appearances in *Altered Straits*, not quite as the legend has it, but among the reconfigured sultans of 1820s Singapore, or Kerajaan Singapura as Malays would have called it.[19]

If information technologies animate *The HDB Murders*, biology, genetic and tissue engineering, neural circuits, nervous systems, artificial intelligence, and databank clouds operate similarly for *Altered Straits*. But, more importantly, if often sub-rosa, so do linguistics, folklore, gender, and ethnic or race relations. The linguistics of a multilingual society such as Singapore, with its creoles and dialects as well as four official languages, provides a conceptual template for multiplicity at many levels, including gender, ethnic sub-identities, and even temporalities (counter-histories, parallel universes). For instance, in *Altered Straits*, announcements on the MRT are made in all the local languages, and at one point the sequence stops pointedly at Cantonese, one of the primary local dialects, rather than Mandarin, the official language that immigrant dialect-speaking populations had to learn (or at least their children are mandated to learn in school).[20] Gender complexity and fluidity in Singapore are metaphorized in part by the cross-species symbiosis and fusion of the hermaphroditic and self-replicating merlions with humans. (They are not unlike the humans of a third kind in Kwa's *Oracle Bone* and the older *Shan Hai Jing*, or *Guideways through Mountains and Seas*, discussed in chapter 3). But more directly, in terms of cultural critique, the novel targets Singapore's situationally applied anti-sodomy laws. Sodomy laws are still on the books, preventing teachers from using plays and novels about homosexuality and such issues in classrooms, but LGBTQ politics are in the open (particularly in the arts and the annual Pink Dot rally), and the government has in essence adopted a "don't see, don't tell" policy, arguing that Section 377A of the Penal Code criminalizing sodomy (since 2007 only for homosexuals) cannot be changed yet because of the conservatism of the heartland electorate.[21] There is a subplot of an elite merlionsman defense corps keeping his homosexual relationship secret, as does a female officer her pregnancy, which is also against the military's code of conduct. The diversity of life is always over-spilling categories and rules.

Like the fluidity of sexuality, the issue of alternative temporalities (or submerged histories) is one of the leitmotifs of the novel operating across three time frames (the 1820s, 1940s, and 2040s), which are scrambled by storytelling, dream work, and traumatic ideation, in addition to the science-fiction genre conventions of time travel. It is one of the virtues of the novel that this mixture of temporalities does not interfere with readability or the forward drive of the plot. One might even argue that the reader's effort to track time frames is part of the authorial intention to illustrate how things could have turned out otherwise. The "what if" component of alternative, speculative, or counterfactual histories (and parallel universes) can, at least suggestively, be a powerful stimulant to creative rethinking about how to re-animate cultural resources—more so than simply negatively protesting that official stories leave out, and enforce ignorance of, the knowledge of minorities or genders (the Bugis, for instance, traditionally have five genders).

Kevin Martens Wong is himself an "Other," an actual bureaucratic category in Singapore's plural society: a Eurasian of Portuguese ancestry.[22] Merlions suggest a different set of "race" categories (which is what Singapore's bureaucracy still calls them despite increasing categorization difficulties due to intermarriage in a post-ethnically segregated immigration society). Wong has a degree in linguistics and anthropology, two disciplines that have long contested racial categories as unscientific, or rather, more critically, as tenacious, socially constructed, and enforced hierarchies of particular power structures. Wong is engaged in a CoLang (the Institute on Collaborative Language Research) project to revitalize Kristang, the creole language of his Eurasian ancestors. The creole is composed of a variable mix of languages across Singapore, Malaysia, Macau, and the Philippines. Operating under the umbrella of the Linguistic Society of America, CoLang is dedicated to teaching speakers of creoles and indigenous tongues, whose languages are at risk of dying out, how to collaboratively keep them alive. Wong teaches Kristang, although he did not grow up speaking it—the last in his family to speak it fluently were his great-grandparents. Most of the people in his classes have no necessary connection to the language other than that Kristang is part of Singapore's heritage. They have fun creating new words to keep the language alive—some inventions take and others do not, just as in other natural languages. One might see at least a metaphorical resonance between the novel and his identity: he is, in a sense, a merlion, come by sea, defending the land.

The merlion becomes thus an interesting invention, giving depth and backstory to what was just a Singapore Tourism Board advertising logo for the city, and a water-spouting sculpture on the shore of Marina Bay. In Wong's imagination, it becomes a species of genetically engineered symbiont paired with elite human soldiers, forming anthronaut incubators for human enhancements such as the regeneration of limbs when injured, or the ability to hold one's breath underwater for long periods of time by using the myoglobin that sea mammals have. The bioengineering pairing of merlion-human symbiont fighters requires biological knowledge that today we are barely on the verge of acquiring: we can graft a nonfunctional ear onto a mammal, we can graft kidneys from one human to another, and do heart, lung, face, and hand transplants, but cross-species grafting of organ replacements is still in the experimental stage, as is most regenerative tissue repair (beyond skin) and growing new organs from stem cells (which require complex three-dimensional vasculature).

But more important culturally, the merlion is also a companion to altering history (or creating parallel universes) in three time-horizons. Wong envisions its presence in the changing social structure of the 1820s (as a short-cut metaphor for the replacement of previous canoe-based naval and mercantile marine forces). What might have ensued, the novel asks, had the British, after five years, been driven out of Singapore (in 1823 or 1824), and rule had reverted to the local sultans (of Johor and Riau) who replaced their previous Seletar marine corps with newly bonded merlions, to use both defensively and offensively against the rival Sulu maritime empire, which had been slave raiding in Singaporean territory?[23] Merlions reappear during the second time horizon, the Cold War (from the 1940 to the 1970s) as part of the anthronaut forces that protagonist Naufal joins against the Sulu forces of the (communist) east. As Singapore prepares, in the aftermath of World War II, first for merger with Malaya, and then for independence, there is a fly-by from the 2040s in the shape of a mid-twentieth-century speculative time-traveling machine using an Alcubierre warp drive, which might have altered that history. What if Lim Chin Siong had become independent Singapore's first prime minister instead of Lee Kuan Yew; or Japan had won World War II; or Dr. A. M. Azahari had succeeded in unifying Borneo as either a separate state under the Sultan of Brunei as a constitutional monarch or as a strong member of a Malay Federation?[24] The time machine flies by, carrying merlion pups, but overshoots and lands instead in 1803. A rescue operation is needed. In the third time horizon of 2039 to 2045, the merlion is re-created as part of a crash military defense program cobbling together elements of the old time machine spacecraft with new energy sources (a Proteus device replaces the Alcubierre warp drive). There are renewed efforts (as in World War II) to weaponize animals (such as the merlion). The post-2045 period is an extension of incipient developments today: ever-expanding and competing information processing entities, like Alibaba or Google (with cloud storage in Singapore's special economic zone for this industry), driven by self-assembling algorithmic (ir)rationalities beyond even those in *The HDB Murders*, privileging the nation over the citizen. The merlions in this period are not only hybridized with human warriors, but their replicating jellies (see below) allow the merlionsmen to merge with whatever biomaterials are around them, which allows them to escape certain, but not all forms of, death.

The earliest of the three time horizons in *Altered Straits* thus is a queering of the 1820s, called the founding era of Singapore by the quite deliberate newly constructed, national-identity-conferring, official "Singapore story" ("from third to first world society in one generation"), which could not afford to blur identities with Malaysia or Indonesia (in terms of ethnic or religious identity). This is quite openly acknowledged to have been an instrumentalized history intended to create a new Singaporean identity out of diverse immigrant communal identities. We get some alternative histories, albeit in the form of vague old men's stories about their time doing national service told at a 1947 party for the protagonist Naufal, who is being inducted into the defense forces. And we get resentments of one of Naufal's cohort who is a Seletar.[25] Only a few British colonial names occur: Col. [William] Farquhar, the first Resident of Singapore (and who is said in the novel to have had a thing for boys), and the "evil" [John] Crawfurd, the second Resident. All of the historical names and politics (of sultans Abu Bakr, Ibrahim, Ismail) are slightly mutated from the historical record with regard to their dates and actions, and the period is slightly shifted to evoke naval battles and alliances of a slightly earlier period against the fifteenth- and sixteenth-century Sultanate of Sulu, which ruled a thalassocratic empire (primarily coastal areas), which at its greatest expanse extended from the coast of Borneo to islands off Mindanao in the Philippines. In reduced form, the empire actually lasted until 1915.

The old men, of course, leave things out: "No one mentioned the Sulu Night of Solace." That is a jump cut, to use a film expression, and a marker of the genre-hybridizing activity of *Altered Straits*. The reference is to the spaceship *Long Night of Solace* from the video game series of that name, a military science-fiction franchise, and some readers may be invited to read the novel in those genre terms. The functions of the counter-history of the 1820s, in which the British and Dutch are hardly present, are threefold: providing a prequel for earlier prototypes or editions of the merlion; recalling from amnesia the history of marginalizing the local indigenous Orang Laut (sea peoples); and supplying a premise for what might have become in the present a society in which Malays could be top-ranking army officers (today they are de facto excluded from such positions for fear of divided loyalties should there be hostilities with Malaysia or Indonesia).

The Seletar merlionsman reflects on the marginalization of his fellow sea peoples after the sultans of the 1820s replaced them with merlions, because they had chosen to follow an unsuccessful claimant to the leadership of the sultanate. Because they had supported Azahar (a conflation of the rivalries to the sultanate in the early nineteenth century with competitions over political unions in the 1960s), he laments, people began to think of them as heretics, sea peoples, inferior to land people. Perhaps the merlions here are also figures for the much larger ships, with their hulls in the sea and their many sails in the wind, of the Bugis and the Chinese, and then the Europeans and Parsis, which rendered the canoes of sea peoples technologically archaic for warfare and long-distance trade.[26] The Seletar nomadic sea peoples lived on both sides of the Johor Straits. Most now live on the Malaysian side, where they are still recognized as one of eighteen Orang Asli (indigenous peoples), while in Singapore they are considered simply Malay. Their language, like Kristang, is on the UNESCO list of endangered languages. Their animistic and sea-oriented life style has been also under pressure in Malaysia. Since especially the 1980s, with the resurgence of Islamic fundamentalism in Malaysia (as elsewhere), they have been under pressure to convert to Islam. Some have converted to Christianity instead, like the Batak of Sumatra, who in an earlier era chose Christianity to ward off pressure to convert to Islam from Aceh to their north. Their mangrove forest coastal environments and resources have been badly eroded or destroyed, and their animism pops up in Wong's novel, as it does in Sandi Tan's *The Black Isle* (discussed in chapter 2) as the powerful black magic that the Seletar are said to still possess, a language of the weak, and of protest against hegemonic ideologies (often retooled as environmentalist care for, and living with, rather than against, nature). Traces remain in Singapore, in the name of Seletar Airport, for example, which served as a British and then the Singapore air force base, and in Seletar Reservoir. Plying the seaways, there is now even a modern oil tanker, built in 2010, named the *Seletar Spirit*.

The old men's stories, vague as history, do contain mythic parables, another of Wong's devices to alert us to the narrative forms he is using. In classic folklore style, the myths come as competing structural inversions of one another, carrying quite different messages. In Farquhar's version (in the novel), the powerful sorceress, Queen of Many Seas, harnesses an ancient sea creature to carry her to fetch tiger's blood with which to cure her ill husband. The Ruler of the Ocean becomes angry at this trespass and turns the Queen of Many Seas into a giant sea serpent. Her husband fails to recognize her and kills her, thereby throwing the kingdom into chaos and fracturing the sea peoples. It is a "just so story" about the decline of the sea peoples, and the consequences of using sorcery to go against the natural order. But Kassim, the Seletar merlionsman, says his people have a different version in which it is an ordinary soldier who wants to save his beloved, and the Ruler of the Ocean is a merlion named Ginggaran (a word for "frustrated" in Indonesian), who is capricious and enjoys frustrating the desires of men. The message here is that it is not the magic that goes against nature, but the ocean that is dangerous and unpredictable.

The two primary action periods of the novel are the 1940s, when Naufal is taken into the anthronaut corps, and a century later, when Titus Ang Chee Howe is enlisted. Naufal ("sea" in old Arabic) enlists (or refuses entitlement to a waiver from conscription) despite the fact that his brother Nabhan ("aware," "vigilant") had lost his mind, screams wildly, and is unable to function after losing his merlion in the Battle of Linga. Nabhan's fate in the service constitutes a warning of the dangers of war and of high-speed prototyping and innovation. Titus Ang Chee's fate will be similar, albeit with an increased capacity and risk of merging with whatever is around him—it is ambiguous as to whether this merging is physical (advanced biotechnology), in dreams (dream work), or in ideation caused by trauma (mental illness). Despite the fact that the first Sulu War of 1941/2 (Japan's occupation of Southeast Asia) is over, in the following Cold War fighting, Naufal is not spared the kinds of trauma that his brother experienced, but he does not lose his merlion, who is able to bring him back from some of the worst of the fighting to safety. The first Sulu War was brutal: on one side Singapore and Aceh lose over 39,000 fighters; on the other side, Sulu loses 50,000. The Treaty of Makassar is essentially a temporary stalemate. We follow Naufal through his grueling training, his changing body, and his resistance to merging his mind with others. In his training he is stripped naked and pushed into the cold, alien water, a double metaphor of both personal transformation (stripped naked) and perhaps climate change: the water around Singapore today is warm, approximately the same temperature as the human body (see Fischer 2023, ch. 4). The cold water thus is a shock, but it is also metaphorical of the alien biological modifications he is being made to undergo. The army keeps a tight lid on the changes, and their mental health consequences.

The fear of expanding hive minds—as gestalt, concordance, and antaboga—in one form or another is central to the novel. In the 1940s (the early days of computers, game theory, operations research, simulations), hive minds are in their early stages. Naufal resists his multiplication (cloning, prototyping, gradual augmentation) and the notion of a "we Naufal," but ever so gradually he becomes used to being mentally and telepathically one with his merlion, who in turn is one with the community of merlions, a configuration the novel calls a "gestalt," giving the anthronaut, or human-merlion hybrid, something of a collective emotional agency and sensing of one another when lost or in need. The word "gestalt" (something perceived as more than the sum of its parts, an easily perceived shape that has its own integrity) comes from early twentieth-century German social psychology, and in *Altered Straits* we experience twentieth-century anxieties about, and tensions between, individuation and sociality, the social nature of egos constructed by their mirroring in the reactions of others, and the coercive internalization of social norms. This becomes intensified in Cold War ideological hysterias and political regimentation. Most troubling to our protagonist Naufal is his feeling of being trapped in a memory but not knowing whose memory it is.

A century later, the forces of hive minds become even more intense with the Concordance hive attacking Singapore in 2039 and again in 2045, when our second lead protagonist, Lt. Titus Ang Chee Howe, has enlisted. This is an age of global war of a nebulous kind, and a geopolitics that seems to scramble the world as we know it in 2020. Titus, for instance, trains with the Pyongyang cadre. Singapore keeps in touch through secret data bursts of communication with places almost entirely in the eastern hemisphere: Pyongyang (North Korea), Thimphu (Bhutan), Dushanbe (Tajikistan), Irkutsk (Siberia), Harbin (China), Brisbane (Australia), Grytviken (South Georgia and the Sandwich Islands). Only Montreal (Canada), Santiago (Chile), and Tikal (Guatemala) are in the Western Hemisphere. One suspects that Tikal, a Mayan archaeological site, is like Seletar and Kristang, a gesture at endangered languages and cultures; Montreal is known for its bilingualism, while Santiago is a gesture at south-south relations, and also has indigenous languages. Grytviken, a stop on the way to Antarctica, is a colonial outpost no longer inhabited all year round.

It is ambiguous to what degree these places constitute an alliance against other places on earth (Sulu, for instance); an alliance against interstellar aliens of the Concordance hive that has conquered other places on earth (Concordance alludes to the Covenant CSO-class supercarrier in the Halo military science-fiction video game series); or, most interesting, a global struggle among competing and expanding AI and big data systems. Both Concordance—which seems to be in 2020 terminology a "cloud" storage entity—and its deep-sea opposite, the antaboga, are described as monsters consuming whatever sentient beings they can. Concordance tries to upload intact nervous systems of all sentient beings, humans and others, to ensure neuro-cybernetic uplinking and system upgrading. It is an "anti-weapon," disabling firearms, and "lifting up human nervous systems into one blissful whole, only using sharp *kris* [Malay ceremonial daggers] like claws to kill, and occasional bombs to flush out humans [for debraining]" (Wong 2017a). The antaboga, similarly, is said to have been originally formed by the fusion of two merlions. It is ecstatic in fighting and consuming the wreckage of battles, expanding until it sinks down into its watery grave in contentment. "The Concordance fought back, held in rapture by this strange new thing, this huge intelligent thing that was yet intelligent and unthinking at the same time" (332). Like the distinction between dumb drones that can only seek out certain kinds of biosignatures and intelligent drones that have human pilots, so here Concordance consumes cognitive capacities while the antaboga is "intelligent" but "unthinking" (smart algorithms come to mind).

The merlions in this third time horizon are the product of Singapore's crash defense efforts after the Concordance invasion of 2039 that devastated the city. They are pair bonded with the most highly selected and bootcamp-surviving human elite troops. These pair-bonded merlionsmen form the elite anthronaut platform for enhanced capacities of a new human and a human-merlion chimera. Human recruits in the 1940s grew fins, which are now replaced by impenetrable chitinous carapaces and powerful tails that harness the waves and release the waves in bursts of energy that superheat the water around prey, killing it instantly, and can accurately target it from 200 meters away. Of some ten thousand thirteen-year-old draftees, like our first protagonist Naufal in his intake cohort, only 216 are found suitable for pair bonding, and of these only thirty-six are taken for merlionsmen of the anthronaut corps. Others are sent to other elite units: the Garuda Aerial Corps, the Tulpari Mounted Police, and the Toenayat Regiment. Tulpar is a line of light tanks manufactured by Turkish firm Otokar, named after a mythic winged horse; Garuda is the eagle-human vehicle of Vishnu. The counterpoint to these flying steeds of the sky is the equally chimeric merlion of the ocean depths.

The building of the post-2039 version of the merlion is assigned to ST BioEngineering (a play on a real corporation, ST Engineering, a global privatized government-spawned company). What is left of Singapore after the 2039 attack huddles in the underground network of MRT stations and tunnels such as the Marina Coastal Expressway (completed in 2013), which is a gateway to Singapore's New Harbor District (replacing the old Keppel container port, which moved north to the new port at Tuas in the 2020s). The merlions are part of a defense-sensing network including whale pod sensors, air force balloons, dumb army drones (that can only look for Concordance biosignatures), more intelligent Home Affairs drones with human pilots, tenuous connections to the last two astronauts alive on an American colony, and members of a Dutch colony at Chryse Pantitia (on Mars). There are also secret data bursts and a relay station on Bougainville for messaging various of the Republic of Singapore's naval fleet, the RSS *Incalcitrant* and RSS *Indomitable* deep in the Pacific, and the RSS *Intransient* off Batam (these names are not unlike those of today's navy ships). The drone carrier vessel is pointedly named the RSS *Lee Kuan Yew*, while a new aircraft carrier is named the *Parmeswara* after the fourteenth-century ruler of Singapore who then founded also the Sultanate of Malacca; the two allude to two different founder stories.

Most of the prototypes for the new merlion failed or took too long to grow, but one survived. In addition to a suite of biomimetic enhanced human genes, including accelerated cell regeneration, it was supposed to have echolocation derived from dolphins, and a tail that could serve as artillery underwater, shooting superheated air bubbles at two hundred meters and vaporizing targets.[27] Merlions produced a jelly on their sides that is a replicator for building new merlions, and that new human recruits are made to swim through as part of their augmentation, particularly to give them the ability to breathe under water longer using myoglobin used by sea mammals. The problem was to figure out how to accelerate the time taken for merlions to grow, and here theories of time travel enter. If the pups could be sent back in time they would have time to grow and be useful in the current war. This is tried, albeit unsuccessfully, by A*STAR (Agency for Science, Technology and Research), which had some aging Orion spacecraft. So A*STAR then gets help from the one remaining astronaut on the American space station, *Liberty*, who had previously worked on a time travel project for NASA in the 2020s. Not able to reconstruct a Cold War Russian design of the Alcubierre warp drive, which had been devised in the Soviet Russian Korolev space center, A*STAR scientists devise an alternative called Proteus, which consumed so much energy it created a blackout on the island, but eventually is launched.[28] Targeting accuracy, however, was slightly off, and the merlion pups are misdirected in time and space to 1803 in Marina Bay East, which would have been underwater at the time (it was created through land reclamation in the 1970s and 1980s). So now they have to try to rescue the pups, targeting a window of time between the Japanese defeat and the new vigilance of independent Singapore's naval ability to interfere with strange incursions or arrivals. Any further accidents would "create time paradoxes we'd rather not handle" (Wong 2017a). Given that these time paradoxes are hard to solve, and since they are creating parallel universes, it is argued that it was "better to defeat Concordance in another parallel universe than letting them finish defeating us in this one."

The novel ends in a whirl of further scrambling of time; dreamworlds and traumatic ideations, in which Titus and Naufal coexist; punishments for violations of the Military Code of Conduct are exacted (caning, being put through a meat grinder); and fears of dismemberment and dissolution (metal slicing bodies, zorgs being loosed, and boundaries of bodies dissolving or morphing). At issue now is less twisted histories, or untwisting official stories, but psychic effects. The merlion Bahana bonded with Naufal keeps Naufal from fragmenting into madness like his brother; and inversely, Bahana's loyalty to Naufal gives Bahana the strength to separate from the gestalt. When Naufal is punished with thirty-one lashes for disobeying a direct order, Bahana helps him psychologically by telling him to focus on him (Bahana). When Naufal is mortally wounded in battle, Bahana carries him to safety in the curve of his tail, even though this means abandoning the battle, a violation for them both. The main problem with merlions like Bahana, in the eyes of the army, is that they are fiercely loyal, "often found putting the needs of their human partner over the needs of the army and the country. . . . But to an organization that required bureaucratic, exacting precision and deference, it was difficult to say whether on balance they [such merlions] were more of a burden or an asset" (315). For the gestalt as well, such merlions are double-edged, having to care for more fragile bodies, but "it was rumored that the gestalt had always sought to be more human, to take on aspects of human individuality that it could not comprehend as a hive mind" (89).

The tension between more communal and more individualistic societies or disciplinary regimes has been a long-standing staple of political theory and punditry. Much of the novel is about transgressions against overly rigid social norms, rules, and bureaucratic procedures. "Where everyone knows everyone and everyone knows everything" (58), it is hard to create spaces for secrecy or heterotopias. Titus's sister tries to protect him against discovery of his illegitimate relations with Akash, a Singapore Survey Corps officer, and he in turn not only worries about his sister's safety in a chaotic world, but in one of the last moments of the novel, though battered himself, his anxieties are set to rest when learns that she is safe. Naufal dreams of days of fishing with his brother and father in their youth.

But the scenes at the end of the novel are ones of traumatic transitions between universes, mind worlds, frames of reference, and the unmaking and remaking of stories. Forms merge and shape-shift, are violently ripped apart and reemerge as parts of other beings. Salehah, once an intimate of Titus, gives Titus the silent treatment: "they had been each other, she knew all about him and rejected him, during the transition between universes"; the engineer Kartik becomes part squid-eating Akash; and Naufal and Bahana each have dreams of being torn apart and being rebuilt.[29] Bahana is shocked by one of these transformations: "The human was nothing like Bahana had ever seen. . . . It was as if reality bent around her—no, as if reality and her couldn't really agree on where she was supposed to be, or why. As if the jigsaw was incomplete, and she, as the last piece, wasn't quite the right fit. . . . Something was out of place. . . . Other things appeared like that, of course. The garuda. The antaboga. The dragons. And the merlions themselves" (317). All of these traditional mythic creatures are composite figures of other animals or animals and humans. The merlion is described in one place as sleek, bottle-nosed, gray, with smooth skin, a serrated tail ending in sharp quill-like points, fins or flippers two thirds of the way up with an additional dorsal fin on its back, a head with snake eyes, a dog nose, a snout sharp and protruding like a shark, and a mane more like quills than hair. The quills of its whiskers are sharp enough to pierce skin. The effort to send these creatures back in time, at least in the scientists' models, would change things only minimally, "because we're only sending animals back that would occupy ecological niches without causing ecosystem wide havoc, and at *the same time would satisfy some of the myths and legends that already existed* in various cultures around the world" (95, emphasis added). Among the modes of communication are the songs of merlions calling for their lost siblings and human partners.

ANALYTIC MONSTERS AND HUMAN REMAINS

> This thing called human nature / is less human than you think / 'cause most of it is nature / where life is on the brink / We've moved out from the jungle / But jungle laws remain . . .
>
> ALFIAN SA'AT, "PEOPLE ARE DANGEROUS" (SONG SET TO FLAMENCO MUSIC IN WILD RICE'S PRODUCTION OF *MADAME WHITE SNAKE*)

> You only have to look at Medusa straight on to see her. And she is not deadly. She's beautiful and she's laughing.
>
> HELENE CIXOUS, "THE LAUGHTER OF THE MEDUSA"

Another way of thinking about the present and future is through what I might call "analytic monsters" repurposed from folklore, as in *Altered Straits*, as well as through new video games and their simulations of algorithmic and feedback-metric machineries that have become management infrastructures, as in *The HDB Murders*. Dragons and white snakes are among the most well-known of such monsters in Chinese tradition. Especially interesting is *taowu*, "the monster that is history," whose meanings David Der-wei Wang (2004) recovers as an analytic figure. *Taowu* is the name of a ferocious divinatory imperial tomb animal-guardian, made up of a combination of animal parts, that sees into the past and future, and is also the name of a genre of historical writing that "because of its fiendish nature . . . compels the ancients to remember and recount its wickedness so as to take precaution," "where poetic justice contends with legal justice or in more volatile terms, where ink demands blood," "registering what is immemorial and yet unforgettable" (Wang 2004, 3, 6–7). This genre of historical writing encrypts the "affective intensities of private and inadmissible truth" in official histories "so dictated by the ideological and institutional imaginary as to verge on a discourse of make-believe" (Wang 2004, 3), much as "the Singapore story" has come to feel, and against which so many novelists are now writing, trying to excavate alternative suppressed histories and truths, and sometimes having to deploy retooled analytic monsters. Freud could not have said or done it better.

Madame White Snake is another such analytic figure in the realm of desire, sex, and spiritual zen, with many retellings, in oral storytelling, films (including animated works), operas, musicals, television serials, and novels.[30] Drawing on a figure that has been operating since the ninth century CE (and earlier in the goddess figure of Nuwa), these works explore the permutations of illicit love and betrayal, divine or demonic seduction (and the stealing of male "essence"), immortality (of the snake) and mortality (of men), and liberation from Buddhist, Confucian, and Daoist gender categories, and from meditation's transformative powers.[31] They also explore women's roles, from evil sorceresses and enchanting femmes fatales, to liberated womanhood, and use the melodramatic plot line of having the courage to follow one's heart—"the immortal snake's quest for love represented us all, we watched to have our hearts broken again and again" (Luo 2021). Additional themes include the homosexual and transgender upending of male/female and human/nonhuman categories, the celebration of women's writing and creativity (and *écriture féminine*), and the "metaphor [of] the indominable spirit defying destiny."[32] There are three recent reworkings of the story with Singapore connections. First, the Pulitzer Prize–winning opera *Madame White Snake* by the Singapore-born, American librettist and founder of activist-social justice opera Cerise Lim Jacobs, and the Beijing-born, American composer Zhou Long, which brilliantly brings Chinese and Western music into conversation (Zhou and Jacobs 2010).[33] Second, the Wild Rice theater company's musical *Mama White Snake*, with music by Elaine Chan and lyrics by Alfian Sa'at, and starring gender-bending Ivan Heng and Glen Goei as the "sister act" of Green Snake and White Snake, set firmly in the pharmacy and pharmakon (poison-healing) trope that has been a key if minor motif for centuries (Chan and Sa'at 2017). And third, the novel by Malaysian-Singaporean writer Nuraliah Norasid, *The Gatekeeper* (2017), written as an allegory of Singaporean stratification and the marginalization of the Malay population within a hard-driving, metricizing, and consumer-driven Chinese majority.

Norasid's *The Gatekeeper*, winner of the 2016 fiction prize of the Singapore-based publishing house Epigram Books, combines the Greek myth of Medusa (lit., "guardian, protector")—one of three gorgons, winged female children of marine deities with snakes in place of hair—with that of the Chinese White Snake.[34] In the Greek-derived versions, Medusa turns those who look her in the eye to stone. Her head, severed by Perseus, becomes a shield to ward off evil, and she increasingly is described as "drop dead" beautiful, and ambiguously as an image of female rage or laughter (in Hélène Cixous's interpretation).[35] In one Chinese version, retold by Li Bihua in her novel *Green Snake* (1986), and adapted into film by Tsui Hark (1993), the two sisters—named Barani ("rain") and Ria ("small river") in *The Gatekeeper*—come to earth above a brothel. The elder sister, intrigued by the human women's snake-like waists twisting in the wild dancing, joins in, while the younger sister is attracted to a bookstore next to the brothel, where she meets a young man with whom she falls in love. Ria is described as reading books, and trying to keep alive the ancient Tuyunri language, keeping her distance from the nearby brothel district.[36] Ria looks up to the elder sister as the beautiful, unapproachable one, and it is she, the younger sibling, who is a green snake—at least in being, at critical moments, the envious and wild, impulsive one. It is her bookish characteristic that bonds her to Eedric (lit., "rich and powerful"), the mixed-race son of a powerful member of the ruling class of Manticura (the rapidly gentrifying and inegalitarian city that is Singapore's simulacrum above ground). For having objected—with her terrible power to stare and turn men to stone—to the rapid segregation, gentrification, and destruction of nature, the sisters flee the police to the slum-underworld of Nelroote. Both Manticura and, from time to time, Nelroote are policed with sophisticated surveillance or heavy-handed (and booted) police raids, interrogation, and torture, picking up themes from *The HDB Murders* and *Altered Straits*.

The Gatekeeper gestures toward the recovery (or creation) of the Tuyunri language, á la Kevin Martens Wong's work with Kristang, along with Malay words scattered through the novel.[37] Tuyunri is given a glossary, along with an appendix intended to supply a mytho-historical time line, which also is a superfluous artifact to the reading of the text. Both the

Tuyunri and the (untranslated) Malay words are perhaps meant to provide an alienation effect for the English-language reader (the language in which the novel is written) to simulate the feeling of being a minority. The prominent Singaporean playwright Haresh Sharma, who, although Indian in terms of Singapore's census categories, grew up speaking Malay and incorporates Malay characters and language in his plays, blurbs the novel as "an impressive piece of writing—confident and effortless." But these aspects of the novel (story line, the combining of mythologies, and vocabularies) are less to the point than Norasid's acknowledged effort to emulate the "world making" of video games. And yet, it is the structural features of the old mythologies that give the novel both coherence and *analytic* purchase in both senses (the unconscious drives of desire; the structural myths that make up the code for interpretation). There is the basic agonism between surface and underworld/watery deeps, ancient knowledge and contemporary forgetting, purity and hybridity, weakness and strength (oscillating from the whiteness of the snake as shimmering beauty or pale decaying ash, and the greenness of green snake as like fresh leaves of desire or debilitating jealousy), love triangles (and even motifs of one man, two women; and one woman, two men), and inversions of gender positions.[38] Ideological claims of the Tuyunri language being grounded in the land (we need to return from destructive political economies to living with nature) are hardly borne out in the novel: aside from the names of the sisters, there is little evidence in the glossary of attention to the local ecology beyond the simple terms of forest, and catacombs as the refuge or last resting place of the ancestors and marginals.[39]

As analytic monsters, dragons, white and green snakes, merlions, and antabogas are logical operators, refracting mirrors (reflecting awry) of our biologies, and transformations of our unrecognized desires or drives. They are also, as in *Altered Straits*, biological mirrors of convergences and assimilative infrastructures managing logistics and formalizing and replacing social norms with what can or cannot be done in more rigid human-designed "ontologies" of rules. The monster of history as a dragon remains extraordinarily potent, albeit no longer invoked in daily discourse in quite that way; the monster of algorithmic and cybernetic control systems that increase productivity, manage logistics, and achieve metrics of success are in fact invoked in daily discourse, albeit again often in ways that express and intensify fears projected in paranoid imaginations that in turn become stress, motivation, and feedback.

Are our dreamworlds and abilities to reconfigure our futures (as in markets, investments, and bets on the futures we *will have been* making) able to work around the rigidities of "ontologies" that have lived beyond their expiration dates (hence becoming monsters), rewriting them for newer realities? What is this world that we inhabit? What are these dreamworlds? Why do the categories morph? And how do we fuse and individuate, bond and break apart? The COVID-19 pandemic has put all these questions under a slightly different aspect: the surveillance tools we worried about before the pandemic have become better friends particularly in Asian countries, amid nonetheless growing concerns about privacy, security, and reliance on digital infrastructures beyond any individual's capacity to understand them. Their failures or limitations have clarified the degree to which merlions depend upon humans. The merlions in this case are airborne viruses, swimming in the air, tiny, imperceptible, and teaching us many things we never knew about our biologies and ecologies. We morph again. These considerations raise again the question of the place of addictions to rationality and smartness in algorithmic prostheses and folkloric structures of thought.

CONCLUSIONS

> Never abandon the sinuous path / Don't follow the direct path / Walk following the ways and roads of the old sages.
>
> KHMER SAYING, EPIGRAPH TO LYDIA KWA'S *SINUOUS*

> On no account acknowledge what your folktales imply.
>
> ALVIN PANG, *WHEN THE BARBARIANS ARRIVE*

This chapter has looked at three first novels in three different genres or modes—detective story, science fiction, and social justice advocacy through revisionary mythopoeisis—to further explore anxieties and tensions embedded in future thinking. "Ethnographically," they focus on bureaucracies and algorithms; bioethical boundaries and linguistic-cultural creolizations; and advocacy in mythology (social justice for minorities via Medusa, and the White Snake Project). All three have elements that, once read, one cannot get out of one's mind, becoming social critiques of the oblique but powerful kind: the challenging dispersion of responsibility in systems of rationales not merely social but also algorithmic; the moral boundaries of bioengineering; and the vital resistances of inequalities, repressions, and erasure of the histories of how we got here. Among the generators of such power are the ability to draw upon both Eastern and Western archetypes.

For me, Daren Goh's *The HDB Murders* updates Michael Young's satirical *The Rise of the Meritocracy*, made particularly trenchant today by the global competitive and destructive metrics-auditing of liberal university education that threatens all noninstrumental educational programs, in Britain as well as Singapore, and elsewhere. Singapore too began as a social democratic experiment. The Lockean, Fabian, and Labour Party agendas of the post–World War II era of reconstruction of society remain vital if contested. Neoliberal reason is increasingly under challenge and seen as corrupting, but the struggle to articulate the philosophy of a humanistic or humane social good, where individuals and groups can be nodes or spaces for slowed-down moral reasoning in new technological worlds, remains work in progress. *The HDB Murders* can just as easily be read through Chinese political philosophy, particularly that of Han Fei, whose name has appeared several times in chapters 2 and 3, as the hard-fisted guiding rules or ruler operating as an unseen center whose effects are felt everywhere. This is not just ancient philosophy, but at the root of debates over the Singaporean and Chinese models of efficient governance in contrast to the messiness of democracy.

Likewise, for me, Kevin Martens Wong's *Altered Straits* is an invitation to pierce through the management-speak of the neoliberal state, including its fast-changing branding campaigns for governance including the attraction of foreign talent, foreign labor, and tourists as Singapore transforms itself into a transnational platform. There are at least three levels of metaphor: the merlion's chimerical fusion of lion and fish as metaphor for a sovereign port dependent on the sea; as a metaphor of bioengineering projects that quite literally play with DNA and tissue engineering; and as a metaphor for the underappreciated endangered languages, dialects, and histories that compose the flexibility and endurance of present and future society. At the heart of this novel, at the risk of overreading it, is the author's CoLang project of saving the Kristang language as well as a tribute to Portuguese-Asians (a more specific history than the umbrella category Eur-Asian) from whom the author is descended. The Kristang language in its varying instantiations across Singapore, Malaysia, Macau, and the Philippines is a reminder of diasporic minorities that continue to contribute to the textures of contemporary society and keep the pores of state membranes receptive and flexible, countering the closed-border and typologizing mentality of the video-game-like naval battle space and apocalyptic plot. More explicit within the novel are the gay, lesbian, and other nonnormative sexualities, and the lives of intermarrying communities, or culturally mixed backgrounds of the anthronauts themselves, again lightly reflecting current cultural politics within Singapore. Kristang itself is both East and West, nonexistent without their mixture, and the struggles over sexuality are being reassessed in literatures of both East and West, as finally the White Snake in *The Gatekeeper* attests.

For me, Nuraliah Norasid's *The Gatekeeper* provides one of the clearest literary or mythopoetic assays into the contemporary (rather than historical) racial stratifications and inequalities generated in the meritocratic state focused on feelings in the Malay community.[40] It brings together ancient Greek myth and ancient Chinese myth, East and West, and does so with a feminist and *écriture féminine* mode of writing the body. If Medusa is more foregrounded, reflecting perhaps the more Western-oriented Singapore education system, the incredibly rich dramatic reinterpretations of the White Snake/Green Snake pairing lie not far behind the theater mask. The snake imagery is geographically complicated. It can be said the *naga*s of the great rivers (Indus, Ganges, Brahmaputra, Irrawaddy, Mekong) are continental—albeit not metaphorically relevant in the context of the island and coastal sea worlds of Singapore and the Malay archipelago, as Charles Lim's *SEA STATE* artwork dramatizes (see Fischer 2023, 104). Still, the doubleness and sinuousness of the snakes and *naga*s—bringing both fertility and destructive floods, protectiveness and death, sloughing off an old skin and generating a new one, the hood of the (multiple) cobras and the venom of their bite—play out quite well in the sexual economy of shape-shifting charisma and jealousy, anger and renewal, coiling and uncoiling, *gui-shen* 鬼神 (meaning, in folk idiom, "ghost or spirit," but more philosophically or cosmologically meaning "movements of contraction and expansion" [Wang Jing 2021, 200]). And Medusa is part of the Greek thalassocratic world: Perseus comes by sea. Thalassocracy in the Malay world, too, is created at the mouth of smaller rivers, places where trading posts can be set to tax the sea lanes as well as the transfer of goods between coast and upland. To push all this underground, *The Gatekeeper* indicates, is to invite constriction at the top and tension from below, not unlike that described in *The HDB Murders*.

Afterword

Portals to the Future: MRT Stations, Universities, and the Peopling of Technologies

Physical entryways are often portals to the future. Singapore's underground stations on its Mass Rapid Transit (MRT) system are not only entries for transit but also sites for public art, sponsored by Art-in-Transit, a program of the Land Transit Authority of Singapore. So too are the entryways to two of Singapore's experiments in creative new university education. I select these three entryways or portals as icons, symbols, and indexes of key themes in this volume, and their forward signaling. Icons, symbols, and indexes were American pragmatist, logician, and semioticist C. S. Pierce's categories of signs; he will not mind if index becomes index fingerprint or thumbprint in Singaporean artist Boo Junfeng's installation at the MRT station at Upper Changi, the entry to the Singapore University of Technology and Design, or if icons include calligraphy as well as phoenixes in the layered art of Tan Swee Hian at the Chinatown MRT, or the symbolic elephants, camphor tree, and rebus mural at the entryways to Tembusu College in the University Town campus of the National University of Singapore. Icons, symbols, and indexes are visual tokens of information compression, and have only become more omnipresent in or at (@) technological societies.

ICONS @ THE MRT STATION For the theme of the use of cultural tinder or resources from the past to rework and create new aspirations for the future, which was also a key theme in the companion volume, *Probing Arts and Emergent Forms of Life* (Fischer 2023), I invoke the Chinatown MRT station, which uses Tan Swie Hian's calligraphy and symbolically stylized phoenix (itself a symbol of continual rebirth and reinvention). It encompasses transitions from past to present, that is, from calligraphy and immigration in ships to fully automated, driverless rapid transit. The Chinatown MRT station opened in 2003, and became an interchange with a second line in 2013. The station is attached, not coincidentally, to one of Singapore's iconic modernist architectural and urban planning experiments, the People's Park Centre and People's Park Complex, completed in 1973. That complex was designed to help pioneer mixed-use, tropical architecture, around atriums and free flow of cooling air.[1] The idea was that it would be a node in the community fabric, encouraging people from the neighborhood to flow through, rather than being a self-contained isolate.

SYMBOLS @ THE UNIVERSITY For the theme of upgrading human capital, and of creating a more humane future society, I invoke the (aboveground) multiple entryways and portals to Tembusu College, one of the four indigenous residential liberal arts colleges of the National University of Singapore (NUS). These four colleges were initiated in the second decade of the twenty-first century, intended to loosen the rigid siloed courses of study at NUS, which itself in the previous decade was transformed from a teaching university to a globally recognized research university. The colleges were to bridge the two-cultures division of sciences and engineering versus the humanities, and instead to build advanced technologies with humanities-informed and people-centered approaches to the world. These four colleges were experimental pilots, each with a slightly different focus, but each drawing students into common classrooms from across their varied disciplines for initial two-year, liberal arts–style college experiences. Such experiences were meant to be formative before disciplinary specializations put obstacles (even just time pressures) in the way of the very interdisciplinarity that would allow them to succeed in an ever more complex world. Tembusu College was built on the relatively new, but increasingly important field of STS (science, technology, and society), in parallel with an STS research cluster of NUS's Asia Research Institute (ARI), both under the leadership of Gregory Clancey, professor of Japanese history of technology. Another college had a focus on drama and the arts, a third on social work outreach, and a fourth on ecology. Painted elephants, a camphor tree from Hiroshima, and a rebus mural signal and symbolize these intentions.

INDEX FINGER PRINTS @ THE SINGAPORE UNIVERSITY OF TECHNOLOGY AND DESIGN For the theme of new digital and visual technologies of AI, computational engineering and biology, design thinking and teamwork production, new materials and additive manufacturing, quality control and surveillance, and physical and cognitive enhancements—all parts of the so-called fourth industrial revolution or new spirits of capitalism and neoliberalism, with potentials of both good features and troubling implications—I invoke the MRT station at the Singapore University of Technology and Design, my third ethnographic home (after Tembusu College and the Genome Institute of Singapore) in observing Singapore's experiments in creative university innovation. The artwork here is a potent reminder of a focus on the peopling of technologies for the future worlds in which we want to live. The artwork is created from the fingerprints and free associations of the pioneer generation of students in the school—enigmatic body marks and puzzled mental feelings.

MRT STATIONS: ART IN TRANSIT @ CHINATOWN

Calligraphy by Tan Swie Hian (see the introduction): three rhyming couplets provide a "footnote" (his pun) to a mural of a soaring phoenix in multiple forms, representing the journey of Singapore's Chinese immigrants. The phoenix, a creature in the *Shan Hai Jing* (*Guideways through Mountains and Seas*) flies over rocks (the Dragon's Teeth Gate, the once perilous entry to the island, near today's Keppel Harbour) that are themselves shaped like two *kris* (Malay ceremonial daggers). Five virtues are inscribed on the phoenix's body (virtue, righteousness, civility, benevolence, credibility), which in another section of the mural is surrounded by a myriad of birds, and in a third section, the birds merge with the phoenix—shades of the Attar's Simorgh, discussed in chapter 5.

UNIVERSITIES: STS/HUMANITIES PORTAL @ TEMBUSU COLLEGE

Two elephants greet you at the entrance to Tembusu College's four buildings. The one known as Blink of an Eye raises his legs and shows off his Band-Aids. His eyeballs reflect a rifle-toting hunter who attempted to kill him and poach his ivory tusks. The other, known as Precious Ties, kneels. His feet and knees are tattooed with the other four endangered species that also

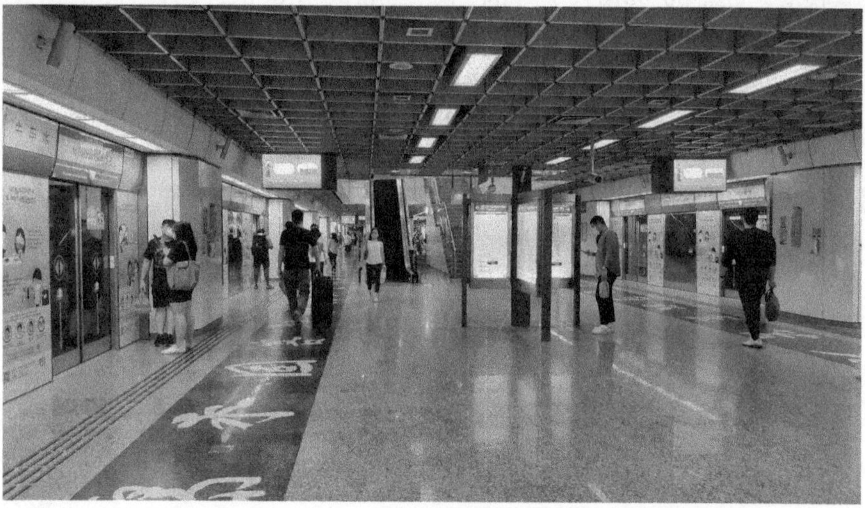

A.1 Art in Transit, Chinatown MRT station NE4. Calligraphy by Tan Swie Hian.

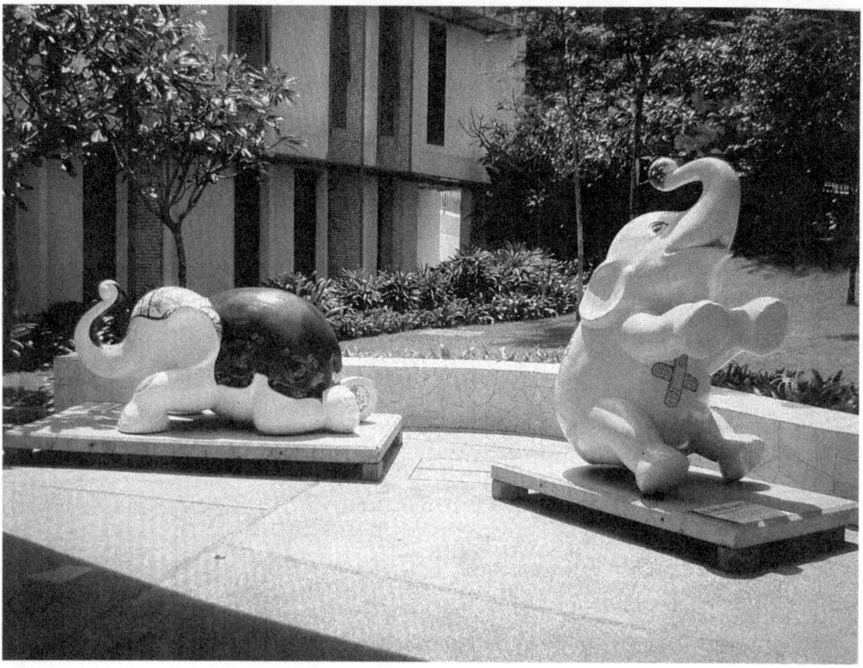

A.2 Tembusu College entrance with elephants Blink of an Eye and Precious Ties. Photo: M. Fischer.

serve as totems for the five "houses" into which the college is divided. The totems were selected by the first class of students, and to the bemusement of the staff, the choices, the students later revealed, were informed by the animals in the DreamWorks film *Kung Fu Panda* (2008). They are (with their Chinese names): elephant (Gaja House), red panda (Ponya House), Komodo dragon (Ora House), snow leopard (Shan House), and red-crowned crane (Tancho House). A *tembusu*, pictured on the Singapore five-dollar bill, is an evergreen hardwood that grows 10 to 25 meters, is impervious to termites or weevils, and is thus good for floors that can last a century. A large *tembusu* stands in the upper courtyard of the Educational Resource Center next to the college, a sort of modernist Metabolist building of curves, with computer facilities, an auditorium and seminar rooms, but no books. The lower courtyard, looking onto the large green of University Town, has a popular Starbucks, and a large covered patio and computer plug–ready tables. Nearer the elephants stands a young camphor tree, grown from one of the seeds that survived the bombing of Hiroshima. Such seeds are disseminated from Hiroshima as peace tokens, memory of both the bombing and the recovery from the war. It was planted on Earth Day in a ceremony with someone from the Japanese Embassy and Dr. Rethy Chem, a radiologist and historian of medicine, who at the time was working at the International Atomic Energy Agency (IAEA). Chem, in collaboration with Gregory Clancey, the master of Tembusu College and a historian of Japan, organized a series of IAEA-sponsored conferences in Japan and at Tembusu on radiation effects after the 2011 meltdown and radiation release at the Fukushima nuclear plant. On a hill behind Tembusu College, two large pieces of the Berlin Wall with colorful graffiti are set up like memorial stellae. The elephants, painted by Tembusu students, were auctioned by Sotheby's during the Elephant Parade Singapore 2011, a fundraiser for the conservation of Asian elephants. Tembusu College bid for and got Blink of an Eye for $7,000, while Precious Ties sold for $45,000 and was donated back to the college by its purchaser, Tangs Department Store.

The elephants are among a series of public artworks created by Tembusu College students under the supervision of resident artist and faculty fellow Margaret Ai Hua Tan. They signal more than just a feel-good concern for the environment or student art projects. One of the core courses at Tembusu College is on climate change, another on model cities (including efforts at greening them), a third on biomedicine and society, and a fourth on animals in the city. Students repaint the elephants every few years, partly due to the climate, but mainly as a ritual so new cohorts of students will feel ownership.

A.3 Blink of an Eye. Photo: M. Fischer.

A.4 (*Opposite left*) Precious ties: snow leopard. Photo: M. Fischer.

A.5 (*Opposite right*) Precious ties: crane and red panda. Photo: M. Fischer.

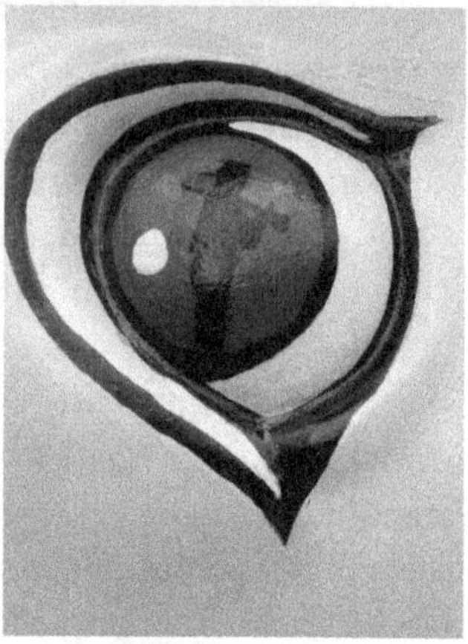

For a while, someone also put a plastic container of water in front of one of the elephants as if for Ganesh, the god of both good luck and learning.

The arts as communicative forms are central to the pedagogy of a number of the course instructors, both for teaching and for students to learn to think with, and learn to work with in changing media environments. They can be matters of political awareness as well. An anonymous person complained on social media that the camphor tree should not be planted because of what the Japanese did during the occupation of Singapore in World War II, and there was a worry that the tree might be harmed (which did not happen). Similarly, someone wrote to complain that the Berlin Wall pieces brought evil spirits with them and should not be located close to colleges, as they would bring bad luck. Performative arts, including debate forums on issues sensitive in the public sphere, are regular features organized both by students and by the rector of the college, law professor and ambassador Tommy Koh, who also managed to arrange the opportunities for the elephants and the Berlin Wall pieces.

A second key piece of student public art, a mural composed of rebuses satirizing contemporary internet culture, also produced under Margaret Tan's supervision, adorns one of the entry halls to the college's Learning Lobe (classrooms, library, and activity rooms). A boy sits cross-legged, thumbs up. His head is a book titled *All About Me*. Next to him, a girl presses "send" on her iPhone and the trap doors of her skull are open, releasing a bird (bird brain). The bird is being chased by a large grinning figure with a butterfly net (the title character, Big Friendly Giant, in Roald Dahl's *The BFG*). The Big Friendly Giant's chest is covered with the icons of Facebook,

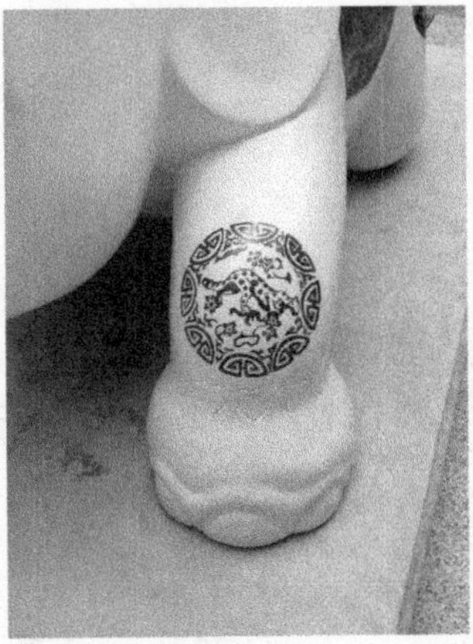 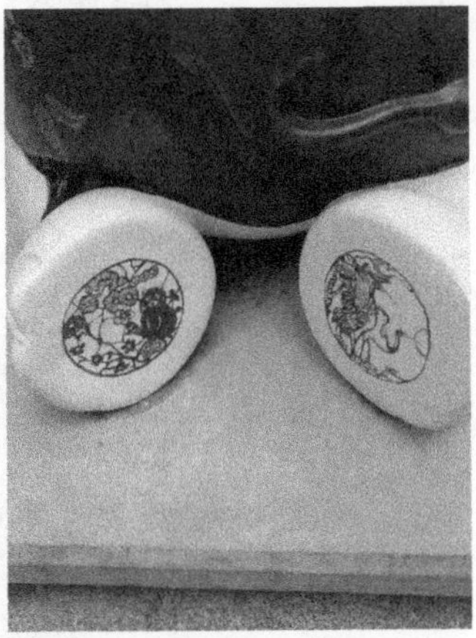

LinkedIn, and other digital icons (seeking to capture the desires released on social media for resale to marketers). The bird flies toward a camera-headed barefoot girl in tank top and jeans who holds up her hand: "Hi!" Nearby, a fish-headed fisher with a fishing pole stands by a tombstone (which reads "RIP Meg Aupload 2005–2012"), phishing for passwords in the skull of a bespectacled figure walking with a cane, perhaps to upload the terabytes of previous generations' knowledge. A wind-blown tourist couple with cameras floats above a ghostly woman's head with Microsoft icon eyes. A detached hand tosses an eye-popping, jaw-dropping head; and a conveyor belt carries more eyes on strings (i-devices). A man in bathing trunks and a woman in a shift hold their detached heads on strings, perhaps signifying the disconnect between online character and the real person. The mural is signed by the respective artists and dated 2013.

The mural provides several useful metaphors. Are the strange metamorphic creatures called global universities distancing machines, analogous to the printing press so criticized in the Muslim world at the time of the Napoleonic invasion of Egypt, allowing the projection of cultural power at a distance, ever more globally (through metrics and rankings, such as the global rankings compiled in Shanghai and London, A- and O-Levels from the United Kingdom, or the dissemination of Taylorian metrics to enforce greater and greater productivity)? Or is the picture of the world in 2013 rather one of students at Starbucks and elsewhere holding textbooks and exercise books open with one hand, the other checking their teachers' archived video lectures on their smart phones, and taking notes on iPads or writing pads? Truth for them is to be discovered by triangulating among

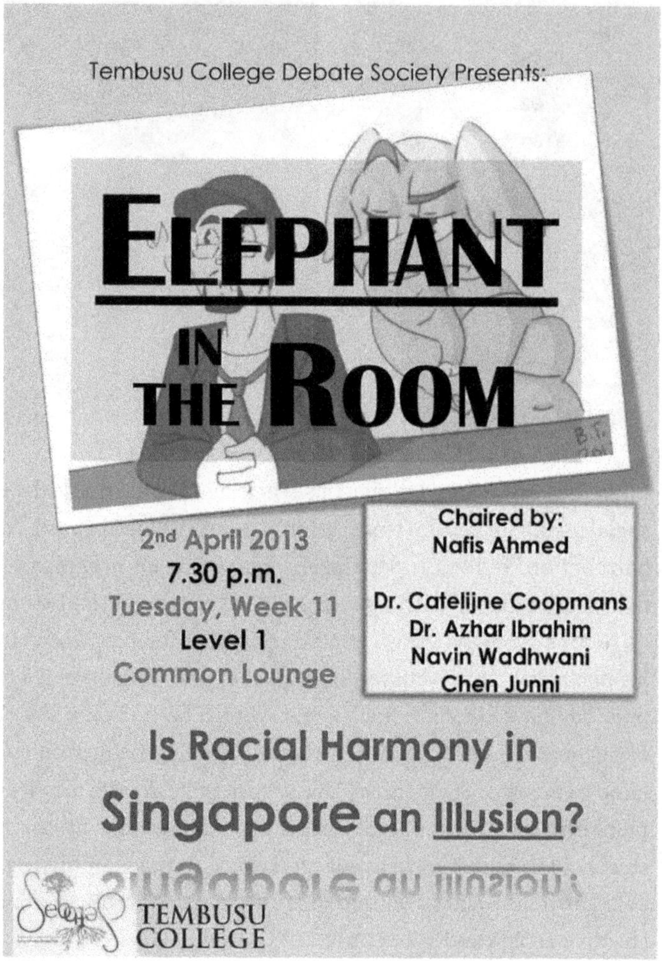

A.6 Elephant in the Room (poster): Is Racial Harmony in Singapore an Illusion?

updated lectures on video (as research updates the science), canonic platforms of knowledge codified in more slowly updated textbooks, and peer help. Truth lies in the shifting of heads between smart phone, iPad, textbook, and colleague at the next table, sharing, correcting, testing. Are they self-empowering, learning, discerning, and creating? As they turn their heads back and forth, cycling through their devices from lectures to workbook, to chat, to textbook, and back, they are looking into the sociocultural and technological infrastructures of new globalizing universities, and they do so with humor, social critique, judgment, as well as a sense of new possibilities. The classroom is already half flipped. "Flipped classrooms" and

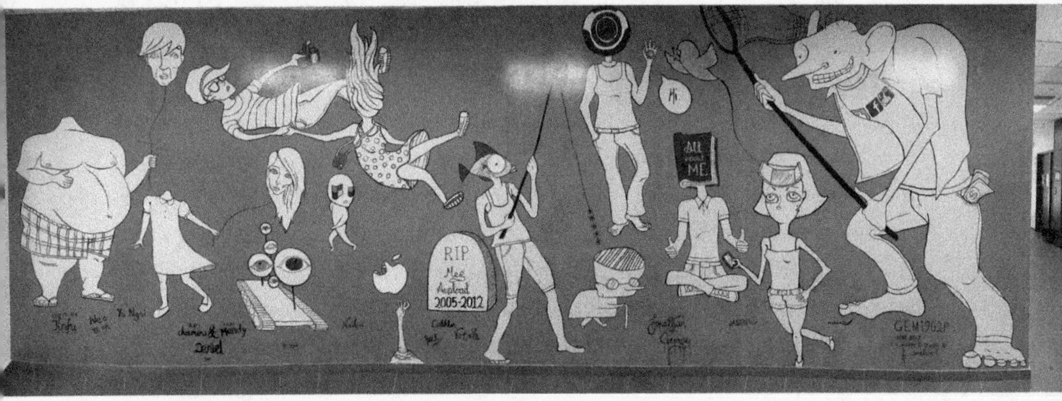

A.7 Rebus mural, Tembusu College. Courtesy of Margaret Tan.

"blended classrooms" were terms of art from the early days of massive open online courses (MOOCs): by presenting study materials online (video lectures, readings, and tutorial problem sets), classroom time theoretically can be devoted less to information delivery and more to coaching and face-to-face, individualized, and shared teaching. The limits of this vision, as well as the opportunity to turn each local class, special lecture, and symposium into venues for global participants, were tested in the year of lockdowns caused by the 2020/21 COVID-19 pandemic.

But the metaphors go deeper: what seems like the mindless fun of a bird escaping Facebook chatter to be captured as commercial data is not so far removed from the three main ranking systems that drive administrators and ministries to seek ever more metrics and rankings by which they can advertise and sell their institutions. This is big business, and serious business-model survival. Singapore at times thinks it can have a large catchment area. In 2003, the year of the SARS pandemic, there were 23,000 Chinese students in Singapore; Singapore hosts also sizeable numbers from India, and smaller numbers from Sri Lanka, Malaysia, Indonesia, Vietnam, Thailand, Cambodia, Laos, and Iran. Those not from monied elites come on scholarships. Some were already recruited to come on scholarship for high school. Some paying students also come from Europe and North America. In 2012 there were 11,699 international students at the National University of Singapore alone. Singapore's university initiatives resonate with those in China, UAE, and elsewhere, including start-up universities, new science cities, technology incubator parks, urban "creative districts," maker-spaces, and slogans of hands-on, project-based, entrepreneurial, active learning.

The performativity sought through, and disciplined by, key performance indicators (KPIs), centers of excellence, audit cultures, and business plans—as Bill Readings began to track twenty-five years ago (see Readings 1996)—has elevated educational reform into central policy concerns for ever-changing economies. Readings argued that universities were undergoing a shift from being centers of nation-building, with national histories and literatures as core features, to nodes in international competition in which metrication of productivity shifted from the nation-building of liberal arts and basic science to entrepreneurial translation (products, patents, jobs, returns on investment, partnerships with industry) in increasing transnational competition. Students become "consumers," and labor forces are monetized as "human capital" with saleable skills, "the birth," as Michel Foucault put it, of neoliberal biopolitics (Foucault 2010), satirized in the novels in chapter 7.

The obsolescence of previous skilled labor and even professionals into cadres of precarity is nowhere more visible than in the taxi drivers of Singapore: former welders, seamen, oil-rig technicians, electronics sales representatives, shop owners, and even engineers and bankers who have been downsized, restructured, or retired. Taxi driving is reserved for citizens only, a domestic labor force cushion. Words too have shifted meanings. Analytic reason now often is replaced by "analytics," referring to large data sets beyond the capacities of individual brains or personal experience, and which underwrite new cultivations of stressed selves in jobs that allow some time for yoga, running, organic food, and mindfulness. The two arts projects—the elephants and rebus mural—described above provide contexts for, and indexes of, these changes. They are also indexes for the educational experiments in response, being pioneered at Tembusu College and Singapore University of Technology and Design (SUTD), to create humanistic interdisciplinarity beyond merely the economic instrumentality of pressures for educational reform to stay competitive in the so-called new knowledge economies. The educational experiments at Tembusu and elsewhere are responses *also* to something "under foot" in the *cultural texture* of fast-changing Asian cities.

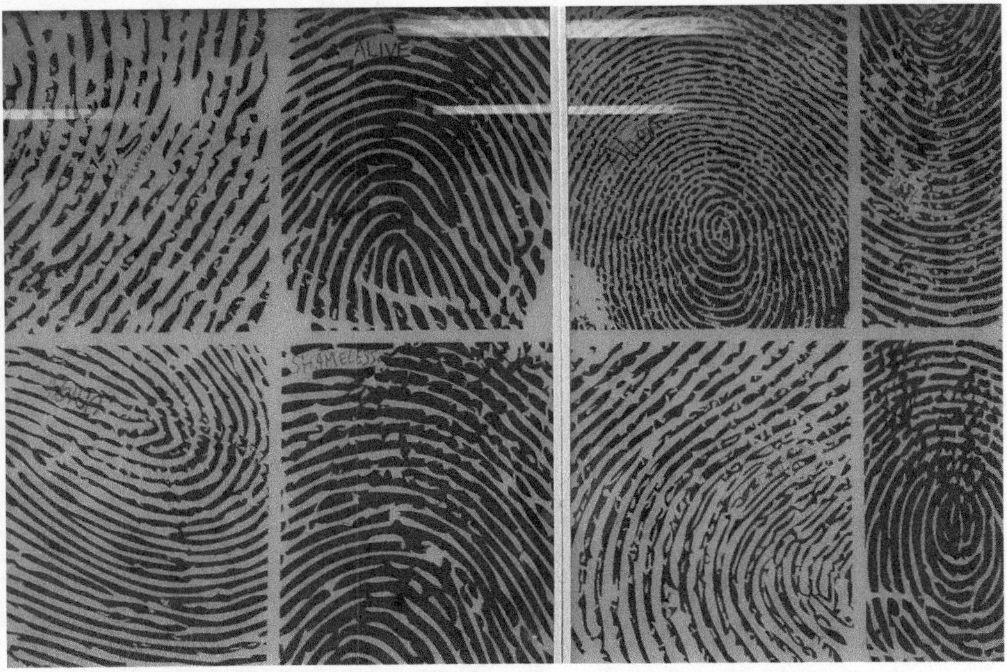

A.8 MRT Upper Changi station at SUTD, Art in Transit: Boo Junfeng, "I Am Anonymous." Photo: M. Fischer.

PEOPLING OF TECHNOLOGIES: I AM ANONYMOUS (MRT STATION @ SUTD)

I Am Anonymous is an Art in Transit installation by Boo Junfeng at the Upper Changi MRT station, with direct entry into SUTD. Boo Junfeng became well known for his film *Apprentice* (2016), about a young Malay who is trained to replace a retiring executioner in Singapore's prison system, a surprising psychological inquiry into both men, and a contribution to the debate over the death penalty; he then was selected as creative director of Singapore's National Day Parade.[2]

I Am Anonymous "comprises prints and texts collected in 2013 from 269 students, the pioneer class, of SUTD, . . . who were asked to complete the statement 'I am . . .' Although written in their own hand and bearing the mark of their fingers, their revelations, nevertheless, remain anonymous."[3] I actually count only 260 fingerprints (nineteen panels of four on

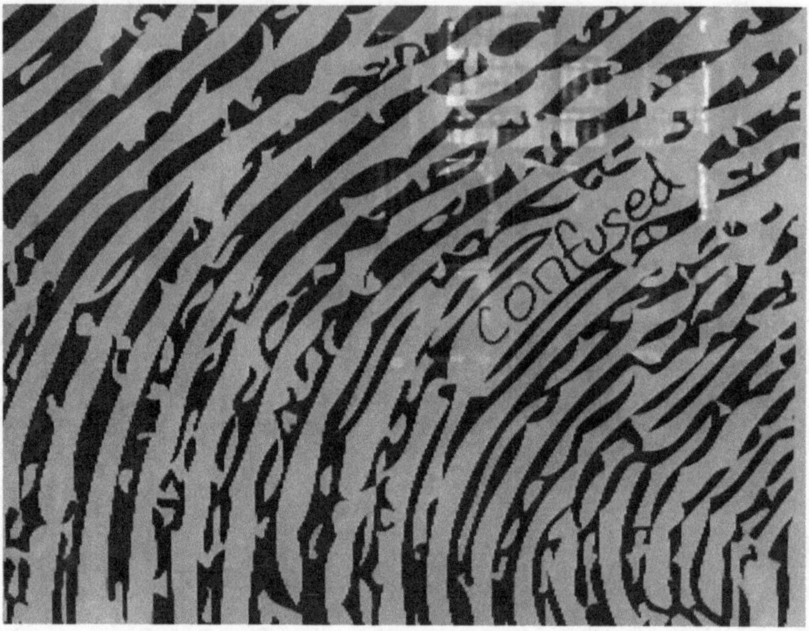

A.9 Boo Junfeng, "I Am Anonymous" (Confused). Photo: M. Fischer.

one wall, and forty-six panels of four along another wall), so maybe nine were smeary or otherwise unusable. As you walk past the long walls of these at first mysterious panels, you suddenly notice out of the corner of your eye that at certain angles words flicker into view: passionate, indecisive, inquisitive, procrastinator, uncertain, messy, grateful, rock concert, awesome, pretty, unique, frivolous, yan-dao, ambivalent, confused, alien. It is indeed a strange, even dark (it is black and white, after all) experience for long hallways, contrasting with the overly cheery slogan boards and banners above ground on the grass outside the entry way: "Great things never came from comfort zones" reads a banner with a picture of the launch of a space shuttle. "A Better World with Design," "Be Fearless in Pursuit of Your Dreams," "The Future Is Yours to Create." The entry walkway above ground, sloping down into the university's ground floor corridor between buildings, is carefully planted with trees and perennials from around the world, each identified with an educational label. As the plants grow, each year the campus becomes greener, emotionally warmer.

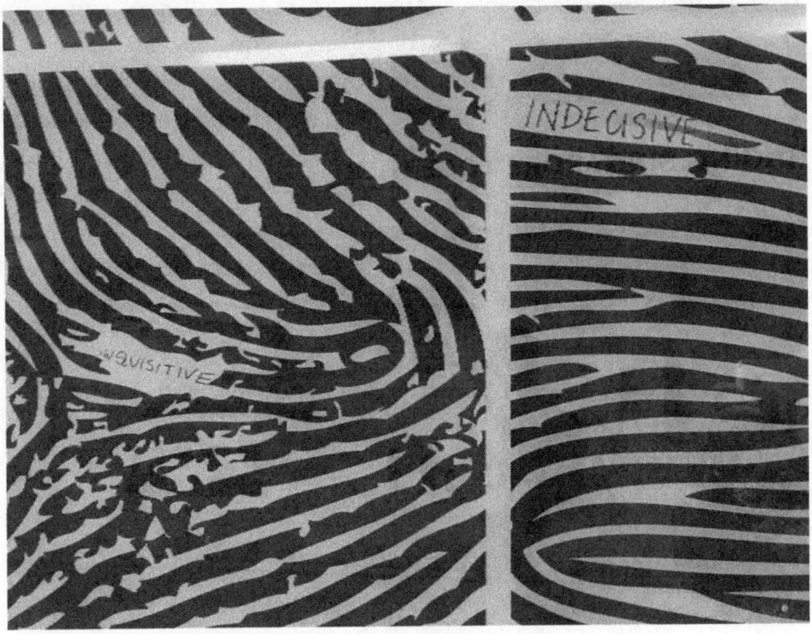

A.10 Boo Junfeng, "I Am Anonymous" (Inquisitive, Indecisive).
Photo: M. Fischer.

So what is the message of an entry by way of fingerprints? One is encouraged to speculate: Cryptic cryptography? Hidden messages? A riff on modern technologies of steganography and cryptographic defenses against hackers? An invitation to programming and new computer languages still accessed largely through fingers and keyboards? A warning about growing pervasive surveillance (even your cell phone as you text while walking past)? Perhaps a decoy to distract from the cameras that surely are embedded somewhere, watching? Is the promised anonymity itself a ruse, a performative contradiction, a double-bind, an aporia? After all, they are actual fingerprints (although Boo Junfeng assures me that the process of reproduction and enlargement distorts sufficiently that they could not be used for identification). And what is one to make of the hidden words that flicker forth, only half hidden, beckoning reassemblage of distributed messages, deciphering codes? And what would a psychiatrist make of these "revelations" of "freshmore" students gambling their parents' money on an untested new university that promises new pedagogies for an emergent world of uncertainties, unpredictable futures, bets with which to challenge engineering thinking (rationality, science, technology, engineering, and math) with the very personalities and differential skills that have given their fingerprints, and will need to learn team work and communication, among other social skills, and the "softer fields of study" that make design viable and equitable, not just livable but contributing to mutual care and aesthetic well-being?[4] The hallway may be more on point than its makers (the artist-filmmaker, the craftspeople, and the pioneer students) and the university faculty and administration might have anticipated, or than it seems at first sight.

Exergue

Bangarra Dance Theatre and the Historical Hinge in Australia

exergue: (1) work outside the main work, (2) reverse side of a coin or below the image giving date, place of minting, etc.

Dance is easy compared to negotiating the *cultural protocols* between North and South—sharing all the mind-fuck stuff with the full-bloods and really digging into the wonderful complexity of Aboriginal culture. White people are always resisting that complexity—it's so much easier to kill it off. . . . But working for the survival of our culture is what we have to do. And it's worth it when a company like the Commonwealth Bank comes aboard as a sponsor of Bangarra to learn something about the *protocols* from us—dealing with *cultural respect*. — STEPHEN PAGE

Respect for cultural protocols, the need for community engagement, and a strong commitment to enforce care for traditional knowledge that is shared, and/or provided through a process of request, invitation, permission and transmission, are all things that need to be considered and upheld as new expressions are created by Indigenous artists. . . . There is no central knowledge source. — BANGARRA DANCE THEATRE, "OCHRES: STUDY GUIDE"

You can't tell the story of aboriginal Australia without featuring Bangarra. "Bangarra" is the Wiradjuri language word meaning "to make fire"—ignition! Key terms here are: respect, cultural protocols, pedagogy, pride, adaptation, diversity of identities, movement, and dance. These are the points of the example, as much as the details that compose it. There are a number of DVDs of the performances mentioned here, and many more short clips on YouTube. By far the best overview is the film *Firestarter: The Story of Bangarra Dance Theatre* (Blair and Minchin 2020).[1]

The following is an analysis not of the film, but of the cultural rise of this dance theater company and its efforts to shift common sense. I am particularly interested in that third space that is beyond what has been called the hybridizing, hyphenating, or creolization of cultures (multicultural, plural, or diverse), or the stopgap notion of cultural trading zones as assemblages, with or without dynamics, and the role that intersectionalities of artforms can model and foster. Third spaces are multidimensional, multilocale, or multi-sited, often multi-scalar, and can allow for both participation by diverse people while at the same time protecting cultural heritages. As Stephen Page says in the film *Firestarter*, it is a restless practice of maintenance and reinvention. It is above all about dignity and respect, listening tactfully with the ear, eye, nose, feel, taste, and the immune, hormone, and pheromone systems, but especially the sixth sense of the (physical and emotional) proximities and distances of others, sometimes available to our companion animals and habitats in ways they are not immediately available to humans, and that we use in fantasy, in our irrationalities, dreamworlds, and poetics.

One of the reasons you cannot tell the story of Aboriginal Australia without featuring Bangarra is that not every Black looks black, hence also Blak.[2] This is a function of Australian policies of removing children from their natal families and placing them with foster families and in residential schools, and the effort to assimilate by breeding out the Blackness in Aboriginals. And it is a function of urban Aboriginals detached from traditional ways of living in the land. The artistic director of Bangarra, Stephen Page, points to himself as an example: descended from the Nunukul people and the Munaldjali clan of the Yugambeh people of southeast Queensland, he grew up in the Brisbane suburbs in a large family of twelve children of different shades of skin tone and facial structure; and, disconcertingly to himself when he was growing up, has light skin, and, confused about his identity, had to repeatedly demand to be allowed into school lines for Blacks. After spending time as a young man in northeast Arnhem Land learning some language and dance, he reports in the film, his father was in tears of happiness at the idea that his son was reconnecting with a cultural heritage that had been cut off by white settlement and Australian government policies.[3]

Another reason you cannot tell the story of Aboriginal Australia without featuring Bangarra is that the dance company became prominent in an important *hinge* period, the three decades of florescence of Aboriginal, Indigenous, Blak, or Blackfella's art, writing, and theater from 1989 to 2019. This came after the 1967 constitutional referendum that included Aborigines in population counts, and began to accord them rights of citizenship. The Aboriginal rights movements existed partly in tandem with movements for Indigenous and Black rights in the Americas. Indeed, the founder of Bangarra and its precursors in the 1970s and 1980s was Carole Y. Johnson, who trained at the Julliard School and was active in the Civil Rights movements in the United States and Australia (see ROH n.d.).[4] Stephen Page, whom she found to lead the company from 1989, says he was lucky to come to the NAISDA Dance College at a good time, from 1981 to 1984.[5] His equally charismatic brothers followed him there: David Page, who first studied music in Adelaide, and who composed much of the music in the early Bangarra productions, and Russell Page, a dancer who has sometimes been called the Rudolph Nureyev or Mikhail Baryshnikov of Australia, or at least of Bangarra. At NAISDA, a mix of tutors in modern dance like Carole Johnson, and elders from various parts of Australia and the Torres Strait teaching traditional dance, came together with young dancers of many mixed backgrounds who were looking to find their identities. In the early days there were two streams of dance taught: traditional and modern. It was the Page brothers who insistently merged the two.

It was a hinge of change first for the company and opportunities for young people, and second, slowly for change in consciousness more broadly in Australian society, signaled by the 1967 referendum, the funding of arts opportunities under the Paul Keating government (1991–1996), and then the public apology to Aborigines by Prime Minister Kevin Rudd in 1998 (shown in the film). Stephen Page says, "Each year during my three years of college study we would go up North to 'real country.' The first one of these trips was the first time I went into a community, a real Aboriginal community" (quoted from Iris n.d.). He was "other" for his skin color ("that yella fella from down south"), lack of dance knowledge (he tried to imitate, they laughed), and lack of language ("If you don't grow up with language you are really flogged out by traditional people, who say, 'If you don't have language you're not Indigenous'" [Munro 2016]). Inversely, for urban kids, as Page points out, "That really rips them apart, because they come from an assimilated culture, of generations where their parents weren't even allowed to be proud of their culture" (quoted in Munro 2016).

> This was the early '80s, you know, when mining wasn't a big issue, and everything still felt quite raw. It was a time where traditional stories were practiced every day for all different reasons—not just for sorry business—and a time where alcohol, drugs, and social poisons weren't in such effect within the communities. It was just really raw and rich when I first went in. Big corroborees took place in a circle and were lit by an old Torana car headlights flashing from somewhere—or from the light of the basketball court that had just been built. You used what you had out there. (Stephen Page, quoted in Iris n.d.)[6]

In the early 1980s there was "a woman's language that only women spoke and you don't hear about that anymore" (Page and McLean 2015). By the early 1990s, Paul Keating was prime minister, and reconciliation and the arts were two of his priorities. As Page recollects: "There were resources there, funding systems set up. There was this really big push for Indigenous storytelling through visual art, through performing art and by the end of the 1990s Bangarra was given the status of a major performing arts company, guaranteeing it triennial Australia Council funding" (quoted in Maley 2020).[7] It was also a period of flourishing of Black art and theater more generally.

Among Bangarra's breakout productions were *Praying Mantis Dreaming* (1992), *Ochres* (1994), and *Fish: An Unborn Soul* (1999). *Fish* was presented in Edinburgh to enthusiastic audiences, but the critics grumbled, as Steven Page recalls: "They wanted us to do the token old work; they didn't want to see us moving into the millennium."[8] Bangarra was synthesizing a new modern dance language for Australia at large, reimagining itself as a plural nation of many cultures, including a diversity of Aboriginal ones. An insistence on identifying the various local communities and dances—"name their names!," as the slogan of the American Black Lives Matter had it in 2020—is critical, so as not to erase respect for diversity, geographic landscapes, and layers of knowledge into a single collective category: "The first big commercial work was *Ochres* in 1994, then it became this crossover, contemporary, and traditional mob working with Torres Strait and Aboriginal and Yolngu mob, with urban mob, assimilated mob. We were all wonderfully dysfunctional, coming in in our own way. We wanted to see how far we could push the traditional boundaries into the contemporary and it just became an addiction; we loved being around each other."[9] In 2000, Bangarra was involved in both the opening and closing ceremonies of the Sydney Olympic

Games, allegedly reaching over 3 billion viewers worldwide. In preparation, the Bangarra team traveled the country collecting diverse troupes, getting elders' permissions, "choreographing a thousand First Nations performers from all over the country, many of whom had never been to the city, let alone performed on a world stage."[10] The performance involved getting them to perform in spectacular formations in the big stadium, with Donny Woolagoodja's giant *Wandjina Namarali* (an image of a round face, derived from a sacred cave painting in the Kimberleys of Western Australia) rising from the earth in the finale.[11]

Important productions kept being created every year: *Skin* (2000), part of which would become the 2015 film *Spear*, directed by Stephen Page himself. There then followed *Corroboree* (2001), *Walkabout* (2002), *Bush* (2003), *Unaipon* (2004), *Clan* (2004), *Boomerang* (2005), *True Stories* (2007), *Mathinna* (2008), *Fire* (2009), *Blak* (2013), *Patyegarang* (2014), *Nyapanyapa* (2016), *Bennelong* (2017), and *Dark Emu* (2018). In the first twenty-five years of the company, it produced thirty-six works with a diversity of inspirations: "First it was the traditional dance and mythological and creation stories and the totemic system, and a little bit of traditional romanticism. Then we went into Black social issues and what's happening in the present moment today. Then we could have a Black perspective about history as well with *Nyapanyapa*, *Mathinna*, *Patyegarang*, *Macq* . . . [and] *Benelong*. . . . And now re-connection works in this urban time about connecting back to the kinships systems (*Miyagan*)."[12] "*Skin* was looking at our social issues through our Black lens," Page says, and was composed of two works: "Spear," about contemporary men's business in both urban and remote contexts; and "Shelter," about contemporary women's business, inspired by the works of late Aboriginal artist Emily Kame Kngwarreye and the cultural practices of women from the Central Desert and Utopia regions.[13] Three to four hundred Central Desert women participated in the Olympic Games ceremonies. Since then, Bangarra has gone back at least twice over the years to perform and work with Pitjantjatjara and Yankunytjatjara women, and has participated in helping with the transfer of knowledge and practice across generations.[14]

The dialectic of men's and women's worlds was already powerfully present in the third of the four-part *Ochres*, originally performed in 1995 and recreated again in 2015. Page has observed that for Bangarra it is a "milestone work . . . that really propelled us into the mainstream, but at the same time empowered our people and our community" (quoted from T. Tan 2019). It begins with "Yellow" (women's energy, the Tjipari Dreaming of the Ngarti language group in the Western Desert, and the Women's Funeral Dance from the Etanyanu language group of northwest Cape York). Then comes "Black," male energy, which begins, as Stephen Page describes it, with "an ash storm [that] has blown over. The call and pain of the initiation can only be viewed from a distance" (quoted from T. Tan 2019). Four boys slowly rise and wipe a hand across their foreheads before covering their hair to symbolize painting ochre on their faces before going hunting. There is animal mimicry, crouching, rearing up, shaking, miming a kangaroo. But there are also hands covering mouths, a political statement about petrol sniffing. There are vocals from northeast Arnhem Land and the Torres Strait, and a buffalo dance and stick dance from northeast Arnhem Land. The third section is "Red," on male and female relationships—playful, sensual, powerful, challenging (youth, obsession, poison, pain), with again vocals from northeast Arnhem Land and the western Torres Strait. Finally comes "White," the new spirit world of the future informed and rejuvenated from the past.

Putting on dance productions is itself a complex choreography and collective endeavor involving many hands, permissions, and *cultural protocols*.[15] The productions themselves also require proposal writers (for three-year government grants), then producers, set designers, lighting designers, composers, singers, dancers, and choreographers. Djakapurra Munyarryun came to NAISDA at the same time as Stephen and they bonded; he joined the company in 1992 and stayed with it for a decade as one of its principal dancers, a key Songman infusing David Page's compositions with chants and Songlines, and is credited in program notes as "cultural consultant."[16] Frances Rings, a dancer, choreographer, and now associate director, remembers David Page's earliest music for the company as a "beautiful contemporary soundtrack, but it was layered with language, and it had this beautiful energy, this rumbling kind of sense of power, it just transported you somewhere else" (quoted in Mahrer 2012). The language, the Songline, was a kind of chanting, a rich rumbling not unlike the lower reaches of the didgeridoo drone (or *yidaki* in Djakapurra's Yolngu language), which Djakapurra also plays. In study guides on the dance company's website, Djakapurra provides notes on the varieties of ochre, the uses of body paint, the moves of traditional dance, and more. He is a large physical presence in many of the productions, and observes in the notes that when he is in body paint, people do not recognize him, and for himself the paint is a mask so that he becomes the being he inhabits. More on *art effects* below.

Djakapurra Munyarryun is from Yirrkala in the Northern Territory, a place of early and continuing inspiration and refuge for Stephen Page, which he first came to as a young man when he needed to escape Sydney. Among others we meet in *Firestarter* who live in Yirrkala are the painter and printmaker Nyapanyapa Yunupingu, born in 1945, a Yolngu woman from the Gumatj clan of northeast Arnhem Land, who learned painting by watching her father, a painter and activist. Crosshatching and other patterns provide a kind of meditative practice for her, "a place of reflection, embedded in her life and history. It reminds me [says Stephen Page] of why I started dancing as a young man—because I had to, because it was my calling, and because it took me to a safe and spiritual place" (Page and McLean 2015). She is a gnarled old woman by the time we meet her in the film, and we get the sense that she has watched the Page brothers grow up as they visited over the years. Her petroglyph-like painting on eucalyptus bark of being gored by a buffalo in 1975 becomes both the backdrop and the inspiration for the dance production *Nyapanayapa* (2016), in honor both of her and her community. The painting toured the United States and elsewhere along with a video that narrated her experience. In 2008 it won the Wandjuk Marika Memorial 3D Prize. She gave permission to use an image of the painting as a backdrop for the dance theater, and was welcomed onto the stage for the premiere, but afterward said she had nightmares of the buffalo and would not paint buffalo again.

Women have been part of the dance company, from the founders Carole Y. Johnson from the United States and Cheryl Stone from South Africa, to generations of dancers, and the women who are nurtured by Stephen Page to move from dancing to choreography, beginning with Bernadette Walong-Sene, his first important choreography collaborator, with whom he worked on *Ochres*. By 2003, Frances Rings joined Stephen Page as a key choreographer and associate artistic director of the company, and in 2007 she and Elma Kris choreographed a double bill, *True Stories*. For it, Torres Strait Islander Elma Kris went back to Murray Island in the Torres Strait to ask permission of the elders to use objects and stories in *Emeret Lu* ("Very Old Things"). Rings, meanwhile, a descendant of peoples who were affected by the atomic tests done at Maralinga in South Australia, went back to that area to work on *X300* (the code name for the test site). Stephen Page notes in the film *Firestarter*:

> The *X300* story presents a confronting fusion of traditional culture and modern science; of the organic and the man-made. Frances and I were

> interested in these contrasts and the very moment of the explosions that somehow brought them together. Such moments as when the heat of the explosion became so intense that the sand crystallized into fractured glass; or moments of blinding light, causing x-ray vision. An image of one's bones and veins begins to represent a complex map of the waterways and waterholes that became contaminated; maps that transform into a method of tracing land and become a way of finding a way home.

Frances makes a different point: "Indigenous people from all over the world have proven that with time they are *adaptive to change* and are still able to *maintain the integrity* of their unique cultures. As the wider community comes to *respect* and learn from its Indigenous people, there will be a greater understanding of the delicate balance needed in order to ensure our future" (Blair and Minchin 2020). Frances helmed the first of Bangarra's ventures into history and biography with *Unaipon* (2004), the Ngarrindjeri man who became a scientist, inventor, anthropologist, and writer. Since 1995, Unaipon's portrait has been on the Australian $50 bill. Born David Ngunaitponi in 1872 on the Raukkan Mission, Unaipon was sent at age thirteen for five years to Adelaide to live with the family of Charles Burny Young, where he got a good education; he died just before the 1967 referendum that allowed Aboriginals to be counted in the census. He mapped the flight pattern of the boomerang, an image captured in the dance, and held a number of patents on mechanical inventions. In 1924 he spent a year walking across South Australia, producing a manuscript, *Legendary Tales of the Australian Aborigines*, which was edited and published in London under the name of the anthropologist and chief medical officer for Australia, William Ramsey Smith. In 2001 it was republished under David Unaipon's own name (Unaipon 2001). Stephen Page says, "I was just so proud to see her [Frances Rings] go back on country and connect with [her] family and the David Unaipon family" (quoted from T. Tan 2019).

Mathinna (2008), the next such historical venture, is a tribute to one of the first of the stolen children, those removed to residential schools or foster parents to be assimilated. Page calls her the archetype of the "stolen child, caught between two cultures," and says the production required considerable research, "including consultation with Elders from the Aboriginal Tasmanian community" (quoted from T. Tan 2019). *Patyegarang* (2014) is the story of the young Aboriginal woman who taught the Eora language and cultural lore to the English botanist and astronomer William Dawes, unwittingly thereby leaving a legacy for her descendants through the meticulous notes taken by Dawes. Vicki Van Hout, a dancer and choreographer herself, and once a member of Bangarra, captures something of the intricate coding carried by dance as well as the music:

> The movement differs slightly from the usual Yolngu inspired locomotive stepping.[17] The women's torsos still bend low toward the ground, heads slightly bowed, but the footwork brushes forward, away from the supporting leg, as opposed to the brush up flicking motion of sand toward the supporting shin/ankle. The men stamp in a simpler singular motion, or shunt, being propelled forward from the back foot, which is sickled with hip and knee slightly rotated outward, instead of an alternating Yolngu drop stomping motion. These subtle *nuances may be lost on mainstream audiences, but* are crucial, an *indication of the different land and relationship to it*, as is *the local language featured in David Page's score* which is peppered with place names that have been appropriated since settlement. . . . Lightning speed when shifting/transferring weight, now and then integrating a subtle quick flick of the head to emphasize the footwork when emulating the perennial hunters, in flight or fight mode. (Van Hout 2014)

Bennelong (2017), similarly, is the story of the Eora and Gadigal man who was one of the first interlocutors with the white settlers in the land that became Sydney. "We were performing down at Bennelong Point: finally we could be in the country, the nation we reside [in], the Eora Nation; we don't talk about 1788 [when the settlers arrived], we go to 1762 . . . the time he [Bennelong] might have been born" (Stephen Page, quoted in Van Hout 2014).[18] *Macq* tells the dark side of one of Sydney's founders, Lachlan Macquarie, governor of New South Wales from 1810 to 1821. Usually seen in white histories in heroic terms, the Bangarra work focuses on the 1816 march intended by Governor Macquarie to create terror, and the massacre of fourteen men, women, and children of the Darawul people by his men. Choreographed by Jasmin Sheppard, events are brought back to light, sometimes with startling resemblances: "a scene in . . . *Macq* [shows the] power struggle between the Indigenous population and Governor Macquarie (with a voice-over quoting from the latter's diary), one dancer representing an Indigenous man and the other the Governor, stalking each other on and around a long table. The resonance with German choreographer Kurt Joos's *Green Table* of 1932—an anti-war statement made just prior to Hitler's rise to power—was there in Sheppard's archetypes and political content writ large" (Brannigan 2014). Again, "Sheppard's section 'Bodies in the Trees' (referring to Macquarie's directive to hang the Indigenous dead in the trees as a warning to others) featured a moving cascade of male bodies passed down on a simple set of steps" (Brannigan 2014). Dance is, the choreographer Jasmin Sheppard says, a better *pedagogy* for the classroom than reading a text. "It speaks without words, but with feeling and the experience of raw emotion, allows you to use all your senses, feel the energy from the dance, and also from the audience, and grabs you in a way reading a book cannot" (Page, in Page and McLean 2015).

For anthropologists who have allowed kinship as a topic to decay, it is good to have *Miyagan* (2016) as a reminder of not just how once upon a time kinship and identity were still bound up together, but how today's assimilated youths "reconnect" and create a sense of identity. The work was choreographed by two cousins of the Wiradjuri nation (western New South Wales), who before meeting in the Bangarra training school did not fully recognize that they were cousins with a common great-great-grandfather who lived on Talbragar Reserve in Dubbo in the early 1900s. Beau Dean Riley Smith tells with a sense of wonder how two paternal aunts (one a lecturer at Sydney University) helped him and his cousin Daniel Riley unravel the (for them) mysterious matrilineal five-level totemic system and moiety system, and how he went back for a family reunion and heard stories from the old people. In still slightly fractured summary, Beau tells an audience roughly how it works. An elder can spell out (or an anthropologist can work out) the system more fully, but not with the same delight in discovery and effort to make the totems dance in story that, at the same time, provides an ever-deepening sense of self and connection for choreographers, dancers, and audiences (including students).

> We are Indigenous men from the Wiradjuri nation, Rileys, cousins, from western New South Wales.[19] We can trace our familial connection back to our great-great-grandfather Jack Riley, who lived on Talbragar Reserve in Dubbo in the early 1900s. We explored this connection with the guidance of Auntie Di and Auntie Lyn, learning of the matrilineal totemic system consisting of five levels: nation, moiety, clan, family and individual. Auntie Di and Auntie Lyn are father's sisters. One is an academic, one lives on country and practices her language and culture back home.[20] They were cultural consultants. Aunty Lyn is a lecturer at Sydney Uni-

> versity and has created a generic genealogy, explaining what is a totemic system, a four totem system and a nation totem (Guga or gowena): location: *wilai* (brush-tail possum), people of Dubbo (Dubuga clan); then family name: Riley or *wambuan*, grey kangaroo for me, Dan is Mari or red kangaroo. Then individual totem, mine is *malian* or wedge-tail eagle. And there are two moieties: Dubi and Kopitem, which create social responsibilities and social behaviors between one another, cultural responsibilities, establish your identity: you are born into it, you know who you are before you are even born. This is what fascinated me about doing a work about kinship . . . I took [Dan] home to meet the family for the first time and he was a little nervous. I took him to my family reunion which just happened to be just a week after we started creating *Miyagan*. The reunion had been planned two years in advance, but just happened to be at that time and that place for us. We heard stories and made weavings.

As Stephen Page sums it up, "Kinship and the bonds we all share as indigenous people of this land are what connects us to land, to each other and to our cultural responsibilities. It also influences our social behavior. There is nothing more valuable than *miyagan*—without kinship, family, there is no life."

The three Page brothers are central to *Firestarter*. They are, respectively, the storyteller, the songman, and the dancer. Stephen is the choreographer and artistic director and sometime composer; David combines electronic, classical, and traditional music into distinctive compositions; and Russell is the dancer who says, "I'm not what you would call a technical dancer. A lot is drawn on instinct or becoming that bird or that snake or whatever you are interpreting. I often think of a big red kangaroo and the fact that they can leap high and land so low, but yet they are quite compact kangaroos."[21]

There are two powerful moments in *Firestarter* when Russell (in 2002) and David (in 2016) no longer appear. There were, Stephen tells us, six suicides in his family, a large number, as there in many Aboriginal communities everywhere. In Russell's and David's cases, as so often, the suicides seemed to have come out of nowhere. Russell had just finished a wildly successful show (*Walkabout*). After David's death, Stephen grieves by throwing himself into work so intensively that he nearly destroys the company, as if he and the production were fireworks exploding in a final grand self-immolation. The company survives, as does he: at the end of the film he is shown holding his granddaughter.

The story of Bangarra, and the film which so artfully presents its thirty-year journey, provides for me an example of a *hinge of history*, of a *time-space of cultural change*, not for everyone at the same pace, but for Australia in its public presentation of itself, and not without serious racist incidents still to be worked through.[22]

Notes

INTRODUCTION

1 Intan Paramaditha is an Indonesian film scholar and critic who has also authored a book of short stories and a first novel (see Paramaditha 2007, 2014, 2018a, 2021). I chose this striking image from her writing for two reasons: the more obvious is the impact of the film that every Indonesian child had to watch every year to reinforce the ideological legitimation of the Suharto regime. In feminist terms, as she puts it, "The ethical problem of showing violence to children was never an issue, as every elementary school student of the period was required to see Pengkhianatan G30S/PKI . . . and it was through violence that they were expected to learn about their own vulnerability. . . . [It was] one of the tools of the state to educate citizens about how fragile the nation could be without a strong paternal figure" (Paramaditha 2014, 139). The second, more intriguing, reason is that Paramaditha, in interviews about her short stories, says that as a child, she was fascinated by folktales and fairy tales, both Indonesian and Western, and, like many children, she especially "loved the Brothers Grimm because they were, well, just so grim (*laughing*), really dark and I love the part that is not really Disney, where everything turns violent; it is just so wild for a child's imagination, there is always mutilation involved; I found those stories interesting" (Paramaditha 2020). Indeed, she has said of her short story "Apple and Knife" (Paramaditha 2018a, 165–76), "I wanted to talk about . . . disobedient women, women who have vengeful and monstrous characters, basically to show that there are certain structures that shape the way they behave, why they are really monstrous" (Paramaditha 2020). Her novel *The Wandering* (2021) takes its motif from Hans Christian Andersen's "The Red Shoes," a story she points out that involves the paradox of women's desire to travel while at the same time being punished for that desire, and some of the stories in that novel play out women's intense rivalries that lead them to destroy one another. There is, in other words, a deep interest in the psychodynamics of violence in patriarchy, in the ordering of

the state, in rivalries, and in mother-daughter relations. See also her reading of Nan Achnas's celebrated feminist film *Pasir Berbisik/Whispering Sands* (Paramaditha 2007).

2 For instance, at a foundational level, Bronislaw Malinowski's ethnography was celebrated by his students for providing a sense of "being there" quite different from earlier "armchair," encyclopedic, and synoptic ethnographic efforts. This was in part due to exploring the linguistic and cultural genres of the Trobriand Islanders, their point of view and epistemologies, providing transcripts of their discourse, glosses of lexical and phrase meanings, and then deeper cultural explanations of semantic networks. It was also in part due to his methodological requirement of inquiring if and how what are often separated by theorists as different institutions affect one another, such that, as in ecology, one cannot change *only one* thing, but other things are implicated (what he called after a mathematical function "functionalism"—e.g., the kula system simultaneously implicating economics, politics, ritual, regional integration, etc.). His several volumes of ethnography were also celebrated for being information rich beyond what he himself could understand or properly theorize, so that future generations could return to his texts, reanalyze the information, and come to different or better conclusions. This has fruitfully been the case: see, e.g., Annette Weiner's reanalysis of rituals with a much richer access to women's roles, perspectives, and ideological understandings (Weiner 1976); and with more recent issues, Lepani on HIV in the Trobriands (Lepani 2012). Malinowski's ethnography of the ceremonial exchanges of the kula ring became a basis for Marcel Mauss's *Essai sur le don* (in English, *The Gift*; see Mauss 1954) and for the proliferating field of exchange theory, as well as inquiries into how political structures can emerge otherwise than from social contract theory. Similarly his essay on magic, science, and religion (Malinowski 1925) spawned debates over modes of pragmatism and rationality grounded in empirical observation and comparison, rather than mere philosophical thought. For an account of how the explanatory forms with which ethnographies have coevolved, see Fischer (2009, 1–113).

3 See, e.g., the eight-volume series *Late Editions*, produced by a collective under George Marcus's editorship (Marcus 1994–2000).

4 Synthetic biology is the attempt to bring engineering principles to biology, for instance, to build biological systems with standard interchangeable parts, called bio-bricks. This version of synthetic biology is promoted in a college and high school competition, the International Genetically Engineered Machine (iGEM), with teams from all over the world. In 2010, in a slightly different sense of synthetic biology, the J. Craig Venter Institute claimed to have created a synthetic cell, one that can divide and reproduce, from man-made genetic instructions. In 2021, the artificial intelligence company Deep Mind in collaboration with the European Molecular Biology Laboratory produced Al-

phaFold, a protein-folding predictor, and public data base that will help "shot on-goal" pharmacology, and largely replace the slow work of crystallography, or at least speed it up. The promise is to make novel molecules, new materials, novel uses for known biological systems, and in general to be able "to write biology," not just read or decipher it.

5 *The Singapore Story* is the title of Lee Kuan Yew's two-volume autobiography and account of his role in the making of modern Singapore. But it is also a colloquial term for what elsewhere is more generically called the "official story." It is built around two founders, Sir Stamford Raffles, the founder of British colonial Singapore in 1819, and Lee Kuan Yew, the leader of independent Singapore. As in all such stories or mythic charters, the roles of others are occluded, as are those of opponents.

6 "Deep play" is the notion that Clifford Geertz (1972) developed in reaction to Jeremy Bentham's reduction of gambling to utilitarian ethics (Bentham wanted to outlaw gambling, arguing that the stakes rapidly become so high that no rational person should engage in it). Geertz pointed out that what is important in gambling is the way a series of deep existential and social meanings are worked out; that gambling, from betting on sports to financial investments, in short is not irrational (said and done) but is meaningful, and often the higher the stakes the more they expose what is culturally important or is contested in a society. The investments are psycho-symbolic, not just calculative. "Social drama" is the notion that Victor Turner (1974) developed from Freud's analyses of symbolic investments, from Max Gluckman's analyses of legal cases, and from Arnold van Gennep's ideas about the processual form of rituals, with stages of separation of a celebrant or initiand, a liminal stage, and a move into a new social or ritual status. He stressed the liminal phase in rituals is one of con-fusion (fusing together) of bodily, visceral, emotional poles of meaning together with cognitive, semantic, and symbolic meaning. The processual form of social drama has proved to be productive for many analyses of conflicts and how conflict resolutions play out.

7 Fausto quite incisively reviews the "so-called anthropology of art" debates among Alfred Gell, Philippe Descola, and Eduardo Viveiros de Castro, noting archly (and correctly in my view) that models of art "cannot resolve to two terms and cannot be stabilized by a foundational anthropomorphism" (Fausto 2020, 13). Quite to the contrary of Gell, Descola, and Viveiros de Castro's premature theoretical reductions ("the film, not the footage"), Fausto suggests the Amerindian problematic or ambition involves "generating the most complex and paradoxical images with multiple referents, recursively nested, oscillating between figure and ground" (22). This, it strikes me, is a far more felicitous basis for a general anthropology of art that is not forever bound to Christian theological obsessions with images and presence—which both he and, even more in depth, Carlo Severi analyze. It is a fascinating dis-

cussion, but my net is wider than Fausto's. Fausto frames his inquiry around "the genesis of presence in ritual" (2020, 8). He wants to undo the Protestant Reformation (Bruno Latour's purifications), and so to reverse the undoing of Amerindian cosmologies and rituals by missionaries, both Protestant and Catholic. Fausto's work builds, in a way, upon Claude Lévi-Strauss's fundamental understanding that binary oppositions, like those in linguistics, are generative rather than static, and so is able to build upon his work, as well as situate his analyses of Amerindian myth and ritual within the much larger and growing corpus of ethnographic work.

8 Garcia builds upon the work of three sets of scholars and artists, *Native Americans* (legal scholar John Borrows; Anishinaabe poet, novelist, and scholar Gerald Vizenor; Acoma Pueblo poet Simon Ortiz; Cherokee artist Jimmie Durham; Modoc healer Kate Gordon; and Ojibwe novelist Louise Erdrich), *ethnographers and anthropologists* (Frances Desmore, Claude Lévi-Strauss, Dennis Tedlock, Michael Taussig, Marisol de la Cadena), and *modern poets* who are in an artistic dialogue in more than superficial ways with these artistic languages (Jaime de Angulo, Charles Olson, William Burroughs, Cecilia Vicuña, Gloria Anzaldúa). Garcia is engaged with some of the central issues of contemporary anthropology, poetics, and postcolonial or de-colonial theory, including the work of "the *Writing Culture* group" (he does not cite me, but my essay in that volume fits neatly with what he does here, especially on Gerald Vizenor and the importance of irony), Elizabeth Povinelli, Nancy Munn, Carlo Severi, and Walter Mignolo.

9 I use these terms as overlapping pluralizations of one another. The terms have slightly different valences and genealogies, but form a semantic network or family of resemblances. Gadamer (1960) provides a magisterial overview of the notion of the *sensus communis*, roughly translated as "common sense," developed especially by Giambattista Vico as a kind of social constructivism, that we know the world insofar as we make it, and that this is the basis of civic life and civilization. *Common sense* has at least three sources: (1) widely held opinions, beliefs, sensibilities, practical judgments, and moral sentiments that evolve as society does; (2) hegemonic understandings of how things naturally are or how legitimate domination works (Karl Marx, Max Weber, Antonio Gramsci); (3) active democratic or anti-monarchical civic formation, the sense of the populace as the foundation of good governance, and of the public as not a preexisting entity but rather as what is called forth during crises or government failures (Thomas Paine, C. S. Peirce, John Dewey). *Structure of feeling* is the gap between official discourse and popular responses, resistances, or alternative sources of legitimacy, often rooted in everyday class or ethnic difference (Raymond Williams). *Culture* as anthropologists developed it was in resistance to elitist definitions of taste or high culture as the best an art or culture produces (Mathew Arnold). As a counter to such upper-class efforts at

naturalizing their taste cultures as a mode of domination, anthropologists pioneered ideas of culture as changing as social formations do rather than as universal achievements, and thus also as fields of contestation (see Fischer 2009, 1–49; and, for a case study of Iran, Fischer 1980). *Consciousness* or the *conscience collective* as formulated by Émile Durkheim, and used by social anthropology, is simultaneously socially formed and viscerally felt. It is in Durkheim's pun both consciousness and conscience. It is viscerally felt such that if for instance a food taboo is violated, it might cause one to vomit; but it is also a set of cognitively and publicly justified moral sentiments. *Habitus* (viz. habit) is similarly the embodied dispositions that organize how people perceive and act in the world (Marcel Mauss, Pierre Bourdieu). *Communities of practice* is a term developed to acknowledge differences among disciplines, focusing both on what people do more than what they think their words mean, and on their specialized linguistic usages that differ from ordinary language, or the same terms used by a different community with different meanings (Lucy Suchman, Melissa Cefkin; the Ethnographic Practice in Industry Conference).

10 The discussions on "concept work" perhaps begin with Gilles Deleuze's manifestos that philosophy should be a machine for producing new concepts, not just a scholastic commentary on European philosophy since Aristotle and Plato; and Michel Foucault's historical and historicizing work showing how concepts in European discourses—from mental health and medicine to penal systems and technologies of disciplining the self—have arisen and are replaced, rather like Thomas Kuhn's notions of paradigms in the history of science. Ulrich Beck has shown how many concepts in sociology have become zombie-like in outliving their original relevance, and now exert a false sense of scientific legitimation. In anthropology, Paul Rabinow has been among the more forceful in promoting the idea of concept work, perhaps most successfully as a pedagogical tool for training graduate students who have produced innovative work on new topics. More recently, drawing on Wittgenstein, Andrew Brandel and Marco Motta (2021) have edited a volume on *concepts*, and one might assimilate to this discussion Bruno Latour's efforts to add to American pragmatism's understanding of concepts (Dewey, Peirce) the French names Gilbert Simondon and Gabriel Tarde. Concepts, like words, often take their meanings through differentiations in semantic networks rather than as singular terms or mathematics-like axiomatic definitions.

11 This is not to say that critical events, or chains of critical events, within evolving sociopolitical dynamics cannot be useful rubrics, but like dates in history that students memorize to help understand heuristic periodization, historians themselves are always reevaluating their terms of significance, and marking new evaluations with new dating markers. My use of social dramas and hinges of history is an effort to include the social processes underlying the markers.

12 See, e.g., Lattimore (1950) and Wheatley (1971). Lattimore was among the

earliest inspirations for my interest in Asia as an undergraduate, Wheatley being an influence somewhat later at Chicago. Important recent follow-ups on Lattimore include my former colleague Peter Perdue's wonderful survey of Qing period Central Eurasian politics (Perdue 2005); Judd Kinzley's account of resource investment and competition between Russia, the Qing, Chiang Kai-shek's Nationalists, and the People's Republic of China (Kinzley 2018); and Rian Thum's account from Uyghur sources of the history of Altishahr or the oases and trade routes in southern Xinjiang (Thum 2014).

13 The title *To Paint a Smile* is taken from that of a 2008 painting by Tan Swie Han, which at first sight seem seems purely decorative, with blue birds above, and flowers and red lava flows below. A yellow stripe moderates one's perception of the red, as the painting (sequencing of colors) proceeds to deep green. Tan Swie Han comments, referring to the Sichuan earthquake: "When the earth is torn apart we also see the flight of a hundred birds and a hundred flowers bloom. . . . This painting shows the complete *smile*, an understanding that there are both joys and sufferings [*satori* and *dukka*]. What is most important is we know they are intertwined and we must transcend it, so that the necessary pain is shorter and the joy or happiness is sustained" (Woon 2008, 201–3).

14 Symbolically the crowning achievement of these monumental calligraphies is the boulder inscribed with Tan Swie Hian's celebratory essay for the birthday of the Yellow Emperor, placed at the entrance to the 180 steps up to the oldest imperial tomb in China. All three of these astounding sites are described in Woon (2008, 146–57). See also Tan Swie Hian (2017a, 2017b), the first a video of a Tan lecture and explication of a poetic image that has persisted across centuries of Chinese meditations, the other a retrospective catalog of some of his work.

15 Wikipedia, s.v. "Zhang Xiaogang," last modified August 20, 2022, 19:26, https://en.wikipedia.org/wiki/Zhang_Xiaogang.

16 These are comments I heard from gallerists in Singapore. They are of course hyped up. But I. Nyoman Masriadi's *The Man from Bantul (The Final Round)*, painted in 2000, was among the first of the new generation to command more than US$1 million. In 2008 it sold for $8 million at Sotheby's Hong Kong. Hendra Gunawan's *Ali Sadikin Pada Masa Kemerdekaan* (*Ali Sadikin during the Independence Struggle*), painted in 1978, sold in 2014 for $4.29 million at Sotheby's Hong Kong; and his *Pandawa Dadu (The Dice Game from the Mahabharata Epic)*, painted in 1971, sold in 2015 for $3.39 million at Sotheby's Hong Kong. Of older painters, Raden Saleh, Sindudarsono Sudjojono, and Affandi also have sold for multimillion-dollar amounts. But other well-known Indonesian artists like Heri Dono and Entang Wiharso are no strangers to the international stage.

17 For an overview of Singapore's swings in positioning between East and West, see Barr (2020) and Meaney (2021).

18 See, e.g., Fischer (2015) on the growing aging cohort of seniors in Singapore as a pressure point.

19 The three main rankings are the Shanghai Ranking Consultancy Academic Ranking of World Universities, the Times Higher Education University Ranking, and Quacquarelli Symonds World University Ranking.

20 Other developments include those of more recent American feminists and queer theorists. Elizabeth Freeman's "erotohistoriography" (Freeman 2010), for instance, is a touchstone for Narumi Naruse's work on Singaporean novels, read through the lens of the ways in which the diaspora is positioned by the state as a fungible or retrievable resource (Naruse 2014). More inventively, cross-linguistically, and cross-culturally, Jing Wang (2021) juxtaposes "sonic feminine new materialism" or "speculative realism" and "agentive realism" of critics such as Karen Barad, Rosi Braidotti, and Salme Voegelin with, and in contrast to, *contemporary* Chinese *qi* thinking about sound, by way of electronic and experimental music. Indeed, her account of *qi* is consistent with its use by Kwa (2014). I find it useful to think with the older work of Cixous et al. for two reasons: (i) it still seems a useful reference frame for later feminist (I think especially of Gayatri Spivak and Donna Haraway) and queer "waves" of thinking; and (ii) there is a literary aesthetics to the writing of these authors which I would like to find in the Southeast Asian novels, not as copy of form but as fusion of style and content, in which the very language is itself transforming and generative. To my ear (or fantasy of sound) *écriture féminine* does different work than the English "women's writing," something creatively embedded in the linguistic liveliness, not just a token of gender. I hope that at least some of the novels show that potential, especially through their play with multiple languages and idioms, and with cultural references that operate philosophically and not just descriptively. I am committed to the appreciation of, and *deconstruction* and *reinterpretation of,* the cultural references, rather than flattening them into mere illustrations of theories about neoliberalism, capitalism, and patriarchy.

21 Aside from Derrida, Cixous celebrates male writers who write in forms of *écriture féminine*: Genet, Shakespeare, Rilke, Kleist. Moreover, for her, the prelinguistic fetus can become either sex, the body is bisexual. And in any case, any rooting in a hypothesized pre-Oedipal stage is a site of the imaginary.

22 There actually is a connection between the two words. Hysteria comes from the Greek for uterus, *hustera* (ὑστέρα); hysteresis from the word for delay, *husteros* (ὕστερος). The delay of the expelling of the placenta after the birth of a child was the connection between the two (Jimenez 2017).

23 Hence, the hysteric's speech is full of gaps, sequences of events are scrambled, connections lost, and s/he cannot clearly speak the story of the trauma suffered. Or as Pierre Janet put it: "It is only for our convenience that we speak of it as a 'traumatic memory.' The subject is often incapable of making the necessary narrative which we call memory" (quoted in Kwa 2013, 26).

24 The literature on Aboriginal land and marine management is growing. Two introductions are Sveiby and Skuthorpre (2006)—the former a management professor and the latter a Nhunggabarra elder, painter, and educator from northern New South Wales—and Pascoe (2014), a subaltern-style rereading "against the grain" and "meta-analysis" of early colonial accounts of Aboriginal agricultural and environmental management modes by a writer of Bunurong, Tasmanian, and Yuin heritage. A growing number of university dissertations and academic articles explore this topic both in relation to "pre-contact with Whites" as well as for contemporary sustainable use, e.g., Ayre (2002), Ayre and Verran (2010), Ayre and Mackenzie (2012), and Hoverman and Ayre (2012).

25 There are several books on Australia's atomic bomb tests as well as government inquiries, e.g., Bayly (2009), Walker (2014), and Tynan (2016). Bayly's account of surveyor and road-builder Beadell's work is particularly well illustrated, with a helpful map, and corrects prior accounts as well as one misconception in Tynan about whether Beadell had been present at the first test.

26 Stephen Page, quoted from *Firestarter* (Blair and Minchin 2021).

27 Symbolic anthropology was the name given to the research program at the University of Chicago in the 1960s and 1970s. To be clear, symbolic anthropology stressed the performative (Victor Turner was one of the key figures at Chicago), and symbols were part of a Piercean hierarchy of signs, icons, and symbols. Symbols could grow and decay, just as metaphors can. Still, the effort often was to locate key symbols that organized constellations of metaphors and meanings, and were thus socially constituting or constructing the epistemologies and phenomenal worlds for extended periods of time. The work of Berger and Luckman (1966) was an important popular translation from the German tradition of phenomenology, foreshadowing the language of social constructivism. But the primary figure for Chicago was Alfred Schutz (1967) and his attempt to provide a philosophical foundation for the sociology of Max Weber. Symbolic interactionism was also an influence stemming from the work of Barney Glaser and Anselm Strauss (1957), which in turn drew from and fed the study of symbols in advertising and psychological persuasion (Cefkin 2010).

28 Stephen Page, quoted from *Firestarter* (Blair and Minchin 2021), at 29:29.

29 Stephen Page, quoted from *Firestarter* (Blair and Minchin 2021), at 29:38.

30 The story is that the sage Valmiki saw a hunter kill the male of a mating pair of *krauncha* birds; the female burst into such wrenching wailing that Valmiki spontaneously recited a *sloka* (or poetic verse), and as he did so his disciple committed it to memory so that he could recite it further to the community. With this poetic form, Valmiki began the *Ramayana*. See the extraordinary *krauncha* dance pose in *Sharira: Fire/Desire*, choreographed by Chandralekha and performed by Tishani Doshi (Fischer 2023, 186).

31 During the 2020 pandemic lockdown, Cerise Lim Jacobs initiated Sing Out Strong, with the call letters SOS, a community initiative to pair young composers and writers, and to experiment with how to produce concerts with performers in different places synchronized through Zoom or Zoom-like video conferencing platforms. Her company further developed this technology for three operatic productions: *Alice in the Pandemic* (2020), fusing animation with remote performances by three live singers (a novel use of a game engine making this technically possible); *Death by Life* (2021) on systemic racism and incarceration, using texts by prisoners and scores by five black composers; and *A Survivor's Odyssey: The Journey of Penelope and Circe* (2021) on sexual violence, women's stories, and 3D environments created by the game development program Unreal Engine.

32 The work in question was, however, praised by the literary critic Edward Said, and there was talk of doing it as a short book in a series he was contemplating. He also praised my first book on Iran. I also remember being marked down in an English class at Johns Hopkins by an overzealous teaching assistant in thrall to the then dominant rules of "new criticism" for trying to read Shakespeare plays in their historical context. "Read only what's there in the text. Don't do any research on historical contexts: that is not literary." New criticism would shortly be overturned by new historicism (borrowing heavily from anthropology) and deconstruction. Such also is historical context.

33 The artworks have been made available on the web by the Land Transit Authority by the name of the station, as well as in a series of coffee-table books under the Art in Transit program. For an overview, see LTA (2022).

34 The fingerprint artworks are by Boo Junfeng, who is also a filmmaker and the director of *Apprentice* (2016), about the death penalty in Singapore. Delicately handled, the film is the story of a chief executioner (hangman) retiring and teaching a young Malay former prisoner to take his place. Coercion and compassion are omnipresent: the young man needs a job in an environment where he is discriminated against on several grounds; the hangman wants to teach him how to make hanging as humane as possible while still making sure that the job is done properly. The filmmaker is aware that public opinion in Singapore favors the death penalty, so he does not try to persuade them otherwise but explores what it means for everyone involved, beginning with the perspectives of the hangmen. Boo was put in charge of the National Parade a few years later, and tried to make it also something that people might think about and not treat as purely entertainment or merely a state show.

35 Regarding this film, see the chapter epigraphs by Indonesian writer Laksmi Pamuntjak to the introduction and to chapter 6.

CHAPTER ONE. OILED HINGES

1 On the history of performance art in Singapore, see Langenbach (2003), Lee Wen (2006), and Yap (2016); see also note 13. Lee Wen was one of its more celebrated practitioners. Performance art is part of the experimental arts scene that began with Tan Da Wu and the Artists Village, and continued at the Substation with Zai Kuning (on whom, see Fischer 2023, ch. 5) and others. Also see Tang Da Wu (2016) for a partial retrospective, and Chan Li Shan (2022).

2 Tan Pin Pin is a cofounder of the Fly by Night video challenge, which over seven years led to the making of several hundred shorts, and a founding member of a collective of independent filmmakers, *filmcommunitysg*. She served for seven years on the board of The Substation (one of Singapore's fecund arts centers) and for two years on the board of the National Archives; and she was on the team in 2011 that lobbied the Singapore Film Commission to include documentaries and films with artistic and cultural merit in the New Talent Feature Grant Scheme.

3 Jasmine Ng, interview with the author, Forty Hands Cafe, Singapore, February 4, 2020.

4 Jasmine Ng's films have remained within the documentary category but have expanded into working with new audiences, installations, and civic action. *Pink Paddlers* (2007) is about breast cancer survivors who make up a dragon boat racing crew. In *Prism* (2012), made for the Lee Kuan Yew School of Public Policy, she did an installation at the Drama Center Black Box (National Library Board), using interactive films screened on the walls to create an immersive space, within which people could talk about what they thought would become obsolete in ten years.

5 Each sequence of four or so shots lasts about two minutes, lingering on the final shot, setting a mood of melancholy. Some of the shots are quite beautiful, as for instance the golden light in the windows of the mosque reflected in the pooling water on the floor. Some are sanitized, sterile, and stark, like photo shoots in an architecture magazine, as are the shots around the swimming pool at 36A Draycott Park. Some are noirish, with street lamps and the whoosh of passing motorcycles and cars, as those by the Seletar Expressway; or looking down in the dark from the twenty-fifth-floor landing between apartments. And some advertise the stunning architecture overlooking the Kallang River and Marina Bay and Barrage, with a side note of a seedling tree and white death condolence notes in the dry grass, marking the accident and collapse of an underground tunnel in building a MRT station entrance. The voice-over uses excerpts from reports in the *Straits Times*. Most places are given an address on screen: this is real, not fiction, even if the whole story can never be known. The seven are: an abandoned house in which a skele-

ton had been found; the side of the Selatar Expressway near Exit 8 at night, where a Sambar deer was hit by a car and lay there for four hours before being put down; a swimming pool at the townhouses and Housing and Development Board (HDB) flats at 36A Draycott Park, where a teenage boy committed suicide; a burned-out mosque, dripping, peeling, and buckling, where another teen had meant only to burn a book or two; a drainage canal beside 182 Bukit Batok Avenue 8, where a teenage girl drowned; a double suicide or murder of two young women off the twenty-fifth floor of the HDB flats at 179 Toa Payoh Central; and the site of the death of a foreman during tunnel construction for the entrance to the MRT at Nicoll Highway, leaving behind in remembrance a small tree and white papers in the adjacent grass.

6 "Punctum" is the term introduced by Roland Barthes in his reflections on photography in *Camera Lucida* and refers to the disturbing element, an "accident which pricks, bruises me," which conveys meaning without invoking a symbolic system or the more general "studium" cultural, linguistic, and political interpretation (Barthes 1981). The program notes unintentionally overdetermine or over-cue interpretation, thus moving into the realm of studium, rather than remaining in the film's lingering and melancholic effort to allow for a punctum.

7 Tan Pin Pin, speaking at the Q&A session, National Archives, Singapore, January 19, 2020.

8 His name is spelled Han Tan Juan in a 2010 dialogue (Tan Pin Pin 2010, 277–78), where Tan Pin Pin describes his hesitancy to be in the film until the very last edit, but in the end he is pleased with the results, and despite his disappointment at the little impact he seemed to have made in his National Library speech, he continued to give talks at high schools. As others of his generation note, young people do not know these histories, but through oral histories and archives they are there to be looked up, and increasingly accessible through the internet.

9 Chopin is said to have been watching a little dog chasing its tail; it is a little waltz taking only one and a half to two and a half minutes to play, done *molto vivace* (very lively). The dog was Marquis, George Sand's dog.

10 "Master shots," Francis Ford Coppola says, are the widest shot possible, from which, if you have enough resolution, you can take various shots for coverage—close-ups, two shots, etc. He is musing about the use of only one camera, an 8K camera, in Barbet Schroeder's *Amnesia*. "It reminded me of a book we studied in film school, *The Way of Chinese Painting*, in which it was demonstrated how a large painting could be broken up into many closer compositions that were very beautiful" (Coppola 2017, 14–15).

11 Kwan Im Thiong Hood Cho Temple is one of the oldest and richest Buddhist temples in Singapore, on Waterloo Street. It was originally built in the 1880s, and rebuilt in the 1980s. I assume the building in the film is the school across

the street, which has had various interesting incarnations, including being the Japanese school before World War II, and the Stamford Girls School after World War II.

12 The modernist addition to the National Museum opened in 2006; it is on the site of the important former Drama Center, in a partially hollowed-out part of Fort Canning Hill.

13 The reading here differs somewhat from that of Edna Lim, to whom I am indebted for the term "sound bridge" (E. Lim 2018). I argue it might be more fruitful to find the formal semiotic and sociolinguistic, or cultural-logics, that compose the film, and thereby challenge the judgment, often used to dismiss the arts, of being subjective or arbitrary. While Lim does not intend to dismiss the film, she reads it as showing that what is considered "performance" is "subjective" and "arbitrary," that there are many kinds of performance. This argument itself has a cultural politics context. "Performance art" became politically contentious at one point in Singapore when Lee Wen and others were banned on three grounds: (1) that free-form happenings or performances are not scripted and thus not subject to censorship; (2) that the censors could not understand the form as fitting into any of the traditional categories of art that they could recognize; and (3) that there was political content. *Singapore GaGa* can be read as a comment on that period (and continued ongoing negotiations with censors), but should not be limited to this. After all, performance is an ordinary word, an odd-job term that ranges from implicit cultural patterns (see Goffman 1956) to what happens in concert halls or theater stages to religious rituals and to busking. "Performance and theater arts" has a specific historical lineage, critique, and reinvention of form, directed against traditional theater as much as politics. And its history across Southeast Asia is fascinating, both in reacting against older forms and in influencing today's international performance and theater arts, repaying the earlier reintroduction by Singaporeans and other Asian performance artists returning from the United States, England, and Australia.

14 The song is "Wasted Days and Wasted Nights," music and lyrics by Wayne Duncan and Freddy Fender, first released in 1975. "Wasted days and wasted nights, I have left for you behind. / For you don't belong to me, / Your heart belongs to someone else. / Why should I keep loving you / when I know that you're not true? / Why should I call your name / When you're the blame for making me blue?"

15 Margaret Leng Tan is an internationally acclaimed musician who worked with John Cage for the last eleven years of his life and became one of the leading exponents of Cage's music, as well as a world virtuoso toy piano player (she owns eighteen of them). Trained at Juilliard School and the first woman there to get a doctorate in musical arts, she was born in Singapore, the daughter of Tan Chye Cheng, the former Straits Times Press chairman. She performed Cage's

Suite for Toy Piano (1948) for her debut with the instrument at the Lincoln Center in 1993. In *Tan Pin Pin's Singapore GaGa*, she also does an interview in which she recalls not being well received in Singapore the first time she performed *4'33"* but got rave appreciation on her return performance.

16 The China Broadcasting textbook lists six qualities of *boyin qiang*: normative (*gui fan xing*), solemn (*zhuang zhong xing*), agitational (*gu dong xing*), modern (*shi dai gan*), measured (*fen cun gan*), and cordial (*qin qie gan*). "These six qualities define the monumentality of this broadcasting tone of voice that performs the sovereign power of the nation-state and constitutes the acoustic milieu of the collective memory of a particular Zeitgeist in Chinese history" (Wang 2021, 174). Jing Wang also notes that Xiang Zhibing performed this voice on CCTV (China Central Television) for twenty-eight years (1981–2009), and it became a subject for commentary in the satirically titled "Water: Standard Dictionary Version," a 1991 video artwork by Zhang Peili (Wang 2021, 174).

17 Parallel to "sound bridges," Tan Pin Pin also uses very short "visual bridges" as transitions across otherwise different scenes, as well as using returns to the same character across different parts of the film. There are three of these visual bridges in particular: First, bridging or stitching together the scene with the four older men singing their Latin song and the scene with Margaret Leng Tan playing *4'33,"* we see public housing flats with laundry poles, a man on a bicycle riding by the elevator, putting his bicycle against a wall, and another man walking by, as does a woman going to the mailboxes. This is a purely "vernacular" or "ordinary life" scene, albeit of an older time (laundry poles), contrasting with the highly formal toy piano scene, and yet in a later scene, Tan Pin Pin stitches back the world of a yet older vernacular soundscape of the *karung guni* and *tok tok mee* men. Second, and similarly, there is the scene of men lighting a lantern to launch into the night sky as we hear the fading sound of the toy piano that preceded it, and the song of the tissue seller which we are about to see and hear. Third, there is the scene of "Happy Birthday" being sung to an older woman, which stitches together the scene with Guo Ren Huey singing "Red Blood" and that with Margaret Leng Tan bringing her toy piano like a suitcase onto a polished-wood theater floor, and reminiscing about her first performance of *4'33"* in Singapore in 1991 at the arts festival, when it was received with consternation and indignation. One realizes that the woman whose birthday it is cannot be Guo Ren Huey's wife, unless at a much earlier time, and that the semiotic chain or logic here is different, of generational succession. A fourth visual bridge perhaps is the repeated use of MRT stations.

18 Abisheganaden was born in Sri Lanka in 1926, raised in Singapore, and at age fifteen witnessed the fall of Singapore to the Japanese. The family was unharmed by the Japanese because of the Japanese alliance with the Indian National Army. Self-taught on the guitar, he played it in an Indian orchestra for

Azad-Hind Radio. After the war he studied the double bass under Hungarian cellist Feri Krempl, and in 1960 became the first person in Southeast Asia to receive a licentiate of the Royal Schools of Music for performance on the double bass. With a grant, he spent a year at the Royal College of Music in London studying voice, double bass, and guitar, and was later mentored by the Australian guitarist John Williams. He started the Singapore Classical Guitar Society, and in 1970/71 produced twenty-six episodes for television of *Music Making with the Guitar*. He composed pieces for teaching such as "Katong Blues" (for his television program), as well as larger complex pieces such as the 1995 double concerto for sitar, erhu, and guitar, *Huan Yin Vanakam*, blending Chinese folk melodies with the rhythmic tempo of songs sung by Indian workers he remembered from his childhood. His daughter Jacintha is a founding member of the Singapore-based performance company TheatreWorks. See Loh (2017).

19 "After the pleasing youth and annoying old age, we shall live in the soil."

20 As Tan Wah Piow recalled in an interview: "During my secondary school and the pre-university, that was the time of the Vietnam war. . . . which made me think a great deal about what's going round in our region. I mean, that was time of anti-war movement in the West . . . the Paris student unrest and the revolution of the generation . . . 1966, you have Cultural Revolution. So the young in the world, whether it's the East or the West, were questioning. Questioning systems, questioning the relationship with authorities" (Tan Wah Piow 2020).

21 Lee Hsien Loong, "Interviewed by Tommy Koh on *To Singapore with Love*," October 3, 2014, https://www.youtube.com/watch?v=UjQvdrBK8h4. The prime minister's argument (repeated essentially verbatim by Yaacob Ibrahim, the minister for communications and information and put on the website of the Media Development Authority) is that the individuals in the film "gave the impression that they are being unfairly denied their right to return to Singapore. They were not forced to leave Singapore, nor are they being prevented from returning. The government has made it clear that it would allow former CPM [Communist Party of Malaya/Malaysia] to return to Singapore if they agree to be interviewed by the authorities on their past activities to resolve their cases. Criminal offenses will have to be accounted for in accordance with the law." A few years later, on October 22, 2019, the issue remaining a sore spot, Ambassador Tommy Koh, once again taking up his diplomatic skills, negotiating among factions as he had his entire career since his university days in the Socialist Club (to which Lee Kuan Yew, Hsien Loong's father, had also belonged), and addressing the much-discussed efforts to identify a new "fourth generation" leadership to succeed Lee Hsien Loong, said publicly that the government should not have banned Tan Pin Pin's film *To Singapore with Love*. Nor should it have withdrawn grants for the graphic novel *The Art of Charlie Chan Hock Chyue*, by Sonny Liew, and for the novel *The State of*

Emergency, by Jeremy Tiang—both about events in the history of Singapore. Both would go on to receive awards and are now freely available in Singapore. Warning that success had made the government more conservative, Koh said, "The contestation of ideas is a necessary part of democracy. We should therefore not blacklist intellectuals, artists, writers because they criticize the government or hold dissenting views." Especially, he noted, when they love the country. (Quoted in G. Z. Tan 2019.)

22 The film stars Sidney Poitier. The title song is performed by Lulu (born Marie McDonald Lawrie). E. R. Braithwaite's novel, on which the film is based, was published in 1959.

23 "*Ini ya riwayat* (this is our story) *kitab*, / We have a story to tell you of how we worked hard to make this part of our motherland (*tanah ayahkuh*) / Our fathers came from the mainland and other lands far away. / They made the old Sri Temasek the thriving city of today. / *Dari du. lu sompa iskaran* (from then until now) / *sepabinas schola* (who built schools) *dan ari kan bangunan ya laksa muyah bakya kitah* (and erected buildings)? / They were built by the people. / So, as a child of my island, / I know the ink is not dry. / Our story is still yet unwritten. / Today I'll join my people's cry." The song is titled in Malay "Anak Pualau Singapura" (Son of the Island of Singapore), composed and performed by the late Francis Khoo. It appears as the closing song in *To Singapore, with Love.*

24 Again, Roland Barthes's term "punctum" (note 6 above) is useful: the point in a photograph that breaks through the "studium" or manifest surfaces to seize the viewer with a disturbing moment of the psychologically "real."

25 "Consociality" is a temporal term for people who relate to one another in the same time horizon, contrasting to their relations with predecessors and with successors. It is a term from the sociological phenomenology of Alfred Schutz.

26 Tan Wah Piow notes that as an architecture student he was sent out to do surveys in Jurong, and that is how he became connected with workers there. He then took a gap year, spending it with the Jurong Industrial Mission, of which his wife was then the director. By then it had come under attack "because they were supported by ecumenical churches, and so on. So I spent eventually a year with them, all doing voluntary work and it would be almost equivalent to the Geylang Centre except that we were just volunteers. People like Vincent Cheng, Paul Lim, these are the names that you hear in 1987 Operation Spectrum. And they were then working with my wife, so I spent a year there before I went back to the university. And later became the president" (Tan Wah Piow 2020).

The illegality was that workers had to be paid in cash. Paying them with vouchers to be spent at the union store is a classic company-town mode of control. The story of getting the workers to confront their union leadership is told in the Thum interview. The head of the union (the Pioneers Industry Employees Union) was Phey Yew Kok, appointed by Lee Kuan Yew to control the Chinese workers. He was also a member of parliament and assistant to Devan Nair (head of the National Trades Union Congress, who would become Singapore's third president). He was accused years later of stealing money from the union.

27 In the previously cited recent interview, Tan Wah Piow states: "The more I try, the more I reinvent [myself] the more I return to where I was, as a 24 year old because problems, not just in Singapore but in various parts of Southeast Asia have not changed. I mean, recently I was in the Philippines and I gave a talk there to students and I was talking to some of the old activists, and it looks like they are back to where they started. They tried with revolution. They tried with people's revolution, they tried the parliamentary process and they are back to where they are. And that is the, problem, not just in Singapore, but in our part of the world. . . . But the question is not just the issue of rights. It's true, lah, in Singapore where rights continue to be restricted by the government, by the regime. But there is also a question of income distribution and so on, which are systemic economic problems. And although generally Singapore is much richer, very, very much richer, than when I was [young], but there is still the inequality, which is a problem" (Tan Wah Piow 2020).

28 "Yes, you see the meaning of the struggle is to make the people especially the younger generation aware that our society today is not a free society. And our society today is suppressed by the people in power. And these people who are in power to day has been the people, a continuation of the people in power even in our days, during our struggle. So in that sense, in my opinion, the struggle continues" (Tan Wah Piow 2020).

CHAPTER TWO. FILMIC STUTTER, TAPED COUNTER-TRUTHS, AND MUSICAL SUTURES

1 Marrie Lee (Doris Young) starred in the 1978 film *They Call Her Cleopatra Wong* ("She purrs like a kitten . . . makes love like a siren . . . fights like a panther") and two sequels, produced and directed by Filipino filmmaker Bobby A. Suarez. Quentin Tarantino told the *Straits Times* in 2003 that *Cleopatra Wong* was "a gigantic inspiration" for the Uma Thurman character in his *Kill Bill* series (Tarantino 2003, 2004). The character Cleopatra Wong was obviously inspired by Cleopatra Jones, James Bond, and Bruce Lee, and drew on a mix of martial arts and spy films, and technological gadgetry.

2 In another interview, Sandi Tan notes that Celler did not actually know how to use After Effects, but taught himself along the way (S. Tan 2018a).

3 The quote is taken is taken from my recording of an author Q&A event, Brattle Theater, Cambridge, MA, September 17, 2018 (see also S. Tan 2012b).

4 See, e.g., Margaret Tan's "Smart Apron" project, and her website for her early projects (M. Tan 2004). More recently she has been doing public murals, one

with students at Tembusu College, described in the afterword. Shirley Soh's project with incarcerated women using art to design objects that also tell about their lives was displayed at the Singapore Biennale, 2013. She did the artwork for the MRT Blue Line station exit at the Botanical Gardens.

5 Author Q&A event, Brattle Theater, Cambridge, MA, September 17, 2018.

6 Vladimir Propp ([1928] 1968) showed how folktales could be structurally analyzed on two axes, a synagmatic one of functions (kinds of actions, verbs, plot) and a paradigmatic one (actors). Lévi-Strauss (1955) used a modified version of Propp's approach to show in the case of the myth of Oedipus that myths operate with binary oppositions that express existential dilemmas or aporia that are unsolvable, such as claims over being autochthonous people in a land or foreigners (impossible, since all peoples come from somewhere), and so people invoke gods to establish their claim to autochthony.

7 The story told in the film is that both Georges Cardona, American film instructor, and the film literally disappeared. Other versions of this history say that the film was, as with so many unfinished film projects (described in chapter 1 in one of Tan Pin Pin's films), simply stashed away, and when Cardona left town he deposited it (or had someone else deposit it) at the National Film Archives, from where eventually someone withdrew it. It is likely that some literary license was taken to heighten the dramatic effect.

8 The word "puncta" here works in both senses: a stopping point of reflection, a still; and, following Roland Barthes (1981), an element within any photograph, a seizure that captures the eye with a particular force of visceral reality, what Lacan also might call the real beyond signification or the symbolic.

9 Unless otherwise noted, all the quotations in this section are from the film.

10 The characters mentioned in the film are identified at the end with their full names and what has become of them.

11 Elsewhere, Sandi says they also would go to the Malaysian border where they could get pirated films not available in Singapore.

12 "I kept almost all of the mail I got for *Exploding Cat*, the zine I ran when I was 16—from a lonesome poet in Ohio, an Israeli experimental musician, several men serving life sentences in California state prisons. Also, back in the pre-Internet, I wrote an insane amount of letters and postcards—sometimes two a day to the same friend, mailed in the AM and in the PM, constituting an ongoing real-time diary of the whirling, frenzied off-kilter triple-axels that were going on in my teenage head (mostly thoughts about movies and French guys). Two of my teenage correspondents (who, unbeknownst to me, had kept *all* of my letters to them) were kind enough to share them with me" (quoted in S. Tan 2018a).

13 At the present time, Sophia Siddique Harvey is chair of the English Department at Vassar College.

14 There were three Cleopatra Wong martial arts films shot in Singapore star-

ring a Singaporean actress as an Interpol agent. Made by Filipino filmmakers Bobby A. Suarez and Romeo N. Galang, they were variants of the blaxploitation film *Cleopatra Jones* (Starrett 1973). *Medium Rare* (Smith 1992) was also shot in Singapore, produced by Singaporean Errol Pang and scripted by Singaporeans Margaret Chan and Rani Moorthy. It was about a Singaporean serial killer, who was played by an American, and directed by an Australian. It failed at the box office. There was also a slick 1990 American-made film called *Homeland*, commissioned by Singapore as part of its twenty-fifth anniversary celebration.

15 Starring Julie Christie and Tom Courtney, *Billy Liar* is one of the British New Wave films using real locations in Bradford to give it a documentary feel. To escape boredom, Billy Liar daydreams, fantasizes, and makes up stories about himself and his family.

16 Truffaut adapted the Davis Goodis novel into a comic thriller starring Charles Aznavour. A former classical pianist changes his name and plays in a down-and-out Paris bar, where his brothers show up and ask for help while on the run from gangsters they have scammed.

17 Guy Hamilton's *An Inspector Calls* (1954) is based on the J. B. Priestley play, in which the enigmatic inspector is named Goole, a homonym of ghoul, or spirit, haunting. Perhaps also relevant here is *Inspector* (Samanta 1956), the hit Bollywood film starring Ashok Kumar, and *Inspector General* (1949), directed by Henry Koster and starring Danny Kaye.

18 Ben Harrison is the son of Bernard Harrison, the former director of the Singapore Zoo and Night Safari, and brother of actress Sharda Harrison. For the 2018 film, the soundtrack was done from scratch since Harrison's earlier work was no longer extant. The soundtrack for the new film was done by Ishai Adar, an avant-garde musician from Ramot Hashavim in Israel.

19 See *The General* (Bruckman and Keaton 1926).

20 Tyler's version of the *Sex, Lies, and Videotape* story is that he and Larry Black (both part of the original Georges Cardona mafia) had worked on the film, and Georges had felt jealous and left out, especially when it won the Palme d'Or at the Cannes Film Festival. But Georges, as director of photography on another film Tyler was making, also, he suspects, had disappeared some of the processed film, not unlike in the *Shirkers* story.

21 One of the themes of Charmaine Leung's memoir is the path to stability and sometimes upward mobility for prostitutes and female entertainers that lies with marrying as a man's second or third wife and then making their way within the domestic politics of the family (Leung 2017). Stella Kon's *Emily of Emerald Hill*, loosely based on her grandparents, a wealthy Peranakan business family, premiered in 1984 and has been produced over 350 times. Emily makes her way through the force of her wits. Leading actresses Pearlly Chua and Margaret Chan have made their interpretations of the role iconic, and re-

cently cross-dressing, gay activist, and virtuoso actor Ivan Heng has reprised the role a number of times to great acclaim.

22 The figure of the grandmother, in the background, often plays an anchoring role in "locating the tenor of the setting as a source of the spell" (Geertz [1976] 1983, 120). She provides anchoring across social historical horizons, in social geography or place, class and culture, and is a resonator for changes in later generations. A similar grandmother figure anchors Alfonso Cuarón's *Roma* (2018) and Hirokazu Kore-eda's *Shoplifters* (2018).

23 Cuarón's *Roma* was made in large-format digital black-and-white, and Cuarón sees it as an adult's retrospective investigation into the class and racial dynamics of the life of his childhood nanny (to whom the film is dedicated), about which he had no real understanding as a child. Colonia Roma is a neighborhood of Mexico City, but the film's title is also perhaps a reference to Federico Fellini's semi-autobiographical film *Roma* (1972), an intercutting of 1930s and 1970s Rome. Cleo, the name given to the nanny, is a reference also to Agnes Varda's film *Cleo from 5 to 7* (1962). See Tapley (2018).

24 The use of sea and land in narratives is not unlike the mythic structure of land versus sea that Marshall Sahlins finds structuring societies from Polynesia to ancient Greece (Sahlins 2004; see also Tambiah 1986, 1992; Fischer 2013).

25 St. Anne's was on Middle Road, below Emily Hill. It now has been relocated to Bedok.

26 Blood Hill, a reference to Red Hill (Bukit Merah), which will reappear as the site of a founding legend of Singapore.

27 I am indebted to my copyeditor Philip Thomas for this recognition.

28 The diseased black tongue will reappear at independence, when Kenneth and his mates emerge from the jungle to be honored by the British for their guerrilla fight against the Japanese. His tongue has been split by the Japanese, and it takes him great effort to learn not to lisp so as to be easily understood. The density of the symbolism cannot be fully unpacked here, but the forked tongue of the politician, the work of Lee Kuan Yew during the war as an accountant for the Japanese (from which he would say he learned something useful about organization and accounts), and his effort of having to learn to speak Chinese are three of them.

29 The Japanese printmaker Tsukioka Yoshitoshi produced a famous woodcut of this story in 1890, and Kiyohime remains a popular figure in mobile and video games, and in anime.

30 These images will reverberate. The dog-man monster Agnes similarly has a black tongue. The metaphor of two tongued (not speaking straight, lisping) is attributed to Kenneth's deep tongue kiss, "overwhelming me from top and bottom, as if he had two tongues" (S. Tan 2012a, 350), as well as to his dominion of "pregnant pauses, doublespeak, and roundabout thinking" (345).

31 The spot is one of my own favorite haunts, near Bussarah Street, where the

Malay and Islamic publishing houses used to flourish, and where a modern Islamic bookstore now resides, and in whose coffee houses I often would sit and write.

32 Actually, it is the dome rather than the minarets that is gilded, and the floor is carpeted rather than tiled. And nowadays, of course, tourists flood the narrow lanes daily.

33 I take the phrase "learns from the movies what it is to be a woman" from Manohla Dargis (2018). The account of Kenneth and Cassandra's kiss (S. Tan 2012a, 346) could come from Dargis's typology of screen kisses. Cassandra's self-reflexive account of their affair could be a commentary from "I'd begun the dinner on *my* terms, in a position of strength, yet he'd managed to rile me until he was back in control," to "the frequency with which he told me he hated me would have sent feminists up in flames . . . until the word *hate* . . . became a kind of perverse mating call. I suspected he used that word only because he couldn't face uttering its opposite" (347).

34 At a public installation at an HDB housing estate that I attended in 2013, newspaper articles from this period were posted on the walls with stories of ghosts encountered in various places in the city. In England too, after World War II, as Michael Young's satire puts it, "too many people had too sharp a sense of history, along with too dull a sense of what the future might bring, . . . [too much] ancestor worship . . . a form of reverence for old houses and churches, quaint weights and measures, coinage" (Young 1958, 22). Elsewhere, he writes, "the long arm of the aristocracy had productivity securely under arrest" (24). And "there is the same threat of the other country's armaments, trade, and science used to batter down resistance to change . . . it was always a matter of quality . . . for the sake of survival, the country had to meet the challenge" (27).

35 A new five-story wing of Mount Alvernia Hospital was opened in July 1965 by LKY. Meanwhile, Green Spot was actually the name of a soft drink bottling company, and there was a huge Green Spot bottle at the entrance of the Amoy Canning Company.

36 This would be David Marshall, Singapore's famed first chief minister, of Baghdadi Jewish origins, known as one of Singapore's finest criminal trial lawyers, who led the team of negotiators for independence. His bust, sculpted by Hungarian sculptor Peter Lambda in 1956 and donated by his widow, today has a place of honor in the Singapore Management University Law School library. Lee Kuan Yew, as a lawyer for the then militant post office workers' union, positioned himself to the left of the centrist Marshall, but later, to outmaneuver the communists, would move to the right.

CHAPTER THREE. WHITE INK, FAMILY SYSTEMS, FORESTS OF ILLUSION, AND AGING

1 "Moreover, Jack sees that Jill herself knows what Jill thinks Jack knows, but that Jill does not realize she knows it" (Laing 1970, quoted as the epigraph for *Pulse* by Kwa [(2010) 2014]).

2 See Lydia Kwa's book of poems, *Sinuous* (2013). The Woodbridge Hospital appears also in Kua Ee Heok's novelistic account of his work there as a young psychiatrist, caring for elderly survivors of World War II (Kua 2003). I have discussed Kua's work elsewhere (Fischer 2015).

3 Scott Stonington, a physician-anthropologist working with Thai Buddhists at the end of life, reminds us that, at least in Thailand, the word "enlightenment" is something reserved to the Buddha, and that what humans can attempt is to reduce suffering, which is different from pain, and which is achieved by loving kindness (Stonington 2020). The philosophy is similar to the one Kwa writes about in undoing opponents (including possessing ghosts or objects), releasing them from their fears, rather than fighting them.

4 There are seven key characters, almost all beings of a "third kind," with a special "mark," and all with "white ink" relationship to their mothers: (1) Ling ("soul" or "spirit") has two important mothers. The first mother commits suicide after being raped by a bandit (who kills Ling's father, a tea merchant) but first saves Ling from drowning, saying remember your name (which you must not reveal), you must not die, you exist beyond this form; and she later returns in dreams to remind Ling that she has a destiny to fulfill. The second is the Taoist abbess (whom Ling will succeed), who "was her mother in ways her own mother could not be." Ling's special mark is that her eyes are different colors. (2) Qilan ("strange orchid"), a Taoist nun, saves Ling from the bandit on the auction block, is the offspring of a fox spirit and a scholar, and so a being of the third kind. Her mother coaches her in patience and appropriate revenge over a demon (*gui*, "poison") who has possessed her father. Qilan teaches the nuns martial arts, but also the ethics of releasing enemies from the fears that cause their enmities, rather than killing them out of personal revenge. (3) The mother of the imperial secretary Wan'er is kept in the palace with her daughter after Wan'er's father and grandfather are killed by the empress. She has had a dream that Wan'er will "weigh the affairs of the world" under Empress Wu Zhao (by outliving the empress, and being the writer and guardian of three records: the official record, the empress's diaries, Wan'er's own diaries). Both mother and daughter operate under close surveillance, but the mother provides advice and company, and finally encourages Wan'er to break away. Under stress Wan'er strokes her own cheek with the back of her hand as her mother did. (4) Empress Wu Zhao's mother is a cousin of the Sui emperor and second wife of a timber merchant, who is disappointed that this daughter, Wu Zhao, is taking up manly arts (while his sons are not), and

appalled by a diviner's prediction that the girl will become a ruler. These are psychological drivers: she is "grieved that I could not gain that ultimate acceptance from my father," and she has the poison of pride in the prediction driving her to prove that she is up to the ruthlessness needed to achieve and hold power and to become immortal with the aid of alchemical elixirs. She seeks proof in her ambitions by staging the rare *feng shan* ritual, affirming her status as mediator of heaven and earth, while her husband dies of slow poisoning. She tries to get her husband to abandon Buddhism, but it is loyalty to *his mother's* Buddhism that blocks her, a Buddhism he points out that anyway includes many Taoist beliefs. (5) Xuanzang, the monk who brought back the Buddhist sutras from India, has the most interesting "mother," an old woman who gifted him a drawing on silk of a turtle's body without the shell, which he was to keep secret until he identified his successor. He reflects on this maternal counter to paternal traditions of inheritance from fathers and male ancestors, and the path he had first entered in being sent to become a monk and then taking vows of renunciation. (6) The mother of Harelip made his needle cushion for his acupuncture practice. He becomes a healer and apothecary, and Xuanzang's successor. (7) The mother of Baoshi ("precious stone"), the hermaphrodite, could not intervene when Baoshi's father tried to give money to Xuanzang to take him away, yet gave Baoshi his name. Baoshi has flashbacks of his mother naked, but never of his father. (8) It is the *grandmother* of Ardhanari, the sculptor and lover of Xuanzang, who gifts him the songs of Krishna, and he sculpts the androgynous figure of Maitreya Buddha, the female empress of the future.

5 The taking of different pulses (in the plural) is referred to in the novel *Pulse* as a traditional Chinese medical diagnostic practice. Knots can refer to the ropes and knots of the *kinbaku* practice in the novel. It can refer to psychiatrist R. D. Laing's book *Knots* (1970), which provides the epigraph for the novel *Pulse*. It can also refer to Jacques Lacan's use of Borromean knots for the intertwining of the *real*, the *symbolic*, and the *imaginary*, such that cutting of any one releases all three. Later Lacan added a fourth ring, the *sinthome*. Unlike "acting out" in symptoms or signifiers calling for interpretation, the *sinthome* is pure *jouissance* addressed to no one. Lacan takes, from the writing of James Joyce, the idea of the *sinthome* as a form of non-signifying *writing*, an enjoyment of the unconscious in itself and an artificial (synthetic) self-creation (*synth-homme*), which helps prevent the three other rings from coming apart. I use this as an analogy for the "registers and threads" that intertwine in the psychic organization of Kwa's novels, without attempting to fit them scholastically into Lacan's typology.

6 Wan'er, the imperial secretary, acknowledges the crux of one of the complicated psychodramas: "yearning to be loved by one's enemy" and struggling against *hate and revenge*. She is conflicted in her servitude to the empress

who has confided in her, she is complicit in a plot against the empress, and she is a victim of the empress's wrath against her family. As a willful child, she was branded on her forehead by the empress to make her docile. The empress, Whu Zhao, is the daughter of a father who wished she was a son, and could not accept that his most virile offspring was female. Before her mother (cousin of a king and second wife of a king), she undergoes the *shame* of having her head shaved and being sent to a nunnery, before she is able to return and reclimb the ranks of concubines. In her diaries she says she writes her life story on behalf of women who have to make their way amid the power struggles of men. Her court is one of constant soap-operatic intrigues, power games, and use of sexual desire as a calculated, if often uncontrollable, form of power.

7 All of these references appear in Lydia Kwa's book-length poem *Sinuous* (2013), along with Cathy Caruthers, Sigmund Freud, and the Woodbridge Hospital. The latter is Singapore's mental health hospital, a venue that appears also in a novel by psychiatrist Kua Ee Heok (2003), discussed in Fischer (2015).

8 Written with two radicals: *gui* (ghost) and *dou* (ladle, gourd). See the magnificent rubbing of the Kui Xing calligraphic form in figure 3.1.

9 See Pu Songling's eighteenth-century collection, *Strange Tales from a Chinese Studio* (Pu 2006). See also the discussion of this genre below.

10 "The human race would cease to exist. . . . The earth would survive, along with creatures invisible to the eye, those who could proliferate in extreme weather conditions, parasites, and those that could transform themselves to adapt to changing circumstances. The chimeric creatures would triumph, the ones whose minds and bodies could transform in response to the diseases that had decimated purer variants. It would be the fulfillment of *The Classic of the Mountains and Seas* . . . myths becoming fact" (Kwa 2017a, 103).

11 On figures and "ladders of instruction" in the *Mahabharata*, and similar parable forms in the *Shahnameh*, see Fischer (2004, 66–130; 2017b; 2018a, 161–85).

12 I am reminded of cultural protocols of access to knowledge in Bangarra Dance Theatre's study guide for *Ochres*: "Access [through stories] can be referred to as 'outside knowledge'—knowledge that may be shared (as opposed to 'inside knowledge' which by its nature is not be shared outside of a given community)."

13 Both Xuanzang and Harelip refuse to participate in Empress Wu Zhao's grand *feng shan* ceremony, thereby becoming outlaws, hiding themselves, and sequestering themselves on top of a mountain that is difficult to access.

14 See Wheatley (1971) on the cosmological and geometric layout of Asian royal cities.

15 Germaine (Necker) de Staël is a particularly interesting figure in this context in being a best-selling novelist, and advocating for a republican form of gov-

ernance and for women's public roles in that governance. She saw the novel as a marker of modernity against the literary forms of the classics (or "ancients"). Her father, like Rousseau, was from Geneva. He rose to become the French finance minister, but lost that office during a financial crisis brought on by supporting the American Revolution with high-interest loans. Napoleon Bonaparte becomes her image of tyranny, and she likens tyranny to a machine "at once diabolical and mathematical that transforms moral life into a servile tool," a metaphor that foreshadows the debates about tyranny in contemporary China, and about the growing pervasiveness of algorithms and surveillance there and elsewhere (Damrosch 2020, 25–29).

16 In the epigraph it is interesting that Benjamin's use of "clouds" is not unlike the use of clouds in Chinese painting and poetry to indicate the heavens; and beyond, perhaps the use of "the cloud" for contemporary internet or web information and image-storage facilities is similar as something that ordinary people find mysterious, but that approaches infinity and omniscience, which upon reflection is problematic in various ways, not least as energy consumers and heat producers.

17 Yuen Ting Lee (2015) notes that Wu Zhao has been the subject of television serials, notably in the 2014/15 drama series *Wumeiniang chuanqi* ("The legend of the charming lady Wu, or the empress of China"). Lee lists five major achievements of her reign, including women's rights, asserting the ruler as a mother over her children, and encouraging scholars to write biographies of notable women; patronage of Buddhism, literature, and the arts; constructing irrigation systems, reducing taxes on peasants, and sponsoring agricultural manuals; reforms of the bureaucracy; and expanding Tang territories. Lee notes briefly how she was differently treated by historians at times of greater and lesser openness to women. The above television series "appealed to a vast audience as well as provoking state censorship, not just because of its extravagant budget and boldness in production, but also its scandalous depiction of the actress Fan Bingbing in the role of Wu and audience's attitudes about sexuality and women. The drama first aired on commercial satellite station Hunan Television on December 21, 2014, but was canceled a week later because of government censors' objections and resumed broadcasting on January 1, 2015, with almost all the breasts and cleavage of actresses cropped out" (Y. T. Lee 2015, 18).

18 Wikipedia, s.v. "Chuanqi (short story)," last modified November 4, 2022, 21:48, https://en.wikipedia.org/wiki/Chuanqi_(short_story).

19 Pu Songling's "strange tales" or *chuanqi* (Pu 2006) are a source, but also "those crazy movies in Hong Kong cinema—*A Chinese Ghost Story, A Chinese Ghost Story 2*—and then various other films in Japanese film history to do with ghosts" (Kwa 2017b). She also credits Daniel Hsieh's study of how women and love are portrayed in chuanqi (Hsieh 2007), in which he stresses

the pervasive misogyny in the *stories*, portraying fox spirits and ghosts as female and malevolent. "This spurred a feminist urge to write a protagonist that is female, half-fox, half-human, that is motivated by compassion and wisdom" (Kwa 2020).

20 Kwa draws on an article and two books by historian James Francis Warren (1986, 1992, 1993). More recent works include Charmaine Leung's warmly received memoir of growing up in Singapore's Chinatown brothel area (Leung 2017) and the site-specific "walking theater" of Chinatown Crossing, performed by Drama Box Theater in 2018 and 2019 (see Drama Box 2019).

21 Interestingly, Kwa writes in *Sinuous,* "Dianne the waitress still wears her hair in a voluminous roll-up bun, now dyed jet black—looks like she recently stepped out from the Tang dynasty court, voluptuous and swaggering all at once, a cowboy courtesan in the 21st century" (Kwa 2013, 93). In the novel she is called Francis, and while voluptuous, does not have this historical Tang dynasty attribute, and in a dream fantasy is described as pole dancing with a snake.

22 "This country I adopted / has bred a dark history of hatred: / 1885 Chinese Head Tax and 1923 Exclusion Act / racial segregation in schools / theft of aboriginal lands / residential school abuse / internment of Japanese Canadians / the Komagata Maru incident in 1914 / detention of Tamil migrants / and so much more" (Kwa 2013, 81).

Patterson makes much of Kwa's class distance, walking by derelicts in Vancouver, as parallel to her distanced fantasy about the prostitutes in Singapore, which he suggests is a trope often used by ethnics impersonating oppressed people of the past. Patterson also sees class privilege in Kwa's ability to take a year's leave of absence from her job to mainly go to the gym and library (how, with no income, he asks). Patterson hears resentment against her richer clients, identifying with the parallel with sex workers as "affective supporters" of the colonial government, in other words both providing grease to the capitalist economies of their times. Kwa's two lovers in Vancouver are of different classes. Stephanie, she mistakenly thinks at first, is bisexual because a man shares her single bed; but it's Stephanie's brother, since they can barely make ends meet; and Stephanie remonstrates about "you baby boomers!" (who are better off). Francis has a more spacious and elegant place, and in *Sinuous* reappears as Dianne, described in note 21 above.

23 In the poem "In Their Stories," we learn that Mah Mah had found a wealthy match for Mahmee, and when Mahmee chose a poor man of a lower class, Mah Mah kept Kong-Kong's money from her and squanders it on her brother instead (Kwa 1994a, 17).

24 Similarly, in Thailand thinking too much (*khit mak*) often translates as anxiety, and is a "powerfully negative mind state and can lead to self-harm both physical and psychological," and contrasts with *kamlang chai* (heart-mind-energy) which is curative, and confers vitality and life (Stonington 2020, 44).

25 Isa Kamari's novel *1819* (2013) is partly based on the *Hikyat Abdullah*. Anthropologists might know it from Engseng Ho's study of the Hadrami diaspora, extending between Yemen and Southeast Asia (Ho 2006).

CHAPTER FOUR. MINIATURES

Section epigraph: Danielle Lim, quoted in Ho, "Story Collection 'And Softly Go the Crossings' Tops Singapore Book Awards."

Section epigraph: Elderly Rwandan woman, quoted in Sadruddin, "The Care of Small Things."

1 The fires are still controversial. They were used by the government as justifications for replacing postwar slums with modern, new mass housing as in much of the social democratic West and communist East; but suspicions remain that the government had the fires set as a political control measure, amplifying the hygiene and life-style improvements by replacing ungovernable densities of population with more easily surveilled and controlled vertical apartment blocks.

2 See Chong et al. (2013a) for a study of Red Hill done amid renewed debates about building public housing with single apartments for seniors versus reconfiguring apartments for multigenerational living. Chong's practice has included planning and redesign for elder-friendly living, including the residents in the design process. The study of Red Hill was done with students and two research assistants at the Singapore University of Technology and Design. In 2013 I also taught a class at Tembusu College (part of the National University of Singapore) in which students did an architectural design for multigenerational living with the needs of elders as the motive.

3 See Fischer (2013) for accounts of the SARS crisis.

4 There are a number of accounts of efforts to diagnose and control the SARS epidemic in Singapore. Fischer (2013) also provides an amusing account of competing claims for priority and credit, especially between Hong Kong and Singapore.

5 *Mycobacterium leprae* was discovered in 1873 in Norway by Gerhard Armauer Hansen (hence Hansen's disease), the first pathogenic bacterium to be identified. Gerhard Domagk, working for Bayer in the 1930s, found that dapsone, a sulfonamide, cured several bacterial infections, and sulfa drugs became the miracle drug for bacterial infections, after phage therapies, a discovery for which he received the Nobel Prize in 1939 but was forced by the Nazi regime to decline the honor (he received it after the war without the money). Promin in the 1940s was the first effective drug for leprosy, and in the 1950s dapsone was introduced, which is what our narrator remembers. After the war, Domagk also developed isoniazid, now a standard drug for tuberculosis. But it was Shantaram Yawalkar, working for Ciba-Geigy in 1974, who developed

a combination of dapsone and rifampicin (an effective bactericide, introduced by Ciba as Rimactane in 1968) to prevent bacterial resistance, and a triple "multi-drug" therapy was adopted by the World Health Organization in 1981 as the standard of care. See World Health Organization (2022); and Wikipedia, s.v. "Leprosy," last modified January 10, 2023, 8:18, https://en.wikipedia.org/wiki/Leprosy.

6 I take the phrase "the care of small things" from the work of Aalyia Sadruddin (2020a, 2020b), in which it is an important motif for constructing lives in what are called, relatively speaking, "ordinary times" (*ibhihe bisanzwe*). Those ordinary times, and ordinary lives, are often combined with the non-ordinary. This is enacted, for instance, by a woman who lost her husband and daughter, and "often broke into song during our conversation; she told me it was 'easier and more enjoyable' for her to sing, rather than speak about matters that were otherwise too difficult for her to think through in a concise fashion" (Sadruddin 2020b, 70). Cardboard Auntie uses a similar therapeutic practice, collecting cardboard and small things she finds on the ground; the Rwandan woman just mentioned does it by singing about things of which she cannot really speak. One might also call it the language of small things, a semiotics of small things rather than of language.

CHAPTER FIVE. BLUE WIDOW WITH GREEN STRIPES

1 The term *abangan* derives from the Javanese word for red (thus, another question of red); it refers to Muslims who are syncretic in their beliefs and practices. As described in Pamuntjak's novel about small-town Java, this became a source of increasing conflict in the 1950s and 1960s as Islamic fundamentalism spread, propagated by preaching rather than deep learning (as her character Sudariminto puts it). Geertz (1960) popularized for English readers the distinction between *abangan* and *santri* (syncretic versus strict Islamic, *pesantran*-educated), and also observed the increase in travel to Mecca from small towns as a force of change (Geertz 1963). *Kejawen* or *agama Jawa* means literally "religion of Java" and refers to this syncretic mixture, with a stress on mysticism, balance or avoidance of zealotry, and kindness to others bringing returns to oneself. Kindness and service to others are leitmotifs throughout the novel *Amba: A Question of Red*, part of Amba's questioning of others' behaviors, even when not specifically about religious practices.

2 *The Book of Centhini* (1814), set in the sixteenth and seventeenth centuries, is a twelve-volume verse compilation of tales, traditions, magic, eroticism, ceremonies, and other lore framed within a set of travels across Java by three separated royal siblings in search of reuniting, in the aftermath of a war between the Sultan of Giri and the Sultan of Mataram (today's Surakarta). This frame story is taken from the *Babad Tanah Java*, or Chronicles of Java, the

story of the defeat of Giri by Mataram and the dispersal of the children of the Sultan of Giri. The eponymous Centhini is a maid to the beautiful young wife of one of these siblings, who, refusing to believe her husband is dead, sets out in disguise to find him. She finds him in the *alam walikan* (the spirit world). The journeys, collecting knowledge from across Java about the four goals and stages of life, contain mystical meanings. Centhini, as a young maid and maiden, is well placed with her beautiful young mistress to observe the ways of desire and eroticism, and *The Book of Centhini* is thus sometimes called the *Kama Sutra* of Java. In literary form it is a verse compilation of 722 "songs" or cantos. See Soewito (2006); and the Singapore LGBT Encyclopaedia Wiki, s.v. "Serat Centhini," accessed January 11, 2023, https://the-singapore-lgbt-encyclopaedia.fandom.com/wiki/Serat_Centhini.

The *Wedhatama*, from Sanskrit Veda Uttama (esoteric wisdom), is a poem from the 1870s, translated into English first in the journal *Indonesia*, volume 14, 1972, and then by Stuart Robson in 1990, published by KITLV Press, Leiden.

3 Pamuntjak notes, "The Javanese are careful with the names they give their children. . . . The elders have a phrase for this: *keberatan nama*. It means a state of being burdened by a name too great, too portentous" (2). And later she writes, "It was also obvious that his choice of the name for his eldest daughter was willfully corrupting, given what happened to Amba in the great epic. *Won't people think us cruel, giving the name of a fallen woman to our firstborn?* his wife had asked. . . . *What sort of father pushes his own daughter toward a troubled fate?* But it was as if Sudarminto needed to exercise his right to see how far the name would take his first child" (62). Notably this comes in a passage in which Sudarminto is described as thoroughly pragmatic, dismissing superstitious beliefs.

4 The book sold over ten thousand copies in the first six months after its 2015 launch in Germany in a translation by ethnologist and Indonesianist Martina Heinschke; and was listed number one on the list of international fiction translated into German. It was listed among the eight most important novels of the 2015 Frankfurt Book Fair, and received the 2016 LiBeraturpreis managed by Litprom (the Society for the Promotion of African, Asian, and Latin American Literature). Wikipedia, s.v. "Laksmi Pamuntjak," last modified December 23, 2022, 5:11, https://en.wikipedia.org/wiki/Laksmi_Pamuntjak.

5 On "white ink" see chapter 3, especially the section so titled, and note 4 there. Nuniek says of her mother that she married a (lower-status) school principal, but "never complained about life, however shitty it turned out to be," a fighter who refused to lose her dignity. Nuniek says of her, "She told me many times, 'We cooks have the highest intelligence, and we have opinions about everything. Why? Because the qualities we have come to know as 'taste' and 'a deft hand in the kitchen' are essentially courage, and that is the prerequisite to al-

chemy: a set of nerves so steely and seasoned. . . . Cooking is not unlike marriage. Learning to wait, to not put your hand into muddied waters" (80). The passage hints of philosophical discussions of taste as a key social term in common sense, judgment, practical dialectics, and aesthetics (Gadamer 1960). It also is a kind of prolegomena to Pamuntjak's *The Birdwoman's Palate* (2014b, 2018a). On a contemporary parallel to the Nuniek-Amba story in Boneh, Sulawesi, see Pamuntjak (2021b).

6 Among documentary films, see in particular Robert Lemelson's *Forty Years of Silence* (2009), which focuses on mental illnesses of former political prisoners; and Joshua Oppenheimer's two films *The Act of Killing* (2012) and *The Look of Silence* (2014), which focus on the continuing impunity of the perpetrators of the massacres. Among written ethnographies, see Eickhoff et al. (2017a) and the special issue of the *Journal of Genocide Studies* in which that piece occurs; for Bali, see especially Dwyer (2009) and Dwyer and Santikarma (2006, 2007).

7 Physical worship or using the body includes the five daily prostration prayers, fasting, pilgrimage to Mecca, maintaining one's health, and dancing into trance (*raga*). A deeper stage of worship is one of logic, reason, and thought (*cipta*). Yet deeper or higher is worship through the spiritual intelligence of the soul and heart, involving mindfulness and alertness (*jiwa*). Eventually one comes to experience the essence of unity with God (*rasa*).

8 The literature on al-Ghazali is huge, but a nice textual review of his terminology in the *Kitab Adab al-Aql* by Malaysian Islamic scholars stresses, as does Pamuntjak, protecting and safeguarding relations with fellow human beings as well as all nonhuman beings with the goal of training one's perceptions and reason and thereby achieving transcendent or divine bliss (Al-Shafi'i et al. 2018). Pamuntjak lightens the scholasticism and provides an excellent way to read al-Ghazali. For a superb and comprehensive review of al-Ghazali, see Griffel (2020).

9 One could as well invoke here Malaysian-Singaporean writer Suchen Christine Lim's *The River's Song* (2013), built around the return to a much-changed Singapore of a daughter from the United States.

10 To cite only one of many incidents, in 2015 the Ubud (Bali) Writers Festival was told to remove all programs having to do with 1965. See Pamuntjak (2015a).

11 As opposed to everything being merely socially constructed, the sequence of analyses of signaling shows a trajectory of changing and increasing sophistication in analyses. On signals and discerning the difference between knots and kisses, see Pamuntjak (2016, 192–99).

12 On Pamuntjak's own attachment to German culture, see her essay "My Late Father, the German Indonesian" (Pamuntjak 2021a).

13 In other versions, although Srikandi peppers Bhisma with arrows, Arjuna

stands behind her and it is his arrow that Bhisma lets kill him. Bhisma does not abduct the three princesses for himself but to give them in marriage to his half-brother, and when he learns of Amba's love and intention to choose Salva, he sends her to Salva with honors. Bhisma's celibacy vow was because his father had decided to become a householder again and marry once more. He did not want Bhisma to be a rival to a new son for producing a line of succession. Amba goes to the forest to meditate and decide whom she blames the most for her predicament, including herself (why didn't she jump from Bhisma's chariot in the first place?), then tries to get many warriors to avenge her by killing Bhisma, and eventually returns to the forest to practice austerities and become a man in the next life so she can kill him herself. She is born a woman, but is raised as a man (again a number of variations). Since Bhisma will not fight a woman, Amba/Srikandi must appear as a man on the chariot. Pamuntjak simplifies the mythological variations, and turns them into a contemporary sexual awareness and love story.

14 Pamuntjak explores beauty and the Helen figure in her play *Hector and Andromache*, where she also is interested in the role of myth ("since every beginning is a repetition / it starts with myth and ends with myth"; Pamuntjak 2006a, 159; 2006c). She also explores beauty as opposed to goodness: "Beauty is really what sets things off. Goodness is always a solution, not an impetus, it is never a muse" (Pamuntjak 2006a, 193; 2006c).

15 See the Wikipedia account of the complicated political maneuvering during this period, and the questions that remain. Abdul Haris Nasution was a Batak from north Sumatra, who rose to become chief of staff of the army. He escaped the assassination attempt at his home by scrambling over the wall of the next-door neighbor, the Iraqi ambassador. But his five-year-old daughter took three bullets in her spine, presumably aimed at him, and died a few days later, as the novel also reports. Wikipedia, "Abdul Haris Nasution," last modified January 2, 2023, 14:31, https://en.wikipedia.org/wiki/Abdul_Haris_Nasution.

16 Res Publica University was founded in 1960 in response to ethnic quotas for university enrollment. It was sponsored by Baperki (Badan Permusjawaratan Kewarganegaraan), an organization whose members were mainly of Chinese descent, although it also had non-Chinese PKI members. It was a left-leaning university where Pramoedya Ananta Toer taught history for a time. In 1965 anti-communists burned the university down, beginning with the College of Technology, where students had barricaded themselves. Wikipedia, s.v. "Res Publica University," last modified July 23, 2021, 15:39, https://en.wikipedia.org/wiki/Res_Publica_University; and Wikipedia, s.v. "Pramoedya Ananta Toer," last modified January 11, 2023, 16:25, https//en.wikipedia.org/wiki/Pramoedya_Ananta_Toer.

17 Indonesia was the focus of American economists and development work in the early 1950s.

18 Pamuntjak has Bhisma saying "crab-like spiders." The Malay and Indonesian dictionary meaning is "centipede." Centipedes use venom to kill their prey, and their first segment legs operate like venomous claws to hold and paralyze the prey.

19 See Pamuntjak's collection of essays on art (Pamuntjak 2006a), in which she reflects on art and its many interpretations dependent on the viewer, and the implausibility of art for art's sake without appreciation of contexts. Pamuntjak experiments with various relationships between myth or figures like Hector and Andromache, who nurse their private griefs, and are "timeless characters that Homer only sketched for us but live in us as if we had always recognized them" (xvii). The book's short pieces are aporic or undecidably apprentice works or oneiric free association (they are both), in which the main conceit is to look at paintings by George Grosz, Toulouse-Lautrec, Salvador Dali, Max Beckman, Egon Schiele, and Giorgio de Chirico and fantasize women's alternative stories. The essay that gives the collection its title, "The Diary of R. S.," is one of the two pieces not based on a painting, but is one of the more obvious trials for *Amba*. It uses a mother-son, rather than mother-daughter, dyad, but is similarly set in 1964 (in Bandung instead of Yogyakarta): "around us were artists like ourselves," "when everything seemed so up in the air," "those involved in the Cultural Manifesto saying no to [the leftists'] social realism" (17). The birthing (of the boy, Suharto's New Order) is described as painful in the extreme, with "no such thing as a peaceful aftermath" (18). The boy "stopped asking where his father was (dead) but wanted to know *who* he was, *what* he looked like, and I told him he was an artist [instead of a surgeon] who died a political prisoner . . . for a crime he might not have committed" (19). The piece begins promisingly in a hair salon in south Jakarta with women trying to read each other's hidden lives, eyeing and judging each other. As in *Amba* and *Fall Baby*, close attention is paid to the stereotypes and misogyny that one is always warding off, while trying to keep one's face in the world, especially in the stage of "sex and the about to be newly single" (51), and through the lens of one's watching daughter. The daughter, in the second piece not linked to a painting, watches her mother's struggles and comments about a woman "twice scorned," a theme of the *Mahabharata* story in *Amba*. The second half of "The Diary of R. S.," however, veers off into the narrator's nightmare argument with "the good Imam" over inequality between the sexes.

In trying to *unknot* recalcitrant myths, in a meditation on Salvador Dali's *Untitled (Woman with a Head of Flowers)*, Pamuntjak sees a timeless image of the woman (the future) with the skeleton of a man in "her wake": it is "any imaginary younger woman fleeing the grip of an aging once formidable man who may or may not be the artist himself" (xiv). One thinks of Djoko Pekik's *Tuan Tanah Kawin Muda* in the eyes of Siri in *Fall Baby*. A love affair is likened to Adam and Eve ("in the beginning") as surreptitious lovers think they can keep the affair separate from other parts of their lives. And the opening piece ends with a failed effort to explain to the boy the subtle difference between the *kiss* and the *knot*, love and marriage. She has been the male artist's model and mistress, and he has painted her in many roles and poses. They stop seeing each other when the boy enters primary school.

The short pieces in this collection make me reflect on the disciplining that novels impose in contrast to the looser oneiric form, although the stories can be made to work as linked pieces, and Pamuntjak provides suggestions for such a reading in her notes on the collection. The piece, for instance, called "The Prostitute and the Dwarf" (Toulouse-Lautrec's *Madame Poupoule at Her Toilet*), one of the more short-story-form pieces, takes us into a brothel in Jakarta and both the travails of a village girl who leaves a degrading job as a maid and the travails of a dwarf, who also lives in the house, but who labors beyond the capacities of his height to move boxes of goods around in the market. In her notes, Pamuntjak identifies Toulouse-Lautrec as a dwarf (he had pycnodysostosis or Maroteaux-Lamy syndrome), and then links this to "the tragic stand-up comic-cum-magician" or "the clown" splayed out in George Grosz's *Suicide*, his painting of a man in bowler hat holding a cane, lying on the ground, in front of a prostitute in a window, and a second man hanging from a lamppost.

20 Lembaga Kebudayaan Rakyat was founded in 1950, with a first national conference in Surakarta in 1959, which President Sukarno attended. Leading figures such as the painter Affandi and the historian and novelist Pramoedya Ananta Toer were associated with it, and it claimed to have some 200 branches across Indonesia and some 100,000 members by 1963. In the polarization of the times, it became increasingly militant and oppositional to non-leftist writers and artists, and was banned after the September 30 coup attempt and takeover by Suharto. See Wikipedia, s.v. "Lembaga Kebudajaan Rakjat," last modified May 2, 2022, 23:26, https://en.wikipedia.org/wiki/Lembaga_Kebudajaan_Rakjat.

21 When I stumbled upon Matisse's painting *Woman with a Hat*, I had a lightning flash of recognition: yes, that's what Pamuntjak is describing as Ibra's portrait of Amba! I'm indebted to Jessica Stewart (2020) for pointing out the Picasso connection. Gertrude and Leo Stein purchased *Woman with a Hat*, and Gertrude hung Matisse's *Le Bonheur de Vivre* in the room in which she held her weekly salons, where Picasso saw the painting and was so determined to outdo Matisse that he began work on *Les Demoiselles d'Avignon*.

22 The film has the title of the original book, *Aruna dan Lidahnya* (Edwin 2018). See also Gitomartoyo (2018).

23 Called Jagal ("Butcher") in Indonesian, *The Act of Killing* is a 2012 film directed by Joshua Oppenheimer in which he gets participants in the mass kill-

ings of 1965/6 to reenact their roles. This in part was possible due to the impunity of the Pancasila Youth and others who still remain in power.

24 Among the best of the miniature portraits is a love song to Banda Aceh's coffee and passion for songbirds, and the lovely note that the local *sate matang* is actually from an upland village in Aceh, in the regency of Bireun. In keeping with the novel's erotic undersong, she writes that Banda Aceh is a city of a thousand coffee warungs, coffee strained through a sock-like sieve, "almost 100% male; I see men everywhere. Watching. Sipping. Filling the air with their aromas and appetites. . . . So why is it . . . my gaze keeps shifting to the one man beside me, who gives me a nudge with his wiry arm whenever I'm in need of human touch?" (Pamuntjak 2018a, 252–53). Of the song birds, Amir tells her the white-rumped shama is the best, "none can compare in sound quality, stamina, and how many songs it can memorize" (255). As to the food, she admits, as in many places famed for their cuisine, the best is not to be had in restaurants but only in homes.

Restaurant reviews from her food columns reappear as parts of these city descriptions. In Medan: "what can you say about a restaurant that packs it in at seven in the morning and cobbles together Malays, Chinese, Bataks, Javanese, Indians, Muslims, Christians, Buddhists, old, young, males, females, old-timers, out-of-towners, bettor-drivers (bettor is a mix of becak and motorcycle), cops, civil servants, you name it? . . . This restaurant gives us a glimpse of the city's sociology like no other place does, and that alone is worth celebrating" (Pamuntjak n.d.b).

Or in Palambang: "Their *pempek* (the signature dish of Palembang: large dumplings made of boiled fish lightly fried and served with *coko*, a spicy sauce suffused with chilies, dried shrimp, soy sauce, vinegar, tamarind, palm sugar, and a truckload of garlic) is utterly divine, easily the best I've had anywhere, and the basic, run-of-the-mill tile-and-laminex surrounds do nothing to distract you from the perfection in your plate" (Pamuntjak n.d.a.). The place is recommended in *The Birdwoman's Palate* by the dying seventy-two-year-old in the hospital who bribed his nurse to say on his medical record that he had avian flu (Pamuntjak 2018a, 166).

25 See Fischer (2013) for an account of some of the international conundra of Indonesia's refusal to share samples with the World Health Organization without promises of benefits to Indonesia in any future vaccine development.

26 The friend's name, Bono, is of course itself a stage name, that of the singer-lyricist of the rock band U2, Paul David Hewson.

27 In some Teochew communities, before feeding the bride something sweet (a date-sweetened soup with glutinous rice balls, for instance), the groom has to prove his stamina and determination to get through hardship by downing something spicy and bitter (e.g., wasabi washed down with Guinness) or concoctions much worse designed by the bridesmaids (Tan 2011, 113–18).

28 In delightful counterpoint, Cheryl Lu-Lien Tan's memoir of *food and family* (Tan 2011) takes the form of a returning fashion journalist from New York and Baltimore, who tries to recover the cooking skills that as a girl she refused to learn. The memoir takes the form of many contemporary novels of returning professionals after a long period of living abroad, and is humorously joyful in parallel to Pamuntjak's novel, exploring to some extent the differences between the Teochew and Hakka sides of her family expressed in food reciprocity, and ritual form, but is geographically, culturally, and philosophically more restricted.

29 On Paramaditha, see again note 1 in the introduction to this volume.

CHAPTER SIX. FILMIC OBSESSIVE REPETITIONS, DISSOCIATIONS, AND POWER RELATIONS

1 Daniel Hui speaking in a video of the Q&A session marking the release of *Eclipses,* Singapore International Film Festival, September 2011. See Hui (2011).

2 There is a personal account of the period by the parish priest in the Geylang Catholic Centre (Aroçtcarena 2015). There are also a number of memoirs about Operation Spectrum (Tan Wah Piow 1987; Seow 1994; Teo Soh Lung 2010) and also Jason Soo's documentary film *1987: Untracing the Conspiracy* (2015), in which Vincent Cheng, the man held in jail the longest, appears. Cheng also attended the showing of the film. Despite previous jailings, all these books are freely available in Singapore.

3 "Q&A with Daniel Hui after the Premiere of *Eclipses*," 9:45.

4 The house, at 38 Oxley Road, was built in 1898 by a Dutch merchant on what in the 1840s had been a nutmeg plantation and the home of Sir Manasseh Meyer. After World War II it was purchased by Lee Kuan Yew, and the basement became a regular meeting place for the People's Action Party. The fate of the house became a running soap opera when his younger son used Facebook posts to accuse his elder brother (the sitting prime minister) of planning to violate the will. Fearing for his freedom, the accuser and his wife fled to Hong Kong.

5 Born in Baghdad in 1846, Meyer came to live with his mother's brother in Singapore as a fifteen-year-old in 1861, studied at St. Joseph's Institution (now the Singapore Art Museum), worked in Calcutta in his uncle's business, then started his own business in Burma, returning to Singapore in 1873 and making his fortune first in the opium trade and then in real estate, building still-standing iconic buildings. He was a major donor to Raffles College (now the National University of Singapore) as well as to the Hebrew University of Jerusalem. He helped build Singapore's two synagogues, hosted the visit of Albert Einstein in 1922 (who was raising money for the Hebrew University of Jeru-

salem), and served as a municipal commissioner of Singapore from 1893 to 1900. He was knighted in 1929 for contributions to society, and died in 1930.

6 Born in Meerut, India, Gupta is a graduate of St. Stephen's College, Delhi, and the Indian Institute of Management, Ahmedabad, and is now a Singaporean citizen.

CHAPTER SEVEN. MERITOCRACY BLUES, CHIMERAS, AND ANALYTIC MONSTERS

Section epigraph: "People Are Dangerous," song set to flamenco music in Wild Rice's production of *Madame White Snake*, lyrics by well-known playwright Alfian Sa'at.

Section epigraph: Khmer saying, the epigraph for Lydia Kwa's *Sinuous*.

1 Otto Neurath's isotypes were an effort to translate statistics into more humanized and visual forms, and are used to good effect in the *New York Times* and elsewhere (Neurath 2010; Neurath and Kinross 2009).

2 Other future directions are possible: fusions of watery creatures with fish tails and various sorts of heads, Marina Warner (2021) notes, were popular in Europe as Greek traditions interacted with Scandinavian ones.

3 On the confounding ways intense wildfires move by convection, eating air from the sides and then jumping ahead as if live monsters, see Petryna (2022). On myths of nationalism and sovereignty that, like Dracula, outlive themselves, see Naficy (2007).

4 The material/cognitive duality, however, is a separation that comes after an original unity, as with the biblical separations of heaven/earth, darkness/light. In the beginning was the antaboga, who created the world turtle from which other creatures derived, and also rice from its tears. In Hindu texts the antaboga is also called the *Ananta Shesha* or *Shesha Naga* (the endless snake). Vishnu is often depicted as resting on the Shesha Naga, the endless or first *naga* (*Adi-shesha*); as it uncoils, time moves forward and creation occurs, while when it coils back, the universe ceases to exist. Shesha in Sanskrit mathematics also is the remainder when all else ceases to exist. The antaboga is like the Leviathan in the Bible and its cognates in other Middle Eastern mythologies. It is a sea serpent-monster, paired with the earth monster Behemoth, and the air-monster Ziz, who rules the bird kingdom, and is sometimes thought to be cognate with the Persian *simorgh* and the Greek phoenix. Wikipedia, s.v. "Antaboga," last modified December 28, 2022, 17:05, https://en.wikipedia.org/wiki/Antaboga; and Wikipedia, s.v. "Shesha," last modified January 6, 2023, 8:22, https://en.wikipedia.org/wiki/Shesha. Norse mythology also has a world serpent, Jörmungandr or Midgard Serpent.

5 The selection process for the elite Coast Guard Special Task Squadron sounds quite similar to that for the elite Aquanauts: it includes a "hell week," pushing

physical and mental strength to their limits, carrying a 50-kilogram backpack at all times and plunging into seawater from a height of 8 meters to instill confidence in water. The latter is described in a *Straits Times* celebratory notice on the seventieth anniversary of women in the Singapore Police Force, and in 2014 the opening up of this elite unit to women. There are now five women in the unit, which chases smugglers and other intruders (Ng 2019). On projections of humans acquiring marine mammal genetic features, see the speculative fiction of Kobe Abe (1970) and Kurt Vonnegut (1985), among many others.

6 Alcubierre warp drive is named after the work of Mexican theoretical physicist Michael Alcubierre. Using a solution for Einstein's field equations, it is speculated that a spacecraft could achieve "apparent faster than light travel if a configurable energy density field lower than that of vacuum (negative mass) could be created." Wikipedia, s.v. "Alcubierre Drive," last modified January 4, 2023, 9:35, https://en.wikipedia.org/wiki/Alcubierre_drive.

7 Hans Eysenck's *The Uses and Abuses of Psychology* (1953) was perhaps the most popularizing and controversial work of his eighty-book multifaceted career, one everyone in my generation had to contend with. I spent 1965/6 at the London School of Economics, living and breathing the debates described in Michael Young's *The Rise of the Meritocracy* (1958), a satire that hewed very close to actuality and so was often read without seeing the irony, signaled by its diegetic dating in 2035, with important dates in the 1960s and 1980s along the way that could not have been known in 1958, but were already "in mind" and unfolding logics that did come to pass.

8 "Today we frankly recognize that democracy can be no more than aspiration, and have rule not so much by the people as by the cleverest people, not an aristocracy of birth, not a plutocracy of wealth but a true meritocracy of talent" (Young 1958, 17). See also, for instance, Sheila Jasanoff (2005), who contrasts the "civic epistemologies" of Britain against those of Germany and the United States. She shows that the British default mechanism for decision-making over ethically fraught issues in science and technology (such as genetically modified foods, or stem cell research) is to defer to experts and form expert committees precisely to avoid widespread discussion. Young points out that the technocratic, antidemocratic feeling was quite explicit in the 1950s, as it remains in Singapore, albeit in two places with elected parliaments. This struggle between expertise, accountability, and who makes decisions is perennial, not just restricted to these terms or these social polities.

9 The description continues: "*Virtual Singapore* includes semantic 3D modelling, which comprises detailed information such as texture, material representation of geometrical objects; terrain attributes, for example, water bodies, vegetation, transportation infrastructure, etc. Models of buildings encode the geometry as well as the components of a facility, such as walls, floors, and ceil-

ings, down to its fine details, as in the composition of granite, sand and stone in a building material. *Virtual Singapore* will be developed based on geometric and image data collected from various public agencies, and will integrate different data sources to describe the city with the necessary dynamic data ontology. The 2D data and information coordinated through existing geospatial and non-geospatial platforms such as OneMap, People Hub, Business Hub etc. will enrich the 3D Singapore City Model. Advanced information and modelling technology will allow Virtual Singapore to be infused with different sources of static, dynamic and real-time city data and information e.g., demographics, movement, climate" (SNRF 2019).

10 The acronym for some reason reminds me of SIGUR, the conference on information retrieval. Simurgh, of course, is the symbolic bird, the flock of thirty birds that find wisdom in their collective conference, discussed in chapter 2.

11 In Singapore, the best and the brightest get scholarships to study overseas: A*STAR and Presidential Scholarships are among the most prestigious, and frequently lead to fast-track job mobility. In the pioneer generation of independent Singapore, engineers were sent to leading management schools before returning to run the new government. In England, as Young puts it, "By 1944, the most brilliant young men from Cambridge and Oxford were already going into the administrative class, there to guide the destinies of the nation. . . . Today we have an elite selected according to deserts, with a grounding in philosophy and administration as well as in the two S's of science and sociology" (Young 1958, 17–18).

12 For Oxford's real-world PPE program, see University of Oxford (n.d.).

13 These buildings are the same ones that the character Kenneth Kee energetically builds to create a clean city in Sandi Tan's *The Black Isle* (2012a), discussed in chapter2. The HDB mass building of socialist-style high-rise apartment blocks was connected with the mandatory Central Provident Fund state pension scheme. This was a core mechanism for creating the state financially as well as its legitimacy, a forced savings scheme, and a percentage of salary-based rent scheme, that the city could invest to continue building (see Chua 1997, 2017).

14 Eliza was an early artificial intelligence program, devised at MIT between 1964 and 1966 by Joseph Weizenbaum. It was meant to show the superficiality of machine-human communication. Instead, it demonstrated that humans easily attributed sentience to the machine. Its most famous script, Doctor, played the role of psychotherapist by responding with nondirectional questions to user inputs, making users feel listened to. For details and development, see Satran 2022.

15 The poster graphics of moral campaigns were celebrated as nostalgia pieces, and the campaigns satirized with mock posters, in a wonderful large show mounted in the National Library of Singapore in January 2013.

16 The theme of meritocratic behavioral training and entrained instincts, particularly the ability to handle pressure and frustration, is given attention throughout the novel, but perhaps most pointedly in the templates for requests for funds. "The infamous strategic proposal template had to be used, and it had to include an economic strategy, a payoff matrix, a Nash Bertrand competition model, and a GDP contribution roadmap for the next ten years. . . . The biggest challenge wasn't actually completing the template. It was that he had no information of data to work with, and was required to have every detail be factually accurate. A single inconsistency could disqualify the submission" (Goh 2017, 187–88).

17 Among the face-recognition and tracking technologies that have become recently controversial in the United States are Amazon's Rekognition and that used by Oak View Group, the company hired by pop star Taylor Swift to set up kiosks when she played the Rose Bowl in May 2018. The kiosks played videos of her for fans, but also took photos of people looking at the videos and sent them to Nashville, where they were cross-referenced with a database of potential stalkers (Deb and Singer 2018).

18 Facebook renamed itself Meta in 2021, perhaps following the logic of Daren Goh's novel.

19 The Malay term *kerajaan* is sometimes loosely translated as king, but means a community oriented around a raja as both a political and psychological focus, the community ranging in size from a small village to a larger port. For an excellent discussion, see Omar (1993).

20 See also the segment on dialect radio and broadcast English in Tan Pin Pin's *Singapore Gaga* (2005), discussed in chapter 1.

21 It was decriminalized for lesbians and heterosexuals in 2007.

22 The Seletar are a former Orang Laut ("sea peoples") community, now marginalized. The four official "races" of Singapore are Chinese, Malay, Indian, and Other (CMIO). One is required to learn one's mother tongue in school—i.e., Mandarin, Tamil, Malay, or English. This forces some odd choices on children of parents who do not speak the properly correlated language. Chinese immigrants to Singapore historically spoke Cantonese, Hakka, Hokkien, or Teochew, not Mandarin, which was designated the national Chinese language after independence. Indians of course speak other regional languages than Tamil, although the early immigrant community comprised largely Tamil speakers.

23 On the *Orang Laut* as providing impressive decentralized naval forces for the sultans, see Fischer (2023). Kwa Chong Guan (2018) and Kwa Chong Guan et al. (2019) usefully sketch out several cycles of rise and decline that Singapore has undergone, including in the fourteenth and sixteenth centuries. First was the fourteenth-century Temasek, which was a node in the Chinese Yuan dynasty's South Seas trade and declined with the Yuan, but remained a homeland for sea nomad warriors of the sultans of Malacca. The second involved

scions of the sultans of Malacca, who, after losing their emporium to the Portuguese in 1511, moved inland and established a port and *shabandar* (port master) in Singapore to serve the riverine trade on the Johor River with Ming China. Portuguese and Dutch reports describe a thriving harbor in the late sixteenth and early seventeenth centuries, and the Portuguese trader Jacques de Coutre traveling here in 1593–1603 called it one of the best harbors serving the Indies. Admiral Matelieff Cornelis de Jong attempted to negotiate with the *shabandar* in 1606 to create a Johor-Dutch alliance to attack the Portuguese in Malacca. Both the Portuguese and the Dutch had plans to build a fort there, which might have changed history.

24 Azahari is one of the historical references in the novel. Dr. Azahari bin Sheikh Mahmud was a Brunei politician, who fought with the Indonesians for independence, then led the Brunei People's Party to victory in legislative elections, but failed in his attempts to create a unified north Kalimantan union with North Borneo and Sarawak, and prevent Brunei from joining the Malay Federation. The brief Brunei Revolt in 1962 was put down by Gurkhas flown in from Singapore by the British, and he retired to live in Bogor, Indonesia, until his death in 2002.

25 Selatar are a former sea peoples, now marginalized. A verbatim performance of Seletar people's voices/transcripts formed part of the production *Air ("Water")* directed by Adib Kosam, and produced by Drama Box in October 2019 as the second part of *Tanah (Land) + Air*. For a review, see Bakchormeeboy (2019).

26 Among Parsi shipbuilders were the Wardia family, who built many of the eighteenth- and nineteenth-century sailing vessels, including the HMS *Minden*, on which Francis Scott Key wrote "The Star Spangled Banner" in Baltimore harbor in 1812.

27 The Leviathan in the Hebrew Bible, according to the Talmud, when hungry sends forth from its mouth heat that makes the waters boil.

28 The city of Korolev, in western Russia, is named after the Soviet rocket and space vehicle designer Sergei Korolev (1907–1966); it was previously named Kaliningrad. One of the buildings housing A*STAR in Biopolis is named Proteos.

29 Akash is perhaps an allusion to the Nordic kraken, monsters of the sea that are imagined as giant squids.

30 Among these works are Chinese, Malay, Japanese, and Korean films, a 1990s fifty-episode Taiwanese television drama which "took Mainland China by storm," and the 2018 sixty-episode internet drama series produced in China with young and veteran stars of the film and television industry. For a global survey, see Luo (2021); and for a list of operas, plays, films, and television programs, see Wikipedia, s.v. "Legend of the White Snake," last modified April 7, 2022, 22:38, https://en.wikipedia.org/wiki/Legend_of_the_White_Snake.

31 In Cerise Lim Jacob's telling (Zhou and Jacobs 2010), the demon snake desires to find out what human love is, and she meditates for one thousand years and so is turned into a beautiful woman. In Alfian Sa'at's version (Chan and Sa'at 2017), Green Snake tells the son of White Rice who wants to explore the real world outside that he has all the knowledge he needs collected in their library of books. In Nuraliah Norasid's *The Gatekeeper,* Ria mines ancient books and is hungry for the contemporary books that Eederic brings her.

32 The upending of male/female and human/nonhuman categories is to be seen in Tsui Hark's film *Green Snake* (1993), but as Luo notes, it goes back to Taiwanese experimental theater of the 1970s, where the story became an "iconic site of homosexual expression" (Luo 2021). Regarding *écriture feminine*, see Cixous (1976). For contemporary revisions of the White Snake story, see Li Bihua (1986), Yan Geling (1999), and Larissa Lai (2002); and see also the discussion of these works by Cathy Yue Wang (2020). The quote "the indominable spirit defying destiny" is from Cerise Lim Jacobs's introduction onstage to *Madame White Snake*, reprised as a TED talk in 2017 ("Cerise Lim Jacobs," White Snake Projects, n.d., last accessed January 12, 2023, https://www.whitesnakeprojects.org/bios/cerise/).

33 I saw the preliminary presentation of *Madame White Snake* in 2009 at Boston University, and then the full stage premiere in February 2010 at the Emerson Cutler Majestic Theater, Boston. For a rich account of *Madame White Snake,* see chapter 6 in Luo (2021). *Madame White Snake* is part of Jacobs's *Ouroboros Trilogy,* along with the operas *Naga* (Prestini and Jacobs 2016) and *Gilgamesh* (Wheeler and Jacobs 2016), which I saw in 2016 at the Emerson Cutler Majestic Theater. I have also seen Jacobs's three subsequent productions, *Rev. 23* (2017), *PermaDeath* (2018), and *I Am a Dreamer Who No Longer Dreams* (2019), all at the Emerson Cutler Majestic, as well as a Zoom streaming of *Sing Out Strong: DeColonized Voices* (2020), broadcast during the 2020 COVID-19 pandemic.

34 The antaboga too is depicted as a sea serpent with wings.

35 Perseus manages to behead Medusa by looking into a mirror rather than directly at her.

36 Among other elements from the older legends is the motif of stealing silver in an economy of borrowing and repayment; and the pharmacy that is run by Mama White Snake as a major setting in the 2017 Wild Rice musical production, but that in this novel is a little shop which sells odds and ends as well as medicaments. In the legends, of course, pharmacy is a play on the pharmakon, which as Derrida ([1968] 1981) famously reminded us is the double-sidedness of poison and healing.

37 Wong has interviewed Norasid about this aspect of the novel, but with little return from Norasid for his effort. See Wong (2017b).

38 Cathy Yue Wang astutely quotes Li Bihua's revision of Eileen Chang's *Red Rose, White Rose* (2011), that "Every man wishes to have two women. . . . White Snake gradually becomes the pale ash . . . while the Green Snake is the crisp and alluring new leaf. . . . She nonetheless becomes an ageing herb . . . while White Snake turns into the tenderly fluttering first snow" (C. Wang 2020, 189). And inversely, "Every woman wishes to have two men in her life: Xu Xian and Fa Hai," the beautiful boy whose words no longer feel genuine, and the authority figure who after surrendering to you, "you start to hate for his lack of consideration and indifference" (C. Wang 2020, 189).

39 In the early Chinese versions, the white snake is drawn to the human male on a bridge at the West Lake *in the rain*, and at the end they bring down a flood, both water and woman being *ying* to male *yang*, and like the recoiling *naga* they destroy all, leaving nothing to remain until the next cycle of uncoiling and creation.

40 For an ethnographic analysis not of the Malay minority, but of inequality generally in Singapore, see Teo You Yenn (2018).

AFTERWORD

1 It had retail stores, offices, and residential apartments, and has remained vital for fifty years, but is currently slated for redevelopment in the 2020s. Also slated for redevelopment are two other iconic buildings of this period: the Golden Mile Complex (with a staggered, tiered arrangement of apartments, each with an open-air terrace, all facing the Kalang River, with an interior around an atrium and retail mall, also completed in 1973); and the Pearl Bank horseshoe-shaped apartment tower, with 774 apartments, each with a balcony and view, completed in 1976. All three were built by William S. W. Lim and a young generation of Singapore architects (see Lim 1990, 1998, 2002). Lim also built the Marine Parade Community Center with its striking modernist curved facade, housing a library, and in the basement the home of the Necessary Stage theater company.

2 Boo Junfeng has made two feature films, *Apprentice* (2016) and the earlier *Sandcastle* (2010), both shown at Cannes, and ten shorts. His negotiations when he was offered the post of director of the National Day Parade was to insist on artistic freedom and the ability to do things differently than in previous years. I had the opportunity to interview him in January 2019.

3 Quoted from the wall panel explanation by Boo Junfeng.

4 In an effort to compress the normal four-year undergraduate program, the freshman and sophomore years have been hybridized and compressed into what SUTD calls "freshmore."

EXERGUE

Chapter epigraph: Stephen Page, quoted in Jeremy Eccles, "Bangarra at Twenty."

1 Apart from *Firestarter*, two of the best supplementary sources on Bangarra for my purposes are Michelle Mahrer's short *Urban Clan* (2012), clips at 3:15–50 and 6:54; and Bangarra's own compilation video (Bangarra 2011), which contains "Mutton Bird" from *Mathinni* (2008), "Moth" from *Bush* (2003), and "Brolga" from *Corroboree* (2001).

2 Self-naming practices have been shifting since the 1990s. "Blak" was coined in 1991 by artist Destiny Deacon in his exhibition *Blak Lik Mi*, and has become popular. "Aboriginal" and "Indigenous" are used interchangeably by Stephen Page, as well as the increasingly popular term "First Nations."

3 The scenario is not unlike the powerful story that the theorist of settler colonialism Patrick Wolfe tells about Americans who come to Australia to study Aboriginal civil rights, and are oblivious to Native Americans who may live largely assimilated lives among them at home. Wolf repeats the anecdote in a number of his publications (e.g., Wolfe 2006), that when he began teaching Black or Aboriginal history in Australia, he would get a large number of visiting American students. When asked why they came to this class, they would say they were interested in the parallels with African Americans and civil rights in the United States. But when he asked how many Native Americans they knew, they would usually say "none." And he would reply, you probably have met many but you did not know it.

4 Historical materials on these developments, including a chronology in photographs, can be found on the website of Redfern Oral History (see ROH n.d.; see also T. Tan 2019). Amazingly, the Redfern Oral History material was posted on March 7, 2021, as I was writing this chapter. The archive is described as not just history but as "cultural fuel."

5 Originally called Aboriginal Islander Skills Development Scheme (founded in 1975–76), it became the National Aboriginal and Islander Skills Development Association in 1988.

6 The Torana was an Australian-made car, manufactured by the Australian General Motors subsidiary Holden from 1967 to 1980, and closely modeled on the British Vauxhall Viva HB. The name Torana comes from an Aboriginal word meaning "to fly." See Wikipedia, "Holden Torana," last modified December 1, 2022, 23:19, https://en.wikipedia.org/wiki/Holden_Torana.

7 Stephen Page consistently notes that there are twenty-eight designated major performing arts companies, but Bangarra is the only one devoted to or dealing with Indigenous dance and performance (Maley 2020).

8 Stephen Page, quoted from *Firestarter*.

9 Stephen Page, quoted from *Firestarter*. The Australian use of the term

"mob" connects with the collective term for a group of kangaroos who move together.

10 Stephen Page, quoted from *Firestarter*.

11 Donny Woolagoodja was born in 1945 at Kunmunya Mission, and moved with his family to Mowanjum, northern Western Australia, south of their Worrora homeland. Donny Woolagoodja is a well-known Kimberley artist and chairman of the Mowanjum Artists Spirit of the Wandjina Aboriginal Corporation. He watched the elders paint the Wandjinas on bark and boards, learning the stories of Lai Lai (creation). His father, who died in 1979, played an important role in maintaining the sacred Wandjina cave paintings. See Short St. Gallery (n.d.).

12 Stephen Page, in Page and McLean (2015).

13 The National Museum of Australia has an excellent set of explanations of Emily Kame Kngwarreye's work, extending from body painting to batik to canvas (usually black rather than white, as in black skin), and of some of the ways in which her work reflects the environment of her home area, including prominently the pencil yam, an important food source, which appears on the surface as creepers, and that forms part of her name (Kame). She was an Anmatyerre elder, and lifelong custodian of the women's Dreaming sites in her clan country, Alhalkere, in what is known now as Utopia, 230 kilometers northeast of Alice Springs (NMA n.d.). The Australian national airline Qantas had an aircraft covered in designs based on her Yam Dreaming and named the *Emily Kame Kngwarreye* (see Wikipedia, "Emily Kame Kngwarreye," last modified September 14, 2022, 00:01, https://en.wikipedia.org/wiki/Emily_Kame_Kngwarreye.

14 "At Yulara, near Uluru (Ayers Rock), many of the older women have passed on. But what is beautiful is that their children and *their* children know who we are as a company and what we did with the women. And *Inma* dance is such a big part. And they are losing that, and for us to go in and share our dance with their dance, because a lot of the kids think they have to be ninety years old to dance, 'no, that's for old women, that's for old fellas.' So how do we learn it? So in a way they like it to bring in Bangarra to say dance is a huge part of their culture" (Page and McLean 2015).

15 The force of the term "cultural protocols" was impressed upon me during a trip to the area around Wewak in Papua New Guinea, the homeland of the poet, writer, and academic Steven Edmund Winduo. When entering each community, he first used his kin and friendship networks to seek permission. His status was no passport by itself. In one case along the Sepik River, where we had not been able to prepare ahead, we had wanted to hire a canoe and boatmen for a trip to the other bank. The boatmen were willing, though the price seemed to him excessive. And as the air thickened under the superficial friendliness, Steven had us quickly exit. This was only one of many incidents

where careful negotiations were required for access. The term "cultural protocols" is used in Australia as well and is one that I have adopted in teaching about access to places where it may not be so formally named.

16 "It was like he was our calling, he was like our sign, our spirit, our spirit dance man that just came to us, and really when we started to work with him and learn trad song and trad dance, there was nothing else I wanted to do. He saw Russell and I dance together and he wanted to learn what we were doing, and we wanted to learn what he was doing, because our upbringing was completely different. Djakapura was pretty much instrumental in guiding the sense of traditional integrity of the work" (Stephen Page, quoted from Mahrer 2012).

17 Van Hout is here alluding to differences in styles of movement between two Aboriginal groups: the Yolngu, who inhabit northeastern Arnhem Land, Northern Territory, and the Eora, whose country is southeastern Queensland.

18 On the reconstruction of aboriginal life at the time of the arrival of Europeans, see Gapps (2018) and Pascoe (2014), and on Aboriginal sites in Sydney today, see Hinkson and Harris (2010).

19 The Rileys are a well-known family: Jack Riley, who lived at Dubbo ("red soil") on the Talbragar Reservation established in 1898, was the father of Alec "Tracker" Riley (d. 1970), who in turn is the father of well-known photographer and artist Michael Riley.

20 "Aunty Lyn" is Lynette Riley. See, e.g., ABC (2017).

21 From Mahrer (2012) at 10:32. This might be an extract from her 1998 film of the same name, reviewed by Pearlman (1998).

22 Stephen Page (in Munro 2016) cites the booing of Indigenous AFL (Australian Football League) player Adam Goodes after he performed a ceremonial war dance (miming spear throwing) in celebration of victory while playing for the Sydney Swans in 2015. He said it was a dance he had learned from an Indigenous youth team, the Flying Boomerangs, and was meant as a statement of Indigenous pride. He had already been subjected to a number of racist booing incidents between 2013 and 2015, and retired from the game that year. He got formal apologies from the AFL, and there are two 2019 documentaries about the affair. Known for his community work and anti-racism advocacy, he helped create a foundation for scholarships for Aboriginal education in schools and universities. He is the recipient of numerous medals and honors, including being named Australian Man of the Year in 2014, and has been awarded an honorary doctorate by Sydney University.

References

FILMS AND MUSICAL WORKS

Achnas, Nan. 2001. *Pasir Berbisik/Whispering Sands*. Nippon Hoso Kyokai (NHK); Salto Productions; Tanimbar Pictures.

Anderson, Wes. 2014. *The Grand Budapest Hotel*. Fox Searchlight Pictures.

Antonioni, Michelangelo. 1966. *Blow-Up*. Bridge Films; Metro-Goldwyn-Mayer.

Blair, Wayne, and Neil Minchin. 2020. *Firestarter: The Story of Bangarra Dance Theatre*. DVD, Bangarra Dance Theatre.

Boo Junfeng. 2010. *Sandcastle*. Zhao Wei Films/Golden Village Pictures (Singapore).

Boo Junfeng. 2016. *Apprentice*. Clover Films/Golden Village Pictures (Singapore).

Chan, Elaine, composer, and Alfian Sa'at, book and lyrics. 2017. *Mama White Snake*. Wild Rice Drama Company.

Chan, Kent. 2011. *Watching Eclipses*.

Chu, John. 2018. *Crazy Rich Asians*. SK Global; Warner Bros. Pictures

Cuarón, Alfonso. 2018. *Roma*. Esperanto Filmoj.

Desplat, Alexandre, composer. 2004. *Birth*. Original soundtrack, compact disc, New Line Records.

Desplat, Alexandre, composer. 2007. *Lust, Caution*. Original soundtrack, compact disc, Decca Records.

Desplat, Alexandre, composer. 2017. *The Shape of Water*. Original soundtrack, compact disc, Decca Records.

Edwin. 2018. *Aruna dan Lidahnya*.

Greenwood, Jonny, composer. 2007. *There Will Be Blood*. Original soundtrack, compact disc, Nonesuch Records.

Hamilton, Guy. 1954. *An Inspector Calls*. Watergate Productions; British Lion Films.

Herzog, Werner. 1974. *The Enigma of Kaspar Hauser*. ZDF, Werner Herzog Filmproduktion.

Hopper, Dennis. 1969. *Easy Rider*. Columbia Pictures.
Hui, Ann. 1984. *Love in a Fallen City*. Shaw Brothers.
Hui, Daniel. 2011. *Eclipses*.
Hui, Daniel. 2014. *Snakeskin*.
Hui, Daniel. 2019b. *Demons*.
Jacobs, Cerise Lim. 2017. *Rev. 23*.
Jacobs, Cerise Lim. 2018. *PermaDeath* (a video-game engine-driven opera).
Jacobs, Cerise Lim. 2019. *I Am a Dreamer Who No Longer Dreams*.
Jacobs, Cerise Lim. 2020. *Sing Out Strong: DeColonized Voices*.
Kore-eda, Hirokazu. 2018. *Shoplifters*.
Koster, Henry. 1949. *Inspector General*.
Kwek, Ken. 2012. *Sex.Lies.Family Values*.
Kwek, Ken. 2014. *Unlucky Plaza*.
Lee, Ang. 2007. *Lust, Caution*. Focus Features.
Lemelson, Robert. 2009. *Forty Years of Silence: An Indonesian Tragedy*. Elemental Productions.
Mahrer, Michelle, dir. 2012. *Urban Clan*. Australian Film Finance Corporation/Music Arts Dance Films. YouTube video, uploaded January 16, 2012. https://www.youtube.com/watch?v=iyUWXM_8WAM.
Malick, Terrence. 1978. *Days of Heaven*. Paramount Pictures.
Ng, Jasmine Kin Kia. 2007. *Pink Paddlers*. Green Mango Productions.
Ng, Jasmine Kin Kia, and Kelvin Tong. 1999. *Eating Air*.
Noer, Arifin C. 1984. *Pengkhianatan G30S/PKI*. Perum Produksi Film Negara.
Oppenheimer, Joshua. 2012. *The Act of Killing*. Final Cut for Real, DK.
Oppenheimer, Joshua. 2014. *The Look of Silence*. Final Cut for Real, DK.
Prestini, Paola, composer, and Cerise Lim Jacobs, lyricist. 2016. *Gilgamesh*.
Reed, Carol. 1949. *The Third Man*. London Film Productions.
Rossellini, Roberto. 1951. *Europa '51*. Lux Film.
Sa'at, Alfian, book and lyrics, and Elaine Chan, composer. 2017. *Mama White Snake*. Wild Rice Drama Company.
Samanta, Shakti. 1956. *Inspector*. Pushpa Pictures.
Schlesinger, John. 1963. *Billy Liar*. Vic Films; Waterhall Productions.
Smith, Arthur. 1992. *Medium Rare*. Derrol Steppeney Pty. Ltd.
Soderbergh, Steven. 1989. *Sex, Lies, and Videotape*. Outlaw Productions.
Soo, Jason. 2015. *1987: Untracing the Conspiracy*.
Suarez, Bobby. 1978. *They Call Her Cleopatra Wong*. BAS Film Productions.
Tan Pin Pin. 2001. *Moving House*.
Tan Pin Pin. 2003. *Gravedigger's Luck*.
Tan Pin Pin. 2005. *Singapore GaGa*.
Tan Pin Pin. 2007. *Invisible City*.
Tan Pin Pin. 2013. *To Singapore, with Love*.
Tan Pin Pin. 2017. *In Time to Come*.

Tan, Sandi. 2018d. *Shirkers*. Netflix.
Toro, Guillermo del. 2017. *The Shape of Water*. Fox Searchlight Pictures.
Truffaut, François. 1960. *Tirez sur la pianiste/Shoot the Piano Player*. Les Films de la Pléiade.
Tsui Hark. 1993. *Green Snake*.
Vertov, Dziga. 1929. *Man with a Movie Camera*. All-Ukrainian Photo Cinema Administration (VUFKU).
Wheeler, Scott, and Cerise Lim Jacobs. 2016. *Naga*.
Yared, Gabriel. 1999. *The Talented Mr. Ripley*. Original soundtrack, compact disc, Sony Classical.
Zhou Long and Cerise Lim Jacobs. 2010. *Madame White Snake*.

OTHER WORKS

ABC. 2017. "Dr Lynette Riley Explains the Concept of Skin Names." *ABC News*, January 12. https://www.abc.net.au/news/2017-01-12/university-of-sydney-skin-name-explainer/8172978?nw=0.
Abe, Kobo. 1970. *Inter Ice Age 4*. Translated by E. Dale Saunders. New York: Knopf.
Almeida, Ronaldo de. 2020. "Bolsonaro, the Evangelicals and the Brazilian Crisis." *Fieldsights*, Society for Cultural Anthropology, January 28. https://culanth.org/fieldsights/bolsonaro-the-evangelicals-and-the-brazilian-crisis.
Al-Shafi'i, Mohammed Muneer'deen Olodo, Mohd Safri Ali, Engku Ibrahim Engku Wok Zin, and Abdulsoma Thoarlim. 2018. "Al-Akhlaq (Ethics) Perceptions in Islam: A Textual Interpretation through Imam Muhammad Al-Ghazali." *International Journal of Academic Research in Business and Social Sciences* 8, no. 10: 315–29. https://hrmars.com/papers_submitted/4737/Al-Akhlaq_(Ethics)_Perceptions_in_Islam_A_Textual_Interpretation_through_Imam_Muhammad_Al-Ghazali.pdf.
Aroçtcarena, Guillaume. 2015. *Priest in Geylang: The Untold Story of the Geylang Catholic Centre*. Singapore: Ethos.
Austin-Broos, Diane. 2009. *Arrernte Present, Arrernte Past: Invasion, Violence, and Imagination in Indigenous Central Australia*. Chicago: University of Chicago Press.
Ayre, Margaret. 2002. "Yolngu Places and People: Taking Aboriginal Understandings Seriously in Land and Sea Management." PhD diss., University of Melbourne.
Ayre, Margaret, and John Mackenzie. 2012. "'Unwritten, Unsaid, Just Known': The Role of Indigenous Knowledge(s) in Water Planning in Australia." *Local Environment* 18, no. 7: 753–68.
Ayre, Margaret, and Helen Verran. 2010. "Learning to Be an Aboriginal Ranger: Inductions into a Strategic Cross-Cultural Knowledge Domain." *International Journal of Learning in Social Contexts* 1:2–18.

Bakchormeeboy. 2019. "Interviewing the Creatives behind Tanah Air, a Play in Two Parts by Drama Box." *Bakchormeeboy*, October 15. https://bakchormeeboy.com/2019/10/15/interviewing-the-creatives-behind-tanah%E2%80%A2air-%E6%B0%B4%E2%80%A2%E5%9C%9F-a-play-in-two-parts-by-drama-box/.

Bangarra (Bangarra Dance Theatre). 2011. "Bangarra and 'Wild Things: Animals on Stage' Exhibition in Melbourne." YouTube video, uploaded October 6, 2011. https://www.youtube.com/watch?v=mfF_NquI2RM.

Bangarra (Bangarra Dance Theatre). 2019. "Ochres: Study Guide for Teachers and Students." https://www.bangarra.com.au/media/jienje3x/ochres_study guide.pdf.

Barr, Michael. 2020. *Singapore: A Modern History*. London: Bloomsbury.

Barthes, Roland. 1981. *Camera Lucida: Reflections on Photography*. New York: Hill and Wang.

Baudelaire, Charles. 1857. "Correspondances." In *Fleurs du Mal*. Paris: Auguste Poulet-Malassis.

Baudrillard, Jean. 1984. "The Evil Demon of Images," translated by Paul Patton and Paul Foss. In *The Evil Demon of Images*, 13–34. Sydney: The Power Institute of Fine Arts. Accessed March 29, 2023. https://monoskop.org/images/4/47/Baudrillard_Jean_The_evil_demon_of_images_1987.pdf.

Bayly, Ian. 2009. *Len Beadell's Legacy: Australia's Atomic Bomb and Rocket Roads*. Dromana, Vic.: BAS Publishing.

Begum, Jinat Rehana. 2015. *First Fires*. Singapore: Ethos Books.

Behrouzan, Orkideh. 2016. *Prozak Diaries: Psychiatry and Generational Memory in Iran*. Stanford, CA: Stanford University Press.

Benjamin, Walter. (1928) 1979. "Fire Alarm." In *One Way Street and Other Writings*, 80. London: NLB.

Benjamin, Walter. (1936) 1969. "The Story Teller: Reflections on the Work of Nikolai Leskov." In *Illuminations*, translated by Harry Zohn, 83–110. New York: Schocken.

Berger, Peter, and Thomas Luckmann. 1966. *The Social Construction of Reality*. New York: Anchor Books.

Berman, Marshall. 1982. *All That Is Solid Melts into Air: The Experience of Modernity*. New York: Simon and Schuster.

Biddle, Jennifer Loureide. 2016. *Remote Avant-Garde: Aboriginal Art under Occupation*. Durham, NC: Duke University Press.

Biehl, João, and Peter Locke. 2017. *Unfinished: The Anthropology of Becoming*. Durham, NC: Duke University Press.

Boey Kim Cheng. 2017. *Gull between Heaven and Earth*. Singapore: Epigram.

Boltanski, Luc, and Eve Chiapello. 1999. *The New Spirit of Capitalism*. New York: Verso.

Braithwaite, E. R. 1959. *To Sir, with Love*. London: Bodley Head.

Brandel, Andrew, and Marco Motta, eds. 2021. *Living with Concepts*. New York: Fordham University Press.

Brannigan, Erin. 2014. "The Strength and Limits of Form: Dance Clan 3." *Real Time* 119. http://www.realtimearts.net/article/issue119/11466.

Bryant, Shelley. 2021. "Rewrites." In *Fish Eats Lion: New Singaporean Speculative Fiction*, edited by Jason Erik Lundberg, 97–110. Singapore: Math Paper Press.

Byrd, Antawan I., et al. 2013. *Art Cities of the Future: 21st Century Avant-Gardes*. London: Phaidon.

Cabral de Oliveira, Joanna, and Marisol Marini. 2020. "Why Is Bolsonaro Afraid of Anthropology?" *Fieldsights*, Society for Cultural Anthropology, January 28. https://culanth.org/fieldsights/why-is-the-bolsonaro-government-afraid-of-anthropology.

Cavignac, Julie A. 2020. "Threatened Rights and Resistance: For a Politically Engaged Anthropology." *Fieldsights*, Society for Cultural Anthropology, January 28. https://culanth.org/fieldsights/threatened-rights-and-resistance-for-a-politically-engaged-anthropology.

Cefkin, Melissa, ed. 2010. *Ethnography and the Corporate Encounter: Reflections on Research in and of Corporations*. New York: Berghahn.

Celler, Lucas. 2018. "'Blissful Madness!' Lucas Celler on Editing Sandi Tan's Documentary *Shirkers*." *Filmmaker Magazine*, January 24. https://filmmakermagazine.com/104301-blissful-madness-lucas-celler-on-editing-sandi-tans-documentary-shirkers/.

Centipede Collective (Brandon Chew and Olivia Lee). 2021. "Energy." In *Fish Eats Lion: New Singaporean Speculative Fiction*, edited by Jason Erik Lundberg, 321–34. Singapore: Math Paper Press.

Cesarino, Letícia. 2020. "What the Brazilian 2018 Elections Tell Us about Post-Truth in the Neoliberal-Digital Era." *Fieldsights*, Society for Cultural Anthropology, January 28. https://culanth.org/fieldsights/what-the-brazilian-2018-elections-tell-us-about-post-truth-in-the-neoliberal-digital-era.

Chan Li Shan. 2022. *Searching for Lee Wen*. Singapore: Epigram Books.

Chan, Robin. 2013. "Meritocracy: Vision of S'pore as Society of Equals." *Straits Times*, April 19. https://www.straitstimes.com/singapore/meritocracy-vision-of-spore-as-society-of-equals.

Chang, Eileen. (1943) 2007a. *Love in a Fallen City*. Translated by Karen S. Kingsbury and Eileen Chang. New York: New York Review of Books.

Chang, Eileen. (1979) 2007b. *Lust, Caution*. Translated by Julia Lowell. New York: Anchor.

Chang, Eileen. 2011. *Red Rose, White Rose*. Sydney: Penguin.

Chng Suan Tze, Low Yit Leng, and Teo Soh Lung, eds. 2017. *1987: Singapore's Marxist Conspiracy Thirty Years On*. Singapore: Function 8.

Chong Keng Hua, Debbie Loo Chia Hui, and Judy Zheng. 2013a. "Redhill: Multi-

Dimensional Narratives." Research report. Singapore: Singapore University of Technology and Design.

Chong Keng Hua, Yow Wei Quin, Debbie C. H. Loo, and Ferninda Patrycia. 2013b. "Social-Psychological Well-Being of Seniors in Singapore's High-Density Public Housing: A Case Study of Redhill." Working paper. Singapore: Singapore University of Technology and Design.

Choy, Lee Weng. 2001. "McNationalism in Singapore." In *House of Glass: Culture, Modernity, and the State in Southeast Asia*, edited by Souçhou Yao, 95–118. Singapore: ISEAS Publishing.

Chua Beng Huat. 1995. *Communitarian Ideology and Democracy in Singapore*. London: Routledge.

Chua Beng Huat. 1997. *Political Legitimacy and Housing: Stakeholding in Singapore*. New York: Routledge.

Chua Beng Huat. 2017. *Liberalism Disavowed: Communitarianism and State Capitalism in Singapore*. Singapore: National University of Singapore Press.

Cixous, Hélène. 1976. "The Laugh of the Medusa." Translated by Paula Cohen and Keith Cohen. *Signs* 1, no. 4: 875–93.

Cixous, Hélène, and Catherine Clement. 1975. *The Newly Born Woman*. Translated by Betsy Wing. Minneapolis: University of Minnesota Press.

Clancey, Gregory. 2012. "Intelligent Island to Biopolis: Smart Minds, Sick Bodies, and Millennial Turns in Singapore." *Science, Technology, and Society* 17, no. 1: 13–35.

Clancey, Gregory (with Catelijne Coopmans and Francois Amar). 2016. "The College as an Emergent Global Form: One Experience at Building a Trans-National College-to-College Partnership." In *With Honors: Challenges and Promises in the Future of Honors Education*, edited by Robert Glover and Katherine O'Flaherty. New York: Rowman and Littlefield.

Clancey, Gregory. 2017. "Singapore's Collegiate Model: Combining Teaching, Research, and Residency." In *The Collegiate Way*, edited by Martyn Evans and Tim Burt, 17–31. Rotterdam: Sense Publishers.

Coppola, Francis Ford. 2017. *Live Cinema and Its Techniques*. New York: Liveright.

Damrosch, David. 2020. *Comparing the Literatures: Literary Studies in a Global Age*. Princeton, NJ: Princeton University Press.

Dane, Gabrielle. 1994. "Hysteria as Feminist Protest: Dora, Cixous, Acker." *Women's Studies* 23, no. 3: 231–56.

Dargis, Manohla. 2018. "Women, What Did You Learn from the Movies?" *New York Times*, November 14. https://www.nytimes.com/2018/11/14/movies/women-learn-from-movies.html.

Das, Veena. 2000. "The Act of Witnessing: Violence, Poisonous Knowledge, and Subjectivity." In *Violence and Subjectivity*, edited by Veena Das, Arthur Kleinman, Mamphela Ramphele, and Pamela Reynolds, 205–25. Berkeley: University of California Press.

Dean, Kenneth, and Zhenman Zheng. 2009. *Ritual Alliances of the Putian Plain*. Vol. 1, *Historical Introduction to the Return of the Gods*. Leiden: Brill.

Dean, Kenneth, and Zhenman Zheng. 2010. *Ritual Alliances of the Putian Plain*. Vol. 2, *A Survey of Village Temples and Ritual Activities*. Leiden: Brill.

Deb, Sopan, and Natasha Singer. 2018. "Taylor Swift Said to Use Facial Recognition to Identify Stalkers." *New York Times*, December 13. https://www.nytimes.com/2018/12/13/arts/music/taylor-swift-facial-recognition.html.

Debord, Guy. 1994. *The Society of the Spectacle*. Translated by Donald Nicholson-Smith. New York: Zone Books.

Derrida, Jacques. (1968) 1981. "Plato's Pharmakon." In *Dissemination*, 63–171. Chicago: University of Chicago Press.

Doggett, Margaret. 1957. *Characters of Light*. Singapore: Donald Moore.

Dostoyevsky, Fyodor. (1871) 2008. *Demons*. Translated by Robert A. Maguire. London: Penguin Books.

Drama Box. 2019. *Chinatown Crossing*. On-site "walking theater" productions, performed in 2018 and 2019. http://www.dramabox.org/chinatowncrossings/.

Dwyer, Leslie. 2009. "A Politics of Silences: Violence, Memory and Treacherous Speech in Post-1965 Bali." In *Genocide: Truth, Memory and Representation*, 113–46. Durham, NC: Duke University Press.

Dwyer, Leslie, and Dagun Santikarma. 2006. "Speaking from the Shadows: Memory and Mass Violence in Bali." In *After Mass Crime: Rebuilding States and Communities*, edited by Beatrice Pouligny, Simon Chesterman, and Albrecht Schnabel, 190–214. Tokyo: United Nations University Press.

Dwyer, Leslie, and Dagun Santikarma. 2007. "Post-Traumatic Politics: Violence, Memory and Biomedical Discourses of Suffering in Indonesia." In *Understanding Trauma*, edited by Laurence J. Kirmayer, Robert Lemelson, and Mark Barad, 403–32. New York: Cambridge University Press.

Eccles, Jeremy. 2009. "Bangarra at Twenty: Circle of Connection." *RealTime* 92. http://www.realtimearts.net/article/92/9515.

Eickhoff, Martijn, Donny Danardono, Tjahjono Rahardjo, and Hotmauli Sidabalok. 2017a. "The Memory Landscapes of '1965' in Semarang." Special issue, *Journal of Genocide Studies* 19, no. 4: 530–50. https://www.tandfonline.com/doi/full/10.1080/14623528.2017.1393945.

Eickhoff, Martijn, Gerry van Klinken, and Geoffrey Robinson. 2017b. "Living with the Indonesian Massacres." *Journal of Genocide Studies* 19, no. 4: 449–64. https://www.tandfonline.com/doi/full/10.1080/14623528.2017.1393931.

Emont, Jon. 2015. "The Propaganda Precursor to 'The Act of Killing.'" *New Yorker*, October 24. https://www.newyorker.com/news/news-desk/the-propaganda-precursor-to-the-act-of-killing.

Eysenck, Hans. 1953. *The Uses and Abuses of Psychology*. London: Penguin.

Falardeau, Paul. 2020. "#957 Transmission of the Queer." *British Columbia*

Review, November 6. https://thebcreview.ca/2020/11/06/957-falardeau-kwa-walking-boy/.

Fausto, Carlos. 2020. *Art Effects: Image, Agency, and Ritual in Amazonia*. Translated by David Rodgers. Lincoln: University of Nebraska Press.

Fischer, Eric, Robert D. Campbell, and Eldon S. Miller. 1967. *A Question of Place: The Development of Geographic Thought*. New York: Beatty.

Fischer, Irene. 2005. *Geodesy? What's That?*: My Personal Involvement in the Age-Old Quest for the Size and Shape of the Earth. New York: iUniverse.

Fischer, Michael M. J. 1980. *Iran: From Religious Dispute to Revolution*. Cambridge, MA: Harvard University Press.

Fischer, Michael M. J. 1984. "Toward a Third World Poetics: Seeing through Short Stories and Film in the Iranian Culture Area." *Knowledge and Society* 5:171–241.

Fischer, Michael M. J. 1990. "Bombay Talkies, the Word, and the World: Salman Rushdie's *Satanic Verses*." *Cultural Anthropology* 5, no. 2: 107–59.

Fischer, Michael M. J. 1994. "Autobiographical Voices (1, 2, 3) and Mosaic Memory: Experimental Sondage in the (Post)Modern World." In *Autobiography and Postmodernism*, edited by Kathleen Ashley, Leigh Gilmore, and Gerald Peters, 79–129. Amherst: University of Massachusetts Press.

Fischer, Michael M. J. 2004. *Mute Dreams, Blind Owls, and Dispersed Knowledges: Persian Poesis in the Transnational Circuitry*. Durham, NC: Duke University Press.

Fischer, Michael M. J. 2009. *Anthropological Futures*. Durham, NC: Duke University Press.

Fischer, Michael M. J. 2013. "Biopolis: Asian Science in the Global Circuitry." *Science, Technology, and Society* 18, no. 3: 379–404.

Fischer, Michael M. J. 2014. "Philosophia and Anthropologia: Reading alongside Benjamin in Yazd, Derrida in Qum, Arendt in Tehran." In *The Ground Between: Anthropologists Engage Philosophy*, edited by Veena Das, Arthur Kleinman, Michael Jackson, and Brighu Singh, 188–217. Durham, NC: Duke University Press.

Fischer, Michael M. J. 2015. "Ethnography for Aging Societies: Dignity, Cultural Genres, and Singapore's Imagined Futures." *American Ethnologist* 42, no. 2: 207–29.

Fischer, Michael M. J. 2017a. "Silver Tsunami—Paradigm Shift—New Urban Creativity." In *Ageing Creative Cities*, edited by Keng Hua Chong and Mihye Cho, xiv–xv. Abingdon: Routledge.

Fischer, Michael M. J. 2017b. "Urban Mahabharata: Health Care, Ordinary, Traditional, and Contemporary Ethics." *Medical Anthropology Theory* 4, no. 3. https://doi.org/10.17157/mat.4.3.475.

Fischer, Michael M. J. 2018a. *Anthropology in the Meantime: Experimental Ethnography, Theory, and Method for the Twenty-First Century*. Durham, NC: Duke University Press.

Fischer, Michael M. J. 2018b. "A Tale of Two Genome Institutes: Qualitative Networks, Charismatic Voices, and R&D Strategies—Juxtaposing GIS Biopolis and BGI." *Science, Technology, and Society* 23, no. 2: 271–88.

Fischer, Michael M. J. 2018c. "Teaching under the Tembusu Tree: Mandala, Sandbox and Heterotopia." Working Paper 18, no. 1. Singapore: STS Cluster, Asia Research Institute.

Fischer, Michael M. J. 2023. *Probing Arts and Emergent Forms of Life*. Durham, NC: Duke University Press.

Fischer, Michael M. J., and Mehdi Abedi. 1990. *Debating Muslims: Cultural Dialogues between Tradition and Postmodernity*. Madison: University of Wisconsin Press.

Fong Hoe Fang. 2009. *That We May Dream Again*. Singapore: Ethos Books.

Foucault, Michel. [1966] 1970. *The Order of Things: An Archaeology of the Human Sciences*. New York: Random House.

Foucault, Michel. 2010. *The Birth of Biopolitics: Lectures at the Collège de France, 1978–79*. New York: Picador.

Freeman, Elizabeth. 2010. *Time Binds: Queer Temporalities, Queer Histories*. Durham, NC: Duke University Press.

Gadamer, Hans-Georg. 1960. *Truth and Method*. London: Sheed and Ward and Continuum.

Gapps, Stephen. 2018. *The Sydney Wars: Conflict in the Early Colony, 1788–1817*. Sydney: University of New South Wales.

Geertz, Clifford. 1960. *The Religion of Java*. Chicago: University of Chicago Press.

Geertz, Clifford. 1963. *Peddlers and Princes: Social Development and Economic Change in Two Indonesian Towns*. Chicago: University of Chicago Press.

Geertz, Clifford. 1966. "Person, Time, and Conduct in Bali." Cultural Report Series No. 14. New Haven, CT: Southeast Asia Studies, Yale University.

Geertz, Clifford. 1972. "Deep Play: Notes on the Balinese Cockfight." In *The Interpretation of Cultures*, 412–54. New York: Basic Books.

Geertz, Clifford. 1980. *Negara: The Theater State in Nineteenth-Century Bali*. Princeton, NJ: Princeton University Press.

Geertz, Clifford. (1976) 1983. "Art as a Cultural System." In *Local Knowledge*, 94–120. New York: Basic Books.

Ginsburg, Faye D. 2002. "Screen Memories: Resignifying the Traditional in Indigenous Media." In *Media Worlds: Anthropology on New Terrain*, edited by Faye D. Ginsburg, Lila Abu-Lughod, and Brian Larkin, 39–57. Berkeley: University of California Press.

Ginsburg, Faye D. 2011. "Native Intelligence: A Short History of Debates on Indigenous Media and Ethnographic Film." In *Made to Be Seen: Perspectives on the History of Visual Anthropology*, edited by Marcus Banks and Jay Ruby, 234–55. Chicago: University of Chicago Press.

Gitomartoyo, Wening. 2018. "'Aruna dan Lidahnya' Tells You to Savor the Little

Things." *Jakarta Post*, September 21. https://www.thejakartapost.com/life/2018/09/21/aruna-dan-lidahnya-tells-you-to-savor-the-little-things.html.

Goffman, Erving. 1956. *The Presentation of Self in Everyday Life*. New York: Doubleday.

Goh, Daniel P. S. 2010. "State and Social Christianity in Post-colonial Singapore." *Sojourn: Journal of Social Issues in Southeast Asia* 25, no. 1: 54–89.

Goh, Daren. 2017. *The HDB Murders*. Singapore: Math Paper Press.

Gomes, Catherine. 2015. *Multiculturalism through the Lens: A Guide to Ethnic and Migrant Anxieties in Singapore*. Singapore: Ethos Books.

Good, Byron. 1976. "The Heart of What's the Matter." *Culture, Medicine, and Psychiatry* 1:107–38.

Good, Mary Jo DelVecchio, and Byron Good. 2013. "Perspectives on the Politics of Peace in Aceh, Indonesia." In *Radical Egalitarianism*, edited by Felicity Aulin, Miriam Goheen, and Stanley J. Tambiah, 191–208. New York: Fordham University Press.

Gray, Mary L., and Siddhart Suri. 2019. *Ghost Work: How to Stop Silicon Valley from Building a New Global Underclass*. New York: Fordham University Press.

Griffel, Frank. 2020. "al-Ghazali." In *Stanford Encyclopedia of Philosophy*. https://plato.stanford.edu/archives/sum2020/entries/al-ghazali/.

Gui, Weihsin. 2008. "Residual Nationalism and Postcolonial Anglophone Literatures." PhD diss., Brown University.

Gui, Weihsin. 2017. "Contemporary Literature from Singapore." *Oxford Research Encyclopedia of Literature*. https://core.ac.uk/download/pdf/147829925.pdf.

Haraway, Donna. 2016. *Staying with the Trouble*. Durham, NC: Duke University Press.

Hinkson, Melinda, and Alana Harris. 2010. *Aboriginal Sydney*. 2nd ed. Canberra: Aboriginal Studies Press.

Ho, Engseng. 2006. *The Graves of Tarim: Genealogy and Mobility across the Indian Ocean*. Berkeley: University of California Press.

Ho, Olivia. 2021. "Story Collection 'And Softly Go the Crossings' Tops Singapore Book Awards." *Straits Times*, September 24. https://www.straitstimes.com/life/arts/short-story-collection-and-softly-go-the-crossings-tops-singapore-book-awards.

Hoverman, Suzanne, and Margaret Ayre. 2012. "Methods and Approaches to Support Indigenous Water Planning: An Example from the Tiwi Islands, Northern Territory, Australia." *Journal of Hydrology* 474:47–56.

Hsieh, Daniel. 2007. *Love and Women in Early Chinese Fiction*. Hong Kong: Chinese University Press.

Hui, Daniel. 2011. "Q&A with Daniel Hui after the Premiere of *Eclipses*." Filmed by Liao Jiekai, Singapore International Film Festival, September 24, 2011.

YouTube video, uploaded October 27, 2011. https://youtube.com/watch?v=RerveOVnTfs.

Hui, Daniel. 2016. "Rutgers Visiting Filmmaker Series—Daniel Hui." Vimeo video, uploaded May 10, 2016. https://vimeo.com/166067403. (Also available on YouTube: https://www.youtube.com/watch?v=kRLnxONLtFo.)

Hui, Daniel. 2019a. "Daniel Hui Interview: 'So This Is My Big Fear. That I Can Be Both Victim and Perpetrator.'" Interview by Maja Korbecka. Eastern Kicks, February 27. https://www.easternkicks.com/features/daniel-hui-interview.

Hui, Daniel. 2019c. "Interview with Daniel Hui on *Demons*." Interview by Zsombor Bobák, Forum Section, 10, Berlin International Film Festival. YouTube video, uploaded February 10, 2019. https://www.youtube.com/watch?v=2pxZi7-urfM.

Indhiarti, Tantri Refa, Sri Utami Budi, and Indah Winarni. 2017. "Revealing a Javanese Identity of Prayer in the Wedhatama through Semantic Proposition." *Kajian Linguistik dan Sastra* 2, no. 2: 111–25.

Iris. n.d. "Profile 01, Stephen Page: A Caretaker of Stories." *Iris Magazine* 1. https://www.irismagazine.com/issue-one/stephen-page.

Jasanoff, Sheila. 2005. *Designs on Nature: Science and Democracy in Europe and the United States*. Princeton, NJ: Princeton University Press.

Jiménez, Fabricio. 2017. "On the Origins of 'Hysteresis.'" *AMVA4NewPhysics*, March 16. https://amva4newphysics.wordpress.com/2017/03/16/on-the-origins-of-hysteresis/.

Johnson, Barbara. 1987. *A World of Difference*. Baltimore: Johns Hopkins University Press.

Johnson, Barbara. 2003. *Mother Tongues: Sexuality, Trials, Motherhood, Translation*. Cambridge, MA: Harvard University Press.

Johnston, Adrian. 2018. "Jacques Lacan." In *Stanford Encyclopedia of Philosophy*. https://plato.stanford.edu/archives/fall2018/entries/lacan/.

Jones, Ann Rosalind. 1981. "Writing the Body: Toward an Understanding of *l'Ecriture Feminine*." *Feminist Studies* 7, no. 2: 247–63.

Kamari, Isa. 2013. *1819*. Translated by R. Krishnan. Kuala Lumpur: Silverfish.

Keng Hua Chong, Kien To, and Michael M. J. Fischer. 2017. "Dense and Ageing: Social Sustainability of Public Places amidst Hi-Density Development." In *Growing Compact: Urban Form, Density and Sustainability*, edited by Philip Joo-Hwa Bay and Steffan Lehmann, ch. 10. Abingdon: Routledge.

Ker, Justin. 2021. "0100110101000101010001101010011110101001001011001." In *Fish Eats Lion: New Singaporean Speculative Fiction*, edited by Jason Erik Lundberg, 185–94. Singapore: Math Paper Press.

Khan, Nurhayati. 2017. "Jinat Rehana Begum, First Fires." *Asiatic* 11, no. 1: 312–16.

Kinzley, Judd C. 2018. *Natural Resources and the New Frontier: Constructing Modern China's Borderlands*. Chicago: University of Chicago Press.

Kittler, Friedrich. 1992. *Discourse Networks 1800/1990*. Stanford, CA: Stanford University Press.

Klein, Naomi. 2008. *The Shock Doctrine: The Rise of Disaster Capitalism*. New York: Picador.

Koh, Buck Song. 2011. *Brand Singapore: How Nation Branding Built Asia's Leading Global City*. Singapore: Marshall Cavendish.

Koh, Buck Song. 2017. *Brand Singapore: Nation Branding after Lee Kuan Yew, in a Divisive World*. Singapore: Marshall Cavendish.

Kon, Stella. 1983. *Emily of Emily Hill*. Singapore: Landmark Books.

Kua Ee Heok. 2007. *Listening to Letter from America*. Singapore: Armour.

Kwa Chong Guan. 2018. *Pre-Colonial Singapore*. Singapore: Institute of Policy Studies/Straits Times Press.

Kwa Chong Guan, Derek Heng, Peter Borschberg, and Tan Tai Young. 2019. *Seven Hundred Years: A History of Singapore*. Singapore: National Library Board.

Kwa, Lydia. 1994a. *The Colors of Heroines*. Toronto: Women's Press.

Kwa, Lydia. 1994b. "Father:Mother:Tongue." In *The Colors of Heroines*, 38–39. Toronto: Women's Press.

Kwa, Lydia. 2000. *This Place Called Absence*. New York: Kensington Books.

Kwa, Lydia. (2005) 2018. *The Walking Boy*. Toronto: Key Porter Books.

Kwa, Lydia. (2010) 2014. *Pulse*. Singapore: Ethos Books.

Kwa, Lydia. 2013. *Sinuous*. Winnipeg: Turnstone Press.

Kwa, Lydia. 2017a. *Oracle Bone*. Vancouver: Arsenal Pulp Books.

Kwa, Lydia. 2017b. "Centuries-Old Ghost Stories Guide Lydia Kwa through New Novel *Oracle Bone*." Interview by David Chau. *Georgia Straight*, October 11. https://www.straight.com/arts/979501/centuries-old-ghost-stories-guide-lydia-kwa-through-new-novel-oracle-bone.

Kwa, Lydia. 2020. "Transmitting the Strange: A Conversation with Lydia Kwa." Interview by Yilin Wang. *Augur* 3, no. 2. http://www.augurmag.com/transmitting-the-strange-a-conversation-with-lydia-kwa/.

Kwa, Lydia. Forthcoming. *A Dream Wants Waking*. Hamilton, ON: Buckrider Books.

Lacan, Jacques. (1949) 2006. "The Mirror Stage as Formative of the *I* Function as Revealed in Psychoanalytic Experience." In *Écrits: The First Complete Edition in English*, translated by Bruce Fink, 75–81. New York: Norton.

Lai, Larissa. 2002. *Salt Fish Girl*. Toronto: Thomas Allen.

Laing, Ronald David. 1970. *Knots*. London: Penguin.

Langenbach, Ray. 2003. "Performing the Singapore State, 1988–1995." PhD diss., Center for Cultural Research, University of Sydney.

Lasmana, Viola. 2018. "Shadow Imaginations: Transpacific Approaches to Post-1965 Indonesian Archives." PhD diss., University of Southern California.

Lattimore, Owen. 1950. *Pivot of Asia: Sinkiang and the Inner Asian Frontiers of China and Russia*. Boston: Little, Brown.

Laws, Zach. 2018. "Sandi Tan ('Shirkers' Director) Was Sucked into a 'Vortex of Obsession' to Solve the Mystery of Her Lost Film." *Gold Derby*, November 2. https://www.goldderby.com/article/2018/sandi-tan-shirkers-interview-netflix-documentary-news-842697531/.

Lee, Alfreda. 2015. "Ten Forgotten Theme Parks of Singapore's Past You Won't Believe Existed." The Smart Local, April 22. http://thesmartlocal.com/read/old-theme-parks.

Lee Hsien Loong. 2014. "On 'To Singapore with Love' and the Fight against Communism." Interview by Tommy Koh, October 3, 2014. YouTube video, uploaded October 3, 2014. https://www.youtube.com/watch?v=UjQvdrBK8h4.

Lee Hsien Loong. 2015. "Speech by PM Lee Hsien Loong at the SUTD East Coast Campus Opening on 8 May 2015." Prime Minister's Office, Singapore, May 8. https://www.pmo.gov.sg/Newsroom/transcript-prime-minister-lee-hsien-loong-speech-sutd-east-coast-campus-opening-8-may.

Lee, Jing-Jing. 2013. *If I Could Tell You*. Singapore: Marshall Cavendish International.

Lee, Jing-Jing. 2018. *How We Disappeared*. Singapore: One World.

Lee Kuan Yew. 1966. "Text of Speech by the Prime Minister of Singapore, Mr. Lee Kuan Yew, at the Special Conference of the Socialist International Congress, Uppsala, on Wednesday April 27, 1966, at Goteborg's Nation, Uppsala University." National Archives of Singapore. https://www.nas.gov.sg/archivesonline/data/pdfdoc/lky19660427.pdf.

Lee Wen. 2006. "Performance Art in Context: A Singaporean Perspective." MA diss., LaSalle College of the Arts, Singapore.

Lee, Yuen Ting. 2015. "Wu Zhao: Ruler of Tang Dynasty China." *Education about Asia* 20, no. 2: 14–18.

Leirner, Piero C. 2020. "Hybrid Warfare in Brazil: The Highest Stage of Military Insurgency." *HAU: Journal of Ethnographic Theory* 10, no. 1: 41–49.

Leow, Joanne Chuang Ching. 2015. "Counter-Cartographies: Literary Wayfinding in Transnational Cities." PhD diss., University of Toronto.

Lepani, Katherine. 2012. *Islands of Love, Islands of Risk: Culture and HIV in the Trobriands*. Nashville, TN: Vanderbilt University Press.

Leung, Charmaine. 2017. *17A Koeng Saik Road*. Singapore: Ethos Books.

Lévi-Strauss, Claude. 1955. "The Structural Study of Myth." *Journal of American Folklore* 68, no. 270: 428–44.

Li Bihua. 1986. *Green Snake*. Hong Kong: Tiandi tushu youxiangongsi.

Lim, Danielle. 2014. *The Sound of Sch: A Mental Breakdown, a Life Journey*. Singapore: Ethos Books.

Lim, Danielle. 2018. *Trafalgar Sunrise*. Singapore: Marshall Cavendish.

Lim, Danielle. 2020. *And Softly Go the Crossings*. Singapore: Penguin Random House.

Lim, Edna. 2018. *Celluloid Singapore: Cinema, Performance and the National*. Edinburgh: Edinburgh University Press.

Lim, Suchen Christine. 2013. *The River's Song*. London: Aurora Metro.

Lim, William S. W. 1990. *Cities for People: Reflections of a Southeast Asian Architect*. Singapore: Select Books.

Lim, William S. W. 1998. *Asian New Urbanism and Other Papers*. Singapore: Select Books.

Lim, William S. W., ed. 2002. *Postmodern Singapore*. Singapore: Select Publishing.

Loh, Joy. 2017. "The Guitar Man: Alex Abisheganaden." *Biblioasia* 13, no. 1. https://biblioasia.nlb.gov.sg/vol-13/issue-1/apr-jun-2017/guitar-man.

Loh Kah Seng, Edgar Liao, Lim Cheng Tju, and Seng Guo-Quan. 2012. *The University Socialist Club and the Contest for Malaya: Tangled Strands of Modernity*. Amsterdam: Amsterdam University Press.

Löwy, Michael. 2005. *Fire Alarm: Reading Walter Benjamin's "On the Concept of History."* Translated by Chris Turner. London: Verso.

LTA (Land Transport Authority, Singapore). 2022. "Art in Transit." Land Transport Authority, June 8. https://www.lta.gov.sg/content/ltagov/en/getting_around/public_transport/a_better_public_transport_experience/art_in_transit.html.

Luers, Erik. 2018. "'Shirkers': How a Filmmaker Reclaimed Her Lost Work and Turned It into a Sundance-Winning Doc." *No Film School*, February 2. https://nofilmschool.com/2018/02/shirkers-documentary-sani-tan.

Lundberg, Jason Erik, ed. 2012. *Fish Eats Lion: New Singaporean Speculative Fiction*. Singapore: Math Paper Press.

Luo, Liang. 2021. *The Global White Snake*. Ann Arbor: University of Michigan Press.

Maley, Jacqueline. 2020. "Bangarra's Stephen Page on Pain, Politics, and Pushing Boundaries." *Sydney Morning Herald*, December 24. https://www.smh.com.au/culture/dance/bangarra-s-stephen-page-on-pain-politics-and-pushing-boundaries-20201214-p56nbl.html.

Malinowski, Bronislaw. 1925. "Magic, Science, and Religion." In *Science, Religion, and Reality*, edited by Joseph Needham, 19–84. New York: Macmillan.

Marcus, George E., ed. 1994–2000. *Late Editions: Cultural Studies for the End of the Century*. 8 vols. Chicago: University of Chicago Press.

Mbembe, Achille. 2021. *Out of the Dark Night: Essays on Decolonization*. New York: Columbia University Press.

McGhee, Heather. 2021. *The Sum of Us: What Racism Costs Everyone and How We Can Prosper Together*. New York: One World.

Meaney, Thomas. 2021. "The Singapore Formula: The Bayswater Grocer." *London Review of Books*, March 18, 13–18.

Michon, Pascal. 2010. "Rhythm, Organization of Significance and Subjectivity in Baudelaire's Correspondances." *Rhuthmos*, June 25. http://rhuthmos.eu/spip.php?article78.

Mrazek, Jan. 2019. *Wayang and Its Doubles: Javanese Puppet Theatre, Television and the Internet*. Singapore: NUS Press.

Munro, Peter. 2016. "Stephen Page Takes Spear from Bangarra Dance Theatre to the Big Screen." *Sydney Morning Herald*, October 9. https://www.smh.com.au/entertainment/movies/stephen-page-takes-spear-from-bangarra-dance-theatre-to-the-big-screen-20150918-gjpzb3.html.

Myers, Fred R. 1986. *Pintupi Country, Pintupi Self: Sentiment, Place, and Politics among Western Desert Aborigines*. Washington, DC/Canberra: Smithsonian Institution Press/Aboriginal Studies Press.

Myers, Fred R. 1989. "Truth, Beauty and Pintupi Painting." *Visual Anthropology* 2:163–95.

Myers, Fred R. 1994. "Culture-Making: Performing Aboriginality at the Asia Society Gallery." *American Ethnologist* 21:679–99.

Myers, Fred R. 1995. "Representing Culture: The Production of Discourse(s) for Aboriginal Acrylic Paintings." In *The Traffic in Culture: Refiguring Art and Anthropology*, edited by George E. Marcus and Fred R. Myers, 55–95. Berkeley: University of California Press.

Myers, Fred R. 2002. *Painting Culture: The Making of Aboriginal High Art*. Durham, NC: Duke University Press.

Naficy, Nahal. 2007. "Persian Miniature Writing: An Ethnography of Iranian Organizations in Washington, DC." PhD diss., Rice University.

Naruse, Narumi. 2014. "Imagined Diasporas: Neoliberal Nationalism in Contemporary Singaporean Fiction and State Culture." PhD diss., University of Hawai'i at Manoa.

Neale, Margo, ed. 2017. *Songlines: Tracking the Seven Sisters*. Canberra: National Museum of Australia Press.

Neiburg, Frederico, and Omar Ribeiro Thomaz. 2020. "Ethnographic Views of Brazil's (New) Authoritarian Turn." *HAU: Journal of Ethnographic Theory* 10, no. 1: 7–11.

Neurath, Marie, and Robin Kinross. 2009. *The Transformer: Principles of Making Isotype Charts*. London: Hyphen.

Neurath, Otto. 2010. *From Hieroglyphics to Isotype: A Visual Autobiography*. London: Hyphen.

Ng, Charmaine. 2019. "Milestone for Women in Police Force: She Gets No Concession as a Female in Elite Police Unit." *Straits Times*, February 4. https://www.straitstimes.com/singapore/courts-crime/she-gets-no-concession-as-a-female-in-elite-police-unit.

Ng, Jasmine. 2014. "Behind the Camera with Jasmine Ng, Film Maker and Mentor." Interview by Isabel Ong. Honeycombers, February 24. https://thehoneycombers.com/singapore/noise-singapore/#.

Ng Yi Sheng. 2008. *Eating Air*. Singapore: Firstfruits Publications.

Ng Yi Sheng. 2021. "Agnes Joaquim Bioterrorist." In *Fish Eats Lion: New Singaporean Speculative Fiction*, edited by Jason Erik Lundberg, 29–44. Singapore: Math Paper Press.

Nien Yuan Cheng. 2017. "*1987: Untracing the Conspiracy*, by Jason Soo and Ex-political Detainees." *SEASIAPASTS*, February 14.

NMA (National Museum of Australia). n.d. "Utopia: The Genius of Emily Kame Kngwarreye." National Museum of Australia. Accessed August 28, 2022. https://www.nma.gov.au/exhibitions/utopia/emily-kame-kngwarreye.

Norasid, Nuraliah. 2017. *The Gatekeeper*. Singapore: Epigram Books.

Obeyesekere, Gananath. 1981. *Medusa's Hair: An Essay on Personal Symbols and Religious Experience*. Chicago: University of Chicago Press.

Omar, Ariffin. 1993. *Bangsa Melayu: Malay Concepts of Democracy and Community, 1945–1950*. Oxford: Oxford University Press.

Page, Stephen, and Judith McLean. 2015. "Bangarra's Artistic Director Stephen Page and Professor Judith McLean in Conversation at QPAC." Queensland Performing Arts Centre. YouTube video, uploaded August 30, 2015. https://www.youtube.com/watch?v=nP4kbBayqKM.

Pamuntjak, Laksmi. 2004. "The Poetry of Goenawan Mohamad." In *Goenawan, Mohamad: Selected Poems*. Jakarta: KataKita. https://laksmipamuntjak.com/works/the-poetry-of-goenawan-mohamad.

Pamuntjak, Laksmi. 2005. "Eating and Difference: A Tale of Two Cities." In "Living Together," special issue, *Prince Claus Fund Journal* (the Hague), no. 12. https://laksmipamuntjak.com/works/eating-and-difference-a-tale-of-two-cities.

Pamuntjak, Laksmi. 2006a. *The Diary of R. S.: Musings on Art*. Jakarta: KataKita.

Pamuntjak, Laksmi. 2006b. *Ellipsis: Poems and Prose Poems*. Jakarta: Equinox.

Pamuntjak, Laksmi. 2006c. *Hector and Andromache: A Play*. https://laksmipamuntjak.com/works/hector-andromache.

Pamuntjak, Laksmi. 2006d. *Perang, Langit dan Dua Perempuan* [War, heaven, and two women]. Jakarta: Gramedia Putaka Utama.

Pamuntjak, Laksmi. 2007. "On Reading Woman: Laksmi Pamuntjak's Preface to 'Not a Muse,' a World Poetry Anthology." https://laksmipamuntjak.com/works/on-reading-woman.

Pamuntjak, Laksmi. 2010. *The Jakarta Good Food Guide Update*. Revised 2nd edition. Jakarta: Djambatan and Pena Klasik.

Pamuntjak, Laksmi. 2013. *Amba*. [In Indonesian.] Jakarta: Gramedia Pustaka Utama.

Pamuntjak, Laksmi. 2014a. *Amba: The Question of Red*. Translated by the author. Seattle: Amazon Crossing; and New Delhi: Speaking Tiger (2016).

Pamuntjak, Laksmi. 2014b. *Aruna dan Lidahnya*. [In Indonesian.] Jakarta: Gramedia Pustaka Utama.

Pamuntjak, Laksmi. 2015a. "Censorship Is Returning to Indonesia in the Name of the 1965 Purges." *Guardian*, October 26. https://www.theguardian.com/world/commentisfree/2015/oct/27/censorship-is-returning-to-indonesia-in-the-name-of-the-1965-purges.

Pamuntjak, Laksmi. 2015b. "Indonesia and India: Living with Difference." In *Masala Bumbui*, August 2015. https://laksmipamuntjak.com/works/indonesia-and-india-living-with-difference.

Pamuntjak, Laksmi. 2016. *There Are Tears in Things: Collected Poems and Prose*. Jakarta: Gramedia Putaka Utama.

Pamuntjak, Laksmi. 2017a. "Jakarta: The Unlikely Capital City of Sex and Swinging." *Guardian*, January 13. https://www.theguardian.com/world/2017/jan/14/jakarta-the-unlikely-capital-city-of-sex-and-swinging.

Pamuntjak, Laksmi. 2017b. "On Hope and Despair: Living with Difference in Today's Indonesia." Keynote address, European Southeast Asian Scholars Association, University of Oxford, August 17. https://laksmipamuntjak.com/works/eating-and-difference-a-tale-of-two-cities.

Pamuntjak, Laksmi. 2018a. *The Birdwoman's Palate*. Translated by Tiffany Tsao and Laksmi Pamuntjak. Seattle: Amazon Crossing.

Pamuntjak, Laksmi. 2018b. *Herbstkind*. Berlin: Ullstein.

Pamuntjak, Laksmi. 2019. *Fall Baby*. Singapore: Penguin Books.

Pamuntjak, Laksmi. 2021a. "My Late Father, the German Indonesian: Trauma and Historical Memory." *Globalist*, May 26. https://www.theglobalist.com/my-late-father-the-german-indonesian/.

Pamuntjak, Laksmi. 2021b. "My Life Is My Choice: The Story of Mara." UNICEF Indonesia, April 30. https://www.unicef.org/indonesia/stories/my-life-my-choice-story-mara.

Pamuntjak, Laksmi. n.d.a. "Eating around the World: Pempek Beringin." Laksmi's FOODPrint. Accessed August 21, 2022. http://laksmipamuntjak.com/restaurant/pempek-beringin.

Pamuntjak, Laksmi. n.d.b. "Eating around the World: R. M. Sinar Pagi." Laksmi's FOODPrint. Accessed August 21, 2022. https://laksmipamuntjak.com/restaurant/rm-sinar-pagi.

Pang, Alvin. 2012. *When the Barbarians Arrive*. London: Arc International Publications.

Paramaditha, Intan. 2007. "*Pasir Berbisik* and New Women's Aesthetics in Indonesian Cinema." *Jump Cut* 49. http://www.ejumpcut.org/archive/jc49.2007/PasirBerbisik/index.html.

Paramaditha, Intan. 2013. "Review of Tales of Waria and Children of Shikandi." *Pacific News* 86, no. 4: 970–71.

Paramaditha, Intan. 2014. "The Wild Child's Desire: Cinema, Sexual Politics, and the Experimental Nation in Post-Authoritarian Singapore." PhD diss., New York University.

Paramaditha, Intan. 2018a. *Apple and Knife*. Translated by Stephen J. Epstein. London: Harvill Secker.

Paramaditha, Intan. 2018b. "Coffee Time with Intan Paramaditha." PPIA TV. YouTube video, uploaded October 7, 2018. https://www.youtube.com/watch?v=VQ6k7VbyoLs.

Paramaditha, Intan. 2020. "The Bottom Drawer with Intan Paramaditha." Bagri Foundation. YouTube video, uploaded September 30, 2020. https://www.youtube.com/watch?v=SwPVmnHtcmE.

Paramaditha, Intan. 2021. *The Wandering*. Translated by Stephen J. Epstein. London: Vintage.

Pascoe, Bruce. 2014. *Dark Emu*. Broome, Western Australia: Magabala Books Aboriginal Corporation.

Patterson, Christopher B. 2013. "Transitive Cultures: Anglophone Literature in Malaya, the Philippines and Asian America." PhD diss., University of Washington.

Pearlman, Karen. 1998. "Taking Up the Fight: Karen Pearlman Previews Urban Clan, Michelle Mahrer's Film about Bangarra Theatre's Page Brothers." *RealTime* 25. http://www.realtimearts.net/article/25/4298.

Perdue, Peter. 2005. *China Marches West*. Cambridge, MA: Harvard University Press.

Petryna, Adriana. 2022. *Horizoning: The Work of Projection in Abrupt Climate Change*. Princeton, NJ: Princeton University Press.

Piao, Lily. 2017. "Review of Jinat Rehana Begum's *First Fires*." *Singapore Bound*, September 11. https://singaporeunbound.org/blog/2017/8/30/difficulties-are-fires.

Propp, Vladimir. (1928) 1968. *Morphology of the Folktale*. Translated by Laurence Scott. 2nd ed. Austin: University of Texas Press.

Protevi, John, ed. 2005. *The Edinburgh Dictionary of Continental Philosophy*. Edinburgh: Edinburgh University Press.

Pu Songling. 2006. *Strange Tales from a Chinese Studio*. Translated and edited by John Minford. London: Penguin.

Purdey, Jemma. 2017. "Talking Indonesia: Women, Gender and Activism." Indonesia at Melbourne, April 27. https://indonesiaatmelbourne.unimelb.edu.au/talking-indonesia-women-gender-and-activism/.

Readings, Bill. 1996. *The University in Ruins*. Cambridge, MA: Harvard University Press.

ROH (Redfern Oral History). n.d. "Dance." Accessed August 28, 2022. http://redfernoralhistory.org/Peopleandplaces/DANCE/tabid/321/Default.aspx.

Sadruddin, Aalyia Feroz Ali. 2020a. "After-After-Lives: Aging, Care, and Dignity in Postgenocide Rwanda." PhD diss., Yale University.

Sadruddin, Aalyia Feroz Ali. 2020b. "The Care of 'Small Things': Aging and Dignity in Rwanda." *Medical Anthropology* 39, no. 1: 83–95.

Sadruddin, Aalyia Feroz Ali. 2022. "Death in an Ordinary Time: Reflections from Rwanda." *Medical Anthropology Quarterly* 36, no. 2: 198–216.

Sahlins, Marshall. 2004. *Apologies to Thucydides: Understanding History as Culture and Vice Versa*. Chicago: University of Chicago Press.

Satran, Shai. 2022. "From Craft to Labor: How Automation Is Transforming the Practice of Psychotherapy." *Culture, Medicine, and Psychiatry* (2022): 1–21. https://doi.org/10.1007/s11013-022-09771-8.

Seow, Francis T. 1994. *To Catch a Tartar: A Dissident in Lee Kuan Yew's Prison*. New Haven, CT: Yale Southeast Asia Studies.

Severi, Carlo. 2015. *The Chimera Principle: An Anthropology of Memory and Imagination*. Chicago: HAU Books.

Severi, Carlo. 2018. *Capturing Imagination: A Proposal for an Anthropology of Thought*. Chicago: HAU Books.

Shelley, Mary. (1818) 2018. *Frankenstein*. London: Penguin.

Short St. Gallery. n.d. "Donny Woolagoodja—Biography." Accessed December 22, 2022. https://www.shortstgallery.com.au/artists/212-donny-woolagoodja/biography/.

Simpkin, Julie, and Justine Molony. 2018. *Old Masters: Australia's Great Bark Artists*. Canberra: National Museum of Australia Press.

Sinclair, Upton. 1927. *Oil!* New York: Albert and Charles Boni.

Sindie. n.d. "Production Talk on 'Eclipses' with Daniel Hui." *SINdie*. https://www.sindie.sg/2012/04/production-talk-on-eclipses-with-daniel.html.

SNRF (Singapore National Research Foundation). 2021. "Virtual Singapore." National Research Foundation (Singapore), February 20. https://www.nrf.gov.sg/programmes/virtual-singapore.

Snyder, Timothy. 2021. "The War on History Is a War on Democracy." *New York Times Magazine*, June 29. https://www.nytimes.com/2021/06/29/magazine/memory-laws.html.

Soewito, Santoso. 2006. *Stories from the Serat Centhini*. Singapore: Marshall Cavendish.

Spivak, Gayatri. 1981a. "'Draupadi' by Mahasveta Devi." *Critical Inquiry* 8, no. 2: 381–402.

Spivak, Gayatri. 1981b. "Finding Feminist Readings." In *American Criticism in the Poststructuralist Age*, edited by Ira Konigsberg, 42–45. Ann Arbor: University of Michigan Press.

Staël, Anne-Louise-Germaine de. 1813. *Considérations sur les principaux événements de la révolution française*. Paris.

Staël, Anne-Louise-Germaine de. 1818. *Considerations on the Principal Events of the French Revolution*. New York: James Eastburn.

Stewart, Jessica. 2020. "Five Matisse Paintings That Revolutionized Modern Art." *My Modern Met*. May 11. https://mymodernmet.com/matisse-paintings/.

Stonington, Scott. 2020. *The Spirit Ambulance: Choreographing the End of Life in Thailand*. Berkeley: University of California Press.

Strassberg, Richard E. 2002. *A Chinese Beastiary: Strange Creatures from the Guideways through Mountains and Seas*. Translation and commentary. Berkeley: University of California Press.

Sveiby, Karl-Erik, and Tex Skuthorpe. 2006. *Treading Lightly: The Hidden Wisdom of the World's Oldest People*. Crow's Nest, NSW: Allen and Unwin.

Tambiah, Stanley. 1977. *World Conqueror and World Renouncer: A Study of Buddhism and Polity in Thailand against a Historical Background*. New York: Cambridge University Press.

Tambiah, Stanley. 1986. *Sri Lanka: Ethnic Fratricide and the Dismantling of Democracy*. Chicago: University of Chicago Press.

Tambiah, Stanley. 1992. *Buddhism Betrayed?: Religion, Politics, and Violence in Sri Lanka*. Chicago: University of Chicago Press.

Tan, Cheryl Lu-Lien. 2011. *A Tiger in the Kitchen: A Memoir of Food and Family*. New York: Hyperion.

Tan, Dora. 2012. "Seven Views of Redhill." In *Balik Kampung*, edited by Verena Tan, 81–98. Singapore: Math Paper Press.

Tan, Guan Zhen. 2019. "Tommy Koh Spoke His Mind and Was Full of Quotable Quotes at S'pore Bicentennial Conference." *Mothership*, October 2. https://mothership.sg/2019/10/news-singapore-tommy-koh/.

Tan, Junbin. 2019. "Dementia Care Work in Singapore: Embodied Relations and Power Dynamics." *Medical Anthropology* 38, no. 1: 71–84.

Tan, Margaret. 2004. "Smart Apron." Margaret Tan's website. http://www.margaret-tan.com/Smart%20Apron.html.

Tan, Margaret. 2014. *Singapore as Model City*. Singapore: Tembusu College, National University of Singapore/Future Cities Laboratory, ETH Singapore.

Tan Pin Pin (with Martyn See and Loh Kah Seng). 2010. "Film and the Making and Keeping of Singapore History and Memory: A Dialogue with Martyn See and Tan Pin Pin Moderated by Loh Sah Seng." In *The Makers and Keepers of Singapore History*, edited by Loh Kah Seng and Liew Kai Khium, 272–87. Singapore: Ethos Books/Singapore Heritage Society.

Tan Pin Pin. 2018. "Interview with Julia Tan and Yuka Kamamoto." Perspective Film Festival, November 3. Accessed December 2020. https://www.perspectivesfilmfestival.com/a-conversation-with-tan-pin-pin.

Tan, Sandi. 2012a. *The Black Isle*. New York: Grand Central Publishing.

Tan, Sandi. 2012b. "Sandi Tan on Her Cinematic New Novel, *The Black Isle*."

Vogue, August 6. https://www.vogue.com/article/filmmaker-sandi-tan-on-her-cinematic-new-novel-the-black-isle.
Tan, Sandi. 2018a. "Five Questions for *Shirkers* Director Sandi Tan." Interview by Vadim Rizov. *Filmmaker Magazine*, October 24. https://filmmakermagazine.com/104550-five-questions-for-shirkers-director-sandi-tan/#.YMf3124pBsN.
Tan, Sandi. 2018b. "Sandi Tan on *Shirkers*: Film Comment Talk." Lincoln Center Film Society. YouTube video, uploaded December 6, 2018. https://www.youtube.com/watch?v=nk2f47jiaRA.
Tan, Sandi. 2018c. "Sandi Tan on Sundance Doc, 'Shirkers': 'I Was Trying to Think of It as an Exorcism.'" Interview by Jeremy Kay. *Screen Daily*, January 21. https://www.screendaily.com/features/sandi-tan-on-sundance-doc-shirkers-i-was-trying-to-think-of-it-as-an-exorcism/5125761.article.
Tan, Sandi. 2018e. "Shirkers Documentary Film Q&A with Director Sandi Tan." Recorded on October 1, 2018. YouTube video, uploaded October 12, 2018. https://www.youtube.com/watch?v=K25wDROpH9w.
Tan, Sandi. 2021. *Lurkers*. New York: Soho Press.
Tan Swie Hian. 2017a. *Anatomy of a Free Mind: Tan Swee Hian's Notebooks and Creations*. Singapore: Didier Millet.
Tan Swie Hian. 2017b. "A Thousand-Year Debate on the Imagery of a Plantain Tree in Snow." National Library (Singapore), February 24. YouTube video, uploaded July 29, 2017. https://www.youtube.com/watch?v=qwqMYFQdaoI.
Tan, Teresa. 2019. "Bangarra Dance Theatre Marks Thirty Years with Digital Archive and Exhibition." *ABC News*, December 13. https://www.abc.net.au/news/2019-12-13/knowledge-ground-bangarra-dance-theatre-digital-archive/11785840?nw=0.
Tan Wah Piow. 1987. *Let the People Judge: Confessions of the Most Wanted Person in Singapore*. Kuala Lumpur: Institute of Social Analysis.
Tan Wah Piow. 2012. *Smokescreens and Mirrors: Tracing the "Marxist Conspiracy."* Singapore: Function 8 Limited.
Tan Wah Piow. 2020. "In Conversation with Tan Wah Piow." Produced by Thum Ping Tjin. *New Naratif*, March 14. https://newnaratif.com/in-conversation-with-tan-wah-piow/.
Tang Da Wu. 2016. *Earth Work, 1979*. Edited by Charmaine Toh. Singapore: National Gallery Singapore.
Tapley, Kristopher. 2018. "Alfonso Cuarón on the Painful and Poetic Backstory behind 'Roma.'" *Variety*, October 23. https://variety.com/2018/film/news/roma-alfonso-cuaron-netflix-libo-rodriguez-1202988695/.
Teo, Sharelene. 2016. *Ponti*. Singapore: Epigram.
Teo Soh Lung. 2010. *Beyond the Blue Gate: Recollections of a Political Prisoner*. Petaling Jaya, Malaysia: Strategic Information and Research Development Center.

Teo You Yenn. 2018. *This Is What Inequality Looks Like*. Singapore: Ethos.

Thaiday, Patrick. 2003. "Bangarra Culture: Patrick Thaiday." Interview by Erin Brannigan. *RealTime* 54. http://www.realtimearts.net/article/54/7070.

TheatreWorks. 2013. *From Identity to Mondialisation: TheatreWorks 25*. Singapore: Editions Didier Millet.

Thum, Rian. 2014. *The Sacred Routes of Uyghur History*. Cambridge, MA: Harvard University Press.

Turner, Victor. 1967. *The Forest of Symbols: Aspects of Ndembu Ritual*. Ithaca, NY: Cornell University Press.

Turner, Victor. 1968. *Schism and Continuity in an African Society*. Manchester: Manchester University Press.

Turner, Victor. 1974. *Dramas, Fields, and Metaphors: Symbolic Action in Human Society*. Ithaca, NY: Cornell University Press.

Tynan, Elizabeth. 2016. *Atomic Thunder: The Maralinga Story*. Sydney: New-South Publishing.

Unaipon, David. 2001. *Legendary Tales of the Australian Aborigines*. Melbourne: Melbourne University Press.

University of Oxford. n.d. "Philosophy, Politics and Economics." Accessed January 12, 2023. https://www.ox.ac.uk/admissions/undergraduate/courses-listing/philosophy-politics-and-economics?wssl=1.

Van Hout, Vicki. 2014. "The Intricacies of Dance and History: Bangarra Dance Theatre, Patyegarang." *RealTime* 122. https://www.realtime.org.au/the-intricacies-of-dance-and-history/.

Vogel, Ezra. 1989. *One Step Ahead in China: Guangdong under Reform*. Cambridge, MA: Harvard University Press.

Vogel, Ezra. 2011. *Deng Xiaoping and the Transformation of China*. Cambridge, MA: Harvard University Press.

Vonnegut, Kurt. 1985. *Galapagos*. New York: Dell.

Walker, Frank. 2014. *Maralinga: The Chilling Exposé of Our Secret Nuclear Shame and Betrayal of Our Troops and Country*. Sydney: Hachette Australia.

Wang, Cathy Yue. 2020. "Chinese Folklore for Modern Times: Three Feminist Re-Visions of the Legend of the White Snake." *Asian Studies Review* 44, no. 2: 183–200.

Wang, David Der-wei. 2004. *The Monster That Is History: History, Violence, and Fictional Writing in Twentieth-Century China*. Berkeley: University of California Press.

Wang, David Der-wei. 2020. *Why Fiction Matters in Contemporary China*. Waltham, MA: Brandeis University Press.

Wang Jing. 2021. *Half Sound, Half Philosophy: Aesthetics, Politics, and History of China's Sound Art*. New York: Bloomsbury Academic.

Warner, Marina. 2021. "Splash." *New York Review of Books*, March 25, 15–17.

Warren, James Francis. 1986. *Rickshaw Coolie: A People's History of Singapore 1880–1940*. Singapore: Oxford University Press.

Warren, James Francis. 1992. "The Ah Ku and Karayuki-San of Singapore—Their Lives: Sources, Method and a Historian's Representation." *Southeast Asian Journal of Social Science* 20, no. 1: 80–92.

Warren, James Francis. 1993. *Ah Ku and Karayuki-San: Prostitution in Singapore 1870–1940*. Singapore: Oxford University Press.

Watt, Ian. 1957. *The Rise of the Novel*. Berkeley: University of California Press.

Weiner, Annette. 1976. *Women of Value, Men of Renown: New Perspectives in Trobriand Exchange*. Austin: University of Texas Press.

Wheatley, Paul. 1971. *Pivot of the Four Quarters*. Chicago: Aldine.

Wiersema, Robert. 2017. "'A Crackerjack Read': Lydia Kwa's *Oracle Bone* Is Magical Historical Fiction for Adults, YA-Style." *National Post*, November 20. https://nationalpost.com/entertainment/books/book-reviews/a-crackerjack-read-lydia-kwas-oracle-bone-is-magical-historical-fiction-for-adults-ya-style.

Wolfe, Patrick. 2006. "Settler Colonialism and the Elimination of the Native." *Journal of Genocide Research* 8, no. 4: 387–409.

Wong, Derek. 2018. "Singapore Is Second Most Visited City in Asia-Pacific, Fifth in the World: Mastercard." *Straits Times*, September 26. https://www.straitstimes.com/singapore/singapore-is-2nd-most-visited-city-in-asia-pacific-5th-in-the-world-mastercard.

Wong, Kevin Martens. 2017a. *Altered Straits*. Singapore: Epigram Books.

Wong, Kevin Martens. 2017b. "Constructing Tuyunri in *The Gatekeeper*: An Interview with Nuraliah Norasid." *Unravel*, April 21. https://unravellingmag.com/articles/constructing-tuyunri-interview-nuraliah-norasid/.

Wong Wen Pu. 2017. "Recognizing Racism: Nuraliah Norasid's *The Gatekeeper*." *Cha: An Asian Literary Journal* 37. https://www.asiancha.com/content/view/2873/630/.

Woon Tai Ho. 2008. *To Paint a Smile*. Singapore: Candid Creation.

Woon Tai Ho. 2013. *Riot Green*. Singapore: Candid Creation.

World Health Organization. 2022. "Leprosy." January 11. https://www.who.int/news-room/fact-sheets/detail/leprosy.

Yan Geling. 1999. *White Snake and Other Stories*. New York: Aunt Lute Books.

Yap, June. 2016. *Retrospective: A Historiographical Aesthetic in Contemporary Singapore and Malaysia*. Petaling Jaya, Malaysia: Strategic Information and Research Development Center.

Young, Deborah. 2019. "*Demons*: Film Review." *Hollywood Reporter*, December 27. https://www.hollywoodreporter.com/review/demons-1191259.

Young, Michael. 1958. *The Rise of the Meritocracy*. London: Penguin.

Zuboff, Shoshana. 2019. *The Age of Surveillance Capitalism*. New York: Public Affairs.

Index